A HISTORY
of
CHRISTIANITY
IN AMERICA

A HISTORY

of

CHRISTIANITY

IN AMERICA

———

Mark A. Granquist

Baker Academic
a division of Baker Publishing Group
Grand Rapids, Michigan

© 2025 by Mark A. Granquist

Published by Baker Academic
a division of Baker Publishing Group
Grand Rapids, Michigan
BakerAcademic.com

Printed in the United States of America

Library of Congress Cataloging-in-Publication Data
Names: Granquist, Mark Alan, 1957– author.
Title: A history of Christianity in America / Mark A. Granquist.
Description: Grand Rapids, Michigan : Baker Academic, a division of Baker Publishing Group,
    [2025] | Includes bibliographical references and index.
Identifiers: LCCN 2024004224 | ISBN 9781540963314 (cloth) | ISBN 9781493441495 (ebook) |
    ISBN 9781493441501 (pdf)
Subjects: LCSH: United States—Church history.
Classification: LCC BR515 .G73 2025 | DDC 277.3—dc23/eng/20240401
LC record available at https://lccn.loc.gov/2024004224

Engraving by Theodor de Bry from IanDagnall Computing, Alamy Stock Photo
Cover design by Darren Welch Design

Baker Publishing Group publications use paper produced from sustainable forestry practices and postconsumer waste whenever possible.

25 26 27 28 29 30 31   7 6 5 4 3 2 1

To my teachers, who inspired me
and
To my family, who supported me

Contents

Illustrations

Acknowledgments

I WANT TO GRATEFULLY ACKNOWLEDGE the students who have been my companions in learning over the decades. They have prodded me to hone and develop the ways I examine and explain Christianity in America, and I have learned much from them about how Christianity has developed and broadened over the centuries. Certainly, generations of scholars of the history of Christianity in America have produced books and articles—large and small—that serve as the bedrock of my learning, and I gratefully acknowledge their work. I have also learned much from my excellent teachers at St. Olaf College, Yale Divinity School, and the University of Chicago Divinity School and from my teaching colleagues at St. Olaf College, Gustavus Adolphus College, and Luther Seminary. It is true that we stand on the shoulders of giants, and I humbly admit that I can only hope to measure up to their accomplishments. If this work is in any way insufficient or somehow in error in places, it is certainly not their fault.

I would also like to thank the editorial team at Baker Academic for their encouragement and support as I worked on this project. The original idea for this project was developed in conversation with then-editor David Nelson, and the work was further shepherded by his successors and the staff at Baker. I am grateful to my colleagues at Luther Seminary and elsewhere who read the manuscript in part or in total and offered their excellent suggestions and advice. And, of course, the support of my wife, Kathy, and my adult children, Elisabeth Alderks and Robert Granquist, has been absolutely vital—they are the bedrock of my life, and I thank them for supporting me and bearing with me while I worked on this project. As to my parents and the generations of faithful Christians who preceded me and formed my faith, I give God thanks for them. It is true: we are surrounded by so great a cloud of witnesses!

Soli Deo Gloria.

Introduction

THE STORY OF THE CHRISTIAN PEOPLE in the United States of America is one of endless change—the ebb and flow of vitality and constant development, ever expanding and ever complicating. In this country Christians have found a place to grow their churches and innovate their faith. Their religious forms and ideas have shaped the country in important and substantial ways, even as the country itself has left indelible marks on their Christianity. In America, old forms of European Christianity have found new iterations, and new forms of Christianity have been developed. And through the vitality of Christianity in the United States, American Christian forms and theologies have been exported around the world, influencing growing Christianities in Africa, Asia, and Latin America. In turn, these forms of Christianity have innovated in their places, and these innovations have returned to the United States to further influence American Christianity.

No one book could encapsulate the whole of this complex topic. (Entire reference book sets have pulled together only the essentials of the subject.) And yet, below the surface there are structural and theological elements that many forms of Christianity in the United States have in common. Not all forms of American Christianity have embraced these elements, and some forms have even developed in protest against them. But the structural elements of religious life in the United States—especially voluntary religion, pluralism, and a free and innovating religious marketplace—have left their mark on all forms of Christianity in this country.

Writing a one-volume history of such a vast and complicated subject is an exercise in compromise and selection, sometimes almost impossible compromise and selection. Some of the most important of these decisions surround the scope of the book itself. This book is about the history of only one religious tradition in the United States: Christianity. While there are many excellent books about the wider subject of religion in America, this book attempts to relate and explain the narrative of only one of them, albeit the largest and predominant religion in America. This book also is largely limited to a single country. While the European context from which American Christianity stems is important, for the sake of focus and brevity only elements of this context essential to the main narrative have been included. Some histories of Christianity in North America have woven into their narratives the developments of Christianity in both the United States and Canada. This is an approach that is certainly commendable, yet the differences between the two distinct religious cultures makes an integrated narrative very difficult to attain. For the sake of flow and clarity, this book maintains a singular focus on Christianity in the United States.

This book flows from my experience of teaching these materials in two colleges and one seminary over thirty years. Its approach has been shaped by the knowledge, questions, and experiences of thousands of students. I hope that it will be a helpful resource both for formal students and for general readers who want to learn more about this fascinating subject. My aim has been to provide a readable narrative while not oversimplifying what is, at many points, a very complex story. I hope that readers will be so captured by the narrative that they will seek to find out more about their own stories and traditions and about those individuals, groups, and movements that particularly catch their imagination.

1

The Structure and Theology of Christianity in America

There are countless sects in the United States. Each reveres the Creator in a different fashion, but all agree about man's duties to his fellow man. Each worships God in his own way, but all preach the same morality in God's name. Though it matters a great deal to each individual that his religion be true, this is not the case for society. Society has nothing to fear from the other life, and nothing to hope for, and what matters most is not so much that all citizens profess the true religion as that each citizen profess some religion.

Although religion in the United States never intervenes directly in government, it must be considered as the first of America's political institutions, for even if religion does not give Americans their taste for liberty, it does notably facilitate their use of that liberty. This is how Americans see their religious beliefs. . . . I am certain they believe this to be necessary for the preservation of republican institutions.

Alexis de Tocqueville, *Democracy in America* (1835)[1]

IN THE THIRD DECADE OF THE NINETEENTH CENTURY, a young French lawyer named Alexis de Tocqueville (1805–59) toured the new country of the United States of America. Though his primary task was to explore the

1. Alexis de Tocqueville, *Democracy in America*, trans. Arthur Goldhammer (New York: Library of America, 2004), 335, 338.

1

American political and legal systems, his observations about American society in general and the place of religion in American life are nothing short of brilliant and have rarely been matched. De Tocqueville was trying to explain the new society that was the United States to a European audience that could hardly imagine how such a republican society could operate. To be sure, the forms of Christianity de Tocqueville saw in the United States were based on European models, but they were so modified by several hundred years in North America as to have become new and distinctive forms of Christianity. Europeans often had a

Théodore Chassériau, 1850

1.1. Alexis de Tocqueville.

difficult time understanding these new developments (as many still do), but in the centuries to follow, these new American forms of Christianity would be disseminated around the world. Although the religious world of the United States has become nothing if not more complicated since de Tocqueville's visit, many of his core observations have remained surprisingly accurate and powerfully instructive.

This initial chapter will lay out the structural and theological development of Christianity in America, as a preamble to the narrative history in subsequent chapters.

The Western European Roots of American Christianity

Christianity began about two thousand years ago as a small, divergent sect among the Jewish people in the eastern Mediterranean region, focused on the person and teachings of Jesus of Nazareth, whom his followers understood to be the long-awaited savior, or *Messiah* ("anointed one"—rendered in Greek as *Christos*, from which we get the word "Christ"). Although this movement did not flourish among the Jewish people of the time, the gospel ("good news") of Jesus the Christ was proclaimed also to non-Jews (the "Greeks," or "gentiles"), among whom it found a small but fervent following. By the year AD 300 or so, Christianity had become well established in the eastern, Greek-speaking half of the Roman Empire, and Christians constituted up to perhaps 10 or 15 percent of the population. Christianity was slower to gain a foothold in the empire's western half, as Latin-speaking Romans predominated there. Many rulers of the Roman Empire were deeply suspicious of this new religious group, and sometimes Christians were persecuted by imperial officials and local people.

All this changed in the early fourth century, when the Roman emperor Constantine (d. 337) came to favor the Christians, and eventually became one himself. Constantine made Christianity the favored religion of the Roman Empire; then in the late fourth century, emperor Theodosius (347–95) made it the empire's official religion. Under imperial favor, Christianity grew rapidly in the West and moved northward into the European continent. Even though imperial authority collapsed in the West during the fifth and sixth centuries, Christianity grew among the Germanic and Slavic tribes that came to rule Europe. The Eastern Roman Empire (also known as the Byzantine Empire) remained for the next eight hundred years, but Christianity in the eastern and southern Mediterranean and the Middle East was greatly diminished by the growth of the Islamic empires. Eastern Christianity spread into southeastern Europe and Russia, but the greatest vitality of Christianity was in the Latin West.

Although western European Christianity became strongly identified with the Roman imperial state, and then with the various states and kingdoms that succeeded it, there was still in the West at least a theoretical division between Christianity and these states (a separation between church and state). The church saw as important the maintenance of its own independence, although in many times and places the church sought to work very closely with these states as a means of strengthening and expanding Christianity.

By the fifteenth century, western Europe was almost completely Christianized, and control of Western Christianity was given over to the bishop of Rome (the pope). Much as the feudal lords of western Europe owed their fealty to their kings, the local priests and bishops in the West owed their loyalty and obedience to the pope in Rome. In the areas of papal control in the West, the ideal was of a common culture—Christendom—where church and state worked together. This ideal was rarely achieved, as popes and kings continually vied to dominate each other and to gain advantage, but the ideal of Christendom still says much about how medieval western Europeans understood their world.

Though it is sometimes difficult for us to understand today, these Europeans did not value religious pluralism and diversity. Rather, they saw religious uniformity as a bedrock value, a way of achieving social stability in both church and state. To them, a society divided between different versions of Christianity, or between Christians and non-Christians, was a recipe for disaster. To be fair

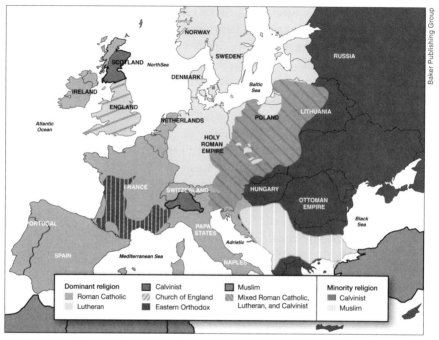

1.2. Sixteenth-Century European Religious Divisions.

to them, this was, in their experience, all too true (as it is, unfortunately, in many places today); wars over religion had often plunged their societies into chaos, and they believed that religious uniformity was preferrable to social and political conflict. Of course, this simply moved the conflict within, and internal battles over religion were common. Yet this was the social, political, and religious system they knew, and it generally kept the peace.

Until the sixteenth century. The great power and wealth of the western medieval church, under papal control, inevitably meant corruption and factional conflict within the church. For centuries, Christian reformers had decried these corruptions and sought avenues to reform and heal the western church, but with little success. Then in the sixteenth century, especially in northern Europe, a new generation of reformers came to the forefront, often supported by local political leaders, eager to rein in papal power. Reformers like Martin Luther (1483–1546), John Calvin (1509–64), and Thomas Cranmer (1489–1556), among many others, intensified the push for reforms, eventually deciding that reform of the medieval, papal church was not possible and that new forms of the Christian church, apart from papal control, were necessary in their areas. This new movement, called Protestantism, divided western Europe, establishing local Christian churches independent of papal control in central and northern

Germany, Scandinavia, Holland, England, Scotland, and parts of Switzerland, France, and Poland. But even in these areas the old ideals of Christendom continued as each territory established its own version of Protestantism as the sole religious option for its citizens. These religious institutions became known as state churches.

What was left of the old medieval church in the West, the papal church, also pushed through a series of major reforms in the Council of Trent (1545–63). These reforms largely eliminated the corruptions in the church that had sparked the Protestant Reformations, while retaining the centralized authority of the papacy. This marks the beginning of modern Roman Catholicism.

As many feared, these religious divisions led to a period of intense conflicts and wars during the sixteenth and seventeenth centuries, mainly between Roman Catholics and Protestants, although there were also inter-Protestant wars, such as in England. The shifting lines of battle and conflict also left many minority populations: Roman Catholics in Protestant regions and Protestants in Roman Catholic regions. This period of conflict eventually led to a stalemate and a western Europe that would be officially divided between different groups of Christians.

But in the midst of all this reform and conflict, groups arose with new religious ideals that discarded the old ideals of Christendom and state churches. These new reform groups, such as the Anabaptists on the Continent and the "dissenting" Protestants in England, began to question whether it was, after all, possible to have a "territorial" church, where everyone in a geographic area was automatically considered Christian at birth. Rather, they felt that the real church was the local gathering of those who were "truly" Christian, only a small segment of the total population. Such groups were often persecuted for endangering the social order and religious peace, but they did not disappear. By the end of the seventeenth century, many western Europeans, exhausted by religious conflict, began to embrace increased religious toleration. It seemed to many that although territorial churches (such as the state churches and the papal church) were still ideal, it might not be possible to force all citizens into them. A de facto pluralism came into wider acceptance.

Religion in Colonial British North America

European colonization of the Western Hemisphere was primarily an economic venture, as European countries looked for trade goods and profit from these lands. Individuals sought land (the primary measure of wealth) and the opportunity to enrich themselves in the New World. Many of the colonies that made up British North America were started initially as joint-stock companies whose investors expected handsome dividends for their investments. Although some settlers came from Europe to North America intending to stay, the early colonial settlements were rather haphazard. Only gradually did settlements of a more permanent nature emerge, but many of their inhabitants still thought of themselves as members of their European homeland countries, just living abroad.

Contrary to what many have been led to believe, overall the religious motivations for emigration were minor. There were a few groups—such as the Pilgrims and Puritans in New England and the Anabaptists and radicals in Pennsylvania—that sought relief in the New World from disadvantages they faced in Europe. But even among these groups, God and mammon vied for the top spot. It is often said that the Pilgrims, for example, came to what is now Massachusetts for "freedom of religion," but this term did not mean the same thing to them in the seventeenth century as it might to us in the twenty-first. To them, freedom of religion meant the freedom to practice their own religion without having to tolerate the presence of anyone who did not agree with them religiously. This was in no way an acceptance of religious pluralism and toleration.

So how did the society that we now know as the United States come to its current understanding of religious freedom? For that story, it is important to investigate the religious upheavals in the British Isles from the sixteenth to the eighteenth centuries. The Protestant Reformation in England followed a different course from those on the continent of Europe. Although there were proto-Protestant reforming movements in England before 1500, the main impetus for the Protestant reform of Christianity in England came from the top down: the decision of King Henry VIII (1491–1547) and his advisers to sever the medieval church in England from the papacy and declare the monarchs of England the heads of the church. What resulted was a state Church of England with some Protestant elements but retaining the episcopacy (rule of bishops) and much of the medieval liturgy and pageantry—a system that would come to be known as Anglicanism. Those English loyal to the papacy resisted, led by some of the great nobles, but eventually Roman Catholicism was driven underground in England.

The second stage of the English Reformation was a protracted struggle between the Anglican supporters of the state church and those who sought to "purify" the Church of England from its medieval, "Romanist" elements, especially the episcopacy and the medieval mass. These *Puritans*, as they came to be known, took their cues from the Reformed, or Calvinist, Protestants on the Continent. Initially, most of them sought only a further reform of the state

Church of England, but in their struggles with the bishops and the monarchs, some of the more radical Puritans began to question the whole state-church model. They wondered, along Anabaptist lines, whether church should be limited to "true believers," rather than understood to automatically comprise the inhabitants of a particular territory. These Reformers—Congregationalists, Independents, Baptists, Quakers, and others—pushed an increasingly radical agenda. In the 1640s, these tensions broke out in civil war, which caused a huge amount of political and religious turmoil, including an attempt to do away with the monarchy altogether.

Eventually, in 1660, the monarchy and the Anglican state church were restored, but the dissenting, or "nonconforming," Protestants were allowed to keep their churches—the beginnings of a rough religious pluralism in the British lands. Only members of the state Church of England (Anglicans) were allowed prominent positions in the military and government, but all Protestants were tolerated. (Roman Catholics, still, were not.)

In British colonial North America, the leaders of each colony determined the religious nature of that colony, following the model of the European state churches. In Puritan New England, the official, governmentally supported church was Congregational, and other Christian groups were not allowed. In the South, from Virginia to Georgia, the Anglican Church was likewise established by law. In Dutch New York and New Jersey, the Reformed church was established, and there were short-lived establishments of Swedish Lutherans along the Delaware River and of English Roman Catholics in Maryland. Only in Pennsylvania and Rhode Island were there no established churches—the Quakers (in Pennsylvania) and the Baptists (in Rhode Island) did not believe that people should be forced into governmentally established churches.

In most places, the arrangement laid out in the above, tidy summary existed only on paper. While Puritanism dominated much of New England and Anglicanism dominated in the South, even in these regions religious uniformity was impossible to maintain. In the middle colonies, from Maryland to New York, the situation was even more religiously fluid, with Presbyterians, Baptists, Anglicans, Lutherans, Reformed, and Quakers all mixed in together. Even more so than in England, colonists were forced into a situation of religious pluralism beyond anything they might have known in the Old World. The strongest colonial establishments of religion—in Massachusetts and Virginia—attempted from time to time to expel or imprison those who "dissented" from the state churches, but this was soon abandoned as impractical. Above all, the primary need in colonial America was for labor; workers were desperately needed to make the colonies profitable, and few employers cared about their workers' religious identities. People kept relocating, and it was virtually impossible to keep a monolithic religious identity within a colony. Religious pluralism was then an established fact, no matter what the colonial authorities wished. Most Americans found that religious toleration was the only possible way for such a mixed religious society to be maintained. This was not yet a situation of religious freedom as a contemporary American might define it, although this religious pluralism was one of the factors that caused such religious freedom to eventually come into existence.

The other important element here was the weakness of religious establishment in the American colonies due to the weakness of most colonial governments, which did not have the funds to pay for state churches. There were very few religious congregations in British North America, and those that did exist were chronically underfunded and often without pastoral leadership for years at a time. This lack of pastoral leadership stemmed, in part, from a critical shortage of ministers in North America, as most European clergy did not want to emigrate to the New World. Apart from Harvard and Yale in Puritan New England, there were few schools in the colonies to educate ministers.

Those who held a membership in one religious tradition or another found that the new situation in North America drastically changed how they organized and practiced their faith. Very few were able to rely on colonial administrations to provide organized religion for them. Religion was voluntary, meaning that if a group wanted a congregation, it was up to them alone to organize their congregation, to pay for it, and to govern it. These voluntary congregations decided their direction and engaged their own pastors to lead them. They could fire their pastors if they did not like them, or members could easily leave a congregation with which they were dissatisfied and find another more to their liking. Colonial religious leaders no longer had the support of either the colonial governments or the religious authorities in Europe, so the power differential between members and their religious leaders was reversed. A new kind of voluntary religious life was slowly being established in the New World, one quite different from that of the European societies.

By 1776—the year of American independence—less than 20 percent of Americans had a formal membership in a congregation, and in frontier areas the percentage was even smaller. This often surprises contemporary audiences, who have heard that, unlike today, "back then" everyone went to church. Even considering that standards for membership might well have been more stringent in colonial American congregations than they are today, this is a startling truth. It is often said that many immigrants came to North America seeking freedom of religion, which is assumed to mean the freedom to join whatever religious group they wished. But it is more likely that many immigrants came to America for freedom *from* organized religion. At least, many came to enjoy such freedom after living for a while in America.

Now, this is not to say that those who were "unchurched" were somehow uninterested or unconcerned with God or things religious; many, if not most, were indeed so concerned. But the key is that they no longer had to rely on organized, established churches to define religious belief for them. They were free to be religious in any way they wished, whether by joining an organized religious group or by keeping their own counsel. Some maintained a general religious indifference, free from compulsory religion. Others became religious "seekers," going from one religious group to another in search of a teaching and a community that worked for them.

By 1776, Europeans (mainly from the British Isles) had been settling in North America for over 150 years, and these colonists had formed an increasingly distinct society of their own, one that had roots in Europe but that was no longer European. The religious world of the North American colonies stemmed from the Protestant Reformation of the sixteenth century and the inter-Protestant struggles in England in the seventeenth century, especially the latter's eventual embrace of Protestant pluralism. Although settlers generally brought with them a traditional understanding of the need for established state churches as a basis for society, the situation in the New World dramatically undercut the possibility of building such a religious arrangement. Rather, the rough pluralism that began and grew, the weakness of colonial governments and their inability to fund the establishments that existed on paper, the freedom of religion that many came to enjoy, and the voluntary nature of religious organizations in general—all these elements together composed the foundation of a distinctly new understanding of the nature and place of organized religion. Religion in the New World had to be different from religion in the Old World.

However, most of these religious developments were more accidental than intentional. Events and situations in the New World forced changes in how organized religion functioned, giving birth to a new, American model of the place of organized religion in society and in people's lives. The previous sentence names no orchestrating individuals or organizations because there was no fully formed intentionality behind this. But these accidental changes soon melded with intellectual developments in eighteenth-century Europe (i.e., the Enlightenment) and with revolutionary ideals from France and elsewhere to provide a rationale for these changes in religion in American society.

Enlightenment and Revolution

The Enlightenment was an intellectual revolution in eighteenth-century Europe that fundamentally changed the way thinkers and leaders in the West understood reality and the world, a revolution centered on the use of reason and the human mind to discover truth. For many centuries previous to this, western European thought was based on forms of static idealism that had their roots in the Greek philosophers Plato and Aristotle. This idealism was blended with Christian theism, resulting in the widespread assumption that an unchanging reality stemmed from the Christian God and that knowledge of God was the starting point for all other knowledge.

The Enlightenment, however, saw the reasonable human mind as the beginning of all knowledge. The mind, using reason and data from the senses, was able to discover and understand everything. It encountered a perfectly created and ordered natural world, made by God but available to all through reason and the senses. Special revelation, such as in the scriptures, was not necessary; in fact, it was holding humanity back. Enlightenment thinkers had supreme confidence in reason and the human mind to discover reality, as long as that mind was well educated and logical. These thinkers were confident in the progressive path of educated humans and optimistic that they could—through reason, education, and science—change human society and the world for the better.

The Enlightenment did still rely on God for the important job of creation. God had created the natural world with all the laws and instructions that humanity would need, should they shed parochial forms of religion and view the creation through reason. This idea, *natural revelation*, was key. After creation, God did not intervene in the world with special messages aimed at one group of people or another. This understanding of God is known as deism: a benevolent God creates the natural world with everything creatures will need and leaves it be, like a watchmaker who creates a watch, winds it up, and then lets it run without interference. Enlightenment deists often had a hazy idea of some form of final judgment at the end of time and equally hazy ideas of some sort of afterlife. Many thought that there had to be some sort of final reward or punishment; otherwise uneducated people would fall into wickedness.

Beyond these basics, the Enlightenment took different forms in the various countries of Europe. Among the intellectuals on the continent of Europe, in German areas and others, the Enlightenment remained an intellectual movement, although it contributed to the formation of rational religion that dominated in areas of the Protestant and Roman Catholic state churches. In France the Enlightenment took on a more radical form, as Enlightenment intellectuals such as Voltaire (1694–1788) spoke harshly against both the established Roman

Catholicism and the monarchy that it supported. In England, the Enlightenment took on a milder form, especially through the influential writings of John Locke (1632–1704). In works such as his *Reasonableness of Christianity*, Locke holds that Christianity, understood through reason, can be a positive force for good in the world. But for this to happen, Christianity would have to move away from its more primitive understandings and focus on the common morality found through the natural world.

Godfrey Kneller, 1697

1.3. John Locke.

The problem, according to Locke, was that most people, at least at this point in time, were neither educated nor rational but ruled by their "base passions" and irrationality. Thus, he argued, organized religion has an important role in reining in such base and irrational passions through the inculcation of a common morality—generally something like the Ten Commandments, the Golden Rule, and other divine laws (hence the need for some sort of final judgment).[2] In England and British North America, Enlightenment thinkers generally supported the churches as long as they pushed this common morality and did not veer off into irrationality and special interest. The churches in America took this as a bargain and saw themselves as the chief guardians of American morality.

In America, many of the Founding Fathers of the eventual republic were Enlightenment deists. Benjamin Franklin (1706–90), George Washington (1732–99), John Adams (1735–1826), Thomas Jefferson (1743–1826), James Madison (1751–1836), and others could hardly be considered Christians in the traditional sense, but they tended to uphold traditional organized Christianity as a means of social good and morals. Washington was a vestryman (lay leader) in his local Anglican parish; though his personal religious beliefs ran more toward deism, he believed it was his duty as a local leader to support the church. Franklin also tended to support organized religion, and as a printer he made money doing so. Although Jefferson leaned more in the direction of the French Enlightenment (which was generally hostile toward religion), he did not

2. John Locke, *The Reasonableness of Christianity*, ed. John C. Higgins-Biddle (Oxford: Clarendon, 1999), esp. 141–54.

directly attack organized religion. Only the radical Thomas Paine (1737–1809), crucial in gathering support for the revolution, was openly and harshly critical of organized religion; horrified at his stance, the other American Enlightenment figures eventually shunned him as doing danger to public morality.

Once the American revolution against Great Britain was successfully completed and a new republic established, the American Founding Fathers wrote Enlightenment ideals into the foundational documents of the new country. When it came to the Constitution, the initial document had almost no reference to organized religion. But the Bill of Rights, the first ten amendments, contained two foundational phrases on religion. One declared the individual right to "free exercise" of religion; the other, the "establishment" clause, forbade Congress from supporting any establishment of religion. This meant no federal support of any kind for organized religion. It was a rather controversial development. Although some colonies had dismantled their support of religion during the revolution, principally Virginia, colonial state churches still existed in Massachusetts and Connecticut. The establishment clause was supported by a strange coalition of deists, like Jefferson, and "dissenting" Protestants, like the Baptists (who did not approve of state churches on theological grounds). While some, like Washington, thought it would be acceptable if the federal government supported religion as long as it supported all religious groups equally, the non-establishment argument won the day.

Thus, by the adoption of the United States Constitution and its first ten amendments in 1789, the basic format of religion in the new United States was roughly in place. Where organized religion existed in the new republic, it was predominantly forms of Protestant Christianity, mainly varieties of Protestantism from the English Reformation. From the beginning of the American colonies, there had been a multiplicity of Protestant groups in each of the colonies, and a rough pluralism was tolerated—a legacy of the English Civil Wars and the Restoration. Though some state-level establishments of religion in New England continued to exist into the early nineteenth century, eventually the twin principles of non-establishment and freedom of religion took hold. Religion in America would be voluntary, and there would be no state support for religion. Americans were free to develop any religious organizations they wished, as long as they ran them and paid for them themselves. Yet despite the rejection of state backing, organized religion was seen as vital in the new republic as a mechanism for ensuring public morality.

Many Europeans were dubious about this new system of religious life. And some European religious leaders were horrified. They believed that, under such conditions, organized religion would fail, leading to the moral collapse of the new nation, and anarchy and lawlessness would prevail. Yet these dire predictions did not come to pass. Those who led religious groups in the new republic eventually figured out how to deal with, and even flourish in, the new situation. When de Tocqueville related his findings on the United States to his European readers in the 1830s, they were surprised to find that, far from being dead, religion was central to life in America.

It can be difficult for contemporary observers in the United States to understand how radical and tenuous this new American religious system was as it came into being at the end of the eighteenth century. Eighteenth-century Europeans—and more than a few Americans—were certain that religious pluralism would lead to bloodshed and armed conflict. And they had good reason to expect this. During the two hundred years since the Protestant Reformation of the sixteenth century, Europe had been racked by wars of religion. Protestants fought Roman Catholics. And, at times, Protestants fought other Protestants in bloody internecine conflicts. The worst of these wars were internal to the European countries. The Thirty Years' War in Germany, the Wars of Religion in France, and the English Civil Wars are but a few of the many examples. No wonder Europeans thought religious pluralism was a recipe for disaster. Even in England, which had the widest religious pluralism in the eighteenth century, there was still an official state church, and pluralism was limited to Protestant groups within proscribed theological limits.

So why did the religious pluralism developing in the United States at the time not lead to the same kind of bloody conflicts that arose in Europe? This is an important question, but it is not an easy one to answer. Perhaps the wide range of pluralism diffused the tensions. Perhaps the fact that there were no state churches and that no one religious faction came anywhere close to representing a majority of the people meant that conflict could not be funneled into a simple binary system. Perhaps Enlightenment attitudes and a popular disgust with the "old" European models meant Americans were more pragmatic about religion, more willing to "live and let live," leaving theological conflict to their religious leaders. These and quite a few other possible explanations have been proposed, and perhaps—taken together—they can explain the lack of religious warfare in the United States.

The Development of an American Religious System

In truth, Americans developed their own particular type of religious establishment. This was not a political or institutional establishment but a cultural establishment of religion based on the idea that to be a good American was to hold to a certain grouping of religious practices and ideas, things that were widely held and tacitly agreed to. These practices and ideas were not derived from any particular form of organized Christianity but, rather, from common threads drawn from the Christian tradition as modified through the Enlightenment: that there was a God who created the world, that one should worship and pray to this God, that there was a common Christian morality in which all people shared, that the foundation of this religiosity was to be found in the Bible, and that there would be a final day of judgment where persons would have to give account for their actions in life. Another of these widely held convictions was that to be a good person and a good citizen of the country, one had to be a member of a religious group (although it did not generally matter which group it was). Though this was essentially a Protestant form of Christianity, there would be room for Roman Catholics and Jews, who eventually found that they could fit themselves into such a common religiosity.

Another important element of this evolving cultural establishment of Christianity in the United States is the distinction between what may be termed *official religion* and *popular religion*. Official religion is the way in which the leaders of any organized religious group understand their movement in theological and ecclesiastical terms. Most religious groups have officially recognized statements of belief (creeds and other such doctrinal formulations) as well as standard forms of religious organization that define their groups and separate them from others. Thus, Christian groups have differing theologies of the sacraments, the nature of salvation, and the authority of the scriptures, among many others. They also differ over church structures (such as bishops, synods, and congregations), traditions of worship and polity, and many other things. These are the official elements that make Baptists, Presbyterians, Roman Catholics, and Orthodox Christians distinct from one another. Popular religion, on the other hand, is what laypeople themselves find to be important in their religious communities and practices. Lay Christians may be unable to list or define the theological and ecclesiastical elements of official religion, and many would not actually be all that interested in them. They might well suggest that these definitions are things that pastors and religious leaders worry about, but which do not really concern them. Lay Christians have also shown that they can and will switch from one group to the next, and they often do so quite readily and without concern for the differences of theology involved.

The importance of this distinction between official and popular religion connects with the voluntary and pluralistic elements of religion in the United States. In a state-church situation, such as in Europe, the official church has little reason to be concerned about popular religion; the state church is not dependent on the direct financial support of the lay Christians but receives its funding through governmental taxation. However, in a voluntary church system, as in the United States, religious leaders must be keenly aware of the religious attitudes of lay Christians, for it is their voluntary support that directly affects the funding and future of any particular congregation or denominational structure. Thus, Christianity in America is a delicate balancing act between what is important to the leaders of the various churches and what is important to the people in the pews. Should this balance be thrown off too far in either direction, the health of that religious group will be in peril.

Freedom of religion, pluralism, and a voluntary religious system thus means that the balance of power for Christianity in America has been reworked in important ways. Without an element of governmental privilege or support, each religious group is forced to compete for members within a religious marketplace where "consumers" of religion have an ever-increasing variety of religious options and, most importantly, the option of no religion at all. To put it bluntly, a religious leader must "sell" an often-skeptical public on the idea that their particular group is a better religious option than all the rest. This means developing both a keen understanding of what people want from their religion (market research) and close personal relations with their people on the local level. To lead a local congregation, pastors or priests must win the people to their side and convince them that their particular tradition has the answers to their religious needs or desires. This means that the elements of popular religion take precedence, for popular religion is indicative of what the people want. American religious officials cannot simply assert the elements of official religion. Rather, they must educate people and convince them that the theologies or practices that define their particular group are, in fact, what lay Christians need or want. This dynamic is crucial. It is also why, in the eighteenth and nineteenth centuries, so many European clergy who came to serve congregations in the United States did not succeed. Nothing in their religious formation or training prepared them for working in this new American marketplace of religion.

As Christian groups developed within this new structure of religion in the United States, after the Revolutionary War and independence from Great Britain, they had to learn how to adapt to the conditions it presented. The problems were substantial: The resources available to fund organized religion were scarce. There were few local congregations and even fewer pastors to lead them. And the opportunity for people to move west and obtain land on the frontier meant that people were moving away from what few congregations there were. Looking forward from the 1790s, one might reasonably project that an already weak American Christianity would simply grow weaker. But any such projection would turn out to be completely wrong.

Christianity in the United States in the Nineteenth Century

After 1800, Christianity in America was poised to begin a dramatic and powerful expansion of its numbers and influence, which saw the percentage of Americans affiliated with some form of organized religion grow from 17 percent in 1775 to around 67 percent by the late 1960s. This was a steady increase over a couple centuries, despite the perceived weaknesses that organized American religion had to deal with.

The reasons behind this dramatic expansion of Christianity in the United States are many and include both practical aspects and religious and theological elements. Practically speaking, the growth happened because many American religious leaders came to embrace the new situation they found themselves in, and even used the new system to their advantage. Since the structures of official religion in the United States were weak, individual pastors and priests could experiment with new religious forms and approaches. Others embraced the freedom of religion and pluralism and moved beyond traditional forms of Christianity to develop new types of Christianity that seemed more suited to the American religious milieu. Christian groups formed seminaries and training schools in the United States to educate pastors attuned to the distinctive elements of religion in America and who could operate successfully within it. Pastors and priests became religious entrepreneurs, discerning how to grow successful congregations. As a result, the country was flooded with congregations and pastors from various denominations. But not all Christian groups were equally willing and able to take advantage of the new situation. Some groups succeeded; others lagged. But the total number of formally affiliated Christians grew and grew. Even though this growth would stall out, and even decrease somewhat, in the late twentieth century and the beginning of the twenty-first, the numbers have remained impressive.

New religious and theological elements also made this growth possible for American Christianity. These elements were clustered together in what would become the dominant form of Protestant Christianity, although this was a general consensus among the ever-widening denominational groups and not the result of formal negotiations or decisions. Key to this emerging consensus was the belief in human free will and the autonomy of the individual. Though this was given a powerful boost by the Enlightenment, these traditions developed within early modern Christianity and were especially significant in the United States, where political democracy and religious autonomy went hand in hand. An important religious element of this was the adoption of the theology of Arminianism, which was promoted initially by the Methodists and was soon widely adopted by many other American Christians (even if their own denominations were officially opposed to it). Contrary to doctrines of predestination, and based on human free will, Arminianism posits that God offers salvation to all human persons, who have the ability to accept or reject that offer. Although the theologians who adopted Arminianism generally understood it in a carefully nuanced manner, popular Arminianism eventually was reduced to a simple formula in which people are challenged to "make the decision" for Jesus, or in other words, to choose to convert.

Given the immense task of "making Christians" of a growing and dispersing American population, religious entrepreneurs used this new theological understanding to develop new methods of making people Christians. These methods, collectively, came to be known as revivalism. Beginning as experimental approaches on the frontier, successful revivals led to the development of revivalism as a formal method for reaching people with religion, a method that would be adopted by a wide swath of American Christianity. Revivalism consisted of intense periods of preaching, music, and worship, all designed to bring individuals to the "point of decision"—that is, to the point of making a decision for God. In some parts of American Protestantism, this decision led to adult baptism, also referred to as believer's baptism. In those parts of Protestantism that continued to practice infant baptism, an adult conversion experience, such as one might have at a revival, was an important element confirming, as an adult, the faith into which one had been baptized as an infant.

Solomon Eytinge, *Harper's Weekly*, 1872

1.4. Revival out in the Field.

Based on Arminianism and revivalism, the emerging Christian consensus funneled the energy and drive that resulted from conversion into many different social and moral crusades aimed at improving the life of the American people, thus establishing Protestant morality as the foundation of civic life. A distinctive development of this effort was the formation of nondenominational societies tasked with some element of social reform—carrying out Christian missions, printing and distributing Bibles, promoting temperance and the elimination of social vices, caring for orphans and widows (and other "unfortunates"), and many, many other causes. Based on a widespread belief that such work could be a means of helping to build, in America, the kingdom of God (a belief connected with the eschatological / end-times perspective known as postmillennialism), many Christians saw the United States as capable of leading the rest of the world into such a glorious future. Even the Protestants and Roman Catholics who did not formally adopt these new theological and religious elements were nevertheless influenced by the general religious attitudes of the time.

The free market of American religion meant that religious entrepreneurs developed new and distinctive forms of Christianity that kept widening the religious options and increasing religious pluralism. Some of these new groups reflected the general Protestant consensus, but many others offered alternatives to that consensus. Communal and millenarian groups flourished with different models of Christian community. Unitarians and Universalists offered an alternative to the conversionist schema. And spiritualists pushed away from Christianity as a whole. The history of religion in America is a story of ever-expanding religious options, whether based on Christianity or on other religious traditions.

Although these diversifying forms of American Christianity were not officially supported by American governmental units, there were novel and important ways by which governmental units provided indirect support to Christian denominations and organizations. Churches and religious organizations received certain exemptions from the government, such as from paying taxes. Christian—mainly Protestant—attitudes and morality were written into law, particularly in the privileging of Christian holidays and in the so-called blue laws, which dictated, among other things, the societal observance of the Christian Sabbath by the closing of businesses and activities on Sunday. In addition, religiously based Christian social service agencies often received direct or indirect financial support from governmental units.

With the then-common consensus that religion was a key element in supporting a democratic society, Christian *morality* was frequently undergirded by the state. The public school systems in many parts of the country taught a generalized Protestant morality and ethos, which is why Roman Catholics and some minority Protestant groups built their own parochial schools. This is one example of how, even as Christianity grew and expanded as the nation itself expanded, by the last third of the nineteenth century, religious and social fissures eventually appeared. The national turmoil over slavery and whether it should be abolished led to a bloody civil war in which the Southern states were eventually defeated and slavery officially ended. But the Civil War also resulted in lingering bitterness and divisiveness over race. From 1840 to 1914, millions of new immigrants continued to expand the spectrum of American religious options, especially as many of these immigrants were Roman Catholics and Continental Protestants. These immigrants did not always share, however, what had become the American religious consensus. Although Protestantism remained the largest general grouping of American Christians, by 1890 Roman Catholicism was the largest unified American denomination and the immigrant Lutheran groups were the third-largest Protestant family.

Still, the old-line Protestant groups maintained their leadership positions in church and society, even if they increasingly lost market share to the newcomers. The two largest Protestant families—Methodists and Baptists—led the way in drawing Americans into congregational membership, which reached 50 percent of all Americans by 1900. The mainline Protestant groups—including Congregationalists, Presbyterians, and Episcopalians—grew much less quickly but still dominated the upper levels of society. Although many Americans, both then and now, would resist the idea that the United States was a class-based society, it has always been so. The difference between the European and American class systems is that class levels in the United States are much more porous and flexible. As Americans moved up social and economic levels, they tended to gravitate toward the mainline Protestant churches. As religious groups became successful, they began to emulate those "above" them. This was especially true of the Methodists, whose origins in outsider, working-class circles were erased by their growth into middle-class respectability.

Toward the end of the nineteenth century, American society was beginning to be transformed by the twin, interlocking forces of urbanization and industrialization. Masses of new immigrants and young Americans sought their fortunes in the burgeoning American cities, slowly transforming the United States from a predominately rural, agrarian society into a leading world industrial power. Along with this growth came social and religious conflict, as new peoples and ideas vied for power with more established ones. Immigrant religious groups, especially Roman Catholic and Jewish, challenged Protestant dominance. New scientific and intellectual ideas challenged traditional worldviews, while social movements such as socialism, populism, and the labor movement pushed for change. The older Protestant groups still had a great deal of control, but the outsiders were pushing them hard.

All these religious, intellectual, and social changes created unrest and challenged the optimistic idea that the United States was on an upward ascent to establishing the kingdom of God on earth. Older Protestant groups struggled with how to respond to this evolving world as many of their basic theological assumptions were challenged by the new scientific and intellectual movements. Darwinian sciences and higher biblical criticism seemed to undermine their bedrock biblical and theological beliefs, while new ideas from Freudian psychology, socialism, and communism called into question the very nature of religious belief.

Protestants began to divide internally on how to respond to such challenges. More liberal-leaning Protestants, having distanced themselves from revivalism, generally thought that these new challenges could be met and overcome by transforming the Christian ethos. They sought to shed what they saw as "premodern" elements of Christianity that no longer worked for modern people. They sought to differentiate the "core" elements and teachings of Christian theology, which were to be maintained, from older accretions to the faith, such as the six-day creation, biblical miracles, and older understandings of salvation and the afterlife. This "evangelical liberalism" still focused on God and Jesus in its own way, but it felt that this new version of Christianity would be attractive and understandable to modern people as well as able to resist the challenges of anti-religious forces.

More conservative-leaning Protestants (along with immigrant religious leaders) rejected the intellectual and social changes as dangerous to the Christian faith. They thought that the whole of Christian tradition (Bible, theology, and ethos) had to be defended from the corrosive forces of modernity and that any concessions to their opponents would open the floodgates to the eventual destruction of the faith itself. Conservative in their leanings, American Roman Catholic leaders sought to reinforce traditional papal and church authority and to limit the full acclimation of American Catholics to American culture. Conservative Protestants began to fire back at both liberal Protestants and modernist critics, doubling down on traditional biblical interpretation and theology. Some Protestants began to question the whole idea of an optimistic postmillennial future. Instead, basing their ideas on the apocalyptic framework of the biblical book of Revelation, they saw the world around them sliding into irreligiosity and demonic control—a catastrophe that would be overcome only by means of heavenly intervention. In the midst of it all, new conservative Protestant options developed, such as the Holiness movement and Pentecostalism.

Christianity in the United States in the Twentieth Century

The liberal-conservative tensions that arose in the nineteenth century became a split in the early twentieth century. Conservative theologians rallied to forceful restatements of traditional Christianity, most notably to those contained in a series of publications entitled *The Fundamentals*. These "evangelical" or "fundamentalist" Christians began to vie for control of the mainline Protestant denominations. "Liberal" or "modernist" Christians fought back and largely repelled these attempts in a series of battles that came to be known as the fundamentalist-modernist controversies. Having lost these battles and having been held up to public ridicule in the so-called Scopes Monkey Trial of 1925, conservatives pulled out of older Protestant denominations and institutions to form their own "Christian" subcultures, with separate denominational and institutional structures. The split of Protestantism into mainline and evangelical wings, so predominant in twentieth-century American Christianity, was complete.

Though the point is sometimes overlooked today, the First World War (1914–18) was perhaps the most important turning point in modern American history. Although the participation of the United States in this war was brief (only about eighteen months), this experience solidified the transition of the country into a major industrial world power and spurred the growth of American government. The war also disrupted and then ended the mass immigration of Europeans to the United States, and nativist and assimilationist pressures accelerated the assimilation and Americanization of those immigrants who had recently arrived. Along with the influence of the war, the development of new technologies—such as automobiles, telephones, radio, and motion pictures—created a truly national culture for the first time. As American Christians looked at the developments during the 1920s, they saw them as ambiguous. Many Christians, especially Protestants, welcomed the imposition of the national prohibition of alcohol, and they decried the

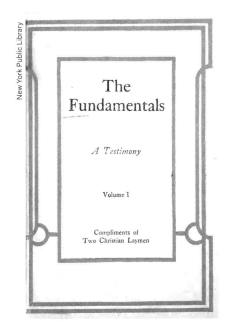

The
Fundamentals

A Testimony

Volume I

Compliments of
Two Christian Laymen

1.5. *The Fundamentals*, 1910–15.

new hedonistic culture of the decade, especially as displayed in the movies. Then came the major social and economic upheavals of the Great Depression (1929–41), which hit American Christianity particularly hard. Since religion was voluntary, essentially a "luxury" or a discretionary part of people's lives, there was a disastrous decline in financial giving to the churches. Along with this, there was also a decline in religious attendance, which is a bit more difficult to understand.

The turmoil of the larger world between the two World Wars also had an impact on American Christianity. Though their side had been successful in the first war, the experience left a bad taste for many, and during the 1920s and 1930s many Americans embraced isolationism and pacifism, despite the upheavals in Europe and Asia. The United States was eventually forced into the Second World War in 1941, and many Americans came to envision the war as a moral and even religious crusade to "redeem" the world for American democracy, a perspective that had more than a slight religious and messianic character to it.

After the Second World War ended in 1945, the United States transitioned to a period of unparalleled prosperity and growth. From 1929 to 1945 the American public longed for a return to normalcy. The desire of a generation to settle down in homes and families had been long delayed. Fueled by the growth of suburban housing and a wave of children (the baby boom), religious groups expanded rapidly. On top of this religious expansion was the Cold War between the Western democracies and the communist world, which was deepened by the grim specter of atomic warfare. This all pushed Americans to embrace organized religion at levels never seen before. Since communism was officially atheistic, to be a "good" American one had to claim a religious affiliation (it did not matter which one). America, it was claimed, was a "Judeo-Christian" nation, built on a (vague and expanded) "biblical" heritage and embracing a common morality (in a very Enlightenment sense).

This period was shaken by events starting in the late 1950s and cresting through the 1960s. Claiming their long-delayed promise, African Americans demanded their rights and equality in the Civil Rights Movement. A long and seemingly pointless war in Southeast Asia brought a revolt of young people against "the system." American religious consumers kept widening their options, exploring newly arrived forms of Asian religions and new, communal forms of Christianity led by charismatic figures. American Roman Catholicism was revolutionized by modernizing currents coming out of the Second Vatican Council (1962–65), which caused significant internal tensions. Perhaps the most transformative development of these decades for American Christianity was the women's movement, which touched all areas of American life and especially the Christian congregations that had long depended on women's contributions while generally not allowing them to occupy leadership positions.

By the early 1970s, it appeared that Christianity in America was following the general trend toward social liberalism that had been growing through the previous decade. While outwardly remaining strong, mainline Protestantism was racked by these social movements and struggled to respond to them, much as their predecessors had struggled a century before. And yet, beneath the trend toward social liberalism there was a strong countervailing force, surprising at the time, of conservative Christians seeking to take their place in the public arena of religion and society. Having spent the previous fifty years in a Christian subculture of their own making, conservative Protestant evangelicals pushed out into the wider stream of American life and flexed their political muscles in various movements, including the Moral Majority and the Christian Right. Conservative Protestants took to the media and dominated religious radio and television with new forms of religious broadcasting, such as talk shows. Long derided as the religion of "backwoods hicks," Pentecostalism emerged into the mainstream with power, and Pentecostal denominations—such as the Assemblies of God—became the fastest-growing religious groups in America. While the liberal mainline denominations began an eventually precipitous membership decline, conservative Christian churches moved into numerical ascendancy through the end of the twentieth century.

The late twentieth century saw American "consumers" of religion seeking a vast array of religious options, willing to pick and choose elements from those options in a form of DIY religion. As always, new and inventive forms of Christianity continued to expand Americans' religious options (along with non-Christian and eclectic forms of religion). Christian entrepreneurial leaders forged new approaches to religiosity with the development of Christian "megachurches" (such as Willow Creek, the Vineyard, Calvary Chapel, and many others), some of which grew into de facto denominations of their own. The decline of liberal denominations though the end of the twentieth century was offset by the growth of conservative Protestant denominations, and so the percentage of Americans claiming a formal religious affiliation remained within the peak range set in the middle of the twentieth century, at about 65 percent of the American population. The percentage of Americans who were Roman Catholic held steady at about 25 percent, a figure that belies a shift in their church: while the numbers of White American Roman Catholics declined, their numbers were replaced by immigrant Roman Catholics, especially from Latin America. Immigrant Christians from Asia and Africa also came in large numbers, especially after the reforms to the immigration system that were set in place in 1965, further increasing Christian diversity.

American Christianity in the Early Twenty-First Century

These general trends in American Christianity continued into the new millennium, and the divisions grew even wider. Up to about 2010, the rate of
religious affiliation in the American public remained roughly steady, at about
65 percent. But since that time, the numbers have sagged, especially among
younger generations, although new Christian immigrants have made up
for some of the decline and have diversified an already amazing spread of
Christian options. The numbers of religious seekers has held steady, and a
growing number of Americans claim no religious affiliation (the "Nones")
or that they have left religion altogether (the "Dones"). Increasing numbers
of Americans claim to be "spiritual but not religious." These developments
are ambiguous and recent, so no trend is yet clear. It is uncertain whether
these represent a regression to an older mean, a clear trend toward a new era
for religion in America, or a new-found honesty on the part of those who
might, in a previous generation, have felt socially pressured to claim some
sort of affiliation.

An interesting recent development is the social polarization over religion
and politics, what is known as the "God gap." Since the 1990s, political scientists have noticed a striking correlation between religious activity and voting patterns. Two-thirds of those who say they attend worship often (weekly
or more) vote for Republican candidates, while two-thirds of those who say
they rarely or never attend worship vote for Democratic candidates. On top
of the other observed polarizations in contemporary American society, this
gap seems to suggest a nation increasingly divided over religious identity and
participation.

Conclusion

The really striking element of this narrative of Christianity in America, however, is the basic continuity of the situation over the past 250 years. American
Christianity has certainly grown increasingly complex and varied in ways
that an eighteenth-century American could hardly have recognized. Yet
under all the developments and expansions and complexity, the basic system
of American Christianity forged at the beginnings of the American republic
has ultimately been consistent for all this time. The bounds of voluntary and
pluralistic religion are wider, but the basic system is still there. The United
States continues to be a marketplace of religious ideas, where entrepreneurial
religious leaders seek to draw adherents to their churches, with ever more
options from which they might chose. America is still a nation of restless

religious seekers looking for the religious options that will serve them best. And if they cannot find options they like, they are always free to develop new ones. Ultimately, this amounts to a dynamic system of American Christianity that still has a tremendous amount of power and resilience. God only knows what the future will bring.

2

The Beginnings
of Christianity in America

Native Americans before European Settlement

Before considering the importation of Christianity into the Americas by European settlers beginning in the sixteenth century, it is good to consider those who were already in the Western Hemisphere when the Europeans arrived. Native Americans, the first human residents on these continents, arrived from Asia at least fifteen thousand years ago, although some scholars think the initial peoples came substantially earlier than that. The best theories suggest that these immigrants came in a number of different waves during the subsequent millennia, spreading quickly throughout the expanse of the Western Hemisphere. Native Americans are divided into hundreds of different tribes or ethnic groups, with many distinctive languages and traditions. Prior to European colonization, they settled in a myriad of different social and cultural arrangements—from large, highly organized communities to small, scattered bands of families and clans consisting of fewer than one hundred individuals. Some developed complex economic and farming systems; some were nomadic hunters, herders, and gatherers; and still others combined elements of both. These human communities adapted their existence to a large range of different climates and topographies—from forests to deserts, coastlines to mountains, and arctic to jungle. Estimates vary widely, but it is believed that at the beginning of the sixteenth century there were perhaps between four and thirteen million Native Americans living in the territory that is now the United States. These Native Americans are often divided into two major categories depending on the patterns of their existence: whether their societies were primarily agricultural or hunting and gathering in nature. Generally speaking, the agricultural societies were located in the American Southeast and Southwest, while the hunting and gathering societies were in the American North.

The older hunting and gathering traditions that these first Americans brought with them from Asia stretch back to the beginnings of human history. These societies were deeply dependent upon food that could be obtained from nature: game from forests and prairies, seafood from the coasts, and naturally occurring plants, wherever they could be found. Some of these cultures had readily available and reliable sources of food within a single area, and thus could be permanently situated. Others were more mobile, following the seasonal availability of game and edible flora from one location to the next. In the American Northeast and Midwest, some groups eventually combined elements of agriculture with hunting and gathering—planting crops in one location in the spring, going elsewhere for the summer, and then returning in the fall to reap the harvest. The availability of food and the need for mobility often limited the size of these groups and brought them into conflict with other groups over the control of resources and hunting grounds. The supply of animals on which their survival depended was carefully considered, and their cultures were based on rituals and practices that ensured successful hunting. Key to this was showing proper respect to the spirits of the natural world that were believed to determine the availability of this food.

These hunting and gathering societies tended to be numerically smaller than those based on agriculture, as the size of these communities depended heavily on often-limited food sources. Within the basic system of the tribe were smaller units of clans and families that represented the core elements of the group, which were also often divided by gender. These tribes' material cultures (their goods and physical artifacts) were often limited by their migrations; they had to transport their goods seasonally, and horses were not introduced into their cultures until the Europeans arrived in the sixteenth century. However, these tribes did develop very rich oral cultures. Stories, legends, and myths were passed down through the generations by storytellers and historians, often the elders of the community. The life of the community was celebrated and regulated by rituals of the lifecycle and the seasons.

Around 3000 BC, in what is now Central America, local societies began to develop forms of agricultural production that eventually enabled the rise of larger and complex societies based on permanent settlement and the cultivation of crops. These societies depended primarily on the production of key crops—notably corn, beans, and squash—along with the domestication of animals, especially turkeys. This economy gradually spread into the American Southeast and Southwest, allowing for the development of permanent settlements that were numerically larger and culturally more complex than had been previously possible. In some areas, especially in the Mississippi River valley and in the Southwest, it allowed for the development of huge, complex communities numbering in the tens of thousands, with elaborate material cultures and highly specialized and stratified societies. This world depended primarily on the organization and coordination of human labor and the social cooperation that could build and farm on a large scale. The huge burial mounds of the Southeast and the Pueblo settlements of the Southwest are enduring reminders of the skill and power of those who built these societies.

These agricultural societies retained many of the social and organizational elements of the older hunting and gathering societies, including the social primacy of clans and families, but now on a scale previously unknown. While many of these groups continued the practice of hunting to supply their communities with meat, the primary focus turned toward agriculture and the elements of the natural world that supported it. The water and the fertility of the land were crucial to the survival of these societies, so much of the life of these communities was focused on the spiritual forces of the natural world that made this fertility possible. When shifting climates and lingering droughts occurred, these could well be devastating to these complex societies.

It is perhaps wrong to speak of Native American *religion*, because that term tends to import into these cultures a western European understanding of spirituality, an understanding that generally locates the divine in a single sector of life. Rather, in Native American understanding, the spiritual (or divine) world was infused into all sectors of experience, so that, in some sense, all of Native American life was oriented around care and concern for the divine. Alongside and throughout the physical, observable world was a parallel world of spiritual power in which all creation—animate and inanimate—participated. Human existence was deeply dependent on these spiritual powers, which could be beneficent, hostile, or each in turn. Much of the energy of Native American societies was spent in understanding, tending to, and, if necessary, appeasing the spirits of the natural world. Rituals and other ceremonial elements of life were developed to regulate human existence and its interaction with the spiritual world so that proper harmony between them could be preserved. Stories—especially the stories of creation, of the origins of the group, and of the ancestors—were crucial elements of Native American life. Properly tending to the dead and to the spirits of the ancestors were important activities and carried out with care.

In many of the Native American groups, these "religious" activities were directed and carried out by individuals whose spiritual awareness and special powers put them in touch with the spiritual powers in an intense way. These individuals, termed *shamans*, lived as it were between the physical and spiritual worlds; thus they were able to help others understand and perform the proper actions and rituals that would maintain or restore the proper balances that made life possible. In some tribes, shamans wielded great power and control.

With the coming of Europeans to North America beginning in the sixteenth century, Native Americans encountered powerful and dangerous societies that transformed and endangered their traditional ways of life. The initial, and often enduring, problem was the introduction into the Native American world of diseases such as smallpox and measles, for which Native Americans had no experience and no natural immunities; as a result, huge numbers of people died. In the Spanish-settled regions of the Southwest and California, Native people were often forcibly gathered into mission settlements. The Roman Catholic faith that they were brought into became a part of their world, but it was often a thin veneer over their existing spiritual understandings and practices. In other areas, Native Americans were forcibly dispossessed of their lands, pushed westward ahead of advancing European settlements, and eventually forced onto reservations meant to contain them. Their complex cultures were often devastated by disease, dispossession, and violent interactions with Europeans.

Though the main motivation for European settlement was economic, there were some Christian Europeans who saw it as their calling to bring the Christian faith to the Native Americans. While some of these Christians sought to assist the Native Americans, their efforts were often hindered by the brutality of the advancing European cultures and by their own limited understanding and appreciation of Native American cultural and religious worlds. Although there were some Native individuals and groups who became Christians, the general results of these efforts were not substantial. Religious groups eventually participated in the reservation system, and the mission schools they developed were often devastating to Native American families and cultures.

The Background of European Christianity

Christianity began as an offshoot of Judaism in the eastern Mediterranean during the first century AD, and it gradually moved from there into the wider cultural world of the Roman Empire. At first it was strongest in the Greek-speaking eastern empire; then it spread into the western, Latin-speaking areas.

In the fourth century, Christianity became an officially recognized and legally protected religion within the empire, and because of imperial favor, it grew rapidly. As the western part of the empire collapsed in the fifth and sixth centuries, Germanic tribes took over control of western Europe, and Christianity slowly made its way into these cultures and regions. After a period of some social and political stability during the ninth century under Charlemagne, the first "Holy Roman emperor," western Europe experienced divisions and struggles and came under attack from non-Christian outsiders, such as Muslims, Vikings, and Huns. But the Christianization of western Europe proceeded, and Christianity was well established in most of this region by the thirteenth century. Though internal divisions remained, many in western Europe began thinking of this region as a single religious unit. This led to what would become known as *Christendom*, a social arrangement in which Christianity and secular governments work together to extend and protect the faith. In reality, this collaboration was rarely harmonious. Nevertheless, medieval Christianity developed a rich and extensive religious culture that came to define and enliven many areas of life in western Europe.

During this period, the Christian churches achieved a measure of internal unity through the leadership of the chief bishop of the region, the bishop of Rome, also known as the pope. Slowly, the medieval papacy sought to extend its power and control, not only over the churches of the region but over its secular rulers as well. The medieval Christian church in western Europe, headed by the papacy, became a very wealthy organization, fueled by the favor of the secular rulers and the donations of the faithful. With wealth came power, both religious and secular. And the leading bishops and cardinals of the medieval church often became powerful figures in society. Some were renowned as patrons of the arts and culture. A significant portion of life in medieval western Europe was controlled by these leaders of the church, and the church had a direct and discernable influence on the daily lives of people. Unfortunately, with wealth and power came corruption, as some individuals were drawn to church leadership for the wrong reasons, and a culture of corruption spread throughout the church, reaching even down to the level of the local parishes.

Though there was still much good in the Western church, there was a growing perception that the church needed reform to return it to its primary religious mission. The need for reform was a constant refrain of some church meetings and officials during the medieval period, but the usually proposed solutions—such as tightening church regulations and electing a "good" (reforming) pope—were often thwarted by those in the church who profited from the system as it was. The ravages of the medieval plagues and a deeply disturbing schism in the Western church (a time when there were simultaneously two, and then three, rival popes) shook people's confidence in the claims of the church to provide religious guidance and salvation. Frustrated by the corruption and "worldliness" of the church, some Christians drew away from the official church into mysticism—forms of popular devotion and community that provided more fulfilling religious experiences. While some of these mystics existed on the margins (or beyond the margins) of orthodox Christianity, most were fairly faithful to the organized church even while they were highly critical of it. Church officials, aided by secular rulers, often persecuted mystical groups harshly as "heretics," which they mostly were not. Reforming groups such as the Waldensians in Italy, the Hussites in Bohemia, and the Lollards in England were forced underground in order to survive.

By the beginning of the sixteenth century, there was fairly widespread agreement in western Europe that the church needed substantial reforms, but there was little consensus on how these reforms should be achieved. Many theologians and intellectuals, such as Erasmus of Rotterdam (1466–1536), favored incremental change within the basic framework of the church system by tightening existing rules, developing new practices, and electing as leaders of the church those who would favor reform. Unfortunately, there were too many in the Western church who opposed substantial reforms, and the incremental proposals rarely achieved any real results. A turning point came with the work of the German monk and university professor Martin Luther (1483–1546). Luther's writings in the late 1510s on reform of the church were widely circulated around western Europe and provoked a firestorm of critique. Though Luther initially suggested only limited changes to the medieval church and the papacy, the church and its secular allies did what they usually did in such cases: apply harsh pressure on critics like Luther to get them to recant and cease their attacks on the church.

The trouble was that such tactics did not work well on Luther. He was increasingly bothered by the disconnect he saw between the Word of God available to him through the Bible and the practices and structures of the medieval church. Luther came to believe that the Western church was fundamentally corrupted and that incremental change from within was useless. Protected by his faith and by the support of his local political leader, Luther responded to church pressure with increasingly harsh critiques of the church. A growing number of Christians in western Europe rallied to his defense. Though he was eventually excommunicated by the church, a significant number of political units in Germany supported him and followed his lead. Beginning in the 1520s, many of these political units began to pull their regional churches away from the control of the papacy and instituted sweeping church reforms independently along the lines suggested by Luther and other, similarly minded reformers. These new churches came to be known as evangelical or Protestant churches, and they adopted practices and theologies that were quite different from those of the medieval church.

Without a single controlling authority, these Protestant churches came to differ from one another in structure and theology. New local churches based in areas of central and northern Germany and Scandinavia followed the pattern set by Luther and his colleagues in common confessional documents; thus they became known as Lutheran churches (though Luther himself was uncomfortable with this name). Reform leaders in areas of southern Germany, Switzerland, and France—such as Ulrich Zwingli and John Calvin—used a different pattern of reform to form other new churches, which came to be referred to as Reformed or Calvinist Protestant churches. This form of Protestantism spread to Holland and Scotland. In England, the royal leaders and their advisers separated the local church from the papacy and formed the independent Church of England—the beginnings of the Anglican Communion. There was also a significant group of Reformed Christians in England, who came to be known as Puritans.

In most of these newly Protestant areas, at least one older pattern was retained—namely, the idea of religious uniformity. All citizens of a particular territory were to be automatically enrolled in the territorial church, or state church, through infant baptism. But small groups of more radical Reformers pushed beyond this, insisting that true Christian churches could only be small congregations of those whose conversion to the faith was ratified by baptism in adulthood. These radical Protestants, known as Anabaptists (or "rebaptizers"), were seen by the territorial churches (Protestant and Catholic) as threats to the religious and social order, so they were persecuted by church and state. Some of these Anabaptists—the Mennonites and the Hutterites, for example—eventually coalesced around influential leaders.

The medieval church under the control of the papacy was slow to react to this new Protestant threat, and it initially sought merely to suppress these protesting groups by means that had worked in the past. But these sixteenth-century reforming movements were of a different intensity, and many had the backing of influential political leaders. Though the papacy retained control over the churches in France, Spain, Italy, and southern Germany, they lost control over the churches in the rest of western Europe. It was finally under the leadership of Pope Paul III (1534–49) that the medieval church realized the new Protestant threat required a new and vigorous response, which came through the Council of Trent (1545–63). The bishops who were the leaders of the council eventually formulated both a sweeping set of internal reforms, to address the corruptions within the church, and also new theological formulations, to respond to the Protestants. It is with the implementation of these new elements that the modern Tridentine ("of Trent") Roman Catholic Church becomes recognizable.

The resulting Catholic Reformation (sometimes referred to as the Counter-Reformation) gave a new spirit and vitality to those churches remaining in communion with the papacy and heartened those who sought significant reforms without breaking with the Roman establishment. In a number of areas in Europe—such as Poland, southern Germany, and France—church and secular rulers began to push back against the Protestant tides, and they made significant progress. New religious orders, such as the Society of Jesus (members of which are called Jesuits), were formed to meet the Protestant threat and spread the Catholic faith. Older orders, such as the Franciscans and the Dominicans, were also revitalized for this same mission. A new religious spirit swept through many Catholic areas, and new forms of spirituality and devotion were developed that engaged lay Catholics and strengthened their faith. This Tridentine form of Catholicism was often austere, devout, sacrificial, and militantly devoted to the spread of Catholic religiosity and the countering of Protestantism.

The European Voyages of Trade and Discovery

During the Middle Ages, western Europeans became geographically boxed into their region by hostile forces: the Vikings to the north, the Huns and Slavs to the east, and (above all) the Muslims to the south. Their main connection to the rest of the world was through the Christian Byzantine Empire in Constantinople, but that empire fell to the Turkish Muslims in 1453. Though the threats from the Vikings and Huns receded after their conversion to Christianity, the Muslim and Turkish threats remained, with the Turks conquering most of southeastern Europe and threatening Vienna in the sixteenth century. On the Iberian Peninsula, a few Christian kingdoms remained in the North after the Muslim conquests that began in the eighth century. These Christian kingdoms struggled for eight hundred years to regain their lost territories, a reclamation that was not complete until the conquest of Grenada in 1492. Though there were certainly Christian groups remaining in the Muslim world and beyond—in countries like India and Ethiopia—European Christians had lost connection with them.

Because of their dominance to the east and south, Muslims controlled the trade that Europeans had with the Middle East and the Far East. It was from these regions, especially Asia, that many luxury trade goods came—goods such as spices, silks, and precious stones and metals. Muslim control of this trade meant very high prices to European consumers. The trip of Venetian explorer Marco Polo through central Asia to China in the thirteenth century was an attempt to find a way around Muslim control of trade. But though the route was possible, it was not practical.

With the end of the Muslim presence in Portugal in the fifteenth century, Portuguese sailors began a series of expeditions into the Atlantic Ocean and southward down the west coast of Africa. By 1488, explorer Bartolomeu Dias had rounded the southern tip of Africa, and, by 1498, Vasco da Gama had sailed through the Indian Ocean to India. This voyage was a momentous one because it bypassed the Muslims who controlled the Middle East and proved that the trade goods of Asia could be obtained directly. Portuguese traders set up trading stations in Africa, India, and beyond, promising great wealth to expeditions that returned to Europe with cargos of luxury goods. European explorers and traders eventually sailed directly to China, Japan, and Indonesia and established trading points with Asian markets for all the goods that Europeans wanted so intensely. These sixteenth-century European voyages to Asia were driven by commerce and profit and, when completed successfully, could be highly lucrative.

Not to be outdone by their neighbors to the west, the newly united Spanish monarchy sought their own routes to the riches of Asia, commissioning an Italian sailor, Christopher Columbus, to undertake such a voyage. Instead of sailing south around Africa, however, Columbus proposed to sail directly west to reach Asia. Despite popular lore, most educated Europeans of the time knew the earth was round; the Greeks had proved this millennia before. However, Columbus was a lousy mathematician and drastically underestimated the circumference of the earth. Had not the Americas and their nearby archipelagoes been there, it is likely that no one would have ever heard from Columbus or his expedition again. As it happened, Columbus found land, but not the land he expected. In 1492, he and his crew landed on a Caribbean island he named San Salvador. By 1502, he had completed three more voyages to the region, still under the impression that he was close to the riches of Asia. But all he found were islands populated by Native Americans, not the spices and silks he sought. The crews and settlers that Columbus brought on these voyages treated the Native Americans very badly, and their presence on the islands introduced European diseases that decimated the local populations. The settlements he founded on Hispaniola (Haiti and the Dominican Republic) suffered from Columbus's own mismanagement and egotistical notions of his importance, and he was soon removed from charge over them. Columbus surveyed much of the Caribbean and the Atlantic coast of Central America, but he never found the passage to Asia that he originally sought.

Even though these first four Spanish voyages found neither valuable trade goods nor a viable passage to Asia, the European discovery of the lands of the

Western Hemisphere (the New World) unleashed even more European voyages of discovery and conquest. With the Treaty of Tordesillas, negotiated by the pope in 1494, the Portuguese and Spanish divided between themselves the known world, for influence and colonial settlement. The treaty established a line that reserved Africa and the Indian Ocean for the Portuguese and cut through the Atlantic Ocean, designating the eastern part of Brazil for them as well, while assigning the rest of the Western Hemisphere to the Spanish. Spanish adventurers and explorers wasted little time in beginning the search for riches and glory in the New World. The first European sighting of the Pacific Ocean came in 1513, when a party of Spanish explorers, under the command of Vasco Núñez de Balboa, crossed the Isthmus of Panama. A more ambitious Spanish expedition, led by Ferdinand Magellan, departed in 1519 to sail around the southern tip of South America and into the Pacific Ocean. Though Magellan was killed in a battle in the Philippines in 1522, remnants of his crew eventually returned to Europe, completing the first circumnavigation of the globe.

Expeditions from Spain soon reached the New World with the intention of founding settlements and colonies. There were already settlements on the island of Hispaniola from the voyages of Columbus. Now other islands in the Caribbean were settled in rapid order, including permanent colonies in Puerto Rico, in 1508, and Cuba, in 1511. In 1513, Juan Ponce de León led the first expedition to Florida, but permanent settlement there did not come until the establishment of the St. Augustine settlement in 1565. The first Spanish incursion into the region of Mexico was an illegal expedition of several hundred adventurers mounted by Hernán Cortés in 1519. With the technological assistance of European weapons, cooperation from Native tribes whom the Aztecs had conquered, and no small amount of luck, a relatively small force of Spaniards conquered the Aztec capital of Tenochtitlán (now Mexico City) in 1521. Control of the rest of the region followed. In 1524, another small, ruthless band of Spanish adventurers traveled south from Panama down to Peru, into the heart of the once-mighty Inca Empire. With the same combination of force and luck, these Spaniards conquered the Incas by 1533. Another exploration party, this one led by Juan Rodríguez Cabrillo, pushed north up the Pacific coast in 1542, reaching as far as what is now San Diego, California. In a relatively short amount of time, Spanish explorers and colonizers had laid claim to a wide swath of territory in the Western Hemisphere.

The Spanish and Portuguese were not the only Europeans to explore the Western Hemisphere in the sixteenth century. John Cabot, in 1497, and Henry Hudson, in 1609, explored areas of North America for the English. Giovanni da Verrazano charted the region of New York in 1524 for the French. And, in 1535, Jacques Cartier pushed up the St. Lawrence River in Canada, also for the

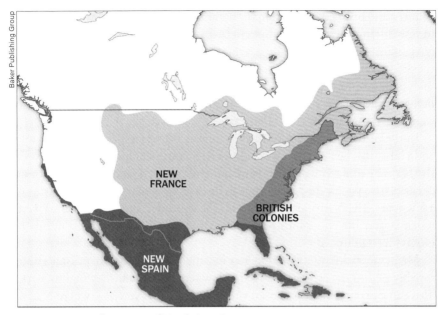

2.1. European Colonization of North America.

French. Numerous European expeditions searched for the fabled Northwest Passage, a route to Asia widely believed to exist around the Canadian Arctic. Many of these voyages ended in frustration or tragedy. In 1579, English explorer and pirate Francis Drake sailed into the Spanish Pacific region as far north as central California. But the Spanish authorities guarded their possessions jealously, so the French and English mainly focused their explorations and colonizing efforts in eastern North America instead, apart from some islands in the Caribbean that they would later seize from the Spanish. The whole of the Caribbean and Central and South America would eventually become known as Latin America, because of the widespread use of Spanish and Portuguese, the so-called Latinate languages.

The nature of the European enterprise in Latin America differed greatly from the European ventures in Asia. In Asia, Europeans focused mainly on trade with the established Asian powers. Though they did eventually seize and colonize some of these areas, initially they tended to take over only the lands they needed for trading. Their profit was in trade and not in conquest. In the Western Hemisphere, on the other hand, there was not the proliferation of finished trade goods for exchange, so the commercial enterprise there was of a completely different nature—in this case, a classical colonial economy. Traditionally, a colony would produce valuable raw materials to trade with the home country, and finished goods from the home country would be sent to the colony in return. The Western Hemisphere had abundant raw materials, especially gold and silver, and eventually developed lucrative plantation economies for the production of sugar, tobacco, cotton, and other raw materials. But to make such colonial efforts profitable, the Spanish needed to conquer the Indigenous nations, control large swaths of territory, and subjugate Indigenous people, who were forced to work for the colonizers.

In the initial settlement of the Caribbean Islands, especially Hispaniola and Cuba, this last element was a disaster. Spanish conquerors tried to force the Native people to work for them, but they resisted, and the vast majority of the Native people died, of European diseases or of maltreatment, after only a few years. The Native populations on the continent of Latin America were much larger, and though diseases decimated many of them, their numbers eventually rebounded.

Medieval Spain was a feudal society in which vast numbers of peasants were forcibly tied to the estates of large landowners, for whom they had to work. This same arrangement was used throughout Latin America, where Native people were subjugated and relegated to the landed estates or mines of European overlords. In such an economy, land was the principal source of wealth, but land was only good if there was labor to make it productive. In the Caribbean and in parts of South America (especially Venezuela and Brazil), the need for labor was so acute that soon the Spanish and Portuguese began importing enslaved persons from Africa to supplement the labor force of the subjugated Native peoples. The English and French also followed this pattern when they took over islands in the Caribbean. Overall, during the colonial period far more enslaved Africans were brought to Latin America than were brought to British North America.

The Spanish conquest in the New World began with the major islands in the Caribbean and then turned to the major empires in Mexico and Peru. The Aztecs in Mexico and the Incas in Peru were themselves conquerors and overlords of many other tribes and peoples, so many Native peoples simply traded the brutal rule of one set of overlords for another. But there were relatively few Spanish overlords and millions of Native people, so the Spanish decided it was necessary to destroy much of the Native cultures and systems (including religious systems) in order to keep the Native people subservient. In much of the Spanish area of colonization, European control was limited to bands of settlement along the coasts, and independent and hostile Native populations existed outside these bands. Only slowly did the Spanish authorities extend their control over these interior regions, and the colonial frontiers were often dangerous places for European settlers.

The Spanish Colonization of North America

Spanish settlement efforts on the mainland of North America were focused on the geographic area that is now Mexico, which the Spanish called New Spain. The initial conquest was in the central part of this territory, around the captured city of Tenochtitlán, which came to be called Mexico City. The settlement of the rest of this territory came incrementally: south, into the Mayan lands, and north and west, toward the Pacific Ocean and what is now the southwestern United States. Discovery of silver and other metals in these latter regions accelerated the process of settlement, but to the north armed Native tribes fiercely resisted Spanish incursions. Once the Spanish conquerors took control of a swath of territory, colonial officials gave large grants of land called *encomiendas*, or estates, along with quasi-feudal control over local Native populations, as a reward to upper-class Spaniards who had assisted the conquest or had aided the king in some way. Other similar grants of land were given to the Church for support of their efforts and institutions. These large estates were focused mainly on agriculture and ranching, and they became the main structures of colonial New Spain.

Colonial society was highly structured and rigidly maintained, especially as there were very few Spaniards ruling millions of Native people. At the top of the social pyramid were the "Europeans," the Spanish ruling class, who controlled the land and the institutions of the colony. This small class was itself divided into two groups. The very highest was the *peninsulares*, those Spaniards actually born on the Iberian Peninsula of Europe. The *peninsulares* controlled all the higher offices of state and church. The other "Europeans" were the *criollos*, the population of Spanish descent born in New Spain. The *criollos* had ruling roles but rarely made it into the highest ranks of society. This caused inevitable conflict, and eventually, in the nineteenth century, the *criollos* pushed for independence from Spain. The two "European" classes maintained themselves by discouraging intermarriage and fraternization with lower classes. The next class down was a larger group of people of mixed heritage, usually the result of the unions of European men with Native or enslaved women, unions that took place because of the persistent shortage of European women in the colony. Those of mixed European and Native parentage were termed *mestizos*, and those of mixed Europeans and enslaved African parentage were termed *mulattos*.[1] Those designated as *mestizos* or *mulattos* often worked in lower-level jobs on estates and in the colonial administration. The largest and lowest of the class groups was the Native population, who made up

1. Today, *mulatto* has come to be an offensive term for someone with one White parent and one Black parent.

the bulk of the colonial workforce. Enslaved Africans were also at this lowest class level, although enslaved Africans constituted a smaller percentage of the population in colonial Mexico than they did in the Caribbean and in parts of South America.

The question of religion in colonial New Spain is complex. Certainly, the Europeans wanted to establish Roman Catholic parishes for those in the higher levels of society and others who were already Christians. The real question concerned the evangelization of the vast number of Native people. The colonial enterprise was geared primarily toward economic gain, not evangelization. Also, colonizers often did not want religious leaders around, as their efforts could disturb the Native workers, and religious leaders could bear witness to, and object to, the mistreatment of the workers. Early in the sixteenth century, as shocking as it sounds today, some Spaniards wondered whether the Native people were truly human, and thus able to be converted. Some in the colonial

Brother Juan de Escalona, "Letter to the Spanish Viceroy" (1601)

The first and foremost difficulty, from which have sprung all the evils and ruin of this land, is the fact that this conquest was entrusted to a man of such limited resources as Don Juan de Oñate. The result was that soon after he entered this land, his people began to perpetrate many offenses against the natives and to plunder their pueblos of the corn they had gathered for their own sustenance; here corn is God, for they have nothing else with which to support themselves. Because of this situation and because the Spaniards asked the natives for blankets as tribute, even before teaching them the meaning of God, the Indians began to get restless, abandon their pueblos, and take to the mountains. . . .

I do not hesitate to say that . . . the conquest (could be) effected in a Christian manner without outraging or killing these poor Indians, who think that we are all evil and that the king who sent us here is ineffective and a tyrant. By so doing we would satisfy the wishes of our mother church. . . .

Because of these matters (and others that I am not telling), we cannot preach the gospel now, for it is despised by these people on account of our great offenses and the harm we have done them. At the same time, it is not desirable to abandon this land, either for the service of God or the conscience of his majesty since many souls have already been baptized. Besides, this place where we are now established is a good stepping stone and site from which to explore this whole land.

George P. Hammond and Agapito Rey, ed. and trans., *Don Juan de Oñate, Colonizer of New Mexico, 1595-1628* (Albuquerque: University of New Mexico Press, 1953), 2:692-95.

Catholic Church, notably Bartolomé de las Casas, strongly attacked the often-harsh colonial treatment of Native people. And in 1537, Pope Paul III decreed that Native Americans were indeed human beings and candidates for conversion. So there were often tensions between the colonizers and those working to evangelize the Native peoples. Yet the Church and many of the evangelizers still treated Native Americans as children and second-class citizens who would be forced to work for the support of the Church.

In the Catholic Church of the time, there were two kinds of workers. There were the *secular* clergy (so called because they were "in the world"), who served the parishes of the diocese and were supervised by the diocesan bishops, and there were the *religious*—that is, members of the religious orders. While some of these religious were ordained priests, many were not. Local tensions often arose because the religious were responsible not to the diocesan bishops but to the heads of their orders. The most important of these orders in New Spain were the Dominicans, the Franciscans, the Augustinians, and the Jesuits. These were all "mendicant" orders, those committed to working among people in the world, rather than being closed up in monasteries. They were mainly responsible for evangelization and education.

The colonial Church was originally supervised by an archbishop from Spain, but in 1546 the pope raised the bishop of Mexico City to the rank of archbishop, meaning that he could directly supervise all the dioceses of New Spain. The pope also granted to the colonial administration of New Spain *patronato real*, direct local control over the Church, which meant that, in many ways, the Church became an arm of the secular colonial government.

The mendicant orders arrived in New Spain as early as 1526 and began the work of converting the Native populations to Christianity. These Christianizers decided that the most effective way to do this was to gather new converts into permanent settlements where they could be controlled and protected. The Native population had to work under the direction of these religious and were subject to discipline that was sometimes harsh. Often, conversions were initially rather shallow, as Native populations were brought into the obedience of the Church without much education or training. The idea was to first bring them into the sacramental grace of the Church and only later to teach them about this new religion. Many Native persons blended Catholic Christianity with elements of their previous religions, creating novel combinations. Many elements of popular Mexican religion—including veneration of the Virgin of Guadalupe and practices surrounding the Day of the Dead (*Día de los Muertos*)—show this fusion at work. Over the centuries, this new religiosity became deeply entrenched in the hearts and minds of the Mexican people.

2.2. Spanish Missions in the American Southwest.

After several generations, as the new faith took hold among the Native populations, the village settlements of converted people (called *doctrinas*) became an object of contention between the religious orders and the secular Church in New Spain. The local bishops claimed that, after such a period of time, the Native parishes should be transferred from the control of the orders and handed over to their authority. The orders resisted this, fearing that their work would be undone by the often-lax oversight of the colonial secular clergy. Eventually, in some areas Native parishes were "secularized"—that is, removed from the control of the religious orders.

On the northern frontier of New Spain, in what are now the southern and southwestern regions of the United States, the work of evangelism was institutionalized in the Spanish mission system. On the frontier, far from colonial protection and close to hostile tribes, evangelizers and new Christians were gathered into fortified compounds, called missions, where they were supervised by religious workers; Spanish soldiers protected the entire project. Dozens of these missions were established from Arizona to Florida, and later up the coast of California. Certainly, many of the religious who worked in these missions had genuine concern for the new Native Christians, but they would also discipline them harshly and often sought to destroy the remaining elements of their pre-Christian cultures and religions (which were often one and the same). As in Mexico, religious blending and combining often took place in these areas, and Church officials would sometimes turn a blind eye to practices they did not like as long as the Native people remained obedient to them.

The Spanish Exploration and Settlement of the South and Southwest

The areas that are now the southern and southwestern United States were always on the frontier of New Spain, quite a ways away from the center of the Spanish colonial administration, in Mexico. This distance meant that there was little direct trade or influence between these regions, and any Spanish settlements on the frontier had to be rather self-sufficient. The main Spanish concern in these areas was to use them as a buffer to protect the main portion of New Spain from incursions from unfriendly Native tribes or the encroachment of other European powers. There was little established, ongoing Spanish presence in these areas, especially among the Native populations, save for in the Rio Grande region of New Mexico and southern Texas.

The first Spanish exploration of Florida and the Gulf Coast region came early in the sixteenth century with the initial expedition of Juan Ponce de León, which arrived in the area in 1513 but soon had to leave due to the hostility of Native tribes. Further expeditions and attempts at settlement also failed. An expedition under the command of Hernando de Soto arrived in Tampa Bay in 1539 with hundreds of colonists, along with priests and religious brothers. The expedition searched for gold and riches throughout the southeastern regions of what would eventually become the United States, from South Carolina as far west as Arkansas, where de Soto died. Nothing came from this expedition, or from another in 1549 that was destroyed by a hurricane.

It was only because of an outside threat that Florida was finally colonized. In the 1560s, French Protestants (Huguenots) settled a colony in South Carolina, calling forth a swift reaction from Spanish officials. The Spanish sent yet another, this time stronger, expedition to northern Florida in 1563 under the command of Pedro Menéndez de Avilés, who founded the first permanent Spanish settlement—which was also the first permanently inhabited European settlement—in what is now the United States: St. Augustine. Menéndez de Avilés had a strong military force and used St. Augustine as a base from which to destroy the French colony in South Carolina and ensure the long-term success of this latest colonial venture.

Along with secular priests to establish parishes for the Spanish settlers, Menéndez de Avilés also brought Spanish Jesuits to begin the evangelization of the Native tribes in Florida and Georgia. In 1573, the Jesuits were replaced by Franciscans, who struggled to establish this work in the face of Native hostility. But by the seventeenth century the Franciscans claimed a vibrant mission in the region, with seventy brothers supervising a growing number of *doctrinas*, which comprised twenty-six thousand converted Native individuals. This missionary enterprise was, however, tenuous from the beginning, and Native revolts and outside Native attacks, along with increasing pressure from the English to the north, meant a decline in the missions. By the time the Spanish were forced to cede Florida to the English in 1763, there was little in the way of permanent results from these missions. Spanish explorers were the first Europeans to see much of what would later become the southeastern United States, but since they could not make settlements in the region commercially viable, they eventually abandoned it.

Spanish exploration and settlement in what is now the southwestern United States came as a result of northward expansion in Mexico and generally had longer-term success. In 1540, a Spanish official in northwestern Mexico, Francisco Vázquez de Coronado, led a large expedition north into Arizona, New Mexico, Texas, and even Kansas. Over the next two years, the expedition saw

"A Seventeenth-Century Letter of Gabriel Díaz Vara Calderón, Bishop of Cuba, Describing the Indians and Indian Missions of Florida"

In the four provinces of Guale, Timuqua, Apalache and Apalachocoli there are 13,152 Christianized Indians to whom I administered the holy sacrament of confirmation. . . .

As to their religion, they are not idolaters, and they embrace with devotion the mysteries of our holy faith. They attend mass with regularity at 11 o'clock on the holy days they observe, namely, Sunday, and the festivals of Christmas, the Circumcision, Epiphany, the Purification of Our Lady, and the days of Saint Peter, Saint Paul and All Saints Day, and before entering the church each one brings to the house of the priest as a contribution a log of wood. They do not talk in the church, and the women are separated from the men; the former on the side of the Epistle, the latter on the side of the Evangel. They are very devoted to the Virgin, and on Saturdays they attend when her mass is sung. On Sundays they attend the Rosario and the Salve in the afternoon. They celebrate with rejoicing and devotion the Birth of Our Lord, all attending the midnight mass with offerings of loaves, eggs and other food. They subject themselves to extraordinary penances during Holy Week, and during the 24 hours of Holy Thursday and Friday, while our Lord is in the Urn of the Monument, they attend standing, praying the rosary in complete silence, 24 men and 24 women and the same number of children of both sexes, with hourly changes. . . . They have also a person deputized to report to them concerning all parishioners who live in evil.

Your Majesty's most humble servant and chaplain,

Gabriel, Bishop of Cuba.

Lucy L. Wenhold, trans., *Smithsonian Miscellaneous Collections* 95, no. 16 (November 1936): 12, 14.

many new areas—including the Colorado River and the Grand Canyon—and fought battles with a number of Native peoples; but since they did not find the gold and other riches they sought, the expedition was abandoned as a financial disaster. At about the same time, in 1542, Juan Rodríguez Cabrillo led a maritime expedition up the Pacific coast of Mexico in search of a reputed (but nonexistent) passage between the Pacific and Atlantic Oceans, discovering instead that Baja California was a peninsula and not an island, and landing in San Diego Bay. His expedition sailed as far north as central California before turning back. Permanent Spanish settlement in California would not begin for another 150 years.

After Coronado, another expedition under Francisco de Ibarra pushed into the region of New Mexico in 1563, leading in 1598 to the appointment of Juan de Oñate as the first Spanish governor of the province of New Mexico (known as Santa Fe de Nuevo México). Oñate and a strong force of Spanish, including secular priests and Franciscans, pushed up the Rio Grande valley and established permanent settlements in the region, including the city of Santa Fe in 1610. Though this colony was not much of a commercial success and was expensive to defend, the Franciscans successfully converted several of the local Native Pueblo settlements. The Pueblo society comprised up to twenty different agricultural settlements, where people lived in compact, multistory villages, often referred to as "pueblos." The Franciscans began to work among these Native Americans, and by the 1630s they had twenty-five missions serving nearly fifty thousand converts. By 1637, there were a total of forty-three missions in or around the Pueblo villages. The Spanish were not able to convert or control Native tribes on the outer edges of their territory—such as the Apache, Comanche, and Ute—who remained a constant threat to the Spanish settlers.

Spanish religious and colonial leaders maintained strict control over the Pueblo tribes. This control, at its best, could be described as paternalistic; at its worst, it was brutal. Though Native people were generally compliant with the new religion of Christianity, many also continued to practice their old religious rituals in secret, led by Native shamans ("medicine men"). Spanish officials moved against these religious leaders, causing smoldering resentment that burst into open rebellion in 1680, when Popé, a Tewa Pueblo shaman, led a rebellion (known as the Pueblo Revolt) that drove the Spanish out of New Mexico for twelve years. When the Spanish returned in force, the Native tribes were eventually forced into compliance, and the missions were reopened. The Pueblo tribes resumed practicing Roman Catholicism, while continuing their traditional religious ceremonies. The Spanish settlers in New Mexico developed a permanent culture of interconnected extended families, which focused on often-austere Roman Catholicism and a deep pride in their Spanish (not

Mexican) heritage. The territory of New Mexico became a part of the newly independent Mexican state in 1821, and then in 1848 it was ceded to the United States. The Roman Catholic parishes and missions in the region thus came under the jurisdiction of the Roman Catholic hierarchy in the United States.

Similar to what happened in Florida with the founding of St. Augustine, Spanish colonial activity in Texas was spurred by perceived incursions in the region by French explorers in the lower Mississippi River valley toward the end of the seventeenth century. A French settlement and mission in eastern Texas was briefly established and then quickly abandoned. Another, similar venture was attempted in the early eighteenth century. Spanish authorities reacted quickly by moving into Texas, beginning in 1716, and establishing settlements, missions, and forts in the region. In 1718, the Franciscans established the Mission San Antonio de Valero (popularly known as the Alamo), and eventually there were as many as twenty-six missions founded from the Gulf Coast to El Paso. The missions later waned, and they were eventually secularized by the new Mexican government. In this process, the lands of the religious orders were given to local landowners, and the religious parishes were given over to the control of the Roman Catholic bishops and their secular priests.

During the eighteenth century, there were new efforts in expansion northward from northwestern Mexico into Arizona and California, again spurred by competitive colonial exploration, this time by the British and Russians moving southward down the Pacific coast. The Jesuits had longstanding mission work in northwestern Mexico, including in Baja California and the Sonoran Desert, which was greatly expanded under the leadership of Eusebio Kino (1645–1711) and Juan María de Salvatierra (1648–1717), who explored the region that is now southern Arizona. The Jesuits established a series of missions among the Pima and Yuman peoples, including the famous Mission San Xavier del Bac, founded in 1692 near where the modern city of Tucson now lies. The Jesuit order, however, ran into conflict with the Spanish Crown, and its members were expelled from New Spain in 1767 and replaced in these missions by Franciscans. These missions also suffered from attacks by hostile Native tribes.

The Spanish presence in Alta (Upper) California, a large region including the land that is now the state of California, went back to the explorations of Juan Rodríguez Cabrillo along the southern Pacific coast in 1542. But Spanish interest in California languished because of its distance and cost, until eighteenth-century incursions by the British and Russians. In 1769, Spanish governor Gaspar de Portolá led an expedition into the region, bringing along with him the Franciscan Junípero Serra (1713–84), who founded the first mission in San Diego that year. Serra and his successor, Fermín Francisco de Lasuén (1763–1803), worked tirelessly to establish a string of twenty-one missions in

2.3. Mission San Xavier del Bac, Tucson, Arizona.

California, as far north as San Francisco. As was the usual pattern among the missions, the local Native tribes were coerced into residence at the missions and were converted to Christianity. Mission leaders eventually reported that they had converted over one hundred thousand people. To support the missions themselves, Native Americans raised cattle and sheep, whose hides and wool were shipped around the world. Contact with the Europeans was, as always, very difficult for the Native peoples, and epidemics of disease swept through their communities. Serra is a complex and controversial figure. He worked tirelessly to establish these missions and tried to protect the Native people from exploitation by Spanish settlers, but he also treated the Native people as children and reportedly punished them harshly for disobeying mission rules.

The California missions lasted into the nineteenth century, and the final one, near Sonoma, was founded as late as 1823. But declining Native populations and a lack of vigorous leadership by the Franciscans led to pressures on Spanish officials to shut the missions down. They stayed in operation, however, until 1826, when the new Mexican government issued a "Proclamation of Emancipation" freeing the Native peoples from their obligations to the missions. The missions themselves were eventually secularized and their properties sold to local landowners. Though many of the California mission buildings survived and have been renovated, there is not much left of the Christian communities that once lived and worked in them.

Over the course of five hundred years, Spanish Christians created vibrant civilizations in Latin America, including a rich religious culture that combined sixteenth-century Spanish Roman Catholicism with various forms of Native and African religiosity. The Roman Catholic Church was a pervasive part of colonial life, and to this day it remains integral to the American experience. The religious fusions that were formed in the Spanish colonial period remain influential in the American Southwest, especially among Native and Spanish-speaking populations in New Mexico and, to a lesser extent, in Texas and Arizona. And in the twentieth and twenty-first centuries, immigrants from Mexico, Cuba, Haiti, the Dominican Republic, and elsewhere in Latin America have brought renewed forms of this religiosity with them as they have settled in various regions of the United States.

The French Colonialization of North America

France was a leading power in Europe but slower than Spain to begin exploration and colonization in the Western Hemisphere. Though the French sent explorers to the region in the sixteenth century, mainly to Canada, these voyages did not result in the establishment of permanent colonies. French traders and fishermen established seasonal bases around the mouth of the St. Lawrence River, and there were a few aborted attempts at permanent settlements. There was a short-lived attempt at a French settlement in Brazil, and in the 1560s French Protestants established a colony in South Carolina, which was destroyed by Spanish forces from Florida. The first permanent French settlement was established in Nova Scotia in 1604. From there, the French spread further into the region they called Acadia, which comprised Nova Scotia, New Brunswick, and northern Maine. These settlements survived on agriculture, fishing, and trade with the Native peoples and, after a few very lean years, developed into a viable colonial enterprise.

Not long after, the French pushed up the St. Lawrence River to pursue further fur trade with Native Americans. They founded permanent settlements at Quebec in 1608 and at Montreal in 1642; this is the region the French called Canada. These settlements also developed into permanent colonies with settlers from France who farmed in the region, establishing there a permanent French-Canadian society, centered in what is now the Canadian province of Quebec. During this time, France was convulsed by religious struggles between the dominant Roman Catholics and a French Protestant minority (the Huguenots), which eventually resulted in the exodus of hundreds of thousands of French Protestants. In 1627, by royal decree, the Huguenots were expelled from Acadia

Father Sebastien Rasle, "Letter to His Nephew" (October 15, 1723)

During the more than thirty years that I have passed in the depth of the forests with the natives I have been so occupied in instructing them, and training them to Christian virtues, that I have scarcely had time to write many letters. . . .

The village in which I live is called Nanromtsouak and is situated on the banks of a river which empties into the sea, at the distance of thirty leagues below. I have erected a Church there, which is neat and elegantly ornamented. I have, indeed, thought it my duty to spare nothing either in the decoration of the building itself, or in the beauty of those articles which are used in our holy ceremonies. Vestments, chasubles, copes, and holy vessels, all are highly appropriate, and would be esteemed so even in our Churches in Europe. I have also formed a little choir of about forty young Indians, who assist at Divine Service in cassocks and surplices. They have each their own appropriate functions, as much to serve in the Holy Sacrifice of the Mass as to chant the Divine Offices for the consecration of the Holy Sacrament, and for the processions which they make with great crowds of Indians, who often come from a long distance to engage in these exercises; and you would be edified by the beautiful order they observe and the devotion they show.

They have built two Chapels at three hundred paces distance from the village; the one, which is dedicated to the Holy Virgin, and where can be seen her image in relief, is above on the river; the other, which is dedicated to the Guardian Angel, is below, on the same river. As they are both on the road which leads either into the woods or into the fields, the Indians can never pass without offering up their prayers.

William Ingraham Kip, *Early Jesuit Missions in North America* (New York: Wiley and Putnam, 1846), 2–4.

and Canada, and these colonies became completely Roman Catholic. For most of the eighteenth century, France and England were locked into a series of wars with each other, and these wars often spilled over into North America. In 1710, the English conquered most of Acadia, which was formally ceded to them in 1713 by the Peace of Utrecht. During the Seven Years' War (1756–63), which was known in British North America as the French and Indian War, British and British colonial forces defeated the French; the war culminated with their capture of the city of Quebec in 1759. In the 1763 Treaty of Paris, all of Canada was transferred to British control.

As part of the expanding fur trade, beginning in 1655 the French extended their reach into the Great Lakes and Upper Mississippi River regions. They established permanent settlements at Detroit, Mackinaw City, Sault Sainte

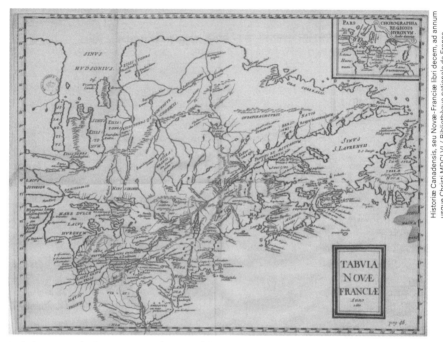

2.4. Seventeenth-Century French Map of the Jesuit Missions among the Hurons.

Marie, and Green Bay. And, in 1659, Pierre-Esprit Radisson reached the western end of Lake Superior. In 1673, a group led by Louis Jolliet and Father Jacques Marquette started exploring the Mississippi River. Marquette founded a mission for Native Americans on the Illinois River at Kaskaskia in 1703, which later became a permanent settlement. Another part of this expedition, led by Father Louis Hennepin, became the first group of Europeans to explore the Upper Mississippi River region; they traveled as far north as the Falls of Saint Anthony (Minneapolis). In 1682, a group under the command of René-Robert Cavelier de La Salle, set off down the Mississippi River, eventually reaching the Gulf of Mexico. La Salle claimed the entire Mississippi River region for France, and the territory was named Louisiana; this became the third French region in North America. The French made attempts to settle regions around the Gulf Coast in Texas, but these settlements were destroyed by the Spanish.

Permanent settlements in Louisiana were founded in Biloxi, Natchez, Mobile, New Orleans, Cahokia, and St. Louis (among others), but the European presence in the region was never very large. Under the terms of the 1762 Treaty of Fontainebleau, the French ceded all of the Louisiana Territory east of the Mississippi to the British and all west of the Mississippi to the Spanish, effectively ending the French colonial presence in North America. The French retained control of some islands in the Caribbean, especially Haiti, Martinique, and Guadalupe. France briefly regained Louisiana in 1801 but then sold it to the new American government in 1803 (the Louisiana Purchase).

Along with French explorers, traders, and settlers, French Catholic missionaries were active in all three regions of French North America, often working at the very edges of this territory. Although there were several different Catholic groups involved in this mission, especially the Recollects and Sulpicians, the leading group was the Jesuits. At the founding of the Acadia colonies, these missionaries fanned out over the region and baptized a number of individuals from the local Micmac tribe. The expansion of French settlement in Canada allowed for the arrival there of the Jesuits, including Father Jean de Brébeuf in 1625. The Jesuit mission strategy among the Native Americans was novel for the time: the priests worked hard to learn the languages of the Native peoples and then lived among them, sharing their ways of life. These Jesuit missions were established without support from the colonial military, and the missionaries were guests of the local tribes. By the 1640s, these missions were becoming effective, with thousands of converts from within the Huron tribe settling in Christian villages. But the hostilities of other tribes, especially those of the Iroquois Confederacy, gravely damaged these missions, and thousands of Hurons were killed or driven west. A number of Jesuits were captured, tortured, and killed, including Brébeuf in 1649; eight of these missionaries were eventually made saints by the Roman Catholic Church. The French missionaries later continued their work, making converts among the Iroquois in Ontario and New York and establishing a permanent Roman Catholic presence among several tribes in this region.

Unlike in New Spain, French women's religious orders were established in Canada with the goal of converting Native women. The most effective of these was the Ursulines, under the leadership of Marie Guyart (1599–1672), also known as Marie of the Incarnation, who established a presence in Montreal in 1639. These women learned the Native languages and translated religious texts into them; they also operated mission schools for girls and women, making converts in this fashion. The mission work among the Mohawk tribe was remarkably effective, and in 1671 Mohawk chief Ganeagowa converted to Christianity. The Jesuits founded a village called Kahnawake, just south of Montreal, for Native converts. One of the first converts was a young Native woman named Kateri (Catherine) Tekakwitha, who became a Christian in 1676. Her tomb became a local shrine, and in 2012 she was made a saint. The Jesuits and other religious orders also developed missions in the Great Lakes and Louisiana regions after 1660, which, despite some initial successes, did not lead to the permanent results seen in eastern Canada.

Mother Mary Nealis, RSCJ, 1924

2.5. French Jesuit Martyrs in Canada.

The French presence in Acadia survived after the region was ceded to the British in 1713, but the British were increasingly worried by the activities of the local French Roman Catholic clergy and missionaries. The Protestant British thought that these Catholic leaders were fanning resistance to British rule within the French population and among the Native tribes. As a result, the British imposed restrictions on French clergy and deported a number of them. Finally in 1755, during the French and Indian War, the British moved to deport all French settlers in Acadia. Some of them retreated to Quebec, but over the next eight years about sixteen thousand others were deported to France or the French Caribbean Islands. After 1763, thousands of these Acadian refugees came to settle in the region of Louisiana around New Orleans. Often referred to as "Cajuns" (derived from "Acadia"), they formed, with other French settlers, a permanent and distinctive local culture in southern Louisiana. Within the borders of the United States, the lasting elements of the French colonial and missionary ventures are the Christian Native Americans in New York and the descendants of French settlers in Louisiana, all of whom are historically Roman Catholic.

Claude Chauchetière, S.J., "The Life of the Good Catherine Tekakwitha, said now Saint Catherine Tekakwitha" (1695)

The cures brought by the invocation with the name of Catherine Tekakwitha and the desire of the French to know her virtue, which were the causes of a longer and clearer recital of what Catherine Tekakwitha has done. . . .

All she touched, which has done cures and as the crucifix that was placed in her hands when she was buried. Her blanket, the earth from her grave and the plate from she ate that have suddenly restored health. . . .

Before Catherine Tekakwitha had come to the Mission of Saint Francis Xavier of the Sault, where the Iroquois professed the Christian religion for twenty-five or thirty years, Our Lord had seemed to prepare the place for this virtuous girl. He began as of 1667, when He had inspired Father Pierre Rafeix to go to the already established settlement of La Prairie de la Madeleine. He made there a sort of a Parish for the French and a Mission for the Natives. . . .

After passing the entire winter in having taught [Catherine] the prayers, teaching her thoroughly and preparing her to receive this Sacrament, which the Father appointed a day to be baptized . . . , He baptized her with the name of Catherine. Although a name already consecrated from the purity of many holy virgins, but she had given greater glory. Then everyone had witnessed the modesty and devotion, which she showed during the ceremony and they made evident the great joy they had in this Baptism. . . . Catherine had not only justified their hope, but surpassed it from the fervour she showed after Baptism and one had reason to believe that the Holy Spirit filled with His grace a soul, which was disposed to receive it from an innocence of life and could be said was angelic.

Internet Archive, accessed July 11, 2023, https://web.archive.org/web/20110725120943/http://www.thelifeofkateritekakwitha.net/en/cc/chapter1.html.

The Russian Colonial Experience in Alaska

The Russian colonial experience was directed eastward across central Asia and Siberia. In 1741, a Russian expedition led by Vitus Bering and Aleksei Chirikov sailed into the Aleutian region of Alaska and claimed the region for Russia. This area of Alaska was used by various groups of Russian traders, mainly seeking the skins of seals and other fur-bearing animals. Overworked by these traders and decimated by European diseases, the Native Alaskan population plummeted by 80 percent during the Russian era. In 1784, a Russian expedition led by Grigory I. Shelikov arrived in Alaska and established a trading company, which eventually became the foundation of the Russian colonial administration. The Russians explored widely around the northern Pacific Ocean and even established temporary forts on the Hawaiian Islands and in Northern California. But the Russian presence in Alaska was never very strong, with never more than about eight hundred Russians controlling only the coastal regions. The Russian colony in Alaska was ultimately deemed unsustainable, and it was sold to the United States in 1867.

The Russian Orthodox Church was established in the colony principally for the Russian settlers. But intermarriage between Russian colonists and Native people and missionary work among the Native groups soon resulted in Russian Orthodox congregations within the Native Alaskan communities. Missionaries sought to make Christianity part of the local culture and encouraged Native leadership in Christian congregations, eventually sending Native candidates to Russia for education and ordination. Missionaries established four schools for Native people and developed an alphabet and written languages for them. A cultural and religious fusion took hold primarily among the coastal Aleut and Alutiiq peoples, and among elements of the Yup'ik and Athabascan peoples in the interior. The Russian Orthodox population among Native Alaskans today numbers about twenty thousand members in ninety Native parishes.

─────────────────────────── BIBLIOGRAPHY ───────────────────────────

Gannon, Michael V. *The Cross in the Sand: The Early Catholic Church in Florida, 1513–1870.* Gainesville: University of Florida Press, 1965.

Grant, John Webster. *Moon of Wintertime: Missionaries and the Indians of Canada in Encounter Since 1534.* Toronto: University of Toronto Press, 1984.

Jaenen, Cornelius J. *The Role of the Church in New France.* Toronto: McGraw-Hill Ryerson, 1976.

Lippy, Charles H., Robert Choquette, and Stafford Poole. *Christianity Comes to the Americas, 1492–1776.* New York: Paragon House, 1992.

Martin, Joel W. *The Land Looks After Us: A History of Native American Religion.* New York: Oxford University Press, 1999.

Orfalea, Gregory. *Journey to the Sun: Junípero Serra's Dream and the Founding of California.* New York: Scribner, 2014.

Ricard, Robert. *The Spiritual Conquest of Mexico.* Berkeley: University of California Press, 1966.

Walsh, H. H. *The Church in the French Era: From Colonization to the British Conquest.* Toronto: Ryerson, 1966.

Weber, David J. *The Spanish Frontier in North America.* New Haven: Yale University Press, 1994.

3

Christianity in British America
to 1700

The British Reformation: A Foundation for North American Protestantism

The Spanish and French religious impact on Christianity in the United States is interesting and important. But the main religious influences on this country in the seventeenth and eighteenth centuries came principally from Protestant Britain and, to a lesser extent, from the rest of Protestant Europe. Certainly, until the middle of the nineteenth century, the United States was an overwhelmingly and intensely Protestant country, and Protestantism is still its leading form of Christianity (and religion) today. Even more than this, America has been primarily molded religiously by the types of Protestantism that were developed during the Protestant Reformations in England and Scotland during the sixteenth and seventeenth centuries. These ongoing reformations, and the eventual religious compromises that determined the place of religion in these societies, were the primary influence on how Americans developed the system of religion and society that today makes this country religiously distinctive. American religious life is built on a system of voluntary religious affiliation, on a generally-agreed-to religious pluralism, and on the separation of church and state. The roots of these three foundational elements can be traced back to

England and Scotland. For this reason, it is vitally important to examine the English Reformation in order to understand religion in America.

Prior to the sixteenth century, England was rather conventionally Christian in the medieval Catholic model. Papal control over the English church was probably stronger than it was in many other European countries—such as France and Spain, which had military and political influence over the papacy. The medieval English church was influential and rich at a time when owning land was the primary form of wealth. It has been estimated that before the Reformation, the church controlled up to one-third of the land in England. There were hundreds of monastic houses throughout the country, and bishops and archbishops were very influential in English political life. There were the customary complaints about abuses and corruption by the church and church leaders, with the typical stories about lazy priests and venal monks. And the fact that many common people farmed land as tenants of the church and had to pay tithes and fees for church services did not improve popular opinion of religious leaders. There had been religious dissidents in England—the so-called Lollards, followers of the reformer John Wycliffe (ca. 1328–84)—who existed underground in the centuries before the Protestant Reformation, but there was little overt religious dissent beyond the common grumbling of the people.

At the time of the sixteenth-century Reformations, the English king was Henry VIII, who ruled from 1509 to 1547. Henry was initially proud of his ties with the papacy and earned the title "Defender of the Faith" in 1521 from Pope Leo X for his (ghostwritten) treatise attacking Martin Luther. But Henry's main concern was for the stability of his kingdom and his ruling Tudor house, both of which required a male heir to succeed him. This concern was legitimate. Twice in its earlier history, England had been torn apart by military conflict because there was no clear heir to the English throne. Henry's first wife, Catherine of Aragon, was a devout Catholic and the aunt of the Holy Roman emperor, Spaniard Charles V. But she produced only one surviving child—a daughter, Mary Tudor—and no sons. Convinced that Catherine was the problem, Henry was desperate to have his marriage annulled by the pope, but the pope was in no position to oppose Charles V and refused to do so. Henry's political and religious advisers, especially Thomas Cromwell and Thomas Cranmer, urged him to sever the English church from papal control. In 1534 Parliament passed a decree declaring that the ruler of England was the head of the English church, allowing Henry to grant himself a divorce from Catherine and to marry Anne Boleyn, who gave birth to a daughter, Elizabeth. The sordid narrative of Henry's six wives continued. The third wife, Jane Seymour, gave birth to a son (Edward VI). But after Jane's death, Henry married three more times.

Henry was not particularly inclined toward Protestant reform of the English church, even after breaking from Rome, and so for the most part he maintained medieval Catholic practice under his own rule of the church. As head of the church, he did close the great English monasteries and seize their assets, and he allowed the open publication of an English-language Bible. Behind the scenes, his Protestant advisers were actively making plans to shift the English church in a more Protestant direction, and those plans came to fruition when the young Edward VI came to the English throne in 1547. During Edward's brief reign, these advisers established the formative Protestant elements of the English church, including the Book of Common Prayer and the Forty-two Articles of Religion—which would become, respectively, the liturgical and doctrinal foundations of the Church of England—both principally the work of the Archbishop of Canterbury. But when Edward died in 1553, the next in the line of succession was Mary Tudor, who was a staunch Roman Catholic and furious with the Protestant leaders of the country. Mary brought the English church back under papal control and executed hundreds of reform leaders. Many more left England for refuge in Calvinist Geneva or elsewhere on the Continent. Mary ruled for only a few years, dying in 1558.

Mary was succeeded by her half sister, Elizabeth I, who had been raised a Protestant. Elizabeth was a shrewd political leader and understood that her position as head of the Church of England could be of immense value to her rule and to the stability of her kingdom. She took the Church of England away from the papacy and sought a broadly inclusive Church of England encompassing the vast majority of English people, from moderate Catholics to most English Protestants. This "middle way" (*via media*) Anglicanism retained the ecclesiastical structure of the medieval church, but with formal worship and instruction in English and a mildly Protestant theology. As a canny and much-loved ruler, Elizabeth became the symbol of resistance to the threat from Catholic Spain and France. England became an intensely Protestant nation during this period, and the remaining English Roman Catholics kept a low profile, with underground priests sheltered in the homes of sympathetic nobles.

After Mary's death, Protestant exiles had returned to England, and they brought with them the Calvinism they had learned in Geneva and elsewhere. These Protestants sought a more thoroughgoing reform of the Church of England along Calvinist lines, seeking to get rid of what they saw as lingering "Roman" elements, such as the bishops, the medieval liturgy, and other "high church" practices. Because they were seeking to "purify" the Church of England, they became known as Puritans, and they became an important force in English life, especially in the House of Commons. As long as these Dissenters (another name for them) outwardly conformed to the religiosity of the Church of England, Elizabethan officials generally allowed them to hold their own separate religious meetings, sometimes supported by sympathetic Anglican priests. The Puritan movement was especially strong in the southern and eastern sections of the country.

Calvinism was also brought to Scotland by returning exiles, especially under the fiery leadership of John Knox, who returned in 1559 and began attacking the corruptions of the medieval Scottish church and the French Roman Catholic influence on the Scottish monarchy. Mary, Queen of Scots, was staunchly Roman Catholic, but this wave of Protestantism drove her out of the country. Calvinist church leaders took over the Church of Scotland and remade it along Puritan lines, ridding the church of bishops and the medieval liturgy and instituting the plain and stern preaching of Calvinism. These Reformers adopted a new structure for Scotland based on the rule of the church by pastors and elders, a system known as Presbyterianism. Scotland became an intensely Calvinist nation, and this ethos was shared by the Scottish settlers in Northern Ireland.

When Elizabeth I died without an heir in 1603, the English throne passed to James I (r. 1603–25), the king of Scotland and son of Mary, Queen of Scots. James was less able to bridge the growing gap between the supporters of the Church of England and their Puritan critics than Elizabeth had been. This debate also took on an increasingly political tone, as proponents of increased royal power (including James) were allied with the great nobles and the Anglican bishops, while the supporters of parliamentary rule in the House of Commons were increasingly aligned with the Puritans. These tensions worsened during the reign of the next king, James's son Charles I, who was an open proponent of absolute royal power, was sympathetic toward Roman Catholicism, and whose queen was herself Roman Catholic. For many Puritans, the final straw came with two actions. First, starting in 1629 Charles attempted to rule without Parliament, which was not called into session again until 1640. Second, Charles appointed William Laud as the archbishop of Canterbury, the leader of the Church of England. Laud was aggressively high church and a royalist who hated the Puritans as much as they hated him. For those who were politically and religiously worried about Charles's actions, the Puritan faction of Parliament became the primary center of opposition.

When Charles was forced to call a new parliament into session in 1640, these tensions erupted into all-out conflict, and civil war broke out in 1642. Parliament raised its own army (the Roundheads or Parliamentarians) and controlled much of the South and East of England. The king raised his own army (the Royalists or Cavaliers), with strength in the North. At the Battle of Naseby, in 1645, the Royalist army was smashed, and Charles was eventually imprisoned. Charles's continuing attempts to conspire against Parliament led to his trial on grounds of high treason. He was found guilty and was executed in 1649. Over the next decade, Parliament and its leader, Oliver Cromwell, attempted to rule the country without a king.

The conflict and chaos of the first half of the seventeenth century brought about an astonishing flurry of new and sometimes radical religious experiments. The Puritans themselves began to differ internally over strategy. Traditionally, they had sought a purified Church of England for everyone, and these Puritans became known as Non-Separatists. But another wing of this movement increasingly began to question whether the true church could be a national, or state, church. These Separatists came to believe that the true church was congregations made up of "true" believers, and they sought to form congregations independent of the Church of England. Eventually this second wing would become the basis of English Congregationalism, and a number of these Separatists left England to form congregations abroad. Increasingly, they required adult members of their congregations to provide some evidence that they had been elected to salvation by God—some kind of (passive) conversion experience was generally expected. Another group of Separatists pushed this even further, deciding that it was only *after* evidence of such election was presented that a person could rightly be baptized. These congregations of English Baptists, small at first, grew rapidly during the chaos of the civil war of the 1640s and were known for their radical advocacy of the absolute separation of church and state and of personal religious freedom, something they called "soul liberty."

This was, however, not the end of radical religious experimentation during this period. George Fox (1624–91) and a group of colleagues organized the Religious Society of Friends, commonly known as Quakers, because of their early ecstatic experiences of God's direct presence. The Quakers were spiritualists who prized above all the direct experience of God's Spirit (the "inner light") in the lives of the believers. They argued that no institution, church, or Bible could claim authority over a believer who had been so enlightened. The Quaker societies (or "meetings") believed in noncoercion and absolute equality between members, even between men and women, and were pacifists. This was extremely radical for the seventeenth century, and the Quakers were violently opposed by Puritans and Anglicans alike. Other groups, such as the Levellers and the Diggers, blended radical and political equality with communism and agrarianism, while the radical Puritan millenarian sect called the Fifth Monarchy Men worked for the establishment of the kingdom of God on earth. Even though many in the English Parliament had only sought a purified Church of England along Calvinist lines, the result was religious chaos.

Oliver Cromwell died in 1658, and parliamentary rule collapsed. In a bid to regain some measure of control, the heir to the throne, Charles II, was invited by

Parliament and the nobles of England in 1660 to restore the English monarchy and the Church of England, even though he was personally a Roman Catholic. The Puritans had lost their opportunity and were once again relegated to a dissenting role. However, Charles II and his successor, James II, badly overplayed their hand in trying to establish royal absolutism. In what became known as the Glorious Revolution of 1688, Parliament moved against James while he was out of the country, inviting royal daughter Mary II to the throne to rule jointly with her solidly Protestant husband, Dutch noble William of Orange. This new monarchy was strictly under parliamentary restrictions, and certain legal rights and tolerances (although not full equality) were granted to Protestant Dissenters (or Nonconformists), though Roman Catholics were still disenfranchised. So, after over a century of strife, the English finally decided on an official state church—Anglicanism—with legal tolerance for other Protestants; this was a pragmatic degree of tolerance and pluralism at the end of a religiously chaotic period. It was this political and religious history that lay behind the settlement of the British colonies in North America and that would have such a profound effect on religion in these new territories.

Religion in British North America—Anglicans and Puritans

The early British settlements in North America were, first and foremost, commercial ventures organized by trading companies seeking profit in the New World. The promise of riches, such as those the Spanish had found in Central America, spurred investment in these companies, which sought royal charters to control areas along the Atlantic Seaboard. Only later did the British government seek to take direct political control over these colonies. Those who immigrated to these colonies in North America did so for any number of reasons—mainly for economic gain, but also for adventure, to escape troubles in Europe, or simply for a fresh start. While some individuals and groups came to North America for religious reasons, these were a decided minority. It is often said that people came to colonial America for religious freedom, but even in those cases where they did, the religious freedom they envisioned was generally freedom to practice their own religion without constraint. But they did not necessarily want to extend that freedom to others. Modern freedom of religion and acceptance of religious pluralism would develop only slowly and much later.

After several failed ventures, the first British settlement was established at Jamestown, Virginia, in 1607. After a rough beginning and the arrival of more settlers, the Virginia Company of London gained a permanent foothold in the region. Initial exploration for gold and other precious metals failed to discover any traces, so the focus of the colony turned to agriculture—especially to a popular new product for Europeans: tobacco. Increasingly, the colony became dominated by great landowners, whose plantations produced tobacco and other cash crops. The Church of England was officially established in the new colony, but the first leaders of the venture had Puritan sympathies, and early moral laws established in the colony had a decidedly Calvinist tone. In 1624, the charter of the Virginia Company was revoked, and Virginia became a royal colony, whose resident governors were decidedly Anglican in orientation. But even though the Church of England was officially established in Virginia, it was a very weak organization, with few resident priests and its ruling bishop across the ocean in London. The scattered Anglican parishes received little funding from

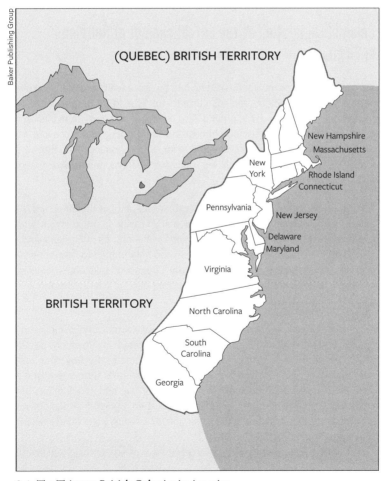

3.1. The Thirteen British Colonies in America.

the colonial government, and the local priests depended heavily on funding and goodwill from the local landowners. Local lay-led parish councils, called vestries, dominated the parishes and the priests. Overall, religious life in early Virginia was weak.

The two major elements of Anglicanism were the liturgical rites of the Book of Common Prayer and the rule of the church by bishops. Bishops customarily confirmed young people into the faith and ordained candidates for the priesthood. While the colonists had access to the Book of Common Prayer, the lack of resident Anglican bishops in North America was debilitating to the early Anglican establishments in Virginia and the other southern colonies. If a candidate in Virginia wished to be ordained as an Anglican

Colonial Legislation on the Establishment of Religion in Virginia

It is ordered, That all ministers residing and being, or who hereafter shall reside and be within this colony, shall conform themselves in all things according to the canons of the church of England. And if there shall be any that, after notice given, shall refuse for to conform himself, he shall undergo such censure, as by the said canons in such cases is provided for such delinquent. And that all acts formerly made concerning ministers shall stand in force, and be duly observed and kept. (March, 1630)

For the preservation of the purity of doctrine and unity of the church, It is enacted that all ministers whatsoever which shall reside in the colony are to be conformable to the orders and constitutions of the church of England, and the laws therein established, and not otherwise to be admitted to teach or preach publicly or privately, And that the Governor Counsel do take care that all nonconformists upon notice of them shall be compelled to depart the colony with all convenience. (March, 1643)

That for the preservation of the purity and unity of doctrine and discipline in the church, and the right administration of the sacraments no minister be admitted to officiate in this country but such as shall produce to the Governor a testimonial that he hath received his ordination from some Bishop in England and shall then subscribe to be conformable to the orders and constitutions of the church of England, and the laws there established, upon which the Governor is hereby requested, to induct the said minister, into any parish that shall make presentation of him. (March, 1662)

William W. Hening, *The Statutes at Large; Being a Collection of All the Laws of Virginia from the First Session of the Legislature in the Year 1619*, 13 vols. (New York, 1823), 1:149; 1:279; 2:46.

priest, he had to return to England, study there, and find a bishop willing to ordain him. In England, bishops defended priests from the financial power of local vestries and ensured that priests were maintained in their clerical positions. But with the bishop an ocean away, Anglican priests in British North America had practically no episcopal support and so had the unenviable task of negotiating their own positions and salaries with the wealthy landowners who dominated the vestries. In practice, these vestries hired and fired their priests at will. Given this situation, along with the poverty of the colonies, it is understandable why few Anglican priests wanted to come to Virginia—unless, of course, circumstances demanded they get out of England. Actually, some very good Anglican priests did make the sacrificial decision to immigrate, but they were not nearly enough to serve all the scattered Anglican parishes in Virginia.

The weakness of this colonial Anglican establishment was replicated in royal colonies in the American south, the colonies that became North Carolina, South Carolina, and Georgia. Again, while the charters of these colonies expected the establishment of the Church of England in their midst, this establishment was generally only on paper, as there were no parishes and no priests in most areas. Official legislation establishing the Church of England often was not approved until the eighteenth century. The first settlement in South Carolina, Charleston, came in 1670, and the first Anglican parish was founded in 1681. But the growth of organized Anglican parishes in South Carolina was very slow. The situation in North Carolina and Georgia was even worse.

In Virginia and Maryland, things started improving toward the end of the seventeenth century. Parish life and the priests were still under the dominating control of the local vestries, but several energetic Anglican priests arrived to enliven the spiritual condition of colonial Anglicans. Thomas Bray (1656–1730) served as a traveling priest and missionary for four years in Maryland to revitalize the Anglican parishes there. James Blair (1656–1743) arrived in Virginia in 1689 as the commissary (representative) of the bishop of London in the colony. Blair brought new life to the Anglican parishes and, in 1693, organized the College of William and Mary, in Virginia, to educate young men for the priesthood. Though this institution struggled mightily in its first years, it eventually became an important part of colonial Anglicanism. Beyond his work in Maryland, Bray returned to England and, in 1701, formed what would become a vitally important Anglican missionary group: the Society for the Propagation of the Gospel in Foreign Parts (SPG). This voluntary society became extremely effective at amassing funds and identifying missionary priests to serve in colonial America. SPG funding and encouragement supported colonial Anglican priests in their parishes in the South and as they established new Anglican mission parishes in the middle colonies of Pennsylvania and New York and even into the heart of Puritan New England.

The Puritan settlements in British North America began with the fabled landing of the Pilgrims at Plymouth, Massachusetts, in 1620. The core of this settlement came from a Separatist Puritan congregation from eastern England that had moved to Holland in 1609 to escape religious pressures in England. But this was not an ideal situation, so they formed a commercial company to finance their trip to North America, departing in 1620 aboard the ship *Mayflower*. Because of storms and poor navigation, they ended up on Cape Cod (rather than in Virginia, as they had intended), and they decided to settle there. Despite a rough beginning, in which many of them died, they formed a small permanent colony at Plymouth, which remained independent until it was absorbed into the larger Massachusetts Bay Colony in 1691. What the Pilgrims envisioned for their settlement was a community in a covenant relationship with God, where the Calvinist social and moral laws would be written into the political regulations of the life of the colony. This was codified in their earliest covenantal document, the Mayflower Compact, signed in 1620. They felt that they could prosper as a society only if they remained faithful and obedient to God.

Although the Plymouth settlement remained small and rather insular, there was soon a much larger group of Puritans who settled in this region: the Puritan settlement under the control of the Massachusetts Bay Company. Worried by the actions of King Charles I and the aggressive high church Anglicanism of his supporters, this group of Puritans left England in 1630 to settle around Boston. By the end of the decade, nearly twenty thousand of them had immigrated to this region, which became known as New England. In a clever move, the ruling stockholders of the Massachusetts Bay Company transferred themselves and the entire company to Boston, effectively providing for their own self-rule in North America, away from any control in England.

Unlike the Separatist Puritans at Plymouth, this much larger group of English Puritans were Non-Separatists, who believed in the ideal of a state-supported church for all residents. They sought a renewed version of a national church, like the Church of England but "purified" along the lines of Calvinism, without bishops and formalized liturgies. Even beyond that, the residents of this new colony would have to be recognized as church members in order to participate in the civic and political life of the colony. They saw in the "wilderness" of North America a chance to bring about the type of religious and political society for which they had been advocating back in England. This experiment in "New" England was to be a sign or example to "old" England of what the home country itself could become, if only it followed the Puritan example. In the words of their first leader, John Winthrop, this new colony would be a

John Winthrop, "A Model of Christian Charity" (1630)

Thus stands the cause between God and us: we are entered into covenant with Him for this work. We have taken out a commission. The Lord has given us leave to draw our own articles; we have professed to enterprise these actions upon these and these ends; we have hereupon besought Him of favor and blessing. Now if the Lord shall please to hear us and bring us in peace to the place we desire, then has He ratified this Covenant and sealed our commission, [and] will expect a strict performance of the articles contained in it. But if we shall neglect the observation of these articles . . . the Lord will surely break out in wrath against us, be revenged of such a perjured people, and make us know the price of the breach of such a covenant.

Now the only way to avoid this shipwreck and to provide for our posterity is to follow the counsel of Micah, "to do justly, to love mercy, to walk humbly with our God." For this end, we must be knit together in this work as one man. . . . We shall find that the God of Israel is among us, when ten of us shall be able to resist a thousand of our enemies, when He shall make us a praise and glory, that men shall say of succeeding plantations, "the Lord make it like that of New England."

For we must consider that we shall be as a "city upon a hill." The eyes of all people are upon us, so that if we shall deal falsely with our God in this work we have undertaken, and so cause Him to withdraw His present help from us, we shall be made a story and a byword through the world.

Collections of the Massachusetts Historical Society, 3rd ser., vol. 7
(Boston: Massachusetts Historical Society, 1838), 31–48.

"city upon a hill" for the whole world to see. These Puritans shared with their Pilgrim cousins the idea that their colony was in a covenantal relationship with God and that their venture would succeed only if, as a society, they remained faithful to God. This colony was not a true theocracy (the rule of a society by religious leaders) because church and state remained separate, although the leading pastors of the Puritan church did have a great deal of influence on the early life of the colony. Pastors rarely sought or were elected to political office, but the magistrates and other political leaders saw their offices as a part of the covenantal relationship the colony had with God.

The founding of the Massachusetts Bay Colony came just at the beginning of the English Civil Wars and direct parliamentary rule during the 1640s and 1650s, and these troubled times had a great effect on the colony itself. As has been seen, this period saw a tremendous amount of religious experimentation in England, and this unrest also found its way to New England. While some new arrivals in the colony from England were disaffected Puritans and other radicals, many others simply sought economic advancement and were less invested in the religious and social vision of the original settlers. One of the first controversies concerned Roger Williams (1603–83), a Puritan pastor of decidedly Separatist leanings, who arrived in Massachusetts in 1631. Williams was opposed to the idea of any state church, even one as purified as the one in Massachusetts, and his agitation for these principles led to his exile from the colony. In 1636, he and some followers headed south to what is now Rhode Island and established their own colony there.

A more difficult controversy of this time involved Anne Hutchinson (1591–1643), who was a member of the Boston congregation led by prominent Puritan pastor John Cotton (1585–1652). Hutchinson was a devout woman who held meetings in her home to discuss Cotton's weekly sermons. The Puritan theology espoused by Cotton held that salvation was wholly a gracious act of God, but Hutchinson took this beyond what Cotton held, saying that no human moral actions or preparations were necessary. She was formally charged with antinomianism (being against the religious and moral law) and in 1637 was tried

The Trial of Anne Hutchinson (November 1637)

Mrs. H: Since that time, I confess I have been more choice and he hath let me to distinguish between the voice of my beloved and the voice of Moses, the voice of John Baptist and the voice of antichrist, for all those voices are spoken of in scripture. Now if you do condemn me for speaking what in my conscience, I know to be truth I must commit myself unto the Lord. . . .

When our teachers came to New England it was a great trouble unto me, my brother Wheelwright being put by also. I was then much troubled concerning the ministry under which I lived, and then that place in the 30th of Isaiah was brought to my mind. Though the Lord give thee bread of adversity and water of affliction yet shall not thy teachers be removed into corners any more, but thine eyes shall see thy teachers. . . . This place in Daniel was brought unto me and did shew me that though I should meet with affliction yet I am the same God that delivered Daniel out of the lion's den, I will also deliver thee. Therefore, I desire you to look to it, for you see this scripture fulfilled this day and therefore I desire you that as you tender the Lord and the church and commonwealth to consider and look what you do. You have power over my body but the Lord Jesus hath power over my body and soul, and assure yourselves thus much, you do as much as in you lies to put the Lord Jesus Christ from you, and if you go on in this course you begin you will bring a curse upon you and your posterity, and the mouth of the Lord hath spoken it.

Thomas Hutchinson, *History of the Colony and Province of Massachusetts Bay* (Boston: 1767), appendix 11.

and excommunicated. Another major factor in this was probably that she was a woman "preaching" and doing theology and so was viewed as undermining Cotton's authority. Hutchinson, her family, and a group of followers left Boston and settled on Long Island, New York, but she was killed in an attack by Native Americans in 1643.

As the Massachusetts Bay Colony grew and expanded, Puritan settlement pushed west and north. One early group that split off from the Massachusetts Bay Colony was led by Pastor Thomas Hooker (1586–1647), who also clashed with John Cotton. In 1636, Hooker and his followers left the colony to settle at Hartford in the Connecticut River valley. One issue Hooker had with Cotton and the Massachusetts Bay Colony was that they allowed only the elect male members of the Puritan church to vote. Hooker held that all male members of the colony—whether members of the church or not—should be eligible to vote, something that was included in the 1639 constitution for the Connecticut Colony. Despite this difference, the Connecticut Colony also established Puritanism as its state-supported religion, and the Puritan influence in this colony was robust.

In 1637, another Puritan colony was established around New Haven, in southern Connecticut. Led by Pastor John Davenport, the Puritan church in this area had, if anything, even more influence than in Massachusetts. The New Haven Colony had no royal charter and later ran into conflict with English officials when it sheltered some of the Puritan judges who had condemned King Charles I to death in 1649. This colony united with the Connecticut Colony around Hartford in 1664. There were attempts at founding other Puritan colonies, especially on Long Island and at Newark, New Jersey. But the areas of Puritan settlement were generally within the boundaries of New England.

Of all the churches in the British colonies of North America, the Puritan churches had the strongest foundation. Because the Puritan church was "established" (state funded), local congregations received financial support from the colonial government. And since these colonies had a measure of religious purpose to them, their laws and mores were based on Puritan principles and generally had substantial support from the people. Unlike those of the Anglican colonies to the south, New England churches had a strong and large pool of pastors to lead them and—with the founding of colleges such as Harvard (1636) and Yale (1701)—had educational institutions within the colonies themselves to prepare young men for the ministry. One question that concerned the Puritans was how to structure their churches: whether to follow the Presbyterian model of the Church of Scotland or to allow more freedom for the local congregations. In an important meeting at Cambridge, Massachusetts, in 1648, the decision was made to adopt the congregational model of church organization, and so the Puritan churches in America became known as the Congregational Church.

The growth and maturation of these Puritan colonies also meant the decline of their original religious zeal. Full membership in the local Congregational church was a key element of the colony, but securing church membership depended on the often long and involved process of being able to discover and to prove that one was chosen—"elected"—by God to salvation through a conversion experience. Only full church members could present their children for baptism into the Covenant. But those of the second and third generations became full church members less often—meaning that they did not report such conversion experiences—and so their children could not be baptized. This provoked both a religious and a social crisis in the community, as fewer and fewer people "owned" the Covenant. This crisis of identity was finally addressed in 1662 with the decision to allow those who had been baptized to present their children for baptism, even though they were not full church members. This compromise, often called the "Half-Way Covenant," relieved the crisis, but it also seemed to signal a betrayal of the original religious purposes of the colony.

The Puritan colonies in New England underwent other significant internal and external religious struggles during their first century. Mention has been made of the expulsions during the 1630s of Roger Williams, Anne Hutchinson, and their followers. The colony itself was also influenced by the events of the English Civil Wars and the Puritan struggles in England to govern without a king. The Restoration of the monarchy and the Church of England in 1660 was a crushing blow to Puritans on both sides of the Atlantic, and the new royal government in England looked with great suspicion on the Puritan colonies in North America. Disaffected Puritans from England immigrated to New England after the Restoration, both adding to Puritan numbers and increasing colonial suspicions of the English government, which attempted to rein in the Puritan colonies. Finally, the Glorious Revolution of 1688 reduced some of these pressures, but it also brought about the end of the Puritan government in Massachusetts. In 1691, England revoked the Massachusetts charter and brought the colony under royal control, with a royal governor. Enfranchisement was expanded beyond male church members. The Puritan experiment seemed to be at an end.

Massachusetts also suffered from incursions by persistent Quakers who kept trying to infiltrate the colony. Being strongly opposed to religious coercion and any kind of state church—Anglican or Puritan—Quakers started coming to Massachusetts during the 1650s. The colonial government soon passed laws against their entry and against any ship's captain that would transport them to the colony. Yet the Quakers came, and came again after being expelled, until

3.2. First Parish Church, Concord, Massachusetts.

Massachusetts authorities had four Quakers executed between 1659 and 1661. Despite this, several Quaker meetings were eventually established in the colony, aided and abetted by Quakers from the nearby Colony of Rhode Island. George Fox, the Quaker founder, visited Rhode Island in 1672, aiding the cause of the movement in New England.

The expanding colonies also had other troubles that hindered their growth. The initial settlements were in part facilitated by the decimation of Native American populations by European diseases, but as the Native populations rebounded and the Europeans pushed inward, armed conflict inevitably arose. From 1675 to 1678, the Wampanoag and their Narragansett allies attacked Puritan settlements, in what became known as King Philip's War, causing a great deal of destruction. Even though the Native forces were eventually defeated, it was a difficult period for the colony. Epidemics and plagues seasonally swept through the colonies, and fires destroyed parts of Boston, leading colonial leaders to wonder whether God was punishing them for having disobeyed their original covenantal agreements. These Puritans often read the events of their day through such a religious or covenantal lens.

Probably the most well-known controversy of this time concerned the Salem witch trials in 1692, when a hysteria swept the village and twenty people were executed as witches before it eventually subsided. It must be noted that in general European history this was a period of intense concern with the uncovering of alleged witches—thousands were executed in Europe, so this was a relatively minor outbreak of a much larger hysteria. Yet the Salem incident was symptomatic of a great deal of social and religious unrest in Massachusetts during this time. Explanations of the Salem incident have pointed to a number of contributing factors—such as poisoned grain, social unrest and hysteria, and misogyny—but the full causes may never be totally understood. Taken in light of the other traumas of the late seventeenth century, however, the Salem witch trials show a Puritan faith community wrestling with its religious vision and mission.

Among the New England colonies, Rhode Island was religiously distinctive in several ways. It was founded by religious dissenters from Massachusetts and from England, and in its small area it contained a few different groups, many of whom were Separatists and so were opposed to any idea of a state church or close connection between church and state. Settlement began here in 1636 with Roger Williams and his followers, and their founding ideals included religious liberty for all persons. God, they believed, would work directly in the hearts of individuals, and these religious folks would gather into voluntary Christian communities, but faith or obedience should not be outwardly constrained. These ideals were embedded in the charter of the new colony in 1647, a remarkable document in American religious history. The new colony soon attracted the attention of the English Quakers, and some of them settled there in the late seventeenth century. Spanish Jews even had a presence in Newport, Rhode Island, as early as 1658, with an ongoing worshiping community and cemetery established in 1677.

The early core of the Rhode Island colony was, however, made up of English Baptists. This movement grew out of the Separatist Puritans in the early seventeenth century and, while they continued to share the belief in the absolute independence of the local congregation in matters of faith and life, they diverged from the Separatist Puritans regarding baptism. The English Baptists came to believe the adult experience of election or conversion demanded by the Puritans should also be accompanied by adult baptism, and that infant baptism (which the Puritans continued to practice) was illegitimate. With the Quakers, they believed that there should be no external religious coercion, something that they came to call "soul liberty." The first Baptist congregation in Rhode Island was formed in 1638, with the assistance of Roger Williams (who remained a member only for a short period of time). An important Baptist leader, John Clarke (1609–76), arrived in Rhode Island in 1639 and established the town of Newport. These Baptist settlements in Rhode Island became a base for the expansion of Baptist congregations in the rest of New England, much to the disgust of the Puritan officials, who hounded Baptist missionaries and congregations wherever they could find them. But the affinities between the Separatist Congregationalists and the Baptists were clear, providing a wedge for Baptist theology outside Rhode Island. Even one of the first presidents of Harvard College, Henry Dunster (1609–59), became an advocate of adult baptism and in 1654 left Harvard to become a Baptist. Rhode Island and (later) Philadelphia became the centers of the Baptist tradition in colonial North America.

Other Religious Groups in British America—the Middle Colonies

Although there were attempts at religious uniformity and established churches in both Puritan New England and the Anglican colonies in the South, these were, as has been seen, rather weak establishments. Even the strongest of them, Puritan New England, could not prevent inroads made by Baptists, Separatist Congregationalists, and Quakers. In many places, the Anglican establishments existed only on paper. However, in the middle colonies, from Maryland to New York, even such weak establishments of religion were hardly known. In this region, religious pluralism reigned, whether by design or by chance. The overriding need in these early colonies was for labor, so excluding able workers for religious reasons seemed hardly the best thing to do. Many of these middle colonies had particular religious complexions at their beginnings, but because of the needs of commerce and shifting political fortunes, such early aims were quickly swept away.

A prime example of this was the colony of Maryland, which was originally envisioned as an American colony for English Catholics. In the 1620s, under a sympathetic king, English Catholic noble George Calvert (the first Lord Baltimore) petitioned the king for a grant on land in the new American colonies. In 1632, the grant was given to his son Cecil, as George Calvert died five weeks before the new charter was sealed. The first colonists landed in the new colony of Maryland in 1634. Catholicism in England was most popular among some of the great English noble families, so the colony was established on semifeudal lines, with a handful of English Catholic gentry and their indentured servants. But the new colony desperately needed workers, and soon the English Catholics became a minority in their own colony, although the Calvert family still controlled the colony itself as proprietors. As early as 1639 the colonial assembly passed laws allowing for the freedom of worship, which would be codified in Maryland's Act of Toleration in 1649.

During the English Civil Wars in the 1640s, the restive English Protestants in Maryland frequently pushed back against the Catholic leaders and the Calvert proprietors, and more than once they seized control of the colony itself.

In 1650, Protestant forces defeated the colonial government and ordered all Catholic priests to leave the colony. Eventually a compromise was reached with the Calverts, but there were continual religious clashes over the next decades, and in 1689 the Protestants again took control of the colony. The proprietary ownership of the colony was abolished in 1689, and it became a royal colony instead. Eventually the Anglican Church was established in the colony, but this was a very weak arrangement with few parishes and priests. English Catholics remained a force in the colony, especially as great landowners, and Maryland was the center of English Catholicism in British North America.

New York was originally established as the New Netherland colony on Manhattan Island by the Dutch West India Company in 1623. The Dutch, newly independent from Spain, were in an expansionistic mood and aggressively establishing trading colonies around the world. Dutch settlement pushed up the Hudson River to Albany and across the river into New Jersey. Being a Dutch colony meant that the Dutch Reformed Church was officially established in New Netherland, and soon Dutch Reformed pastors arrived to found congregations. But the West India Company had profits—not religion—as its main focus, and pastors were costly. Between the first pastor's arrival in 1628 and the English conquest of New Netherland in 1664 (at which point the colony was renamed New York), the company sent only fifteen pastors to the colony, and only about a dozen congregations were formed. The Dutch Reformed pastors battled on several fronts: against the colonial leaders for more support of the official religion and against other religious groups who sought to establish their own congregations. Dutch Lutherans, for example, sought to form a congregation and call a pastor, but the Reformed pastors and the colonial officials blocked this until the English took control.

With English rule came talk of replacing the established Dutch Reformed Church with an Anglican establishment, but commercial consideration and fierce resistance from the Dutch settlers postponed this action for decades. As in Maryland, the overriding need in New York was for labor and commerce, and religious considerations took a back seat. A rough religious toleration was

3.3. John Campanius, Frontispiece to Luther's Small Catechism Translated into Algonquin.

developed under the British, though the Dutch Reformed Church was still officially established. Ironically, the Dutch Reformed congregations grew quite a bit stronger after the English takeover in 1664. These congregations became the center of Dutch resistance to English control, and dynamic new pastors from Holland gave new life to the congregations. British governmental authorities did attempt to establish Anglicanism in New York after the Glorious Revolution (1688), aided by the Society for the Propagation of the Gospel in Foreign Parts. But, as elsewhere, the attempt at exercising royal and Anglican control was not widely supported by the colonists.

South from the Dutch colony of New Netherland, the Swedish monarchy established its own colony, New Sweden, on the Delaware River in 1638. This colony, which stretched from Wilmington, Delaware, to Philadelphia, was the project of an ambitious Swedish king who was eager to get into—and profit from—the colonial trade. This was always a small colony, but the Lutheran Church of Sweden sent pastors to establish congregations there. The Dutch saw this colony as an intrusion into its territory and conquered it in 1655. The Dutch, and then the English after 1664, left the Swedish Lutheran congregations alone, and these were served by pastors from Sweden, although there were long gaps in this service. Around 1689 there was a renewed interest in these congregations by the Church of Sweden, which sent a number of able Lutheran pastors to serve them. But by the end of the eighteenth century the Swedish language was dying out among the colonists and, lacking a viable English-language Lutheranism in North America (or anywhere), the remaining Lutheran congregations affiliated instead with the Protestant Episcopal Church—this being the name taken by the newly reorganized Anglican, formerly Church of England, congregations after their separation from the English establishment during the American Revolution.

Reformed Protestants from the British Isles, known as Presbyterians, also took root in the middle colonies. Presbyterians were among the Puritan Dissenters from the sixteenth and seventeenth centuries. Theologically, they were cousins to the Congregationalists. They differed over the question of church structure: while the Congregationalists lodged church authority in the local congregation, the Presbyterians favored a system where pastors and congregational representatives met in regular governing meetings called presbyteries, where these delegates made binding decisions for whole groupings of congregations. Further regional and national meetings were also held. The Presbyterians did not dominate in England, but, under the leadership of John Knox, they took control of the Church of Scotland. Scottish immigrants to Northern Ireland (the Scotch Irish) established Presbyterianism there as well.

There was considerable immigration of Scots and Scotch Irish to the British North American colonies in the seventeenth century, and they established scattered Presbyterian congregations in the middle colonies. In 1683, a presbytery in Northern Ireland sent Presbyterian pastor Francis Makemie (1658–1708) as a traveling evangelist to North America. Makemie traveled the length of the colonies and established a Presbyterian congregation in Maryland in 1684. But it was in New Jersey that the Presbyterian influence was the most pronounced, and New Jersey soon became the center of colonial Presbyterianism. In 1706, local Presbyterians formed the Presbytery of Philadelphia as their first regional body in North America. Makemie himself continued to travel and establish Presbyterian groups, though he sometimes ran into opposition—as in 1707, when he was arrested in New York for preaching without a license. The Presbyterians would become a major religious force in the middle colonies.

The Quakers, centered in Pennsylvania and the western side of New Jersey, were also influential in this region. The Quakers (or the Religious Society of Friends, as they are formally known) are a group of spiritualists who began in England in the 1650s under the leadership of George Fox. The early Quakers were religious radicals who believed that God spoke directly into the hearts and souls of believers, a phenomenon they called the "inner light." True believers, illumined by such a religious experience, were thus free from the control of any external religious structures—whether church or scripture or doctrine. The inner light of the believer was primary. Early Quakers attacked the churches and social structures as enemies of the true faith. They believed that the true church was in the heart of the believer, not in a building or organization. As religious and social radicals, they were persecuted and ostracized, and many, including Fox, were imprisoned. The Quakers gathered in meetinghouses (not churches), and they emphasized equality among believers and decision-making by consensus.

There were scattered Quakers in British North America as early as the 1650s, and Fox himself made a tour of the colonies during the years 1671 to 1673. Fox debated the Baptist leader Roger Williams in Newport, Rhode Island, in 1672. And Williams later wrote a book attacking Fox. There were early Quaker settlements in western New Jersey in the 1670s. But the major Quaker settlement in North America began with the founding of Pennsylvania. William Penn was a highly connected Englishman who became a Quaker in 1666 and was imprisoned for his beliefs. In 1681, Penn prevailed on King Charles II, who owed the Penn family a large debt, to grant him a large tract of land in North America as payment for the debt; this was the territory that became Pennsylvania (Penn's Woods). Penn intended Pennsylvania to be a "Holy Experiment," a colony where the Quakers and any other religious groups could practice their religious

beliefs without harassment. Philadelphia
(the City of Brotherly Love) was founded
in 1682, and the Quaker elites soon
came to dominate the new colony.
Ironically, the Quakers, who had
suffered as a small minority in
England, came to be the ruling
class of the new colony. But they
found that such a position was
hard to maintain with their religious beliefs. The early Quakers
did attempt to deal fairly with
Native Americans and pay for the
land they were settling. This did not
resolve tension, and there were Native American attacks on the settlers
on the frontier. As pacifists, the Quakers
would not raise an army for the defense of
the frontier. Already in 1691 Quaker George

3.4. William Penn.

Keith (ca. 1638–1716) wrote a scathing attack on the Pennsylvania Quakers,
accusing them of religious laxity and of abandoning the early ideals of the
Quaker movements. Keith gathered a group of Quaker believers around him
but was "disowned" by the Quaker establishment. He later became an Anglican
(of all things!) and served in America from 1802 to 1804 as a missionary for
the Society for the Propagation of the Gospel in Foreign Parts. A number of
the Keithian Quakers became Baptists.

The "Holy Experiment" in Pennsylvania required some dramatic innovation in how the colony would be governed. In line with Quaker ideals, the
colonial assembly (which Quakers initially dominated) stressed consensus in
decision-making, eliminated the swearing of oaths, allowed the freedom of
religion, refused to establish a militia, and eventually outlawed slavery. But this
experiment was hard to manage. The practical factors involved in running a
colony, along with pressure from non-Quakers in the colony, caused increasing
conflict within the Quaker community. The leading Quaker merchants and
landowners eventually lost political control of the colonial legislature in the
middle of the eighteenth century.

The Pennsylvania experiment soon attracted the attention of many in Europe
who were suffering religious persecution. Religious freedom in Pennsylvania
and the availability of good farmland were major draws to the new colony.
George Fox himself made trips to Germany and the Netherlands to set up

Quaker communities and make contacts with similar groups, such as the Mennonites, who were Anabaptist pacifists on the Continent. A number of these Mennonites immigrated to Pennsylvania beginning in the 1680s, as did members of other similar groups, and the settlement of Germantown was established in 1683 just north of Philadelphia. The German Rosicrucians (mystics and deists) were another early presence in Germantown. And a number of other radical groups were also drawn to the colony.

However, most of the Germans who came to Pennsylvania and the other middle colonies came for economic rather than religious reasons. Constant warfare in Continental Europe and a lack of economic opportunity created a great pressure for migration, which was generally undertaken by individuals and small groups. Many immigrants could not afford the passage to America, so they came as indentured servants who had to work for seven years to pay off their passage. These immigrants were generally Protestants—either Lutheran or Reformed—who settled in German ethnic communities, often in mixed groups along with Mennonites and Moravians.

As previously noted, the first Lutherans in North America were the Swedish Lutherans who settled along the Delaware River beginning in 1638. The first Dutch Lutheran congregation was formed in New Netherland in 1649, but the Dutch officials (pressured by the Reformed pastors) refused to allow entry to European Lutheran pastors coming to serve the congregations. This restriction was lifted with the British takeover of New Netherland (which then became New York), and Lutheran congregations formed along the Hudson River and into eastern New Jersey. Starting in 1669, several Lutheran pastors arrived in the area to serve these scattered congregations, but pastoral leadership was rare, and there were often long interim periods between pastors. These Lutheran congregations comprised a mix of Dutch and German Lutherans, and so ethnic and linguistic differences often caused problems.

The numbers of Dutch and Swedish Lutherans remained small, and German Lutherans eventually eclipsed them. German immigration to British North America was focused on Pennsylvania and surrounding colonies, although there were eventually Lutheran congregations from Nova Scotia to Georgia. Immigrant Lutherans were generally without pastors and worshiped in homes or other buildings, reading from Luther's sermons and singing hymns. The first Lutheran pastor in Pennsylvania was Daniel Falckner, who arrived in 1694. He served as a land agent and established a number of early congregations. His brother, Justus Falckner, was a theological student from Germany who arrived in America in 1700. Justus was soon ordained by the local Lutheran pastors (Swedish and German) and was an itinerant Lutheran pastor serving the Lutheran congregations in New York and New Jersey until his death in 1723.

But for most of the growing tide of German Lutheran immigrants to North America, Lutheran pastors were a rare sight, often only encountered when a wandering (and sometimes self-ordained) Lutheran pastor passed through their communities.

Along with these Lutherans came German Reformed Protestants, and the two groups often lived in the same communities and sometimes cooperated in local congregations (something that was not unheard of, especially in the western parts of Germany). The early German Reformed congregations were originally related to the Dutch Reformed congregations in New York and New Jersey, but linguistic differences soon caused the Germans to go their own way. Much like for the Lutherans, Reformed pastors from Europe were a rare occurrence in the early period, and many communities took whatever spiritual leadership they could find.

This increasingly diverse group of Christians in British North America was generally focused on forming congregations for European immigrants and often had a difficult time accomplishing even this. Yet a wider mission—to bring Christianity to the Native Americans and enslaved and free African Americans—was sometimes on the hearts and minds of Christian leaders, even if such efforts were only rarely carried out. Despite occasional good intentions, the success of such missions was sporadic at best. The initial contacts between Native Americans and Europeans proved disastrous for the Native peoples, who died in huge numbers because of exposure to European diseases for which they had no immunity. Even when this situation improved, the expanding numbers of European settlers pushed the Native peoples farther and farther west and otherwise disrupted their communities and ways of life. The conflicts sometimes turned violent, which usually ended badly for the Native tribes.

There were occasional efforts to bring Christianity to the Native Americans, but too often this was predicated on their adoption of European culture as well. In New England, pastors John Eliot (1604–90) and Thomas Mayhew Jr. (1618–57) had some success in forming Native peoples into settled Christian communities. They also translated the Bible into Native American languages. But the outbreak of King Philip's War (also called the Great Narragansett War) between Native Americans and English settlers, in 1675, poisoned relations on both sides, and the Native communities faltered. There were other occasional efforts to Christianize Native Americans. Swedish Lutheran pastor John Campanius established good relations with the local Native population and learned the local Algonquin language, into which he translated Martin Luther's *Small Catechism*. But Campanius returned to Sweden, and the Native population he was working with moved west, so nothing lasting came of this. Perhaps the most effective mission to the Native tribes was accomplished by Moravian pastor David Zeisberger (1721–1808) in Pennsylvania, who established a series of settlements for Native Christians that honored Native cultures, but these groups were continually harassed and pushed westward by the hostility of advancing settlers. Most European settlers saw the Native populations as problems or threats, rather than as people with whom to share the Christian gospel, and so they often treated them ruthlessly.

Apart from the Europeans, another group of outsiders comprised those persons from Africa whom Europeans cruelly enslaved and brought to North America to labor on farms and plantations. African slavery has its roots in early sixteenth-century Spanish Latin America; the first group of enslaved Africans in British colonial North America was brought to Virginia in 1619. Although African slaves could be found in most of the British colonies in the seventeenth century, the economics of slavery was most lucrative for White settlers in the

John Eliot's Brief Narrative (1670)

Right Worshipful and Christian Gentlemen:

Upon the 17th day of the 6th month, 1670, there was a Meeting at *Maktapog* near *Sandwich* in *Plimouth-Pattent*, to gather a Church among the *Indians*: There were present six of the Magistrates, and many Elders, (all of them Messengers of the Churches within that Jurisdiction) in whose presence, in a day of Fasting and Prayer, they making confession of the Truth and Grace of Jesus Christ, did in that solemn Assembly enter into Covenant, to walk together in the Faith and Order of the Gospel; and were accepted and declared to be a Church of Jesus Christ. . . . The same day also were they, and such of their Children as were present, baptized.

From them we passed over to the *Vineyard*, where many were added to the Church both men and women, and were baptized all of them, and their Children also with them; we had the Sacrament of the Lords Supper celebrated in the *Indian-Church*, and many of the *English-Church* gladly joined with them; for which cause it was celebrated in both languages. On a day of Fasting and Prayer, Elders were ordained, two Teaching-Elders, the one to be a Preacher of the Gospel, to do the Office of a Pastor and Teacher; the other to be a Preacher of the Gospel, to do the Office of a Teacher and Pastor, as the Lord should give them ability and opportunity. . . . Advice was given them, that after some experience of walking together in the Order and Ordinances of the Gospel, they should issue forth into another Church; and the Officers are so chosen, that when they shall do so, both Places are furnished with a Teaching and Ruling-Elder.

Charles W. Eliot, ed., *American Historical Documents 1000-1904*, Harvard Classics 43 (New York: P. F. Collier & Son), 147–49.

southern colonies, where plantation agriculture could generate enough revenue to support the cost of owning enslaved persons. Also, in the colonial period a number of enslaved Africans achieved their independence, so there were free Africans, mainly in the cities.

As in Latin America, in North America there was an initial reluctance on the part of slave owners to share the Christian gospel with enslaved persons, due to two main worries: first, that enslaved persons would somehow be equal to their masters if they were introduced to Christianity; second, that enslaved persons might seize on parts of the Bible's narrative to justify insurrection or rebellion. In the main, Europeans ignored the spiritual needs of Africans. And if they did address those needs, they did so while simultaneously attempting to use the Christian message as a means of controlling the enslaved persons. If Africans were brought to church, they had to sit in the back or in a balcony, and if they were allowed to take Communion, they could do so only after the White congregants were finished. Many enslaved Africans were not allowed to marry or to have their children baptized in Christian ceremonies. This general situation would change in subsequent centuries, but Africans in seventeenth-century British North America—free or enslaved—had little formal exposure to organized Christianity.

The Nature of Christianity in Early Colonial Society

Those Europeans who immigrated to seventeenth-century British North America encountered what was, to them, a new and strange world. Many struggled just to survive, let alone to recreate the social, cultural, and religious worlds they had left behind. These immigrants were used to the European world of Christendom, a Christian civilization where church and state worked together and supported each other. Even though the Protestant Reformations of the sixteenth century had disrupted this situation to a degree, and limited religious toleration in England had stretched the established church even further, organized religion in Europe was still strong and influential. Not so in America. What state-supported, established religions there were in the New World were shells of their European selves—even in Puritan New England, the strongest of the lot. Weak colonial governments had very little money to devote to organized religion, and there were very few pastors and priests to support congregations. Throughout the colonial period, there were never enough clergy to organize and lead churches, especially as settlers continued to push inland in search of new farmland.

It is often said that the early European immigrants came to the New World in search of religious freedom, but this is generally a myth; the primary reason for immigration was economic advancement, or else to start a new life. While there were some who sought religious freedom in America, by "religious freedom" they usually meant the freedom to practice *their* religion, not a general freedom that would have allowed any group to practice whatever religion it preferred. Actually, if truth be told, freedom *from* religion—that is, freedom from the prescribed religiosities of the state churches of Europe—was probably the main religious concern for many European immigrants. And if this was not the first reason they came, then it was something they came to appreciate in this New World. Above all, the new colonies needed labor, and they were not too picky about the religion of the people who came to work.

In this new situation, the enduring essence of religion in America was forged, and this essence was that religion was voluntary. There simply was no way to enforce, or proscribe, religious behavior, and immigrants soon came to realize that they had the freedom to choose whether or not to join any particular religious group. Beyond this, voluntary religion meant a dramatic shift in power in religion away from the clergy and church structures and to the people themselves. If the people wanted a religious community, it was up to them to form the group, to organize it, run it, and pay for it. These religious communities identified and engaged their clergy (when they could find them), and they also had the power to fire them. The power differential shifted here from the clergy to the people, the ones who voluntarily joined and paid for the community. This was true across the religious spectrum, and it was a difficult lesson for the clergy to learn, especially those trained in the European system.

There is another enduring myth about religion in colonial America, and that concerns the general strength of organized religion. Religion in this period is often viewed through a romantic lens—as though it were a religious golden age, a time when everyone was religious. The truth is, organized religion in the colonies was extremely weak, and many colonists had little or no ongoing exposure to organized religion, whether or not that was something they wanted. There were never enough clergy and never enough congregations to meet the needs of the colonists. By 1700, there were fewer than 350 organized congregations in the British colonies, about 150 of which were Puritan congregations in New England. And there were fewer clergy members than there were congregations. Many congregations had no pastors, or they had to share a single pastor with several other congregations. The critical lack of clergy was due to several factors, including the reluctance of many European clergy to immigrate to the colonies and the inability of many religious groups to develop and educate enough of their own pastors in North America.

The weakness of organized religion in early colonial America does not necessarily mean that individual colonists were not themselves personally religious. It is almost impossible to gauge the strength of the religious beliefs of the colonial population as a whole at this time, and it is not clear if they were any more or less religious than Americans in subsequent centuries. But the colonists were coming to realize that they had more power and control over their religious lives in America than they had had in Europe, as well as many more choices, including the choice to not be religious if they did not want to be.

For the leaders of organized religion, this new situation must have initially seemed dire, and some in Europe speculated that colonial America would be a lawless and religionless place. This turned out not to be the case, largely because those religious leaders who were inventive and flexible were able to see beyond the loss of their familiar European religious context and to perceive that this new American religious situation could eventually provide an opening for religious expansion on a massive scale. They realized, however, that while Americans could be persuaded to join and support local religious communities, they could not be required to do so. Religious leaders would have to provide incentives for people to commit to a religious affiliation, rewards for the sacrifices that such an affiliation entailed. People had to be persuaded, and the clergy had to persuade them. As it developed, America would essentially become a vast religious marketplace where increasing numbers of religious organizations vied for the allegiance and affiliation of the American people. This dynamic would fundamentally reshape the old (and new) religious groups that operated in this New World. Christianity in America would never be the same.

────────────────────── BIBLIOGRAPHY ──────────────────────

Bonomi, Patricia U. *Under the Cope of Heaven: Religion, Society, and Politics in Colonial America*. Updated ed. New York: Oxford University Press, 2003.

Fortson, S. Donald, III, ed. *Colonial Presbyterianism: Old Faith in a New Land*. Eugene, OR: Pickwick, 2007.

Gaustad, Edwin S. *Liberty of Conscience: Roger Williams in America*. Grand Rapids: Eerdmans, 1991.

Hall, David D. *A Reforming People: Puritanism and the Transformation of Public Life in New England*. New York: Knopf, 2011.

Kidd, Thomas S. *American Colonial History: Clashing Cultures and Faiths*. New Haven: Yale University Press, 2016.

Miller, Perry. *Errand into the Wilderness*. Cambridge, MA: Harvard University Press, 1956.

Pointer, Richard W. *Encounters of the Spirit: Native Americans and European Colonial Religion*. Bloomington: Indiana University Press, 2007.

Stout, Harry S. *The New England Soul: Preaching and Religious Culture in Colonial New England*. New York: Oxford University Press, 2012.

Sweet, William Warren. *Religion in Colonial America*. New York: Cooper Square, 1965.

Winner, Lauren F. *A Cheerful and Comfortable Faith: Anglican Religious Practice in the Elite Households of Eighteenth-Century Virginia*. New Haven: Yale University Press, 2010.

4

The Growth of American Christianity and Increasing Pluralism, 1700–1775

BY 1700, THE THIRTEEN BRITISH COLONIES along the Eastern Seaboard of North America had achieved a semblance of permanence. There were about 250,000 European settlers in this region at the beginning of the century, as well as Native Americans and free and enslaved Africans. With the formation in 1732 of the thirteenth and final colony, Georgia, the political outlines of the region were set, with the Spanish in Florida to the south and the British and French-Canadian provinces to the north. The British government also wanted to keep the colonial population east of the Appalachian Mountains for several reasons. The primary purpose of colonies was for them to produce raw materials for the mother country and then to consume finished goods from the mother country in return; given the realities of transportation, this necessitated access to the coasts. The American colonies were, accordingly, largely populated along the Atlantic coast, although the search for new lands for a growing population increasingly pushed European settlement inland. This meant conflict between European settlers and Native Americans, something the British wanted to avoid.

The number of colonists had greatly expanded by 1770, reaching 2.1 million. The threat from the French in Canada had been eliminated by their defeat in the French and Indian War (1754–63), which had resulted in the virtually complete withdrawal of the French from North America. But the growth of the American colonies and their newfound powers led to a growing conflict between the colonists and the British government in London. Americans chafed under the regulation of colonial trade and the imposition of taxes to support their defense. The British authorities attempted to rein in the economic and political aspirations of the restive American population and sought to have them pay their share of colonial defense. Although most colonists retained affection for Great Britain, many of them longed for the same political and economic rights enjoyed by British subjects at home. While the colonists still counted their particular colonies as their primary sources of identity, a sense of American identity had begun to develop.

The Growth of American Christianity in the Eighteenth Century

There was a growth in organized Christianity in the American colonies during the eighteenth century, although the formation of congregations lagged somewhat behind the population growth. In 1700, there were 373 organized Christian congregations in the American colonies. That number grew to 1,175 by 1740, and then to 2,731 by 1780. As impressive as this growth would seem, the formation of congregations lagged behind the population growth. There was one congregation for every 670 Americans in 1700, one congregation for every 765 Americans in 1740, and one congregation for every 1,025 Americans in 1780.[1] According to estimates, only 17 percent of Americans were formal members of Christians congregations in 1776. Rates varied by colony, from 26 percent in New Jersey to 7 percent in Georgia.[2] These statistics measure only formal membership, and standards for membership varied by denomination; these standards might have been stricter in the eighteenth century than they would be today. But even with this in mind, it is clear that organized religion in the American colonies in the eighteenth century was weak. To be sure, this is not necessarily to say that the colonists of the time were not personally believers. That would be impossible to determine with any accuracy. But it is clear that our often-romantic image of an intensely Christian world in colonial America is simply not supported by the facts. Actually, there has been a dramatic and sustained growth of organized Christianity in the United States from the eighteenth century through the twentieth. Americans today are three times more likely to be church members than they were in 1776. In the

---

1. Figures for congregations in this section are taken from Edwin Scott Gaustad, *Historical Atlas of Religion in America*. rev. ed. (New York: Harper and Row, 1976), 3–4.
2. Roger Finke and Rodney Stark, *The Churching of America, 1776–2005: Winners and Losers in Our Religious Economy* (New Brunswick, NJ: Rutgers University Press, 2005), 29–31.

eighteenth century, as the number of European settlers ballooned, few became official members of Christian congregations, and those who did often lacked steady pastoral leadership.

The largest Christian group in British colonial America at the time was the Congregationalists, mainly in New England, which grew to almost 750 congregations in 1780. Their traditional competitor, the Anglicans, had about 400 congregations by that year, from New York to Georgia, but centered in Virginia. Two other groups expanded strongly during this century: the Presbyterians, who had nearly 500 congregations by 1780, and the Baptists, with around 450 congregations. These four constituted the major Christian groups in the American colonies and represented the bulk of English-speaking church-goers. German and Dutch Reformed congregations numbered around 325 by 1780, and there were almost 250 German Lutheran congregations as well. The growing pluralism included smaller numbers of Quakers, Mennonites, Amish, Moravians, and an increasing number of Methodists. It is almost impossible to estimate the number of Christian clergy in the colonies during this century, but from reports it seems clear that there were significantly more congregations than there were pastors. Many pastors served two or three congregations, and some congregations had no pastor whatsoever.

The Congregationalists, found predominantly in New England, continued to dominate the region, but increasingly they had to deal with upstart competitors such as the Baptists and Presbyterians. Even the Anglicans made inroads in New England, with the development of three substantial congregations in Boston that attracted the well-to-do. By the beginning of the eighteenth century, it was becoming abundantly clear that although the Congregationalists in New England still wielded great regional power, their original vision of a monolithic Puritan commonwealth was not to be achieved. Losing this vision was extremely disquieting to them. They were not advocates of pluralism, but pluralism happened anyway. Even more difficult were the internal fissures within the Congregationalist world that threatened to divide it. The loss of the vigor and vision of the first generation (as seen in the compromises of the Half-Way Covenant) was bad enough, but religious rationalism (an essentially rational and objective approach to religion) was also increasingly making inroads. The influence of rationalism at Harvard so alarmed the Congregationalists in Connecticut that in 1701 they moved to form their own school as a more orthodox alternative—the Collegiate School, at New Haven, which changed its name to Yale College in 1718. Despite these challenges, with both Harvard and Yale as educational options the Congregationalists had a great advantage over many other colonial religious groups: the ability to educate their own clergy in American schools. With such an advantage, the Congregationalists continued through the eighteenth century to establish more new congregations than any other religious group. The Congregationalists also enjoyed solid financial support from the colonial governments of Massachusetts and Connecticut, support that continued into the early nineteenth century.

These advantages were not enjoyed by colonial Anglicans, who suffered from a lack of both priests and finances. On paper, the Anglicans were officially established and state-supported in the southern colonies, but in reality the southern colonies struggled financially and could not devote many resources to support the existing parishes, let alone to establish new ones. Anglicanism in Virginia and Maryland was fairly stable, but the situation was worse in the Carolinas and Georgia, where there were few parishes outside the major towns. The Anglicans lagged behind the Congregationalists in founding new congregations, and although there were nearly four hundred Anglican parishes in the colonies by 1780, both the Presbyterians and Baptists had moved past the Anglicans in numbers. The other major weakness for the Anglicans was in educating clergy. Although the College of William and Mary in Virginia was formed in 1693, this institution struggled mightily during its first decades and did not produce the numbers of Anglican priests necessary for the parishes. Also, candidates for ordination had to go to England for approval and ordination at the hands of an Anglican bishop, which took considerable time and resources. The lack of a resident Anglican bishop in America was problematic to the Anglicans, though the prospect of such a resident bishop was a great religious and political threat to other colonial religious groups (as shall be seen later).

The Anglicans did, however, enjoy two advantages. They enjoyed the mission support of the Church of England's Society for the Propagation of the Gospel in Foreign Parts (SPG), a well-connected and well-funded society that funded missionary priests in America and provided financial support for struggling parishes. The other major advantage was the support for the Anglican parishes by the monarchy and the royal officials in the colonies. During the eighteenth century, government and military officials were required to be members of the Church of England, and such membership was often socially and commercially advantageous. Especially as Anglican missionaries moved into the middle colonies and New England, these aspects were crucial in the establishment of several influential parishes: Trinity Church in New York City and North Church in Boston, among others. Some prominent "dissenting" ministers, such as George Keith (Quaker) and Timothy Cutler (Congregationalist), transitioned to the Anglican priesthood.

The two fastest-growing religious groups in eighteenth-century America were the Baptists and the Presbyterians. In 1700 there were only 33 Baptist and 28 Presbyterian congregations in America, but both groups had surpassed the

Anglicans by 1780, with around 450 Baptist and 500 Presbyterian congregations. Neither group was state supported (the Baptists were opposed to this), but they both seemed to thrive in the competitive, voluntary, and pluralistic situation that was coming to define religion in America.

The two original centers of Baptist strength were in Rhode Island and Philadelphia, both colonies that had, like the Baptists, expressly rejected any kind of state-supported, established religion. The Baptists (like the Quakers) believed that religious faith must be voluntary and that any form of establishment led to hypocrisy, or worse. From Rhode Island, the Baptists spread into the rest of New England, finding converts especially from the Separatist Congregationalists and other disaffected Puritans, who embraced the idea of a "fully converted" congregational membership made up of "true" believers. The Baptists also pushed into the middle colonies and especially into the interior of the South, through the efforts of preachers Shubal Stearns (1706–71) and Daniel Marshall (1706–84). In the upland frontier of the South, which lacked settled Anglican parishes, the Baptist movement took root. Its expansion was aided by the fact that the Baptists could raise up a larger number of preachers because they were not required to have much in the way of formal education. In the 1760s and 1770s, the growth and success of the Baptists in the South occasioned a reaction from the colonial governments in Virginia and North Carolina, which tried to imprison or expel Baptist preachers from their territories. Their efforts did not succeed, and they pushed the Baptists even further in the latter's advocacy for the dismantling of state-supported religious establishments.

The growth of the colonial Presbyterians was most pronounced in the middle colonies, especially because of an influx of Scotch Irish settlers into the region. New Jersey became the center of colonial Presbyterianism, especially under the leadership of early pastors William Tennent Sr. (1673–1746) and his son Gilbert Tennent (1703–64), but the movement spread throughout the middle colonies and down into the upland regions of the South. Early educational efforts among the Presbyterians began as early as 1726 and took permanent form with the chartering of the College of New Jersey (now Princeton University) in 1746. Unlike the Baptists, who were strictly congregational in organization, the Presbyterians held to corporate forms of church structure that bound groups of pastors and congregations into regional and national organizations—presbyteries and synods. Under the leadership of Presbyterian missionary Francis Makemie, the first American presbytery was formed in Philadelphia in 1706, and two others were added by 1716 (New York and Delaware). The Presbyterians and the Congregationalists shared a similar Reformed (Calvinist) theology, and in Connecticut, the Congregationalists adopted a Presbyterian church structure in the Saybrook Platform of 1708.

Snyder / Presbyterian Historical Society

4.1. William Tennent Sr.'s "Log College," 1726.

The eighteenth century saw a large increase in German immigration to North America, especially to the middle colonies and most of all to Pennsylvania, where the immigrants developed a thriving German-American culture. With the exception of a few groups of religious or political refugees, this German migration was primarily made up of individuals and small family groups seeking economic advancement. A number of Germans came to America as indentured servants, who, in return for passage to the New World, worked as virtual slaves for a period of time (often seven years). Almost all the German immigrants were Protestants, but they were divided between Lutheran, Reformed, Anabaptist, and radical Pietist groups.

Early on, the Lutherans grew as scattered congregations from New York to Georgia, appealing to Lutheran authorities in Europe for pastors and assistance. Eventually, in 1742, the Pietist center at Halle sent Henry Melchior Muhlenberg (1711–87) to Philadelphia to take charge of three Lutheran congregations. From this base, Muhlenberg worked tirelessly to pull together the scattered Lutheran congregations in the middle colonies, and they formed the Ministerium of Pennsylvania in 1748. Initially, Muhlenberg had to fend off challenges to his leadership from rogue Lutheran pastors and from Moravian leader Count Nikolaus Ludwig von Zinzendorf (1700–60), but eventually Muhlenberg became the recognized leader of Lutherans in the colonies. Continual German immigration swelled Lutheran numbers, and by 1780 there were 240 Lutheran congregations stretching from Georgia to Nova Scotia.

The Reformed (Calvinist) tradition in America included English Congregationalists and Baptists, Scotch Irish Presbyterians, and Reformed Protestants

Henry M. Muhlenberg, "A Pastor's Journal" (November 1763)

November 1: In the forenoon I had all sorts of running in and out and troublesome interruptions. Visit from the late Pastor Steiner's widow, who had many laments to make.

November 5: Saturday. Visit from Josua Pawling, of Providence, who said I must again take over the Providence church and congregation, otherwise everything would go to ruin.

November 6: I went to church with Mr. Brycelius, baptized three children, and preached to a crowded auditorium. As soon as church was over I was taken to Germantown to bury Mr. Jacob Gänsle. About five-thirty in the evening I drove away and arrived home in the dark near eight o'clock.

November 9: I felt unwell, but I had to carry out my promise to go to Mr. [George] Whitefield. He received us very cordially. I received a courteous letter inviting me to visit Chief Judge Coleman and furnish a testimonial to the deceased wife of a certain Lutheran man. I also visited the silversmith, Mr. Carben; had a refreshing visit with the family.

November 16: Learned that the church council had rejected the petitions I had submitted to them. This bewildering and miserable affair is hastening my death and is almost rendering me unfit for my office.

November 17: Today we had the first deep snow and unhealthy, wet weather. Had a visit. . . . The rest of the time I meditated and wrote. Otherwise I was distressed and depressed over the intricate dispute in this poor congregation. . . . My health is suffering from it.

November 21: Visit from the poor widow of a Reformed preacher. She was in great straits.

November 29: Tuesday. Early in the morning I journeyed to Germantown. At home I heard that immediately after my departure on Saturday several dissatisfied persons had come into my house and blustered against me and the church council. At 1 PM I married Daniel Sorg and Margretha Heidel. In the evening we had a heavy rainstorm. Refreshing visit from Mr. Kressler.

Henry Melchior Muhlenberg, *The Journals of Henry Melchior Muhlenberg* (Philadelphia: Muhlenberg Press, 1942), 1:700–716.

from France (Huguenots), Holland, and Germany. The Dutch Reformed in
America survived the loss of Dutch rule in New York and were revitalized during the eighteenth century. This group moved increasingly away from control
by church authorities in Holland, forming their own *coetus*, or association,
in 1747 and declaring their independence in 1755. They organized their own
school, Queen's College (now Rutgers), in New Jersey in 1766, and by 1780 had
127 congregations in America. Immigration also brought a significant number
of German Reformed Protestants to America. While they initially formed
congregations in concert with the Dutch Reformed, geography and language
differences led to the formation of a separate German Reformed *coetus* in 1746
under the leadership of Michael Schlatter. By 1780 there were two hundred
German Reformed congregations in North America. In many places, especially
in Pennsylvania, German Lutherans and Reformed lived in the same areas and
sometimes cooperated in the formation of Union Churches, in which Lutheran
and Reformed congregations shared church buildings and sometimes even pastors. There were also numbers of immigrant French Reformed (Huguenots)
who were refugees from persecution in France. The largest Huguenot settlement was in Charleston, South Carolina, but there were scattered Huguenot
congregations as far north as Massachusetts. These individuals and congregations did not form a denominational structure but tended to affiliate with
other Protestant groups.

German immigration in this period brought Anabaptists and radical Pietists
mainly to Pennsylvania and the middle colonies. The Moravians, Pietists from
Germany, began to arrive in 1735. They formed their own center in Bethlehem,
Pennsylvania, under the leadership of Count von Zinzendorf, who, during a
visit to America in 1741 and 1742, attempted (unsuccessfully) to pull together
all the German Protestant congregations in America into a single organization
under his leadership. There was also a significant Moravian settlement in North
Carolina. Other Pietists, particularly those who tended toward separatism and
adult baptism, also gravitated toward the religious freedom of Pennsylvania,
including the Church of the Brethren (Dunkers), and one of the early communal experiments in America, the Ephrata Cloister, which was founded by
a former Dunker, Conrad Beissel (1691–1768). Though this community did
not survive long after its leader's death, it was a precursor of a number of other,
similar communal experiments.

The Anabaptists were Separatist Protestants from the sixteenth-century
Protestant Reformation in Germany, Switzerland, and Holland who settled
in local congregations emphasizing adult baptism and pacifism. These groups,
especially the Mennonites and Amish, were similarly drawn to the religious
freedom in Pennsylvania. The Mennonites began to arrive in Pennsylvania in

1683 and, under the leadership of Francis Daniel Pastorius (1651–ca. 1720), initially cooperated with Quakers. But linguistic and theological differences arose, and the Mennonites soon migrated west to the rich farmlands of Lancaster County, which remains one of their centers. Their more conservative relatives, the Amish, began arriving after 1727 and settled in the same region. Since the Mennonites and Amish believed in the autonomy of the local religious community, distinct variations emerged in the patterns and practices of their life and worship, and they formed a variety of denominational structures.

To round out this examination of Christianity in eighteenth-century colonial America, two other significant groups need mention: the Quakers and the Roman Catholics. Both had early roots but did not benefit from growth through immigration, and so they did not expand much during this period. Consequently, Quakers and Roman Catholics eventually became minorities in the colonies they had founded—the former in Pennsylvania and the latter in Maryland. As religious and social outsiders, the Quakers were ill-prepared to govern a large and pluralistic society, and in 1756, during the French and Indian War, they opted to give up control of the government of Pennsylvania rather than participate in that conflict. Many Quaker merchants had become wealthy and were economic leaders in the middle colonies, which led to some complacency. But Quaker leader John Woolman (1720–72) sparked the social consciences of the Quakers by writing in opposition to slavery, war, and economic disparity. The small settlement of English Roman Catholics—centered in Maryland and expanding to nearby Pennsylvania—developed its own institutions, but its members were greatly outnumbered by the local Protestants. Protestant antipathy toward Roman Catholics was a constant aspect of American colonial life and flared up at various times, especially during the war against the French in Canada. Roman Catholicism in America would remain small until the great migrations of the nineteenth century.

Religious and Cultural Changes—the Enlightenment

The growth in organized Christianity in colonial America during the eighteenth century occurred in the midst of an intellectual revolution happening on both sides of the Atlantic: the Enlightenment. This movement eventually transformed many of the basic assumptions of the Western world and realistically ushered in the modern age. The Enlightenment was an intellectual transformation that dramatically changed the way people looked at themselves, their societies, the world they lived in, and even God. In the Enlightenment, reason was primary and available through the properly educated human mind.

There was an air of optimism and progress among Enlightenment intellectuals that suggested humans could move forward and transform not only themselves but also their societies and their world.

The reformations of the sixteenth century unleashed a wave of religious unrest for much of the next two hundred years. Theological conflicts between Protestants and Roman Catholics were fought not only with words but also with armies, as religious and political conflicts escalated into war. Not all of these wars were about religion—most were about power—but religious labels often distinguished the combatants from one another. Internally, governments often persecuted their religious minorities (such as in France). The American experiments in religious pluralism seemed destabilizing and dangerous to most Europeans. But these conflicts, usually bloody, were mostly fought to a stalemate. And by the end of the seventeenth century, many Europeans were tired of religious conflict, both theological and military.

Out of this unrest, some theologians and intellectuals crafted a new vision of humanity, God, and the world. In this new vision, human reason was the path to all truth, discovered through a natural world built on rational principles and divinely installed natural laws, accessible to all. Enlightenment thinkers were sure of the natural goodness of the human person, which could be directed through rational education, and that humanity was capable of making moral and social progress. Optimism was in the air, and education was seen as the path to a brighter future. Though it began as a small movement among European intellectuals, the Enlightenment eventually transformed many areas of Western life on both sides of the Atlantic.

The beginnings of Enlightenment thought are usually seen in a circle of British intellectuals—including Isaac Newton (1643–1727), John Locke (1632–1704), and David Hume (1711–76)—and French intellectuals—including René Descartes (1596–1650), Denis Diderot (1713–84), and Voltaire (1694–1778). Broadly, as these new thinkers considered God and religion, they held that both God and the universe God created were rational and ordered and that the rational truths about God and the universe were just waiting to be discovered by the rational human mind. God created reason and natural laws and put them into the world. Thus, the essence of religion was reason, and any parts of religion that were not reasonable were to be rejected. Since God created a world with a singular universal and natural moral law, this single morality (often reduced to the Golden Rule) was accessible to all, despite differences in religious affiliation. Thus, claims by various religious groups to have an exclusive understanding of God, moral standards, and the world were implicitly rejected. It was thought that if they were reasonable, all religions would teach the same God and the same morality. The Enlightenment God, then, set the world into motion and did not interfere in it. There were no miracles, divine interventions, or special revelations. Most Enlightenment thinkers did, however, allow that there would be a final judgment at the end of the world, in which good people would be rewarded and bad people would be punished.

Though Enlightenment intellectuals shared many rational presuppositions, there was a distinct difference between the English and French Enlightenments in their attitudes toward traditional established religions. The differences were, in part, based on the religious histories of the two countries. In France, the Roman Catholic Church was powerful, monolithic, and deeply aligned with the royal structures of power. It persecuted those who differed from it and was deeply resented by many intellectuals and common people. At the end of the eighteenth century, the French Revolution was violently anticlerical and attempted to destroy traditional, organized Christianity. French intellectuals were strongly opposed to the Roman Catholic Church and, during the French Revolution, attempted to establish a substitute "religion of reason" (which turned out to be quite a failure).

The religious situation in England was quite a bit different. The English had a long history of internal conflict as well as an established state Church of England, which was closely aligned with the monarchy and the government. Yet England also had a long tradition of parliamentary democracy and had, through its long period of religious conflict, eventually embraced a rough form of religious pluralism. These English traditions of democracy and religious pluralism were transmitted to its American colonies. The intellectuals of the English Enlightenment, including some top church officials—such as Bishop George Berkeley—were much less critical of traditional organized Christianity than were their French counterparts. They saw value in traditional forms of Christianity as instruments of social stability and of teaching God's natural morality to the masses, who did not have the means of achieving a rational education. If properly led, they reasoned, traditional Christianity could be a vehicle of social improvement and progress. Thus, there was not the same fiercely antagonistic relation between traditional Christianity and the Enlightenment in England as there was in France.

The Enlightenment and rational religion slowly seeped into the religious and intellectual world of Anglo-America, as some pastors and theologians were exposed to these new ideas. Many church leaders saw little conflict between the new religion of reason and traditional Christianity, although they had to minimize or dismiss certain elements of traditional Christianity to harmonize the two. In Puritan New England and among colonial Anglicans, the new religion of reason was finding a home in certain quarters, much to the dismay of some. By the eighteenth century, the religion of reason had made such inroads into

Harvard College, for example, that Connecticut Congregationalists sought to found Yale College in 1701 as an orthodox Puritan counterpoint. Certain prominent Christian preachers—including Cotton Mather (1663–1728) and Charles Chauncy (1705–87)—wrote influential books based on the new Enlightenment principles.

Although for the most part the Anglo-American Enlightenment did not directly challenge traditional Christianity, this school of thought did have a corrosive effect on many traditional Christian doctrines, including human sinfulness and the nature of conversion and salvation, all of which were gently but persistently undermined. But this was not enough for some, who quietly and individually came to reject the essence of Christianity altogether in favor of reliance on reason alone. These thinkers felt themselves rational enough not to need the "crutch" of traditional religion, though they often supported it publicly as a means of maintaining social order and cohesion. This religion of reason is often called "deism," and a number of the prominent leaders in the American colonies were deists, including George Washington, Benjamin Franklin, Thomas Jefferson, and John Adams, among others. It would not be until the early part of the nineteenth century that organized deism was developed in North America, with the formation of the Unitarian and Universalist movements.

The First Great Awakening

As important as the Enlightenment is for understanding eighteenth-century Western religious life, this is not its most important feature. More noteworthy was the widespread revival of religious life during this period, a broad movement of what are sometimes referred to as "religions of the heart."[3] This revival was a disparate conjunction of religious movements that shared a key element: reliance on the subjective, on "feelings" or emotions, as the center of religious experience. In the seventeenth and eighteenth centuries, this subjective approach to religion was taken by many Lutheran and Reformed Pietists, Roman Catholic Jansenists and Quietists, Quakers, Hasidic Jews, and leaders of the Anglo-American evangelical movement. The latter included Puritan and Methodist religious forms, both of which were critical elements of colonial American religion; the Pietist movement was also important among the Lutherans and Reformed. In America, the Anglo-American evangelical movement was most clearly seen in a series of religious revivals of the 1730s and 1740s that came to be known as the First Great Awakening.

3. See Ted A. Campbell, *Religions of the Heart: A Study of European Religious Life in the Seventeenth and Eighteenth Centuries* (Columbia: University of South Carolina Press, 1991).

The Puritans introduced Reformed (Calvinist) Protestantism into Britain in the sixteenth century, including an emphasis on the necessity of a conversion experience (in which a believer comes to true faith) and holy living (sanctification) after one's conversion. For the Puritans, this conversion experience was a work of God through the Holy Spirit in the believer; it was not something the believer *did*, but was a passive conversion experience. Puritans kept seriously and rigorously examining their spiritual state (often over years or even decades) to determine whether God had worked the work of election (conversion) in them. Although it was understood that God might effect the work of conversion in a person through human elements, such as preaching or personal conversation, Puritans strongly held to the passive, God-inspired nature of conversion. What they wished to avoid at all costs was any hint or suggestion of an active human role in the conversion experience—some form of "manufacturing" this conversion by human means—which would taint the process.

However, a passive conversion, accomplished solely by the work of God, would mean that those who are elected by God are so designated by God's grace alone—or in theological terms, that the elect are predestined to salvation. The concept of predestination has often been controversial, suggesting to many that God's salvation is arbitrary, since it is done without reference to human moral action or religious practice. Within Calvinism, a controversial seventeenth-century movement called Arminianism sought to mitigate the problem of predestination by suggesting that God offers the grace of salvation to all persons but that it is up to each person to actively accept or reject this offer. According to the Arminians, God elects, and so predestines for salvation, those whom God foresees will accept the offer of salvation. Arminianism was a theological development hotly contested by orthodox Calvinists, as it suggests that human beings have some sort of role to play in obtaining salvation and that those who reject the offer of salvation can thereby thwart the will of God. Nevertheless—especially through many in the evangelical movement and, later, through Methodism—Arminianism became (and still is) the dominant theological tradition in American Protestantism.

The Evangelical Awakening—or, simply, modern evangelicalism—was the most important religious factor in eighteenth-century Anglo-American Protestantism. This movement, which included Reformed Calvinism and a significant portion of Anglicanism, was centered on four core principles: biblicism (stress on the authority of the Bible), crucicentrism (focus on Christ's atoning work on the cross), conversionism (the need for a conversion experience), and activism (active means of expressing the gospel through human effort).[4] Although

---

4. David W. Bebbington, *Evangelicalism in Modern Britain: A History from the 1730s to the 1980s* (London: Unwin Hyman, 1989).

not all evangelicals adopted Arminianism, over time the vast majority of them did. This evangelicalism became the dominant form of Christianity in colonial America through the religious revivals of the First Great Awakening, which in turn deeply influenced the subsequent structure and development of much of American religious life, whether evangelical or not.

There is much debate about the Great Awakening of the 1730s and 1740s—its parameters, its causes and effects, and even whether there was such a thing at all. Certainly, the title is retroactive, applied later to a series of religious awakenings that happened across the American colonies during these decades. But it is clear that something important and powerful swept through the American colonies during this period. Though individual revivals generally happened independently of one another, knowledge of them spread. Revival tours, such as those of George Whitefield (1714–70), spanned the colonies, further spreading these revivals.

The initial stirrings of what would become the First Great Awakening occurred in New England during the first decades of the eighteenth century through the work of two important Congregational leaders: Solomon Stoddard (1643–29) and Cotton Mather (1663–28). Stoddard served the Congregational church in the town of Northampton, in western Massachusetts, for fifty-seven years. This period was one of unrest and worry among the Congregationalists, with the loss of the original Puritan vision, the challenges of pluralism, and the decline in religious participation. Through many efforts, Stoddard sought to raise the religious level and intensity within his congregation and town. And to his satisfaction, Stoddard recorded that he had witnessed five separate awakenings or "harvests" during the time of his leadership. Cotton Mather, a man of many talents and interests, was pastor at the prestigious Old North Church in Boston. Although Mather opposed a number of Stoddard's religious innovations, he too was influential in religious awakenings and moral reform in Massachusetts during this time.

But the initial major figure of the First Great Awakening—and perhaps the greatest theologian America has ever produced—was Stoddard's grandson and ministerial colleague at Northampton, Jonathan Edwards (1703–58). While working at this church on the colonial frontier, Edwards managed to spark a series of religious revivals within the area that soon became known throughout New England and the rest of the colonies. But, beyond this, he corresponded with English and European intellectuals and wrote numerous volumes of serious Christian theology and philosophy, some of which are still influential today, and became the intellectual leader of the First Great Awakening.

Edwards began by providing pastoral assistance to his grandfather at Northampton toward the end of Stoddard's career. Then he took over the

Jonathan Edwards, "The Awakening in Northampton, Massachusetts" (1737)

There was scarcely a single person in the town, either old or young, that was left unconcerned about the great things of the eternal world. Those that were wont to be the vainest and loosest, and those that had been the most disposed to think and speak slightly of vital and experimental religion, were now generally subject to great awakenings. And the work of conversion was carried on in a most astonishing manner, and increased more and more; souls did, as it were, come by flocks to Jesus Christ. From day to day, for many months together, might be seen evident instances of sinners brought "out of darkness into marvelous light," and delivered "out of a horrible pit, and from the miry clay, and set upon a rock, with a new song of praise to God in their mouths."

This work of God, as it was carried on, and the number of true saints multiplied, soon made a glorious alteration in the town; so that in the spring and summer following, AD 1735, the town seemed to be full of the presence of God. It never was so full of love, nor so full of joy, and yet so full of distress, as it was then. There were remarkable tokens of God's presence in almost every house. It was a time of joy in families, on the account of salvation being brought unto them; parents rejoicing over their children as new born, and husbands over their wives, and wives over their husbands. The goings of God were then seen in his sanctuary; God's day was a delight, and his tabernacles were amiable.

Jonathan Edwards, *A Faithful Narrative of the Surprising Work of God* (London: 1737), 14–15.

care of that congregation upon his grandfather's death in 1729. Beginning about 1734 and continuing for approximately three years, Edwards led a series of revivals within the area that soon attracted wider attention. Concerned that public religiosity and morality were on the decline, especially among the young, Edwards worked to call hearts and minds to the things of God and salvation. Through a series of sermons on the doctrine of justification by grace through faith, Edwards soon unleashed a revival that spread through western Massachusetts and down the Connecticut River valley as far south as Long Island Sound. This revival, which Edwards called a "surprising work of God," sparked similar awakenings in New England and even into the British Isles. Some of Edwards's twelve hundred sermons were published and achieved great circulation throughout the English-speaking world.

Edwards eventually attempted to tighten up church discipline within the Northampton congregation, reversing Stoddard's open invitation for all to participate in Communion. Edwards pushed to restrict Communion participation to only those members with a demonstrable conversion experience. This caused great friction within the congregation, and he was eventually ousted from the pastorate there. In 1750, he took a call to a Native American mission at Stockbridge, Massachusetts. He wrote a number of his most serious and important theological and philosophical books in this frontier situation. In 1758, he was called to become the president of the College of New Jersey (now Princeton University) but died of complications from a smallpox vaccination after only a few weeks there.

When considering the term *revival*, modern readers might have in their minds the picture of a fire-and-brimstone preacher unleashing thunderous oratory and powerful, emotional calls to repentance and salvation. While this does represent some of what American evangelicalism would eventually become in later centuries, this was not Edwards's type of revival. A careful Calvinist, Edwards's preaching was precise and thoughtful, more akin to a theological lecture than anything else. He was not out to excite the passions of his listeners. But Edwards had an incisive and serious way of getting into people's hearts and minds to turn them to considering God and their religious lives. He was not about to "manufacture" revivals and conversions, though he staunchly defended the awakenings of the 1730s and 1740s as the work of God, against critics who saw other, less divine forces at work in them.

Edwards's theological genius was his ability to combine the theological seriousness of the Calvinist theological tradition with elements of Enlightenment thought, especially the centrality of the human person. In serious theological works—such as the *Treatise Concerning Human Affections* (1746) and *Freedom of the Will* (1754)—Edwards persuasively defended Calvinism against Arminianism while also arguing that humans were capable of genuine religious experiences that were more than just basic emotional experiences. Through careful theological reflection and thought, Edwards sought to maintain the elements of Calvinist theology while still allowing for genuine religious experiences through these awakenings. Several subsequent generations of his theological protégés, the Edwardsians, continued to develop these themes, though none of them was nearly as successful as Edwards himself.

While Edwards provided the theological basis for the awakenings, it was British evangelist George Whitefield who brought the revivals to tens of thousands of Americans through the five preaching tours he took of colonial America between 1739 and 1755. Because of opposition from many Anglican priests, and because the crowds he attracted would not have fit in their church buildings anyway, Whitefield delivered most of his sermons outdoors, to crowds numbering into the thousands. After careful measurement, Benjamin Franklin estimated his audience at one sermon in Philadelphia at twenty thousand people. The crowds sometimes became so enthusiastic about Whitefield's appearances that local authorities had a difficult time maintaining order. These preaching tours spanned the length of the British colonies, from Georgia to Massachusetts, and arguably made Whitefield the best-known person in colonial America. His preaching tours united the colonies and brought the First Great Awakening to many corners of British North America.

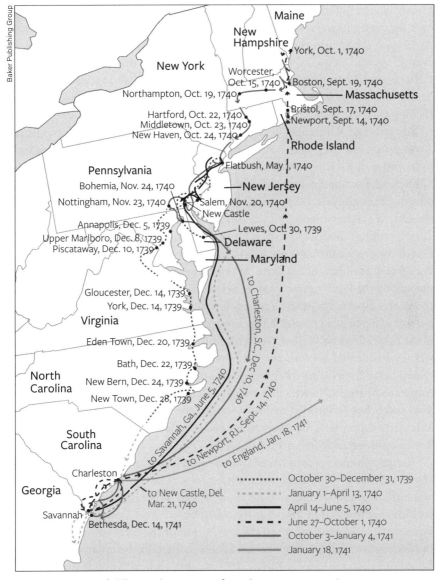

4.2. George Whitefield's Preaching Tours of North America, 1739–41.

Whitefield was the spellbinding orator that Edwards was not—he had to be, in order to preach to thousands of people at a time without amplification. In awe, English actor David Garrick was said to have observed that Whitefield could reduce an audience to tears by simply uttering the word "Mesopotamia." Unlike most other preachers of his day, Whitefield preached extemporaneously (without notes or a written text), and this is perhaps the way he was able to connect so readily with his audiences. It is estimated that Whitefield preached over eighteen thousand times in his career, and his audiences in England and America reached into the millions. He set a standard and example for later evangelists and frequently served as a model for their own efforts. Theologically, he was an evangelical Calvinist, and though he was good friends with the Methodist leaders John and Charles Wesley, he did not adopt their Arminian theology.

Edwards and Whitefield were certainly the major figures in the First Great Awakening, but they were not the only ones. Several other religious leaders independently led their own revivals or followed the examples of Edwards and Whitefield. Even before Edwards and Whitefield, Dutch Reformed pastor Theodorus Frelinghuysen (1691–1748) began, in 1726, a series of revivals among the Dutch congregations in northern New Jersey, attempting to impose the same Communion discipline that Edwards advocated in Northampton. These Dutch congregations saw a growth in religiosity as a part of his efforts. Also in New Jersey, members of the Tennent family were active in pushing for awakening among the Presbyterians, led by William Tennent Sr. (1673–1746) and his three sons, especially Gilbert Tennent (1703–64). Influenced by Frelinghuysen, the Tennents began preaching for conversion among the congregations in the middle colonies, and William set up an informal "Log College" in New Jersey, where he educated his sons and other young men for the ministry. Gilbert is remembered for a rather intemperate sermon in 1740, "The Danger of an Unconverted Ministry," in which he attacked clerical opponents of the awakenings. This and other actions led to a split within the Presbyterians, with the New Side party supporting the awakenings and the Old Side party opposing them. The two sides reconciled in 1758.

The most notorious preacher of awakening in New England, besides Edwards and Whitefield, was James Davenport (1716–57), in Connecticut. Davenport was brilliant but unstable, and in 1741 and 1742 he preached wildly emotional revivals that resulted in his being banished from both Connecticut and Massachusetts, seriously damaging the reputation of the awakening movement. Presbyterian and Baptist revival preachers worked in the upland areas from Maryland through the Carolinas. In 1763, evangelical Anglican priest Devereux Jarratt (1733–1801) preached similar revivals among the Anglicans in

Virginia, influenced by both Whitefield and the Methodists. There were many other local revivals organized by pastors and laypeople alike, including one in Newport, Rhode Island, where a laywoman, Sarah Osborn (1714–96), played a crucial role.

Not all Christian leaders were enthralled with these awakenings and revivals, and some opposed them as dangerous human inventions, rather than genuine movements of the Spirit of God. Some opponents were traditional Calvinists who championed the slow, passive methods of previous times and charged that the new revivalism was "manufacturing" shallow conversions that could not be sustained. Prominent Boston Congregational pastor Charles Chauncy (1705–87) charged that the new approach was undercutting the slow movement

Chauncy against Religious Enthusiasm (1742)

But in nothing does the enthusiasm of these persons discover itself more, than in the disregard they express to the Dictates of reason. They are above the force of argument, beyond conviction from a calm and sober address to their understandings. As for them, they are distinguish'd persons; GOD himself speaks inwardly and immediately to their souls.

They see the light infused into their understandings, and cannot be mistaken; 'tis clear and visible there, like the light of bright sunshine; shews itself and needs no other proof but its own evidence. They feel the hand of GOD moving them within, and the impulses of his SPIRIT; and cannot be mistaken in what they feel. Thus, they support themselves, and are sure reason hath nothing to do with what they see and feel. What they have a sensible experience of, admits no doubt, needs no probation.

And in vain will you endeavour to convince such persons of any mistakes they are fallen into. They are certainly in the right; and know themselves to be so. They have the SPIRIT opening their understandings and revealing the truth to them. They believe only as he has taught them: and to suspect they are in the wrong is to do dishonour to the SPIRIT; 'tis to oppose his dictates, to set up their own wisdom in opposition to his, and shut their eyes against that light with which he has shined into their souls. They are not therefore capable of being argued with; you had as good reason with the wind.

And as the natural consequence of their being thus sure of everything, they are not only infinitely stiff and tenacious, but impatient of contradiction, censorious and uncharitable: they encourage a good opinion of none but such as are in their way of thinking and speaking.

They are likewise positive and dogmatical, vainly fond of their own imaginations, and invincibly set upon propagating them.

Charles Chauncy, *Enthusiasm Described and Caution'd Against* (Boston: J. Draper, 1742), 5.

of God's work among the elect. Others, such as Jonathan Mayhew (1720–66), influenced by the new Enlightenment, pushed back against the whole idea of conversion itself. They argued that, rather than to effect the dramatic turn of "lost" sinners, the point of religion was to further the gradual moral education of autonomous individuals. Some opponents seized on the excesses of Davenport to discredit the awakenings, while others bristled at being labeled as dangerous, "unconverted" ministers.

These fissures about the Great Awakening and its methods eventually erupted into outright divisions within several denominations. Usually these opposing factions were designated "New" and "Old," with the New group being advocates of the awakening and the Old group being opposed to it. The Presbyterians had their New Side and Old Side, which temporarily divided the denomination. And the Congregationalists had their New Light and Old Light parties. In these divides, the New parties usually significantly outnumbered the Old parties. Among the Congregationalists, some of the liberal opponents of the awakenings would eventually form the Unitarian congregations in the early nineteenth century.

The Great Awakening also had a profound impact on African Americans, both enslaved and free. Prior to the awakening, most slave owners ignored the religious lives of their slaves, with some worrying that conversion of African Americans to Christianity would undercut their chattel status or give them "unfortunate" ideas of equality. But awakening preachers had different ideas, and some in the middle colonies and the South included African Americans in their audiences or congregations, although usually apart from White attendees. Religiously converted slave owners became increasingly convinced that it was their Christian duty to have the gospel preached to their slaves, although in a form that was carefully tailored to stress their Christian duty to obey their masters. In the South, especially, Baptist, Methodist, and Presbyterian preachers (as well as Anglicans, though less so) targeted African Americans with the new form of Christianity. The evangelical revivals' emphasis on an individual's experience of God, on a conversion experience that liberated one from sin, and on intense emotion seemed to appeal to many African Americans, certainly more than the formal religiosity of the established churches. Since the awakening movement downplayed the formal distinctions between educated preachers and the laity and held that any converted Christian could proclaim the good news, both White and African American lay preachers became important to the religious life of the South.

In some places, enslaved African Americans were included in the local congregation, often segregated in the back or in a balcony. In other places, preachers led services in the slave quarters. Sometimes in the open, but more often in

Illustrated London News, 1863

4.3. Preaching to the Household Slaves.

secret, African American lay preachers gathered informal congregations. Free African Americans formed their own congregations. Especially early on, these congregations faced hostility and opposition, but many persevered. African Americans seemed to take enthusiastically to the new evangelical Christianity. Although many slave owners saw Christianity as a form of social control, enslaved African Americans could and did subvert their masters' Christianity to meet their own needs, and enthusiastically embraced the new religion.

Growing Political and Religious Tensions, 1750–75

The actual effects of the First Great Awakening are hard to quantify. Though there were numerous reports of large numbers of converts as a result of the revivals, it is unclear whether these revivals led to a great increase in the number of congregational members. Eventually the revivals waned and life in the colonies returned to normal. However, these awakenings had other, nonreligious effects that were equally important and were partly responsible for the American Revolution against the British. The revivals, especially Whitefield's preaching tours, gave many colonists a shared experience and thus contributed to the creation of a new American identity that began to transcend the older allegiances to one colony or the other, or to the British homeland across the sea. The Great Awakening (along with the Enlightenment) stressed personal choice, freedom, and an ability to determine one's own destiny. These elements, in part, may have created an atmosphere where thoughts of colonial self-determination and liberty could flourish.

It is clear that religion and politics were deeply intertwined in the events leading up to the American Revolution (1775–83). The old inter-Protestant tension between the Anglicans and the Protestant Dissenters—and the friction between the supporters of the monarchy and of Parliament—had never quite faded and seemed to come back into play whenever there were tensions between the colonists and the colonial administration. Though the Dissenters in England had been legally recognized, most positions in the British government and military were reserved for Anglicans. The monarchy and the Church of England were intertwined, and attempts to strengthen the power of either in the American colonies were often met with colonial resistance.

Some of the American colonies, especially the middle and New England colonies, were originally "owned" by companies or individual persons, such as the Massachusetts Bay Company or William Penn. But the British government increasingly pushed to take control of these quasi-independent entities, converting them to royal control, with royal governors. Colonial legislatures were still allowed, but this arrangement set up a pattern of conflict between these legislatures and the royal administrations. When the New Netherland colony was taken over by the English in 1664, England installed a royal governor in New York and New Jersey and began to consider similar actions in New England. When the Massachusetts Bay Colony charter was revoked in 1686, resistance to increased royal power was led by the Puritan leaders, with echoes of the passions of the English Civil Wars. Attempts to strengthen royal control over the colonies and attempts to expand Anglican parishes (especially in New England) seemed to be two sides of the same coin.

Beginning in the middle of the eighteenth century, these underlying tensions at times flared into open conflict. Great Britain and France had long contended over the control of North America, and these tensions led to the French and Indian War (1754–63), which resulted in the expulsion of the French from their North American colonies. This war, and the ongoing British defense of the American colonies, was costly. The British insisted that the American colonies bear some of the cost of the war and their continuing defense and attempted to impose a series of unpopular taxes on the colonies. The colonists chafed under British restrictions on their commerce and insisted that they should have some say in their taxation, just as English citizens had some say, through Parliament, in their taxation. The larger question had to do with the status of the American colonists vis-à-vis the British Empire. Did they have rights similar to English citizens at home, or as colonists, were they merely subjects who had to submit to the whims of the British government?

After a rather sluggish beginning in the seventeenth century, the Anglicans pursued much more aggressive expansion in the American colonies during the eighteenth century. They strengthened the older established churches in Maryland and Virginia and instituted newer establishments in the Carolinas and Georgia. There was also an attempt to establish the Anglican Church in New York, but this establishment was strongly contested by the dominant Dutch Reformed Church, and the Anglican establishment was mainly on paper. Though

An Account by an Anglican Missionary of the Middle Colonies (1701)

I. And to begin where I am more immediately concerned, with Maryland. Here, through the Mercies of God, and after many Struggles with the Quakers, 'tis to be hoped, we are in a fair way at last to have an Established Church. . . . And yet these latter Parishes having built their Churches, think they ought to have Ministers as well as the rest: And had I not in my parochial visitation, given them good Words, and fair Promises, speedily to supply them, I fear our Law would not have passed altogether so easily as it did. And yet how to make good that Promise to them, I shall be sadly at a loss, except the Proposals hereafter given may find favour with Your Lordships, and those to whom you shall please to recommend them.

The Papists in this Province appear to me not to be above a twelfth Part of the Inhabitants; but their Priests are very numerous; whereof more have been sent in this last Year, than was ever known. And tho' the Quakers brag so much of their Numbers and Riches, with which Considerations they would incline the Government to favour them with such unpresidented Privileges. . . .

II. As for Pennsylvania, I found too much work in Maryland, to be able to visit personally that Province.

III. Adjoining to this, are the two colonies of East and West Jersey, where they have some pretty Towns, and well-peopled; but are wholly left to themselves, without Priest, or Altar.

IV. From New York, I have an account that a Church of England Clergy are much wanted there: And there will be room for at least two Ministers, besides one which they have already; the one to assist at New-York, the other to be placed at Albany; where, besides the Inhabitants of the Town, which are many, we have two Companies of Soldiers in Garrison, but all without a Preacher.

Thomas Bray, *A Memorial Representing the Present State of Religion on the Continent of North America* (London: John Brudenell, 1701), 5–7.

it was inconvenient that the British government was unsuccessful in organizing an established Anglican presence in the other colonies, this did not hinder the expansion of Anglicanism in the American colonies overall. Anglican parishes were organized in Pennsylvania, New Jersey, and New York, and some of the urban parishes soon became very successful, including Trinity Parish on Wall Street in New York City. Because of their ties to the British monarchy and colonial administrations, the Anglican parishes soon attracted many colonists who found personal and professional advantages in such membership.

This increased Anglican aggressiveness in the American colonies was sparked by the establishment in England of the Society for the Propagation of the Gospel in Foreign Parts (SPG). This Anglican missionary society was formed in 1701 in England by Thomas Bray to provide priests for Anglican parishes in the colonies and to fund outreach to Native Americans. The society soon received a royal charter, and many Anglican priests in England urged their parishes to financially support the society. The SPG was soon funding Anglican priests in the colonies, especially in those places where there were no colonial establishments. The society also sent to America priests and missionaries to establish new parishes, which created controversies, especially when the SPG started work in Congregational New England. Some of the first SPG missionaries, John Talbot and George Keith (the former Quaker), were sent to Boston in 1702, where they founded an Anglican parish. By 1735 there were three Anglican parishes in Boston (the heart of the Puritan commonwealth), and although these parishes relied heavily on SPG subsidies, they did attract some of the leading citizens of Boston to their membership. In a dramatic move in 1722, Yale College rector Timothy Cutler and several other Congregational pastors announced their conversion to Anglicanism. Cutler was reordained in England and, in 1723, returned to New England where he served as a priest at an Anglican parish in Boston for over forty years. Anglican parishes were also founded in Rhode Island and Connecticut; to many New Englanders, it seemed that the Church of England was making a concerted effort to "invade" the Puritan commonwealth, raising old religious and political fears from a century before. The Anglican presence in the American colonies grew from 111 parishes in 1700 to 406 by 1780, although this growth did not match that of other American Protestant groups. By 1780, there were more Baptist and Presbyterian congregations in the United States than there were Anglican parishes.

Another part of the mission of the SPG was evangelizing Native Americans and enslaved African Americans. Initially, an important motivating factor in the formation of the SPG in England was the Christianization of Native Americans, but efforts in this direction did not bear much fruit, as SPG missionaries struggled with the Native languages, and the tribes kept moving away from

European settlements. Thus, these efforts to evangelize Native Americans were generally abandoned. The subsequent SPG mission efforts among enslaved African Americans in the South, however, did not suffer from these problems and were often more successful at getting conversions. Southern colonial legislatures allowed such conversions, but only with the understanding that conversion did not mean freedom for African Americans.

The greatest weakness of colonial Anglicanism was the lack of an Anglican bishop residing in the colonies. Colonial Anglicanism was under the episcopal control of the bishop of London, but that was too far away for effective administration. Colonial candidates for the priesthood had to travel to England for ordination, and colonial priests did not have the direct support of a bishop. But the prospect of a resident Anglican bishop in North America was also controversial in many parts of the colonies. Congregational leaders in New England were particularly alarmed at this idea, especially after 1763, when the Anglican Church was established in neighboring Quebec. Puritan leaders had long memories of their ancestors' "oppression" at the hand of Anglican bishops, and the establishment of such bishops, along with the appointment of royal governors in the colonies, seemed to them (and others) to be a two-pronged attempt to strengthen royal control over the colonies and infringe on the colonists' religious and political rights. It is not clear, either, whether many colonial Anglicans sought a resident Anglican bishop in America. Many of the Anglican parishes were controlled by lay vestries, who held financial power over the resident priests, and a resident bishop might well have interfered with these arrangements. Additionally, not all colonial Anglicans were in favor of increased royal power. For example, George Washington belonged to his local Anglican parish and served on its vestry.

After the end of the French and Indian War, in 1763, relations between the American colonists and the British government worsened steadily. The first major conflict was over the imposition of the Stamp Act in 1765, which taxed all printed materials in the colonies. The reaction against this tax was widespread, and New England clergy railed against the measure from their pulpits as an attack on religious freedom. Though this tax was repealed in short order, British authorities continued to add new taxes on the colonies, especially customs taxes on many items that the colonists imported from England. American merchants and ship owners were also forced to trade directly only with England and other British colonies, which caused further indignation. The British sent troops to Boston to quell the unrest, but when, in 1770, British troops opened fire at a protest and killed five men, the conflict escalated. Though unrest was less fervent in the colonies outside New England, many Americans felt they were being misused and mistreated by the British authorities. It was generally felt that any taxes or customs duties in the colonies should be approved by the colonial legislatures and that direct imposition of duties on the colonies by the British authorities was "taxation without representation." Although many Americans probably wanted to remain part of the British Empire, they were coming to appreciate their own American identity too. Open conflict seemed likely, but it was not yet inevitable.

As religion contributed to the growing American identity, it also played an interesting role in the increasing colonial conflict with the British government. There was nothing approaching unity among religious groups on the way to American political independence. Some, including many (but not all) Anglicans, urged continued maintenance of close ties with the British government. And the new Methodist movements suffered because of John Wesley's strong opposition to American independence. Others endeavored to remain neutral in the growing conflict. The historically pacifist churches, such as the Quakers and the Mennonites, opposed armed conflict. And many of the non-English-speaking churches, including the Lutheran and Reformed churches, felt that this was a problem among the "English" and not a concern of theirs. But other Christian groups felt the need to support the resistance, especially the Congregationalists, the Presbyterians, and the Baptists. Some colonial ministers, especially in New England, preached for resistance and liberty from their pulpits, tying the American cause to the gospel in a more or less direct fashion.

The increasing resistance to British rule—or, as some would have said, *misrule*—came from a growing conception of personal self-determination and liberty (republicanism). Many colonists came to believe that each person should have a say in the matter of the course of their life and of the lives of their communities. This ideal was deeply embedded (theoretically) in the British political tradition of parliamentary rule and in the English Enlightenment. But the increasing insistence on freedom from British rule also stemmed from the pragmatic self-rule the colonists had developed and practiced for over 150 years. Far away from the center of British rule in London, the colonists learned democracy by taking control of their own affairs in town councils, local governments, and colonial legislatures. And democratic lessons were also absorbed by participating in American voluntary religion, where laypeople established, organized, financed, and ran their own congregations. Generations of Americans had learned the elements of representative government by participating in their own congregations. Local congregational life was a laboratory for self-rule and self-government.

The other aspect of the religious background to the colonists' drive for liberty and republicanism was more theoretical. Though they had been tempered in Europe, personal action and liberty lie at the core of Protestantism. This can be overstated, but in the Protestant understanding, the basic relation is between the believer and God. And this relation is direct, not mediated by any church body or organization. The awakenings of the eighteenth century were built on the idea that an individual has the power to influence their own relationship with God. This religious sense of individualism and personal responsibility combined with the growing Enlightenment political ideal of the autonomous person to produce a powerful movement for personal liberty and self-determination.

This convergence of religious and political ideals in support of republicanism was a strong element in the formation of an independent American identity. As American religious historian Mark Noll has suggested: "Republicanism was critical for the relation of religion and politics in the Revolutionary era because the beliefs of American Christians paralleled republican principles in many particulars. This confluence in turn led to the widespread assumption that republican principles expressed Christian values and hence could be defended with Christian fervor."[5] Of course, in practice, the republican benefits of individual power and liberty were generally limited to White men who owned property; these benefits were not extended to the poor, to women, or to enslaved persons. But although they were rarely, if ever, achieved, the republican ideals still became embedded in American life. American colonial resistance to British rule increased as political and religious leaders made common cause, even if they supported that common cause for very different reasons.

The increasing influence of the English Enlightenment can be seen clearly in the patrician political and military leaders of the American colonial cause, in men like Thomas Jefferson, John Adams, Benjamin Franklin, George Washington, and James Madison. Religiously, these men were deists, not traditional Christians. They believed in a creator God, but not in the Christian God of the Trinity, and they were often unclear about the divinity of Jesus Christ. They believed that God set the world in motion with physical and moral laws, but they did not believe in miracles or in supernatural revelation. Generally, these deists believed in some form of final judgment, although many of them were not exactly sure what this entailed. They generally supported traditional forms of Christianity as a means of teaching morality to the common people, but as enlightened, learned men, they had little personal need for traditional religion. George Washington never spoke critically of Christianity and was a long-serving vestryman in his local Anglican parish in Virginia, as this was what was expected of him as a leader in society. But he had little personal investment in traditional

5. Mark Noll, *A History of Christianity in the United States and Canada*, 2nd ed. (Grand Rapids: Eerdmans, 2019), 107.

Christianity. The only Enlightenment figure to break with this consensus was the radical (and plebeian) figure of Thomas Paine, the great popularizer of the revolutionary cause. He also actively attacked the power of the churches and of Christianity, and though his service to the revolutionary cause was recognized, his support of deism for the masses was roundly criticized, and he was shunned.

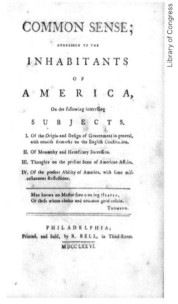

Conclusion

By the eve of the Revolutionary War, in 1775, Christianity in colonial America was growing and gaining a foothold. Despite the impressive growth in the number of congregations and denominations, Christian groups were hard-pressed to keep up with population growth and mobility in the colonies. Christianity was responding to the new situation

4.4. Thomas Paine, *Common Sense*, 1776.

in North America and developing new and distinctive patterns of organization and thought. The revivals of the First Great Awakening instituted new forms of Christianity appropriate to the American context and laid out patterns of religion that continue to the present. The twin systems of the English Enlightenment and Anglo-American Protestant evangelicalism blended with elements of the British political tradition to create a new identity for the American colonies, an identity that would slowly bring them together as a unit distinct from Great Britain. Religious pluralism, supplanting the older ideal of religious uniformity, had taken firm hold in America and forced traditional religious groups into a competition for members and territory. Many practical and theoretical aspects of American religion that were forged in this colonial period eventually became bedrock features of American public life. Slowly but steadily, European religious forms were molded to meet the American context, creating a new and distinctive form of Christianity, one that would influence all other forms of religion brought to America in subsequent years.

———————————— BIBLIOGRAPHY ————————————

Glasson, Travis. *Mastering Christianity: Missionary Anglicanism and Slavery in the Atlantic World*. New York: Oxford University Press, 2012.

Heimert, Alan, and Perry Miller, eds. *The Great Awakening: Documents Illustrating the Crisis and Its Consequences*. Indianapolis: Bobbs-Merrill, 1967.

Kidd, Thomas S. *Benjamin Franklin: The Religious Life of a Founding Father*. New Haven: Yale University Press, 2017.

Marsden, George M. *Jonathan Edwards: A Life*. New Haven: Yale University Press, 2003.

McLoughlin, William G. *Isaac Backus and the American Pietistic Tradition*. Boston: Little, Brown, 1967.

Noll, Mark A. *The Rise of Evangelicalism: The Age of Edwards, Whitefield, and the Wesleys*. Downers Grove, IL: InterVarsity, 2003.

Riforgiato, Leonard R. *Missionary of Moderation: Henry Melchior Muhlenberg and the Lutheran Church in English America*. Lewisburg, PA: Bucknell University Press, 1980.

Schmidt, Leigh Eric. *Holy Fairs: Scotland and the Making of American Revivalism*. 2nd ed. Grand Rapids: Eerdmans, 2001.

Stout, Harry S. *The Divine Dramatist: George Whitefield and the Rise of Modern Evangelicalism*. Grand Rapids: Eerdmans, 1991.

Tanis, James Robert. *Dutch Calvinistic Pietism in the Middle Colonies: A Study in the Life and Theology of Theodorus Jacobus Frelinghuysen*. 'S-Gravenhage: Martinus Nijhoff, 1967.

5

War and a New Nation, 1775–1810

The Revolutionary War (1775–81)

American grievances with British rule developed into armed rebellion in April 1775, when British military attempts to crush resistance in and around Boston failed. American forces encircled Boston and forced the British troops to withdraw by sea to Halifax, Nova Scotia. The American Continental Congress, made up of representatives from the thirteen colonies, selected Virginian George Washington to lead the Continental Army, which was really a coalition of militia forces from the various colonies. In July 1776, the British invaded New York City and routed Washington's army, which retreated through New Jersey. The British ultimately occupied Philadelphia. Though the American forces were close to collapse at several points, the British could not definitively end the rebellion. The British attempt to separate New England from the rest of the colonies failed when a British army force was defeated at Saratoga, New York, in October 1777. The war in the middle colonies then devolved into a stalemate, and when France entered an alliance with the Americans in 1778, the British withdrew from Philadelphia, back to their main station in New York City.

In 1778, British forces under Lord Charles Cornwallis invaded the southern colonies, and for the next two years, the bulk of the fighting was in this region. The British defeated American troops on a number of occasions, but again, they could not finally overcome them. The British thought victories in the South would crush the rebellion, but they found that trying to subdue the colonies militarily was next to impossible. In 1781, Cornwallis moved his forces north to Virginia to await transport by ship to New York City, and Washington marched his army south to encircle the British forces, at Yorktown. French warships defeated the British navy in the Chesapeake Bay, and Cornwallis was forced to surrender in October of 1781, ending most British military activity in the colonies. The British evacuated New York City, and the war was formally ended with the 1783 Treaty of Paris. The Americans were given all British territories east of the Mississippi River and south of Canada. (The Native Americans who lived in these territories were not consulted on the deal).

Such a short, sweeping survey of the Revolutionary War does not do justice to the complexity of the events. It was unthinkable to many that a disorganized rabble of colonists could militarily defeat one of the great European powers. And that they would want to try was even more unthinkable. American attitudes toward war and independence were hardly uniform, and future president John Adams (1735–1826) estimated that one-third of Americans supported the war and independence, one-third opposed it, and one-third were neutral or undecided. Religious leaders could be found on all sides of the issue, and some were bold in declaring their support of one or the other option. Many of the Dissenting clergy, especially in New England, were vocal in support of the cause of independence; some even advocated for independence from the pulpit. Others, especially many of the Anglican clergy, argued a traditional Christian position that the British king was a part of God's secular order and so should be obeyed (see Rom. 13). Still others maintained neutrality, not wanting to mix the sacred and the secular or—in the case of German-speaking Christians— feeling that this was a dispute between the "English." Quakers, Moravians, Mennonites, and others maintained their traditional pacifism, sometimes at a great cost to themselves. But there is no doubt that the war was costly and destructive, especially in the middle and southern colonies, and that organized religious life was at times severely disrupted. At the end of the war, quite a few who remained loyal to Britain left for Canada, the British Caribbean, or England—which badly hurt the Anglican parishes, especially in the North.

The revolutionary cause was adopted by its proponents with something approaching religious zeal, because, in the minds of many, the American cause was in fact God's own cause. From the beginnings of the Puritans in New England, some had believed that the British settlement of North America was part of God's plan, and that the colonists would prosper only insofar as they obeyed God. Though, by the beginning of the American Revolution, many of those who would become the founding leaders of the United States were deists, they still believed that God's plan was written into the orders of creation, and

A Pastor's Report on the Effects of the War in New Jersey (1777-78)

Many people here were plundered on this occasion. The English soldiers are undisciplined and cannot always be controlled. This was one of the main reasons for their slight success, because often both friend and foe were robbed in the most despicable manner, and sometimes with the permission of the officers. . . .

From this time on until the end of June when the English army left Philadelphia conditions here were in a rather wretched state. It looked as though America would soon be conquered. . . . Everywhere distrust, fear, hatred and abominable selfishness were met with. Parents and children, brothers and sisters, wife and husband, were enemies to one another. The militia and some regular troops on one side and refugees with the Englishmen on the other were constantly roving about in smaller or greater numbers, plundering and destroying everything in a barbarous manner, cattle, furniture, clothing and food. . . .

At the end of March, 15 persons were arrested, who had traded with the English; half of them belonged to the congregation. They were kept imprisoned for one night in the schoolhouse at the Raccoon Church and the next morning they were marched off under guard to the country. . . .

At daybreak on April 4, 300 refugees and English troops arrived in three divisions to surround the militia, which escaped with great difficulty. They burnt down the schoolhouse for the simple reason that their friends had been kept prisoners there.

In the month of May a division of American troops was stationed in Swedesborough for some weeks. Although the weather was fine, they, nevertheless, took up their quarters in the church and filled it with filth and vermin, so that no Divine service could be held. I therefore had to preach in private houses, wherever the best opportunity was found.

Nicholas Collin, *Journal and Autobiography*, trans. Amadeus Johnson (Philadelphia: 1936), 244–47.

thus they could say that the new country was a part of the inevitable progression of humanity from the "Old World" of Europe to a better society in the "New World" of North America. In the Old World, rulers were considered to be ordained by God to their positions, and rebellion against these rulers was equal to rebellion against God. But in the new republic in North America, there was an important shift. As historian George Marsden observed: "The United States was the first modern nation systematically to shift public veneration of the government from the veneration of persons [kings] to the veneration of the nation and its principles."[1] In other words, the system of government

1. George Marsden, *Religion and American Culture* (New York: Harcourt Brace, 1990), 44.

(republicanism) and the nature of the nation as a whole now took on religious significance. America's cause was God's cause. This is one important element of American civil religion, and it is a constant theme in and through Americans' understanding of themselves and their nation. The elements of national identity—the flag, the leaders, the holidays (i.e., holy days), and other nation-centered rituals—are, to many, religious elements. Unfortunately, what was lost from the Puritans to the revolution was the sense of a people standing under God's judgment.

The Constitution and the Formation of the United States

But before such a veneration of the nation itself could occur, the former colonists would have to build themselves a stable nation. This was not an easy thing to do, seeing as they were rejecting the older, European models of how a nation should be formed. The general idea was that the new country would be some form of a republic, a federation of the thirteen colonies. But joining thirteen colonies into a single nation was difficult. In 1781, the Articles of Confederation were approved as a first attempt, but this structure was a weak union of thirteen virtually independent states with a joint Congress that lacked any real power. The inadequacies of the Articles were soon realized, and, in 1787, leaders from the states came to Philadelphia for a Constitutional Convention. The resulting constitution was sent out to the states for ratification later that year and provided for a three-pronged federal government: a legislative branch (Congress) with two bodies; an executive branch with an elected president; and an independent federal judiciary, including a Supreme Court. Because of fears of a strong centralized government, the first ten amendments to the Constitution, known as the Bill of Rights, were added in 1791 to spell out in detail the rights of individuals and of the states.

Though these steps were significant, the details of this new national government were only worked out in the coming decades. Crucial to this process was the work of the first president, George Washington (served 1789–97), who alone had the personal standing to pull together the basic elements of the new nation. Though Washington sternly warned against the dangers of conflicting political parties, these began to emerge even within his own cabinet. The Federalist Party, under the leadership of the second president, John Adams (served 1797–1801), urged a stronger, centralized federal government. However, the Democratic-Republican Party—led by the third president, Thomas Jefferson (served 1801–9), and the fourth president, James Madison (served 1809–17)—urged states' rights and a weaker federal government. But despite these often-vicious factional disputes, the elements of the new nation eventually took shape.

The political philosophy of the new nation was republicanism, a theory that has a long tradition in the West, going all the way back to the Greek philosopher Plato. In its modern form, republicanism traces its roots back to the Italian Renaissance, and especially to the political philosopher Niccolò Machiavelli (1469–1527). The Anglo-American strain of republicanism emphasizes the God-given, or natural, rights of individuals and insists that governments exist to support and defend these rights. The American founders saw that because the central element of any system of government consists in the accumulation and exercise of power, the natural trajectory of any government will be to consolidate power for itself, and that will lead invariably to tyranny and corruption. It is not possible to remove this tendency from government; thus, the best government will separate and balance power to avoid concentrating it in any one area. This is the reason behind the separation of powers within the American federal government and for the Constitution's inclusion of a well-defined list of rights for American citizens.

The American founders did not envision democracy. Rather, they feared the unchecked power of the masses of the *demos*, the people, which they thought would lead to anarchy and repression. These thinkers had a realistic understanding of the flaws and foibles of individuals and so sought to balance power in any social or political system. Though most of these founders were not traditional Christians, their view of the human person did parallel, in many senses, the traditional Christian understanding in which the human person is flawed and in need of redemption and salvation. This common ground led to a kind of partnership between American religious and political leaders. A republic, it was believed, would ensure the God-given natural rights and liberties of each individual while seeing that the baser elements of human nature were kept in check.

Republicanism, especially the idea of the involvement of ordinary people (by which the founders meant ordinary White male property owners), also had an important impact on the structure and governance of American religious groups. Lay leadership in religion, which had already begun before the Revolutionary War, accelerated through the end of the eighteenth century and into the nineteenth. Given that religious organizations were, in large part, organized by laypeople—and supported by their direct financial contributions—these same people began to push for more direct control over their own congregations as well as over presbyteries, synods, general assemblies, and other legislative bodies. When, after the Revolutionary War, the Anglican congregations reorganized and renamed themselves the Protestant Episcopal Church, the lay leaders pushed for a legislative House of Delegates (clergy and laity) to balance the power of the House of Bishops. In 1748, the Lutherans formed their initial synod, the Ministerium of Pennsylvania, as a gathering of clergy (a ministerium), but the lay leaders of the congregations quickly sought and won their own representation at the yearly meetings of the Ministerium, especially regarding financial matters. And there are many other examples of such power sharing between clergy and lay leaders across the spectrum of American religion.

Religious Liberty and the First Amendment to the Constitution

One of the most important questions facing the new country and its government, then, was the question of religious rights and liberties. The English model of church and state was a modified state church. The Church of England was established and supported by the British government, and the king was the head of the church. Though other Protestants could "dissent" and opt out of the Church of England, most of the high positions in the British government, military, and other key institutions were reserved for Anglicans alone. Protestant dissenters were tolerated if they were theologically orthodox (Quakers were on the margin here), and they had the right to believe and worship as they saw fit. Roman Catholics had no legal rights to exercise their religion or hold offices. Conformity to the Church of England was, however, rather perfunctory; it tended toward a "lowest common denominator" type of religiosity, even for some clergy.

Most of the American colonies (except for Pennsylvania and Rhode Island) had some sort of official religious establishment, but the details of these establishments varied. Most of these had developed to allow some sort of dissent, along the English line, although there were often restrictions on dissenting activities. In Virginia, for example, dissenting clergy had to be licensed and controlled by the colonial government, and unlicensed preachers were, at times, subject to imprisonment or expulsion. The early arrangement of Massachusetts, in which only members of the Congregational Church could be voting citizens, was eventually modified, but other religious restrictions remained in force. Outside of Virginia and New England, however, colonial religious establishments were rather weak, sometimes existing on paper alone. Dissenting Protestant clergy, especially Baptists and Presbyterians, were very active across the colonies, but especially in the western parts, where political and legal power was less evident.

It seems that many Americans during the eighteenth century were not opposed to some form of state-supported religion. This was the norm in almost all the European countries, and many could not envision how religious life could be maintained without some form of governmental support. Obviously, religious dissenters wanted their own rights and freedoms and chafed against restrictions, but they probably would have accepted some form of governmental support were it available. Some Americans, such as George Washington, thought that one solution was for all Christian groups to receive funding from the states. The worry was that, without stable governmental funding, religious life would cease to exist, leading to moral and religious chaos. This is exactly what many European religious leaders thought would happen in America.

The first major battle over state-supported religion took place in Virginia during and after the Revolutionary War. As early as 1777 Thomas Jefferson (1743–1826) drafted for the Virginia legislature a bill entitled "A Bill for Establishing Religious Freedom," which would have mandated both the total disestablishment of the Anglican Church in the state and complete religious freedom. This bill was introduced into the legislature in 1779 but was tabled indefinitely. It was opposed by the Anglican establishment, as one might imagine, but also by many of Jefferson's deistic allies, who felt that it went too far. The patriot orator Patrick Henry (1736–99) led the opposition to Jefferson's bill and introduced his own in 1779, which named Christianity as the official religion of Virginia. Henry and others sought a new type of religious establishment, one in which each person could designate their tax money for a specific religious denomination. All religious groups then could benefit from the financial support of the state.

Many initially supported this, including many of the moderate deists, who felt that the common morality taught by all religious groups was crucial to the successful operation of the new republic. But Jefferson and others disagreed with this approach and sought to end all state support of religion in Virginia. During Jefferson's absence in 1785, his colleague James Madison introduced a slightly revised version of the original bill into the Virginia legislature, and, despite rather strenuous opposition from Henry and others, the bill passed and religion in the state was gradually disestablished after 1785.

With the adoption of the Constitution and the formation of the federal government in 1789, questions of church and state were moved to national debate. The Constitution itself had very little to say directly about religion in the new republic, other than that there should be no religious tests or requirements for public office. But the question of religion was raised again with the Bill of Rights, the first ten amendments to the Constitution. In the debate leading up to the formulation of the Constitution and the Bill of Rights, a strange alliance—between deists like Thomas Jefferson and dissenting Protestants like the New England Baptist leader Isaac Backus (1724–1806)—developed to push for complete religious liberty in the new republic. Backus himself had been advocating for the disestablishment of the Congregational Church in New England since 1769 and had proved to be a real thorn in the side of colonial leaders. Backus even urged a tax revolt among his Baptist colleagues, suggesting they simply refuse to pay their church tax, figuring that it would be impossible to jail all those who resisted. For Backus and the New England Baptists, this was a matter of conscience. They believed in "soul liberty," the idea that no one should be compelled to believe in or support a religious group with which they disagreed. Dissenters like Backus knew that Jefferson and his deistic colleagues were hardly Christians, but they made common cause with them in attacking religious establishments. Each had their own reasons.

Religious Liberty in the New American Republic

First Amendment to the Constitution of the United States (1789)

Congress shall make no law respecting an establishment of religion, or prohibiting the free exercise thereof; or abridging the freedom of speech, or of the press; or the right of the people peaceably to assemble, and to petition the Government for a redress of grievances.

https://usconstitution.net/xconst_Am1.html

Thomas Jefferson, "Letter to Connecticut Baptists" (January 1, 1802)

The affectionate sentiments of esteem and approbation which you are so good as to express towards me, on behalf of the Danbury Baptist association, give me the highest satisfaction. My duties dictate a faithful and zealous pursuit of the interests of my constituents, & in proportion as they are persuaded of my fidelity to those duties, the discharge of them becomes more and more pleasing.

Believing with you that religion is a matter which lies solely between Man & his God, that he owes account to none other for his faith or his worship, that the legitimate powers of government reach actions only, & not opinions, I contemplate with sovereign reverence that act of the whole American people which declared that their legislature should "make no law respecting an establishment of religion, or prohibiting the free exercise thereof," thus building a wall of separation between Church & State. Adhering to this expression of the supreme will of the nation in behalf of the rights of conscience, I shall see with sincere satisfaction the progress of those sentiments which tend to restore to man all his natural rights, convinced he has no natural right in opposition to his social duties.

https://usconstitution.net/jeffwall.html

The First Amendment to the Constitution deals, in part, with the question of church and state, and it contains the following language: "Congress shall make no law respecting an establishment of religion, or prohibiting the free exercise thereof." This language is traditionally divided into two clauses: the first (the establishment clause) forbids government support of religion and religious groups, while the second (the free exercise clause) allows for citizens to practice their religious faith without governmental interference. These clauses draw from Jefferson's 1777 Bill for Establishing Religious Freedom and suggest a complete separation of church and state. Notice that neither the First Amendment nor the Constitution itself contain the language commonly (and wrongly) attributed to it: the "wall of separation between Church and State." This language was first written in 1802 by Jefferson in a letter to a group of Baptists in Danbury, Connecticut, and only expressed Jefferson's opinion about what the First Amendment meant. Other, later legal scholars have also used this language to describe the meaning of the First Amendment, but it is important to understand that the words *separation of church and state* are not in the actual language of the Bill of Rights itself.

The two religion clauses of the First Amendment did little to determine the relationship between church and state in America, or the place of religion in American life. Rather, these religion clauses ignited a long-running debate about the issues surrounding religion in America, debates that have now been raging for over two hundred years and that show no signs of abating. Every year, courts in the United States deal with hundreds of cases involving issues of religion. The Supreme Court is often left to decide thorny issues of religious life in America, and even all of their carefully crafted decisions have not resolved these questions. As the popular saying puts it, "the devil is in the details," and this is most certainly true regarding the relationship and boundaries between religion and the state in America. Questions arise: Can the government give indirect aid to religious groups (such as religious schools)? Can religious groups receive federal funding for social-welfare activities? If so, what are the boundaries of this? Can individuals claim exemption from certain laws on religious grounds? Are all religious behaviors and practices exempt, or can the government restrict religious practices for nonreligious reasons? The boundaries are constantly being probed and delineated.

Even in the beginnings of the republic, governmental practices blurred the lines set forth in the First Amendment. Religious chaplains, paid for by public funds, serve in Congress and the United States military. Religious groups receive a large amount of government funding, albeit indirectly. Congress and other legislative bodies pass laws restricting some religious activities, such as polygamy, and supporting others, such as Sabbath observances. Christmas is a

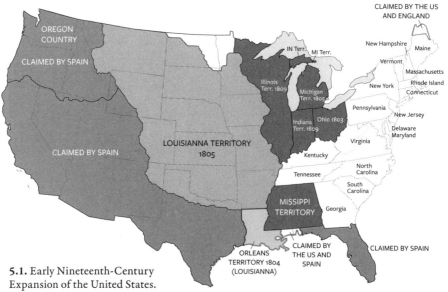

5.1. Early Nineteenth-Century
Expansion of the United States.

federal holiday, but no other religious festival is thus recognized. Various levels
of government give massive aid to religious organizations through tax breaks.
The list could go on quite a ways.

Initially, and for over a century afterward, the rights enumerated in the Bill
of Rights were understood to apply only to the federal government, not to state
and local governments. Though Anglican establishments in Virginia and the
other southern states were quickly dismantled, the New England establishments in Connecticut, Massachusetts, and New Hampshire remained firmly
in place. Their demise (the final one removed was in Massachusetts in 1833)
came about by political and not judicial means; the political climates in those
states shifted so as to bring about disestablishment. They were not struck down
by the courts as being unconstitutional; rather, religious pluralism in New
England meant that the Congregational Church no longer had the political
power to keep the establishments in place. But in many ways, big and small,
religion and the government remained intertwined, and the questions of the
boundaries between church and state continued to be open.

The Movement into the West and the Second Great Awakening

After American independence, restrictions on colonial settlement west of the
Appalachian Mountains were lifted, and scores of Americans moved into the
new territories east of the Mississippi River in search of new farmland. Ignoring

the traditional territories and rights of Native Americans and pushing them continually west, American settlers moved into the Ohio and Mississippi River valleys, across the Great Lakes, and through the Deep South. As populations increased, new states were added to the union: Vermont (1791), Kentucky (1792), Tennessee (1796), and Ohio (1803) were the first. And by 1860 there were sixteen more, for a total of thirty-three. The draw of the frontier (moving ever westward) would dominate American life and culture through much of the nineteenth century.

This drive westward into unsettled territories was yet another challenge to organized American religious life. The traditional colonial denominations were hard-pressed as it was to organize and staff enough congregations in the settled, eastern sections of the country without having to expand into a diffuse and largely unsettled frontier territory. Eastern congregations saw significant numbers of their members suddenly pick up and move west, beyond their reach. When this is considered alongside the disruptions of the Revolutionary War, the battles over disestablishment, and the challenges from religious rationalism and deism, it will come as no surprise that the leaders of the traditional denominations saw this as a time of religious depression and struggle. But they failed to see that new religious groups were on the rise, developing new methods to reach not only those on the frontier but also the mass of those unreached by churches in the East. Sometimes this new religiosity is referred to as a Second Great Awakening, but whether this was a revival of religion or simply a shift in the religious "center of gravity" in the new country is controversial. It is clear, however, that new religious winds were blowing, and these had a dramatic effect on American religious life.

The first signs of a new religious awakening occurred in New England during the 1790s. Although there had been scattered and localized revivals of religion in the decades following the First Great Awakening of the 1730s and 1740s, there were also long periods of declining religious fervor. To the dismay of established Congregational clergy, most of the new religious energy in New England seemed to surround the upstart Baptists and Methodists that were invading their territory. But the theological influence of Jonathan Edwards had only grown after his death, and his followers, the New Divinity Congregational pastors, began a series of revivals in New England in the 1790s and early 1800s. Edwards's grandson, Timothy Dwight (1752–1817), who took over as president at Yale in 1795, played an important role in these revivals. By constant preaching and encouragement to the students (who, to begin with, were largely indifferent), Dwight eventually ignited a religious revival among the students, beginning in 1802, and one-third of the students were converted. The subsequent influence of these students rippled out through the towns and congregations

Peter Cartwright, "Account of the Revival at Cane Ridge"

Somewhere between 1800 and 1801, in the upper part of Kentucky, at a memorable place called "Cane Ridge," there was appointed a sacramental meeting by some of the Presbyterian ministers, at which meeting, seemingly unexpected by ministers or people, the mighty power of God was displayed in a very extraordinary manner; many were moved to tears, and bitter and loud crying for mercy. The meeting was protracted for weeks. Ministers of almost all denominations flocked in from far and near. The meeting was kept up by night and day. Thousands heard of the mighty work, and came on foot, on horseback, in carriages and wagons. It was supposed that there were in attendance at times during the meeting from twelve to twenty-five thousand people. Hundreds fell prostrate under the mighty power of God, as men slain in battle. Stands were erected in the woods, from which preachers of different Churches proclaimed repentance toward God and faith in our Lord Jesus Christ, and it was supposed, by eye and ear witnesses, that between one and two thousand souls were happily and powerfully converted to God during the meeting. It was not unusual for one, two, three, and four to seven preachers to be addressing the listening thousands at the same time from the different stands erected for the purpose. The heavenly fire spread in almost every direction. It was said, by truthful witnesses, that at times more than one thousand persons broke out into loud shouting all at once, and that the shouts could be heard for miles around. . . .

As Presbyterian, Methodist, and Baptist ministers all united in the blessed work at this meeting, when they returned home to their different congregations, and carried the news of this mighty work, the revival spread rapidly throughout the land.

Peter Cartwright, *The Autobiography of Peter Cartwright, Backwoods Preacher* (Cincinnati: L. Swormstedt and A. Poe, 1856), 30–31.

of New England and New York and among northerners moving out into the frontier. Regular periods of revival were seen in these areas for the next three decades. Nathaniel William Taylor (1786–1858), professor of theology at Yale, inherited and passed on Edwards's and Dwight's theological tradition, which became known as the New Haven theology.

The religious situation on the western frontier was extremely difficult. Life in these areas was often brutal and harsh, and the settlers were lightly scattered over wide regions. Elements of settled civilization (churches, schools, towns, and other institutions) were few and far between, and though women were often integral to the establishment of congregations, the frontier had a large preponderance of single men. Scattered Protestant pastors attempted to preach the gospel and found congregations, but this work proceeded slowly. New ideas

Library of Congress / Wikimedia Commons

5.2. A Camp Meeting on the Frontier (Hugh Bridgeport, *Camp Morning*, ca. 1829).

and new structures would be needed to bring religious life to the frontier; these would be developed by Presbyterian, Methodist, and Baptist preachers.

The first stirrings of the Second Great Awakening in the West came through the work of Presbyterian pastor James McGready (1758–1817), who moved west from North Carolina in 1796 to serve three small congregations in southwestern Kentucky: Muddy River, Red River, and Gaspar River. Working with local Methodist pastors, McGready organized a series of successful revivals in these congregations in 1799 and 1800. Influenced by the example of these revivals, McGready and Presbyterian pastor Barton Stone (1772–1844) organized a similar revival for the summer of 1801 in northern Kentucky at Cane Ridge, along with local Baptist and Methodist pastors.

The Cane Ridge revival of 1801 has become a legendary event in American religious history, for both its successes and its excesses. This weeklong revival in August 1801 was not held in local churches (they could not handle the size of the crowds) but in an open-air camp. The event drew an astounding crowd, numbering in the tens of thousands, from all over the region—to see, to be seen, and to hear almost continuous exhortation by Presbyterian, Methodist, and Baptist preachers. Hardened frontier settlers were challenged by these preachers, and many were converted by a simple, direct, and emotional approach. Contemporaneous reports of this meeting emphasize the emotional and

physical responses of many of those in attendance, including crying and weep-
ing, jerking, dancing, and laughing (probably physical responses of religious
and psychological release from the harsh life on the frontier). Reports in the
eastern press were divided between those who saw the meeting as the work of
the Holy Spirit—a new Pentecost—and those appalled by manifestations they
judged "undignified" and even "diabolical." But Cane Ridge was, no doubt, an
enormous success. And similar "camp meetings" were organized over the next
few years from southern Ohio to Tennessee. These meetings, and many more
like them—usually occurring in late summer, between planting and harvest—
were the impetus for the eventual founding of thousands of new Methodist,
Baptist, Presbyterian, and other Protestant congregations on the frontier.

It has been suggested that these camp meetings were modeled, in part, on
the Scottish "Communion fairs" that the Presbyterians brought with them
to North America: religious events lasting several days, a couple times a year,
featuring preaching for repentance and culminating in services of the Lord's
Supper. While this seems very likely, especially given the Presbyterian presence
in their leadership, these new camp meetings were distinctively organized to
meet frontier conditions. The camp meeting became an enduring element of
American Protestantism. Camp meetings and revivals continued through the
nineteenth and twentieth centuries and are held even today by some Protestant
contingents. Also, the influence of the camp meeting can be seen far and wide,
including in American Bible camps and in Chautauqua meetings.

Though reports of camp meetings around the turn of the nineteenth century
concentrated on the dramatic and emotional—indicating, for some, that they
were the spontaneous work of God—these events were, in reality, carefully
planned well in advance and organized to bring about the greatest success. The
transitory nature of these events, which lasted only a week or so, required a new
religious and theological approach. The older, careful, and sustained approach
to conversion—taking months and even years—would not be effective for such
short-term events. To reach hard-living frontier folks, the preaching had to be
dramatic and direct, "hitting them between the eyes" with the gospel message
and urging them to convert right then and there. During a meeting, pastors
would preach all over the camp, wherever they could find a stage or a platform
or even a stump. Not all were in attendance for religious reasons, and preachers
often had to deal with hecklers, sometimes even descending into the crowd to
fight them physically. Reporting on the events, one cynic suggested that the
meetings resulted in more souls being conceived than converted. But in such
rough conditions, the preachers developed a plain, powerful approach that was
often very effective. This approach also became the basis for much of American
Protestant evangelicalism. Theologically, the careful niceties of Calvinism were

discarded. Arminianism was much more effective, with its exhortation to the listener to actively (and immediately) respond to God's call, to accept God's offer of salvation and become a "new creation" (i.e., converted) *on the spot*.

One interesting element of this new approach was what it meant for laypeople, and especially for women. The needs of the frontier required preachers who could speak the language of the people, not college-trained orators. Formal theological learning was suspect; what was needed, it was thought, were converted preachers who could witness powerfully to ordinary people. Any converted Christian could give their own testimony—one did not need education or ordination to do so. Eventually, this meant that women could also share their religious experiences, in women's groups or even to mixed audiences. Though this development moved slowly, eventually some women began to find a greater religious voice through these revivals.

The Development of New Christian Groups

Methodism started as a reforming movement within the Church of England, under the direction of John Wesley (1703–91). The Methodists began their activities in the American colonies during the 1760s, but Methodist societies were slow to organize, and by 1776 there were only about five thousand Methodists in America. As in England, these societies were initially situated near Anglican parishes, mainly in the middle colonies, and relied on Anglican priests for sacramental services. American Methodism suffered during the Revolutionary War, as Wesley was a strong loyalist, and many Methodist missionaries and Anglican priests left the colonies. American Methodists were under the leadership of Francis Asbury (1745–1816), whom Wesley sent to America in 1771 to coordinate Methodist efforts. After the war, Asbury began to reinvigorate American Methodism, with the help of priests ordained by Wesley for work in America. In 1784, the "Christmas Conference" of Methodists in Baltimore, Maryland, established an independent Methodist Episcopal Church in America, and Asbury and Thomas Coke (1747–1814) were elected as its bishops. This independent status predated the separate establishment of the Methodist Church in England, which did not happen until 1795.

Methodism began to grow under the strenuous efforts of Asbury and the traveling Methodist missionaries who emulated him. Known as "circuit riders," these missionaries traveled across the whole of the new country—especially into the new western lands—and established fledgling Methodist congregations wherever they could. Asbury and other Methodist circuit riders rode thousands of miles a year on horseback, reaching thousands of new people.

The Methodists could raise up thousands of circuit riders and pastors because they did not insist on their pastors having formal theological education; they required only that they could preach the gospel in the words of the common people. Peter Cartwright (1785–1872), perhaps the premier Methodist circuit rider, began his career in 1802, and in his first twenty years in the ministry he preached an average of one sermon a day.

With such flexible and energetic pastoral leadership, Methodists established thousands of new congregations, especially on the frontier. The core of their organization was the "class" system, in which groups of about twelve members would meet together weekly for spiritual and social support. These classes could be established virtually anywhere and would often serve as the nuclei for future congregations. Circuit riders would visit these scattered classes on a regular basis to lead worship and provide the sacraments. The whole enterprise was, rather surprisingly, very hierarchical and disciplined, and the entire country was organized into districts in 1796. The central core of this denomination was and is the Methodist *Book of Discipline*, which lays out Methodist organization and principles. It is perhaps ironic that a movement with such broad popular appeal could also be so centrally and hierarchically structured, but the Methodists grew rapidly. From 5,000 members in 1776, they expanded to 65,000 in 1800 and 130,000 in 1806.[2] By the end of the nineteenth century, they numbered in the millions and were the largest Protestant family in the United States.

Aside from its flexible and disciplined structure, Methodism also had a theology that was well suited to the new awakening. John Wesley was an early and eager proponent of Arminian theology and a supporter of both awakenings. Given the optimistic and democratic air of the new country, Arminianism's embrace of human free will and of a perfectible human nature dovetailed nicely with the republican ethos of the new country. Methodism swept away the general passivity of Calvinism and initiated a forthright and practical morality expressed in the great moral crusades that would be fought in the new century.

The Baptists were one of the older colonial groups, with roots in America going back to the 1630s in Rhode Island. The middle colonies were another area of Baptist strength, and the first Baptist organization, the Philadelphia Baptist Association, was formed in 1707. Although Baptists do not require adherence to formal doctrinal statements and creeds, they have developed them at times, such as the Philadelphia Confession of Faith, 1742. The original theological basis of the Baptist movement was in Calvinistic Protestantism, although they rejected infant baptism in favor of adult (or believer's) baptism, which was granted

---

2. Roger Finke and Rodney Stark, *The Churching of America, 1776–2005: Winners and Losers in Our Religious Economy* (New Brunswick, NJ: Rutgers University Press, 2005), 59.

on the basis of a conversion experience and a confession of faith. During the eighteenth century, a split developed in England between Calvinistic Baptists and those Baptists who adopted Arminianism, a division that carried over to Baptists in America. Since the Baptist tradition is strictly congregational, with no larger formation of Baptists having authority over the local congregation, Baptists in America have broken into a large number of different traditions and associations.

In England, the Calvinist Baptists were called the Particular Baptists, but in America they became known as the Regular Baptists—the original core of the movement in America. Being Calvinistic, they resisted the evangelistic practices of the First Great Awakening during the 1740s. During this time in New England, many of the Separatist Congregationalists embraced both the awakening practices and adult baptism, becoming known as the Separatist Baptists, at odds with the Regular Baptists. Other Baptists who rejected Calvinism for Arminianism were the General Baptists and the Free Will Baptists, both of which established their own traditions in America.

Despite their divisions, or perhaps because of them, the Baptists in America grew steadily, from five hundred congregations in 1775 to over eleven hundred by 1800. With the opening of the frontier and the Second Great Awakening, the growth of Baptists increased. There were 35,000 Baptists in America in 1784. By 1790, there were 65,000; and by 1810, there were 170,000.[3] Much like the Methodists, the Baptists were able to quickly raise up large numbers of pastors and congregations, especially on the frontier, and the enthusiasm of the awakening swelled their numbers. Baptists embraced lay leadership of congregations and the autonomy of each congregation. Baptist pastors often began as self-supporting lay preachers who gathered small congregations around them and preached on the weekends. Their lack of formal theological education was not seen as a hindrance; instead, they were judged on their self-taught knowledge of the Bible and their ability to preach with force and effectiveness. Eventually, some local preachers would become formally recognized, or licensed, by one or another of the regional associations.

The Baptists formed dozens of new regional associations across the new United States, sometimes on a doctrinal basis. As was generally true across the denominations by the beginning of the nineteenth century, the influence of Calvinism was on the wane, even among the Regular Baptists. The Regulars and the Separatist Baptists grew closer to each other, especially in the East, and they established a close relationship by 1800 on the basis of the Philadelphia

3. Finke and Stark, *Churching of America*, 59. By the early twentieth century, the Baptists had overtaken the Methodists to become the largest Protestant family in the United States.

Confession of Faith, 1742. The General (Arminian) and Free Will Baptists also moved closer, especially in New England. But this irenic spirit was not apparent on the frontier, where Separatist Baptists resisted closer relations with Regulars and formed their own regional associations, often contesting territory with other Baptist associations. These Separatists wholeheartedly embraced the new revivalism of the Second Great Awakening, and the proliferation of Baptist varieties accelerated. But this internal competition did not seem to hinder the overall growth of the Baptist movement, and it perhaps even spurred the growth.

The postrevolutionary period was a time of religious ferment and competition, as new movements and ideas challenged existing ones and as transformations in government and society created new ways of doing things. On the frontier, competition between the various religious groups—especially Methodists, Baptists, and Presbyterians—was fierce. And even though they sometimes cooperated in revivals and camp meetings, they were in competition for the same audiences. Theological disputes raged—for example, between Calvinists and Arminians, between proponents of infant baptism and proponents of adult baptism, and between congregationalists and those who valued connection with a wider ecclesiastical body. This religious competition probably goaded the various groups to sharpen their messages and expand their reach, but such religious conflict also dismayed many others. This was a time of many nonaffiliated religious seekers who seemed to ask themselves, "Which of these competing groups is right?" Some Christian critics thought that such conflict was "unchristian" and injurious to the preaching of the gospel. "On what basis," they asked, "could Christians come together to be unified and proclaim a common message?"

In the United States, these concerns coalesced into a new Protestant movement uniquely aimed at this situation and the American ethos. Just as Americans were building a new society in North America free from the constraints of Europe, so this movement sought Christian unity free of old divisions in a "restoration" of biblical Christianity as found in the New Testament. This movement, which became known as Restorationism, was and is a powerful religious force in the United States, one that has sought to overcome denominational and doctrinal divisions on the sole basis of the Bible.

The roots of this movement can be seen among scattered groups in New England and the Carolinas during the 1790s, which brought together like-minded congregations on the frontier. But the real genesis of the movement came with dissident evangelical Presbyterians on the western frontier. One such early leader was Barton Stone (1772–1844), a Presbyterian pastor in Kentucky and one of the leaders of the Cane Ridge revivals, who was expelled from the Presbyterian

Synod of Kentucky in 1803 over doctrinal disagreements. He founded a religious union in 1804 of individuals and congregations who were to go solely by
the name of "Christian," or Churches of Christ, with the Bible as their only
creed and manual of discipline. Deciding that infant baptism was "unscrip-
tural," these congregations practiced only adult baptism by immersion. Another
such movement was founded by two former Scottish Presbyterians—Thomas
Campbell (1763–1854) and his son Alexander Campbell (1788–1866)—who
similarly left the Presbyterians in western Pennsylvania in 1809 to form the
forerunner of the later Christian Church (Disciples of Christ) denomination.
Thomas Campbell was famous for his signature dictum that came to define this
movement: "Where the Bible speaks, we speak. Where the Bible is silent, we
are silent." The Restorationist movement was strongest on the western frontier,
especially through the Ohio River valley and the Upper South, and is sometimes
alternately referred to as the Stone-Campbell movement.

Many in the American context have found Restorationism very appealing.
With its biblicism and ahistorical focus, Restorationism could ignore eighteen hundred years of Christian history in favor of a simple restoration of the
church of the New Testament. But this restoration was not nearly as simple
as it seemed. First, the history of the intervening years could not be easily
overcome, and the "churches of the New Testament" that they sought to revive
ended up looking suspiciously like nineteenth-century American evangelicals. Second, the Restorationists quarreled over the parameters of the biblical
church and over which elements of the past were to be adopted. Some thought
that the Bible forbade any musical instruments in worship, and they eventually founded what would become the Churches of Christ (noninstrumental).
Third, despite their calls for Christian unity, the Restorationist movement
has often been internally divided. The irony is that a movement that sought
to overcome the multiplication and division of Christian denominations has
itself resulted in the formation of new Christian denominations. Still, this
call for the restoration of biblical Christianity has become an enduring part
of American Christianity.

African Americans were some of the most enthusiastic converts in the new
churches (especially in the Methodist and Baptist churches), responding to the
revivals of the Second Great Awakening, although they were routinely discour-
aged and discriminated against by White congregants in these denominations.
Some of the first African American congregations were organized in the South,
including the Silver Creek church in South Carolina around 1773, which moved
to Savannah, Georgia, in 1778. Andrew Bryan (1737–1812), an enslaved African American, overcame intense opposition (included being whipped and
jailed) to form an African American congregation in Savannah, Georgia, in

1788—which eventually led to the formation of other such congregations in the area. However, formally established and independent African American congregations were not allowed in most areas of the South, and African Americans were limited to segregated sections in White congregations, where they could be carefully monitored and controlled. African Americans were sometimes allowed by slave owners to preach in the slave quarters of plantations, but in other situations African Americans had to meet secretly in the woods for religious services.

In the northern states, some supported the abolition of slavery in the 1790s, around the time of the adoption of the Constitution. But this support faded over time, especially as slavery was gradually abolished in the North and the transatlantic slave trade was ended. But racial division and discrimination were still very common in the North, and the free African Americans there often faced severe treatment. Despite this, African Americans were present in significant numbers in the Protestant denominations. It is estimated that of the 60,000 Methodists in America in 1790, 20 percent were African Americans. And they seem to have been present in similar numbers in the Baptist congregations. The revivals of the Second Great Awakening undoubtedly added significantly to these numbers.

African American Lemuel Haynes (1753–1834) was ordained in 1785 as a Congregational pastor in New England. But African Americans, including Haynes, faced harsh discrimination in White churches. Because of discrimination in his local Methodist congregation in Philadelphia, in 1787 Richard Allen (1760–1831) began to preach informally to other African Americans, and in 1794 Allen formed the independent Methodist Bethel Church. Though Bishop Francis Asbury (of the Methodist Episcopal Church) ordained Allen as a Methodist deacon in 1795, local Methodists continued to harass Allen and his congregation. But they persevered, and, in 1816, Bethel and other African American congregations officially formed the African Methodist Episcopal (AME) Church, the first African American denomination in the United States. Asbury consecrated Richard Allen as the bishop of the new group.

Other African American congregations were also formed in northern cities around this time. Absalom Jones (1746–1818), a friend and colleague of Allen, founded an African American Episcopal congregation in Philadelphia in 1794 and was ordained as the first African American Episcopal priest in America in 1802. Daniel Coker (1780–1846) led the formation of an African American congregation in Baltimore around 1801 and was a part of the initial organization of the AME in 1814. Coker later went to Africa, where he formed congregations in Liberia and Sierra Leone. James Varick (ca. 1750–1827) established the Zion congregation in New York around 1796, which became

The Essentials of Restorationism (1809)

1. That the Church of Christ upon earth is essentially, intentionally, and constitutionally one; consisting of all those in every place that profess their faith in Christ and obedience to him in all things according to the Scriptures. . . .

2. That although the Church of Christ upon earth must necessarily exist in particular and distinct societies, locally separate one from another, yet there ought to be no schisms, no uncharitable divisions among them. . . .

3. That in order to do this, nothing ought to be inculcated upon Christians as articles of faith; nor required of them as terms of communion, but what is expressly taught and enjoined upon them in the word of God. . . .

4. That although the Scriptures of the Old and New Testaments are inseparably connected, making together but one perfect and entire revelation of the Divine will, for the edification and salvation of the Church, and therefore in that respect can not be separated; yet as to what directly and properly belongs to their immediate object, the New Testament is as perfect a constitution for the worship, discipline, and government of the New Testament Church, and as perfect a rule for the particular duties of its members, as the Old Testament was for the worship, discipline, and government of the Old Testament Church, and the particular duties of its members.

5. That with respect to the commands and ordinances of our Lord Jesus Christ . . . no human authority has power to interfere . . . by making laws for the Church; nor can anything more be required of Christians in such cases, but only that they observe these commands and ordinances. . . . Much less has any human authority power to impose new commands or ordinances upon the Church, which our Lord Jesus Christ has not enjoined. . . .

10. That division among the Christians is a horrid evil, fraught with many evils. It is antichristian, as it destroys the visible unity of the body of Christ; as if he were divided against himself, excluding and excommunicating a part of himself. . . .

13. Lastly. That if any circumstantials indispensably necessary to the observance of Divine ordinances be not found upon the page of express revelation, such, and such only, as are absolutely necessary for this purpose should be adopted under the title of human expedients, without any pretense to a more sacred origin, so that any subsequent alteration or difference in the observance of these things might produce no contention nor division in the Church.

Thomas Campbell, *The Declaration and Address of the Christian Association of Washington, Pennsylvania* (Washington, PA: Brown and Sample, 1809), 16–18.

the founding congregation of another African American group, the African Methodist Episcopal Zion Church. These initial congregations—and many others like them—persevered in the face of intense hostility and discrimination.

Reforming among Established Christian Groups

The years after the Revolutionary War also saw a significant period of necessary reforms among the more established Christian groups in the new United States. The challenge from the new revivals and fast-growing denominations, especially the Methodists and Baptists, was difficult. Some of the existing denominations, such as the Anglicans and Roman Catholics, had to rebuild after cutting ties with European structures, while the German-language churches faced the realities of a difficult period of language transition and the challenge of becoming fully American denominations.

The most difficult transition was experienced by the Anglicans, whose congregations were decimated by the war and its aftereffects. As many Anglican laypeople and priests were Loyalists during the war, a good number of them left America after the war for other parts of the British Empire. In Virginia, two-thirds of the Anglican rectors supported by the Society for the Propagation of the Gospel in Foreign Parts left after the war. The loss of state support, such as in Virginia (in 1785) and elsewhere in the South, compounded the difficulties, as did the necessary rupture between American Anglican congregations and the bishops in England. The key question was how such a hierarchical and British-oriented denomination could survive in the newly republican United States. The Anglicans themselves were divided: those in the North were generally more high church and loyalist, while those in the middle colonies and the South were more democratic and supported the revolutionary cause.

The first attempt at rebuilding came from the New England parishes, when Connecticut Anglican Samuel Seabury (1729–96) was selected and sent to Scotland in 1785 to be ordained by bishops in the Scottish Episcopal Church (British law forbade English bishops from ordaining him). In a General Convention of Anglicans from the middle colonies and the South, two additional candidates were selected to become bishops: William White (1742–1836) and Samuel Provoost (1742–1815). After the British law was changed, White and Provoost were ordained by the archbishop of Canterbury in 1787. White was a supporter of the revolution, served as chaplain to the Continental Congress, and had a close relationship with George Washington. White and his supporters were strong advocates of democratic reforms within American Anglicanism. In 1789, the two "streams" of American Anglicanism merged into a single organization called the Protestant Episcopal Church in the United States of America. Under White's urging, the new denomination instituted a dual legislative structure, with a House of Deputies (made up of equal parts laity and clergy) balancing the House of Bishops. The new Episcopal Church had, however, fallen far behind the other American denominations. In numerical terms, during the colonial period, the Anglicans had been roughly on par with the Congregationalists and Presbyterians, but the new Episcopal Church had fallen behind them, and far behind the surging Methodists and Baptists. It would take decades for the Episcopalians to regain any sort of momentum.

The Roman Catholics in the new United States also faced a period of reorganization, although not nearly as drastic as the Episcopalians. In the colonial period, the small Roman Catholic presence was centered in Maryland, especially around Baltimore, and the church was under the supervision of the Roman Catholic bishop in London. There were a number of priests (mainly former Jesuits) and a few educational institutions, but Roman Catholics in the colonies attempted to maintain a low profile given the intensely anti–Roman Catholic inclinations of most American Protestants. But many American Roman Catholics supported the revolutionary cause, and one of them, Charles Carroll (1737–1832), was a signer of the Declaration of Independence. In 1784, his cousin John Carroll (1735–1815), a priest, was designated by Roman authorities as the "Superior of the Mission" in the United States and then ordained as the first bishop of Baltimore (and head of the American church) in 1789.

Like the Episcopalians, the American Roman Catholics faced problems with the republican spirit of the new United States. In particular, control of the local Roman Catholic parishes by lay trustees was a major issue. Under the prevailing American law, in order to have legal protection, church property had to be vested in the hands of local lay Roman Catholics. Lay control over the property and the funding of these parishes clashed, however, with the Roman Catholic understanding of episcopal control and of the traditional powers of the bishops and priests. Long-running

Catholic Historical Research Center of the Archdiocese of Philadelphia

5.3. John Carroll, First Roman Catholic Bishop in the United States.

battles were fought during the early nineteenth century over this issue of trust-eeism. The matter was eventually resolved in favor of the church authorities, but the church still had to deal with the strong elements of democracy within its parishes.

The Congregationalists and Presbyterians did not face the type of reorganization needed by these other denominations, but they still faced serious challenges after the Revolutionary War, especially the challenge of the frontier and the competition from the Methodists and Baptists. The Congregationalists and Presbyterians grew slowly, but their growth was eclipsed by that of these other denominations, and their share of the religious "market" shrank appreciably. In 1776, these two were the leading denominations in the United States, with approximately 20 percent each of the religious market, but by the early nineteenth century their percentages had dropped into the single digits. With their insistence on an educated, professional clergy, the Congregationalists and Presbyterians simply could not raise up enough pastors to compete on the frontier or among the unchurched masses back East. They disdained the Methodists and Baptists and yet were losing to them.

Overall, the Presbyterians were in a better position than the Congregationalists, and many Presbyterian pastors worked on the frontier and participated in the camp meetings and revivals. They did lose some of their pastors and congregations to the Restorationist movements on the frontier, but these losses did not significantly affect their growth, which was steady (but not spectacular). The Congregationalists fared worse. In New England, they lost pastors and congregations on the conservative side to the Separatists and Baptists and on the liberal side to the Unitarians and Universalists. New England Congregationalists managed to hold on to their state funding for a while, but these state establishments were eventually dismantled politically. In 1801, the Congregationalists and Presbyterians agreed on a Plan of Union, a mission strategy in which each group would avoid head-to-head competition with the other, especially in founding congregations on the frontier. This seemed like a rational use of resources, but it limited both groups in the long run, the Congregationalists most of all. The Presbyterians were ahead of the Congregationalists on the frontier, so they were able to found many new congregations in the Midwest and the South, while the Congregationalists were practically disadvantaged and remained confined primarily to New England.

After the Revolutionary War, the German-speaking Lutherans, Reformed, Moravians, and Anabaptists and the Dutch Reformed struggled with pressure to transition to the English language and to otherwise assimilate to the new American culture. The war delayed these transitions, but pressure increased after the war, with the loss of ties to Europe, the flourishing of revivalism, and the new republican spirit. The transition to English was a sharply fought battle, mainly along generational lines; but the tide of younger English-speakers was unavoidable, and within several decades this transition was essentially complete. German was maintained in some of the rural areas and among separatist groups like the Mennonites and the Amish, but on the whole the triumph of English was complete. These groups slowly acculturated and became part of the wider American religious scene and the new evangelical revivalism.

Alternative Religious Visions

The decades after the Revolutionary War also saw the beginnings of a trend in America toward religious experimentation and innovation, something that has defined religion in America ever since. The widening of religious pluralism and the freedom of religious expression as enshrined in the Bill of Rights meant that all religious options were on the table, and inventive and visionary religious leaders have continually explored new options. The Second Great Awakening during this period was certainly one such form of experimentation, though much more with form than with substance, as the theology of the new awakening groups was rather traditional Christian doctrine. But there were many other religious seekers who sought to push beyond the traditional boundaries.

The deism of the eighteenth-century Enlightenment was a rather individualistic movement among intellectuals and leaders. As we have seen, American deists like Thomas Jefferson and Benjamin Franklin tended to support traditional forms of Christianity to an extent, as means of inculcating republican moral virtues in the masses. And some leaders, such as George Washington, supported local congregations without fully participating in them. Radical deists of the French Revolution attempted to establish a separate "religion of reason" among the people to supplant Christianity, but this failed miserably. Radical deist Thomas Paine (1739–1809), hero of the American Revolution, also sought to demolish Christianity through his book *The Age of Reason* (1794), but he was sharply opposed not only by Christian leaders but by many of the American deist leaders as well.

One of the key disagreements between the deists and traditional Christians was over the nature and person of Jesus Christ. The deists rejected the traditional Christian understanding of Jesus as the divine Son of God whose death on the cross led to the salvation of humanity. They rejected the Christian Trinity—God as Father, Son, and Holy Spirit—preferring to concentrate on the essential unity and oneness of God. They saw Jesus as a human prophet whose teachings pointed the way to the Creator God, but certainly not as divine or as a miracle worker. Jefferson took a pair of scissors to the Christian Gospels and cut out all the parts of the stories about Jesus he could not believe. What was left, essentially Jesus's teachings, Jefferson pasted in a notebook he entitled *The Life and Morals of Jesus of Nazareth*. Others in America agreed with Jefferson's approach.

These modes of thinking began to make inroads among a number of the more liberal elements of Christianity in America, especially the idea of a rational world with a rational God behind it, a stark contrast to the sometimes-wild emotionalism of the revivals. Religious rationalism had been circulating for decades among Presbyterians, Episcopalians, and (above all) New England Congregationalists—especially among those who opposed the First Great Awakening during the 1730s and 1740s. This religious rationalism, along deistic lines, slowly became referred to as Unitarianism (the belief in the essential oneness of God and the rejection of the doctrine of the Trinity). After the Revolutionary War, elements of early Unitarianism could be seen in places such as King's Chapel—which was originally an Anglican church but became the first Unitarian church in America in 1785—and in a number of New England Congregational churches. To the shock of many, Harvard College essentially became Unitarian in 1805, pushing more conservative Congregationalists to establish a separate institution, Andover Theological Seminary, in 1807, for the purpose of training more orthodox pastors. English deist philosopher Joseph Priestly (1733–1804) arrived in America in 1794 and attempted to establish several Unitarian congregations in Pennsylvania, but these efforts were unsuccessful. Establishment of a formal Unitarian movement would come later.

The Universalists were another group developing during this period. Often linked with the Unitarians (with whom they would merge in 1961), the Universalists had origins quite distinct from the Unitarians. The central question for the Universalists concerned the Christian doctrine of salvation: Who would be saved and go to heaven? Universalists believed that a good God would not commit anyone to hell or damnation, so they denied the existence of hell (they were sometimes known as the "no-hellers") and affirmed the universal salvation of all people. Though elements of this theology could be seen in New England throughout the eighteenth century, it was advocated especially by John Murray (1741–1815), who established a Universalist congregation in Gloucester, Massachusetts, in 1779, and by Elhanan Winchester (1751–97), a New England Congregationalist who became an evangelical Baptist and a revivalist preacher. The Universalist movement was strongest in the rural areas of New England and among the Separatist Congregationalists and Baptists.

Though these new groups advocated new religious ideas, they tended to retain traditional religious forms and social modes. But in the religious ferment

Internet Archive Book Images / Wikimedia Commons

5.4. Shaker Women from the Sabbath Day Lake Community.

of the new nation, there were others who sought to push religious and social boundaries even further. Restorationist groups on the frontier wanted to restore New Testament Christianity, but they did not adopt the communism and communalism seen in the book of Acts. There were experiments in communalism in eighteenth-century America though, especially the Ephrata Cloister in Pennsylvania, and the post–Revolutionary War period saw an upsurge in the formation of such groups, which would accelerate further in the early nineteenth century.

One of the earliest and most successful of these communal groups was the United Society of Believers in Christ's Second Appearing, popularly known as the Shakers. This group originated among the Quakers in England, led by visionary leader "Mother" Ann Lee (1736–84), who held that the second coming of Christ had come through her and that she and her followers were to establish the millenarian kingdom of God on earth. Mother Ann and her followers came from England to New York in 1774 and began establishing a series of communal settlements in New York and New England. In these settlements, envisioned as the first outposts of this new kingdom of God—literally, heaven on earth—celibacy and sharing of goods in common (communism) were the rule. After Mother Ann's death in 1784, leadership of the communities passed to a line of male and female disciples, ruling jointly. During the Second Great Awakening, the Shakers established new settlements in Indiana and Kentucky, pushing the number of settlements to eleven. They are now more remembered for their simple and elegant furniture and crafts, and less for their unconventional religious beliefs and practices, especially their patterned religious dancing.

There was another, similar communal group that came to America from Germany around this time, the followers of German Pietist leader George Rapp (1757–1847), who immigrated to Pennsylvania in 1803 to form a similarly celibate religious colony. The group moved to western Indiana in 1814, where they formed the New Harmony settlement. This utopian community, built on New Testament models, was organized like the Shakers in the millenarian expectation of Christ's second coming, although in their theology they were closer to Christian orthodoxy than were the Shakers. Many other communal religious experiments would be established in America in the early nineteenth century.

──────────────── BIBLIOGRAPHY ────────────────

Conkin, Paul K. *Cane Ridge: America's Pentecost*. Madison: University of Wisconsin Press, 1990.

Den Hartog, Jonathan J. *Patriotism and Piety: Federalist Politics and Religious Struggle in the New American Nation*. Charlottesville: University of Virginia Press, 2015.

Gaustad, Edwin S. *Faith of Our Fathers: Religion and the New Nation*. San Francisco: Harper & Row, 1987.

Heimert, Alan. *Religion and the American Mind: From the Great Awakening to the Revolution*. Cambridge, MA: Harvard University Press, 1966.

Hughes, Richard T., ed. *The American Quest for the Primitive Church*. Urbana: University of Illinois Press, 1988.

Kidd, Thomas S. *God of Liberty: A Religious History of the American Revolution*. New York: Basic Books, 2010.

Richey, Russell E. *Early American Methodism*. Bloomington: Indiana University Press, 1991.

Stein, Stephen J. *The Shaker Experience in America: A History of the United Society of Believers*. New Haven: Yale University Press, 1992.

Wood, Gordon S. *Empire of Liberty: A History of the Early Republic, 1789–1815*. New York: Oxford University Press, 2009.

Wright, Conrad. *The Beginnings of Unitarianism in America*. Boston: Starr King, 1955.

6

New Frontiers, Renewal,
and Growth, 1810–50

THE FIRST HALF OF THE NINETEENTH CENTURY was a time of
great ferment and growth in the new United States. Physically, the nation
acquired territory that stretched all the way to the Pacific Ocean through the
purchase of the Louisiana Territory from France in 1803, through the purchase
of Florida from Spain in 1819, through the annexation of the Republic of Texas
in 1845, through the addition of the Southwest and California to the union
after the defeat of Mexico in 1848, and through the final treaty settlement of
the northern boundary of the country with the United Kingdom in 1846. By
the end of this period, the shape of the continental United States was generally
fixed in its permanent configuration. In terms of population, the country grew
from 7.2 million inhabitants in 1810 to 23.2 million in 1850. Immigration from
Europe, which had stalled during the American Revolution and the Napoleonic
Wars, began anew with 600,000 immigrants during the 1830s and 1.7 million
during the 1840s. Fourteen new states were added to the union, including all
the territory east of the Mississippi River, as well as Arkansas, Missouri, Iowa,
Texas, and California. The westward expansion of the population continued.
Americans pushed into the West and to the Pacific coast via the Santa Fe,
Oregon, and California trails. This westward expansion came at the expense
of the Native Americans, who were pushed out of the eastern states by the
Indian Removal Act of 1830, one brutal element of which was the expulsion of

the Native tribes in the Southeast to Oklahoma and Kansas via the infamous Trail of Tears in 1838.

The United States experienced two wars during this period. The eponymous War of 1812 (1812–15) with the United Kingdom was largely an unnecessary event, fought to a standstill, and its greatest victory (at the Battle of New Orleans) was conducted after the peace treaty had been reached. Still, the war showed that the new republic could stand up militarily against a major European power, both in North America and on the Atlantic Ocean. A further development was the issuing of the Monroe Doctrine in 1823, in which the president declared that the United States would resist European intervention in the Western Hemisphere. This did not prevent the United States from intervening itself, as it did when it annexed the Republic of Texas in 1845, leading to the Mexican-American War (1846–48), in which Mexico was defeated and the southwestern territories were added to the United States.

With all this activity, the internal growth of the United States continued its rather tortuous path. The partisan politics of the previous generations continued, although often in different guises. The old Federalist Party collapsed in the 1830s, and the Democratic-Republican Party split. Elements of the latter joined with many of the old Federalists to form the Whig Party, while

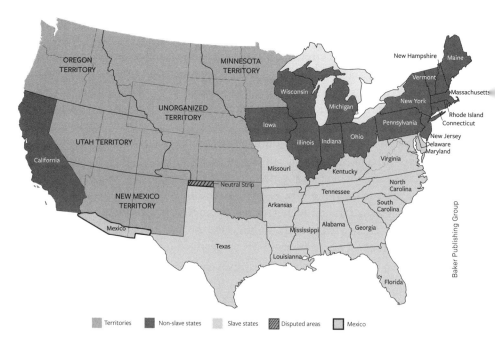

6.1. States and Territories of the United States of America, September 9, 1850–March 2, 1853.

the other part formed the new Democratic Party. The election of Andrew Jackson as president in 1828 is sometimes known as the "Second American Revolution," the triumph of democratic-style populist politics over the older aristocratic republicanism. Internal divisions were rife between those who sought a strong federal government and those who favored the primacy of states' rights. Sectional struggles were a constant, mainly between northern and southern interests, but also between eastern and western. An important development during this time was the increasing self-definition and growth of the federal judiciary, especially the Supreme Court, as a recognized third element of the national government.

The growth of the country was fueled by dramatic developments in commerce, industry, transportation, and technology. Especially in the North, Americans embraced the new Industrial Revolution, and factories were rapidly erected to mass produce goods for a growing population. Steam power and mechanization drove this revolution. While most Americans continued to live on farms or in small towns, the growth of industries and mechanization was transforming their lives as much as it was transforming the lives of Americans in the burgeoning cities. The demand for raw materials for the new industries increased mining and agriculture, but it also constituted a new economic engine propping up the enslavement of African Americans. Unfortunately, the monetary system of the country lagged behind the Industrial Revolution, which led to economic fluctuations such as the Panic of 1837.

The geographic expansion of the country necessitated a parallel revolution in transportation. Initially, steam-powered vessels plied the coastal and inland waterways. The limitations of this mode of transportation led to the digging of canals, such as the Erie Canal, which linked the Hudson River to the Great Lakes by 1825. But canals were expensive to build and were soon supplanted by the railroads. The first American railroad was opened in 1827, and by 1850 there were nine thousand miles of track in the country. Along with this revolution came new means of communication. During this period, hundreds of newspapers were begun and an efficient postal service was formed. But the most dramatic development was the introduction of the telegraph, which came into practical use during the 1840s, delivering almost instantaneous communications across hundreds of miles.

A new and self-aware American identity was also on the rise. This new national culture can be seen in the literary works of a new generation of writers and thinkers, including Henry Wadsworth Longfellow, Edgar Allan Poe, James Fenimore Cooper, Nathaniel Hawthorne, Herman Melville, and Ralph Waldo Emerson.

Consolidation and Growth in American Christianity

As fast as the new United States was expanding and developing during the first part of the nineteenth century, American Christianity was growing even faster. During the dramatic population and territorial increases of this time, Christianity spread to all corners of the new nation while also managing continued growth in areas that were more settled. In 1776, it is reckoned that approximately 17 percent of all Americans had a formal membership relation with an organized Christian congregation. By 1850, that proportion had doubled, to 34 percent, even as the population of the country had grown exponentially.[1] In 1776 there were an estimated 2.5 million people, and by 1850 there were almost 24 million, which means the number of church members increased from 425,000 in 1776 to over 8 million in just seventy-five years. This is even more impressive when one considers that standards for church membership were, in many of the fast-growing Christian groups, rather more stringent than they are today. And this is not to say that the other two-thirds of Americans, those not formally affiliated with Christian congregations, were secular. They may, in many cases, have attended local congregations without formally joining.

Almost all the major American Christian denominations grew during this time, but some grew much faster than others. In 1776, the four largest Christian denominations were the Congregationalists (20 percent of all Christians), the Anglicans (16 percent), the Presbyterians (19 percent), and the Baptists (17 percent). The other groups were much smaller, including a small number of Roman Catholics and recently arrived Methodists. In contrast, by 1850, the Methodists (with over two million members) constituted 34 percent of all Christians and the Baptists (with over one million members) constituted an additional 20 percent, meaning that the bulk of membership growth in American Christianity occurred among these two denominations. Though the older, established denominations did grow modestly during this period, they had lost their share of the religious "market." By 1850, the Congregationalists constituted only 4 percent of all Christians, the Episcopalians 3.5 percent, and the Presbyterians 12 percent. Having dramatically lost ground to the Baptists and Methodists, these older denominations now represented less than 20 percent of American Christians. A new group pushing ahead were the Roman Catholics, who had grown to nearly 14 percent of the Christian total by 1850.[2]

Much of this growth was accomplished through the formation of thousands of new Christian congregations across the country, and it was here that the

1. Roger Finke and Rodney Stark, *The Churching of America, 1776–2005: Winners and Losers in Our Religious Economy* (New Brunswick, NJ: Rutgers University Press, 2005), 23.
2. Finke and Starke, *Churching of America*, 56.

Methodists and the Baptist excelled. By 1850, the Methodists had over thirteen thousand congregations in the United States, and the Baptists had over nine thousand, while the next four denominations had a combined total of around seven thousand.[3] The Methodists and Baptists opened thousands of new congregations because of their flexible and low-cost ministry structures (pastors and leaders) and because there was little outlay of capital needed to do so. While many of these new congregations were established in the frontier territories as they were occupied by settlers, the Methodists and Baptists also founded many new congregations in the settled, eastern portions of the country.

Although it is clear that much of this growth can be attributed to the religious awakenings that occurred between 1790 and 1810, these sporadic and episodic events were certainly not the whole story, or even necessarily the most important part of it. For such religious growth to be sustained over time, the religious fervor of these awakenings had to be channeled and continued through organized means, through the major denominational structures. Someone had to take the occasional and ad hoc religious revivals and mold them into a religious movement that could be organized and repeated thousands of times in towns and villages across the nation. That someone was the New York lawyer-turned-evangelist Charles Grandison Finney (1792–1875).

The earlier revivals were carefully planned, but they tended to be localized. What Finney did was spread the essential insights and theology of the awakenings across all the country's Christian denominations. Converted in 1821 and ordained into the Presbyterian ministry in 1824, Finney began organizing a series of revivals in the towns and villages of upstate New York between 1824 and 1831, revivals that were so successful they attracted national attention. Finney's revivals also took place in a number of eastern cities from 1827 through 1832. When poor health stopped his itinerant career, Finney served congregations in New York City and Oberlin, Ohio. And after 1835, he served first as professor of theology and then as president at Oberlin College.

Besides leading his own revivals, Finney quite literally "wrote the book" on revivals. His hugely successful *Lectures on the Revivals of Religion* (1835) has been the manual for revival leaders ever since. Unlike those who worried about "manufacturing" conversions and bypassing the Spirit of God, Finney insisted that a revival was nothing miraculous, but simply "the *right* use of the appropriate means,"[4] and that revivals could be organized and planned. Human beings could be influenced and converted by the rational use of those

3. Edwin S. Gaustad, *Historical Atlas of Religion in America*, rev. ed. (New York: Harper and Row, 1976), 176.

4. Charles G. Finney, *Lectures on the Revivals of Religion*, rev. ed. (New York: Fleming N. Revell, 1868), 13.

"appropriate means." Finney introduced many of the now-familiar elements of revivalism, including the "protracted meeting" (community-wide services over days and weeks), special prayer meetings for different demographic groups, and the "anxious bench" (a pew in the front of a revival service where those wavering about their conversion could come and be prayed over). Conversion need not be drawn out, according to Finney. It could be the simple acceptance of grace, simply "giving one's life to the Lord." Finney also encouraged women to give their prayers and testimonies in public in the revival services. These were some of the first times that women could be heard witnessing to God in public worship. Later evangelists would refine the elements of revivals and add their own nuances, but Finney established the basic outlines of revivalism that have lasted to the present day.

With the beginnings of this revivalism, the broad outlines of American evangelical Protestantism were established. The base of this was evangelicalism

Finney on the Revivals of Religion

Revivals were formerly regarded as miracles. And it has been so by some even in our day. And others have ideas on the subject so loose and unsatisfactory, that if they would only think, they would see their absurdity. For a long time, it was supposed by the church, that a revival was a miracle, an interposition of Divine power which they had nothing to do with, and which they had no more agency in producing, than they had in producing thunder, or a storm of hail, or an earthquake. It is only within a few years that ministers generally have supposed revivals were to be promoted, by the use of means designed and adapted specially to that object. . . .

It used to be supposed that a revival would come about once in fifteen years, and all would be converted that God intended to save, and then they must wait until another crop came forward on the stage of life. Finally, the time got shortened down to five years, and they supposed there might be a revival about as often as that. . . .

And yet some people are terribly alarmed at all direct efforts to promote a revival, and they cry out, "You are trying to get up a revival in your own strength. Take care, you are interfering with the sovereignty of God. Better keep along in the usual course, and let God give a revival when he thinks it is best. God is a sovereign, and it is very wrong for you to attempt to get up a revival, just because you think a revival is needed." This is just such preaching as the devil wants. And men cannot do the devil's work more effectually than by preaching up the sovereignty of God, as a reason why we should not put forth efforts to produce a revival.

Charles G. Finney, *Lectures on the Revivals of Religion*, rev. ed. (New York: Fleming N. Revell, 1868), 18–19.

as formed in eighteenth-century England. It was a Reformed Protestantism with four major principles: biblicism, crucicentrism, conversion, and an active outward expression of the gospel. Nineteenth-century American evangelicalism added to this human free will as expressed in Arminianism, organized revivalism, a postmillennial outlook, and the formation of mission and benevolent societies to carry out the Christian witness in word and deed. This American evangelicalism produced a remarkable religious consensus among the Christian denominations in the United States, a consensus that tended to transcend confessional boundaries. Of course, these tendencies were strongest among the groups with roots in Reformed Protestantism, but they also had an important impact on other religious groups, including Episcopalians, Lutherans, and even, to an extent, Roman Catholics.

The most important of these developments was the widespread adoption of human free will and Arminianism, which had begun already in England but became dominant in America through the fast-growing Methodists. Traditional Calvinists held that God is the sole determiner of human salvation (that salvation is *predestined*) and that humans cannot thwart the will of God in salvation (that grace is *irresistible*). In reaction to this, Arminianism held that although God offers grace to humans, humans have the free will to accept or reject this offer and can persevere in faith by their own efforts. At the same time, for the Arminians, God knows in advance (has *foreknowledge* of) who will accept faith and continue in it.

Though many of the colonial Protestants were Calvinist—including the Congregationalists, Presbyterians, and Baptists—the Great Awakenings divided these denominations into "New" and "Old" groups (the former being pro-revival, and the latter anti-revival). Many of the Old groups held to traditional Calvinism, but by the early nineteenth century, the triumph of the New parties was virtually complete, and traditional Calvinism was routed. American revivalism—as formulated by Finney—leaned decidedly in the Arminian direction, which seemed to encapsulate in religious terms the optimism and positivity of the new American republic.

Added to this, and equally important, was the increasing adoption of postmillennialism. In Christianity, the "millennium" is the thousand-year rule of Christ on earth ahead of the final judgment (Rev. 20:4–6). Over the centuries, Christians have speculated about the events leading to the end of the world, especially how the millennial kingdom would come about. Some, taking the biblical book of Revelation as a literal road map to this end, believed that the world would slide into a traumatic period of destruction and evil, to be overcome by Christ and the heavenly armies at the battle of Armageddon. Those holding this view became known as premillennialists. But another group of

Christians held, instead, that the millennium would be a gradual process in which humans and their societies would be improved through cooperation between human effort and the leadership of the Holy Spirit. This would quite literally mean building God's kingdom on earth. This belief is known as post-millennialism and includes an optimistic view of history, one much more in tune with the spirit of early Republican America than premillennialism. Thus, postmillennialism spread widely among American Christians.

The new American evangelicalism had strong ties to similar movements in England and Scotland, and there were definite transatlantic ties that brought together much of Anglo-American Protestantism. In 1846, a group of British and American evangelical leaders gathered in London to form the Evangelical Alliance, a pan-denominational ecumenical organization. Among the seventy-five American leaders at this meeting were Presbyterian Robert Baird (1798–1863), Congregationalist Lyman Beecher (1775–1863), and Lutheran Samuel S. Schmucker (1799–1873). The formation of this organization was derailed by controversies over the abolition of slavery, and it was decided that each nation would form its own national organization, but this did not happen in the United States until 1867.

The growing evangelical Protestant consensus led to a powerful wave of Christian activism. Conversion unleashed the energies of new believers, who were urged to work for the moral improvement of both their own lives and the societies around them. The optimism of the times—expressed in postmillennialism—and the freedom of human beings to join their lives with God's mission on earth meant that Christians had the power and the obligation to begin building God's earthly kingdom and to spread the Christian gospel around the world. With a characteristically American response to such a challenge, nineteenth-century American Christians organized a vast array of voluntary benevolent societies (i.e., societies for "doing good") to organize and further God's work on earth. Hundreds of such groups, generally pan-Protestant, were organized during this period: Bible, tract, and educational societies; groups to raise up and send out missionaries; and groups focused on working for moral reform at home and abroad. These national groups depended on vast networks of local societies for their support and were often run by interlocking groups of Christian leaders (many of them leading Christian laypeople). Scholars have named this the "Benevolent Empire" or the "Evangelical United Front." These voluntary religious organizations quickly became an enduring feature of American Christianity across all the denominations. Almost every denomination had its mission and reform societies, which led to a massive expansion of Protestant mission work on the American frontier, in the fast-growing American cities, and around the world (especially in Asia, and later, Africa). It is difficult to gauge the impact of these groups, but one indicator of the scope of their work was that, by the 1840s, the largest of these benevolent groups had aggregate annual expenditures greater than that of the federal budget.

The expansion of evangelical Protestant Christianity was a chief goal of many of these groups, whether within the boundaries of the United States or around the world. One of the largest of these home mission societies was the American Home Missionary Society, formed mainly of Congregationalists and Presbyterians in 1826 to coordinate the work of state and local societies. A competing American Baptist Home Mission Society was formed in 1832, and most other denominations had similar organizations. These groups sought to form and support congregations of Americans moving into the western territories, as far west as Oregon and California. These societies did not generally work among Native Americans on the frontier, but they did increasingly work among new immigrant populations back east.

One of the major emphases of this era was foreign mission work, something pioneered by European Protestants toward the end of the eighteenth century. Americans soon took up this cause as their own, and during the nineteenth century thousands of American men and women went out into foreign mission fields. Congregational and regional mission societies were formed around the United States to raise funds and awareness for the cause. Young men and women caught the evangelical and postmillennial vision of saving souls and saving the world, and they applied to become missionaries. Conditions overseas were harsh, and some of these missionaries (and their family members) died abroad, becoming martyrs for the cause.

The first major national foreign missions society was the American Board of Commissioners for Foreign Missions (ABCFM), formed in 1810. Initially, some of its "foreign" mission activity was directed toward Native Americans, including the Cherokee in the Southeast and the Dakota in Minnesota. In 1835, the ABCFM sent Marcus Whitman (1802–47) and Narcissa Whitman (1808–47) to Oregon to work among the Native Americans there, but in 1847 their small mission was attacked and they were killed. This initial work among the Native Americans then faltered.

American mission work overseas became an increasing focus. In 1819, the ABCFM sent a party of missionaries, including Hiram Bingham (1789–1869) and Asa Thurston (1787–1868) to the then independent Kingdom of Hawaii, in the Pacific Ocean. These missionaries were the first of many sent to Hawaii, and they established a thriving Native church on the islands, a church that included many members of the Hawaiian royal family. Descendants of the missionaries often stayed on the islands and became powerful and influential business

6.2a and b. Adoniram and Ann Judson, Missionaries to Burma.

leaders in the kingdom. ABCFM sent thousands of missionaries abroad during the nineteenth century, especially to China, Southeast Asia, India, the Middle East, and Latin America.

The ABCFM also sent Adoniram Judson (1788–1850) and his wife Ann Judson (1789–1826) and Luther Rice (1783–1836) to India and Burma in 1812. But, as they became Baptists aboard the ship en route to Asia, they had to leave the employ of the ABCFM and went on to spearhead the formation of a rival national missionary society among the Baptists. The work of the Judsons especially flourished in Burma, where a strong Indigenous Baptist church was established.

Not all foreign mission work was successful, initially or otherwise. It was dangerous and often discouraging work, and the numbers of converts could be rather small, even after several decades. For the most part, these early missionaries went to regions outside Western colonial control, so they often depended on the goodwill of local communities for their survival. These days, missionaries are often stereotyped—portrayed either as self-sacrificing heroes, on the one hand, or as witless and culturally inappropriate colonial dupes, on the other. The reality of these nineteenth-century missionaries was probably much more complex than such stereotypes suggest. They were often young and idealistic and sent into difficult conditions with little training or preparation, but the more successful missionaries learned how to deal with local mores and proclaim their message within cultural contexts that were very unfamiliar to them;

others never learned this lesson, or they died. These missionaries introduced Protestant Christianity to many areas of Asia, Africa, and Latin America (the Global South). In many of these places, Christianity eventually took root and became a thriving Indigenous religion. As a result, now in the twenty-first century, some two-thirds of all the world's Christians live in the Global South.

In the United States, evangelical Christians mobilized and organized hundreds of voluntary organizations, whether pan-Protestant or specific to different denominations, to work for the building up of the kingdom of God in America. Although these institutions were based on earlier English models, American evangelicals seemingly perfected those models for the religious and moral reform of the country. Given the historical Protestant emphasis on Bibles, Bible reading, and religious literacy for all people, many of these groups concentrated on the printing and distribution of such material. There had been a proliferation of local and regional Bible societies in the United States since the late eighteenth century, and a national organization, the American Bible Society, was organized in 1816 in New York City to coordinate their work. This group concentrated on printing Bibles and organizing the work of up to 130 different local and regional partners. An associated group, the American Tract Society, was a merger in 1825 of several groups and focused on printing religious tracts and pamphlets. The American Tract Society flooded the country with inexpensive publications that could be ordered in bulk and passed out during evangelistic efforts and campaigns. It was estimated that at the time they produced five pages of printed material for every person in the country.

A related organization, formed in 1817 and named the American Sunday School Union in 1824, targeted religious education. Sunday schools began in England as a way of providing general education to working men, women, and children whose only time available for such pursuits was on Sundays. Through the Methodist class system, Sunday schools became a means of regular religious education and evangelism. Sunday schools were often established in working-class areas of cities or towns, and some eventually became the nuclei for congregations. The American Sunday School Union was a means for coordinating these efforts and for developing a standard curriculum that would become widely used in Protestant congregations across the United States. Starting in 1832, the Union also organized national Sunday school conventions that brought together educators and evangelists from around the country. Through the efforts of this society and the Bible and tract societies, the literary and educational message of evangelical Protestantism was widely disseminated across the nation.

Also important to this "Benevolent Empire" were the huge number of organizations developed to encourage personal and societal moral reforms, an

important element of the postmillennial push
to work toward the kingdom of God on earth.
Driven by the Methodist push for personal
moral perfection, these societies endeavored
to assist individuals with their moral lives and,
increasingly, they also pushed for the incorpo-
ration of Christian moral principles into the
institutions and laws of the nation.

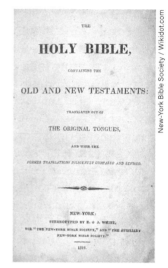

New-York Bible Society / Wikidot.com

One early and important example of these
moral crusades was the movement against the
production and use of alcoholic beverages, the
temperance movement. The colonial and early
United States was awash in alcohol, which was
drunk by all ages and at all levels of society; so
much alcohol was produced that one historian
has named it the "Alcoholic Republic."[5] Initially,

6.3. An Early Publication of
the American Bible Society,
1816.

the reform movements emphasized "tempering"
the use of alcohol and eliminating the use of hard
liquor, to which end a national organization, the
American Temperance Society, was formed in Boston in 1826. But soon the aim
of the movement shifted to the complete elimination of the use of any kind of
alcohol, and millions "took the pledge" not to drink alcohol at all. An important
new element of this crusade was its shift toward addressing the issue on societal
and political levels. Seeing how the abuse of alcohol could devastate working-
class families and communities, more radical leaders in the movement began
to push for laws restricting or eliminating alcoholic beverages altogether. The
first such was the "Maine Law" prohibiting alcohol on a statewide level. This
law became the model for nine other states that adopted similar laws before
the Civil War. And though some of these laws were thrown out, the trend was
toward increasing restrictions. The Maine Law was also an important precedent
for Christian moral principles being written into public laws.

All kinds of other organizations were formed to address moral and societal
issues, large and small. If there was a moral concern, there was a voluntary
society to address it. There were organizations to rescue young women from
prostitution (Magdalen societies), to provide relief for the poor, to supply aid
to immigrants, to oppose the use of tobacco, and to address many other vices.
Importantly, there were groups that addressed prison reforms. Conditions in

5. W. J. Rorabaugh, *The Alcoholic Republic: An American Tradition* (New York: Oxford University
Press, 1981).

American prisons were generally dreadful and focused on punishment. Beginning in the 1790s, Quaker activists championed a new form of incarceration, the "penitentiary," where offenders would be placed in cells to be, well, penitent—to reflect on their crimes and repent for them through Bible reading and counseling. (Similar societies to address the question of slavery will be discussed later in this chapter.)

The new Protestant educational institutions fed this activism that came after 1800, most of which embodied the elements and principles of the evangelical consensus. Through the nineteenth century, states gradually began to require compulsory public education for elementary students, which resulted in the decline and disappearance of the older, church-based schools. Protestants generally thought this was acceptable because, although the public schools were nonsectarian, they inculcated a generic Protestant biblicism and morality into the students, and various denominations supplemented this public education with forms of Christian education. In most areas of the country, there was no public education beyond these primary schools, so it was at this level that Christian groups aimed their educational efforts through the establishment of religious academies (high schools) and colleges. Hundreds of such institutions were established before the Civil War by religious groups and even private individuals.

Most of these academies and colleges had rather insubstantial and shaky beginnings. Individuals or groups (often pastors) would open their homes or church buildings for a few dozen local teenaged students. The curriculum was rudimentary and the facilities sparse, and many of these institutions did not last long due to chronic underfunding. Stronger institutions grew, and some eventually added collegiate programs. Some students would come for a time and then leave when their funding ran out, especially if they were boarding at the schools. School staff were expected to serve as parental authorities (*in loco parentis*) and enforced strict Christian morality. There were usually formal courses of study leading to degrees, but many students did not stay long enough to complete their degrees. Only a few institutions were co-educational, although this period saw the formation of a substantial number of women's educational institutions, sometimes called ladies' seminaries (*seminary* here being a generic term for an educational institution).

With this educational push, theological seminaries were established to produce pastors for the growing numbers of American churches. The older apprenticeship model proved woefully inadequate for producing enough pastors, and by 1860 over sixty Protestant seminaries had been founded in the United States. Like the academies and colleges, these seminaries often relied on shaky resources and were led by a few better-educated pastors. Of course, the older

Protestant denominations, with their emphasis on a learned clergy, led the way in the establishment of these institutions, but they were soon joined by the Methodists and even the Baptists. It was still possible in many denominations to become a pastor by the older means, but these new seminaries produced many more pastors, and more efficiently.

Women increasingly played vital roles in this new evangelicalism and its various benevolent societies. American Christian women had long supported local congregations, but the new activism and the organization of mission and reform groups was largely fueled on the local level by women. Frozen out of clerical leadership in their congregations, women found new leadership roles in the revivals and in the benevolent work of the societies.

The revivals, especially those related to the expanding Methodist and Baptist denominations, downplayed formal theological learning as a requirement for leadership, requiring instead a knowledge of the Bible and a converted life. Women were converted during these revival events, many in what were called "promiscuous" meetings (at the time, *promiscuous* simply meant mixed meetings of men and women). There, women might be led by the Spirit to pray and offer testimonies in public. Some women were allowed to become evangelists, which meant they could preach freely but not lead a congregation (which was reserved for men alone). One such woman, Phoebe Palmer (1807–74), became known nationally and internationally for her revival preaching and spiritual writings. Other women longed to work in the mission fields. The mission boards would certainly not send out women alone to do mission work, but neither would they send out single young men, for fear of "temptation." In several instances, young women quickly married male missionary candidates so that both would be eligible to go abroad, such as in the cases of the previously discussed Narcissa Whitman and Ann Judson, both of whom contributed greatly to the mission work.

On the local level, many women became involved in the work of the benevolent societies, providing the workforce and funding that made these organizations possible. In some denominations, the women themselves formed devotion societies and women's missionary societies to express their piety and benevolent activities. In many Protestant denominations, these local groups were eventually organized on the national level and became important sources of funding to support the mission work.

Alternatives to the Protestant Consensus

Although the evangelical Protestant consensus, as it came together during the first half of the nineteenth century, was widely adopted among many American denominations, this time of growth also saw the development of significant alternatives to this consensus. Many of these alternatives were reacting against one or more of the elements of the consensus, seeking to provide a different path forward for American Christianity. This shows that although Americans were increasingly becoming formal church members, there was a wide range of religious options for the religious "seekers" of this time. And there were many religious seekers. Even though the percentage of Americans who were religiously affiliated had doubled from 17 percent of the population in 1776 to 35 percent in 1850, this meant two-thirds of all Americans were still religiously unaffiliated.

Revivalism was a controversial part of the Protestant consensus. Although it was undeniably effective in bringing people to religion, at least in the short term, some religious leaders were repelled by revivalism. Like the Old-party critics of the Great Awakenings, these leaders ridiculed the revival preachers as uneducated and unpolished and charged that they were artificially manufacturing religious conversions that would not last. Their worry was that, in the pursuit of short-term goals, these revival preachers were ultimately doing more harm than good. In the more settled congregations, some of the more flamboyant elements of frontier revivalism were toned down by this time. Ironically enough, by following Finney and making revivals something that could be planned and repeated, leaders turned many of the elements of revivalism into more formalized rituals, even liturgies.

But the critique of revivalism went deeper than this. Revivalism, as with the rest of evangelicalism, was centered on a conversionist pattern. The core of this idea was that the human person needed to be converted, and in revivalism this was expected to be a rather sudden and often dramatic transformation. Those who were converted spoke of their preconversion lives as dramatically bad and about how, in being converted, their lives had instantly gone from "darkness into light." But this pattern was disputed by more liberal Protestants, who rejected the idea that humans were initially bad before such a dramatic turnaround. Rather, these Protestants held that human beings were essentially good from their beginnings and that this goodness only needed to be cultivated across time. The key to human improvement was a gradual and steady Christian moral education, a growth in religiosity that would last. One of the foremost proponents of this viewpoint was the Congregational pastor and theologian Horace Bushnell (1802–76), who led a prominent New England parish. His 1847 book *Christian Nurture* was widely influential as an alternative to the conversionist pattern. In his 1849 book *God in Christ*, he argued that all religious language was poetical and not literal and that building grand theological systems was ineffective. This book was very controversial, and Bushnell was tried for heresy in 1850, though he retained his pulpit and became even more famous in liberal circles.

A number of the liberal Protestants of this time, like Bushnell, were reimagining some of the older Christian theological positions, but quite often they were not public or specific about their theological reforms. However, there were other liberal Protestants who were willing to make radical revisions to Christianity and to make their proposals very public, including the Unitarians and the Universalists. These two developing movements, with roots in the eighteenth century, came to form definite structures in the early nineteenth century.

The Unitarians pushed against the traditional Christian doctrines of the divinity of Christ and the Trinity—God as Father, Son, and Holy Spirit. Stemming from religious rationalism and deism, they rejected both doctrines in favor of a stress on the oneness and "unity" of God as Creator. They saw Jesus Christ as something other than the one God—perhaps a prophet or some other God-filled person whose works and teachings were important and true. It is possible to see the beginnings of these developments in congregations and pastors in eastern Massachusetts in the mid-eighteenth century, but a twenty-year struggle over these doctrines was kicked off in 1805 when Harvard went Unitarian. A key moment came in 1819 when Boston Unitarian pastor William Ellery Channing (1780–1842) preached a provocative sermon in Baltimore entitled "Unitarian Christianity," a strident defense of this position. Finally, in 1825, representatives from about 125 congregations gathered in Boston to form the American Unitarian Association. Most of these historic congregations were based in eastern Massachusetts, which led to the old gibe that the Unitarians believed in the "Fatherhood of God, the Brotherhood of Man, and the Neighborhood of Boston."

Parallel to this, but distinctly separate, socially and religiously, was the formation of the Universalist Church of America in 1833. The Universalist congregations, many of which came from the ranks of the New England Baptists, reacted against the traditional Christian teaching that not all human beings would be saved by God. Their idea was of universal salvation: that God intended to save all human beings. Socially, the Universalists represented the rural areas and smaller towns in New England, eventually spreading into other areas of the United States. In the twentieth century, the Unitarians and Universalists would gradually move toward each other and eventually merge into a single association.

The Transcendentalist movement, led by New England literary figures such as Ralph Waldo Emerson (1803–82) and Henry David Thoreau (1817–62), grew out of Unitarianism. The early Unitarians were generally rationalistic and maintained the essential uniqueness of Christianity, as they conceived of

Emerson on True Religion (1838)

Jesus Christ belonged to the true race of prophets. He saw with open eye the mystery of the soul. Drawn by its severe harmony, ravished with its beauty, he lived in it, and had his being there. Alone in all history, he estimated the greatness of man. One man was true to what is in you and me. He saw that God incarnates himself in man, and evermore goes forth anew to take possession of his world. . . . Thus is he, as I think, the only soul in history who has appreciated the worth of a man.

In this point of view we become very sensible of the first defect of historical Christianity. Historical Christianity has fallen into the error that corrupts all attempts to communicate religion. As it appears to us, and as it has appeared for ages, it is not the doctrine of the soul, but an exaggeration of the personal, the positive, the ritual. It has dwelt, it dwells, with noxious exaggeration about the *person* of Jesus. The soul knows no persons. It invites every man to expand to the full circle of the universe, and will have no preferences but those of spontaneous love. But by this eastern monarchy of a Christianity, which indolence and fear have built, the friend of man is made the injurer of man. The manner in which his name is surrounded with expressions, which were once sallies of admiration and love, but are now petrified into official titles, kills all generous sympathy and liking. All who hear me, feel, that the language that describes Christ to Europe and America, is not the style of friendship and enthusiasm to a good and noble heart, but is appropriated and formal,—paints a demigod, as the Orientals or the Greeks would describe Osiris or Apollo. Accept the injurious impositions of our early catachetical instruction, and even honesty and self-denial were but splendid sins, if they did not wear the Christian name.

Ralph Waldo Emerson, "Divinity School Address," https://emersoncentral.com /texts/nature-addresses-lectures/addresses/divinity-school-address/.

it, and the Transcendentalists were part of the broad early nineteenth-century romantic and idealistic reaction against the Enlightenment and Enlightenment rationalism. This movement argued for a broader understanding of religion that would encompass all of human religious experience and spirituality. The key moment of this movement (which never did take institutional form) was the 1838 sermon by Emerson at Harvard Divinity School, in which he attacked the Unitarians. Transcendentalism was, essentially, an intellectual and literary movement, although there were several attempts to put this into a social form, including the short-lived communal experiment at Brook Farm, in 1841, and Thoreau's retreat into solitude at Walden Pond, in 1845.

Brook Farm was only one of dozens of communal religious experiments that were attempted in the early United States. The common millennial expectations and possibilities of establishing God's kingdom on earth led thousands of individuals to seek out societies where this heavenly kingdom could be established in the present time. The Shakers and New Harmony were early examples, to be followed by such communities as Hopedale, Oneida, Amana, Fruitlands, Bishop Hill, the North American Phalanx, and the Icarians. There were at least twenty-five such groups before the Civil War, though many were short-lived. Often these religious communities shared their goods in common and featured living arrangements that focused on the community as a whole and not on the individual. Some of these groups, most notably the Shakers, regulated human relationships and sexuality by requiring celibacy for their adherents. The Oneida Community in New York, led by Christian perfectionist John Humphrey Noyes (1811–86), took a different direction, known as "complex marriage," in which each male member of the society was (theoretically) married to each female member. To scandalized outsiders, this reeked of gross immorality (although it was actually tightly controlled), and eventually Noyes himself had to flee to Canada to avoid legal action. In time, the community returned to traditional family and economic patterns and became famous for its silverware industry.

While these groups were shaped primarily by the optimistic, postmillennial vision of the building of God's kingdom on earth, other seekers carefully read their Bibles and discovered in its apocalyptic writings, especially the book of Revelation, a darker vision of the coming millennium. Rather than a gradually progressing world, this vision, called premillennialism, saw instead a world that was morally and religiously declining, falling under the control of Satan and the power of evil. This reign would be overcome only in the (imminent) end of the world, when Christ returned to earth with the heavenly armies to destroy evil once and for all. Only then would the millennial kingdom be established by God. Although this apocalyptic vision of the end has been a part of Christianity from the beginning, at certain times it has been pushed to the fore.

The New England lay preacher and theologian William Miller (1782–1849) was a prophet of this premillennialism. Converted from deism in 1816, Miller set out to study the Bible thoroughly for some understanding of the coming millennial kingdom and of how and when Jesus would return to establish it. After intense study and calculations, Miller decided that he had cracked the hidden codes of the Bible, which spoke in vague and metaphoric terms of the coming of the end of the world, and he put his ideas into print in 1832. Miller's writings were widely distributed, and thousands of people responded to his message, which was picked up and further disseminated by others. From 1834 to 1839, he toured and lectured around the country. When he was pressured by his followers to give a definite and public date for the end of the world, Miller decided, after further

William Miller on the Coming End of the World (1842)

Question.—You believe that the Lord is to make his second personal appearance on earth next year. Will you tell for what purpose he is coming?

Answer.—"He cometh to JUDGE THE EARTH." Psalm xcvi. and xcviii. "He shall judge the world in righteousness, he shall minister judgment to the people in uprightness. The wicked shall be turned into hell, with all the nations that forget God. For the needy will not always be forgotten: the expectation of the poor shall not perish forever." Psalm ix. 8,17,18.

Q.-What particular events will take place at his coming?

A.-The Lord himself shall descend from heaven with a shout, with the voice of the arch-angel, and with the trump of God: and the dead in Christ shall rise first, then we which are alive and remain shall be caught up together with them in the clouds, to meet the Lord in the air; and so shall we ever be with the Lord." 1 Thessalonians iv. 16, 17. . . .

Q.-Will the new earth be inhabited?

A.-Yes. "Blessed are the meek, for they shall inherit the earth." Matthew [chapter 5,] verse 5. . . .

Q.-Then I understand your belief to be, that next year, the year 1843, is the time fixed in counsels of eternity for consummation of all the grand events spoken of by the prophets concerning the final destiny of all men?

A.-Yes. Sometime in the course of next year, being one thousand eight hundred and forty-three years from the birth of our Saviour, one thousand eight hundred and ten years from his crucifixion, and two thousand three hundred years from the going forth of the commandment to restore and build Jerusalem. I expect to see what Daniel saw, viz. "One like the Son of Man," who "came with the clouds of heaven."

William Miller, "End of the World," *Voice of Warning*, Boston, 1(1), October 1, 1842.

calculations, that the end would come in 1843 or 1844, and he eventually settled on October 22, 1844. Thousands of his followers expected and planned for the world to end on that date only to fall victim to what they would later call the "Great Disappointment." Miller himself died several years later, still fully expecting the very imminent end of the world. Despite the Great Disappointment, premillennialism was and is still an important ideology in American Protestantism, and the Millerite movement eventually resurfaced later in the nineteenth century in several disparate contexts, including among the Seventh-day Adventists; adherents of the Bible Prophecy movement; and, later, the Jehovah's Witnesses.

The evangelical Protestant consensus and its elements filtered into every corner of American Protestantism, including the Quakers. Many of the leading families in this movement, centered in and around Philadelphia, had prospered as merchants and traders and had become very wealthy. The original zeal of the Quakers had died down in many to a quiet religiosity, and rationalism had made inroads into the community. The leading group of Quakers, the Philadelphia Meeting, had settled into a comfortable respectability, although under the influence of John Woolman (1720–72) they had been early advocates for the abolition of slavery and for women's rights. But not all Quakers were rich Philadelphia merchants. There were also working-class Quakers, one of whom was Long Island farmer Elias Hicks (1748–1830), who led a new movement within the Quaker tradition. Serving scattered Quaker communities across the country, Hicks was an advocate for human reason within this tradition and represented the democratizing elements of American culture in the 1820s. For Hicks, the Quaker inner light came through the innate rational abilities of the "untainted" common person—the farmer, the trader, and the like. He rejected a number of traditional Christian doctrines, along with other movements and causes popular among American Christians of his day, including missionary work, Bible societies, public schools, and even the Erie Canal. His work brought him into conflict with the aristocratic leaders of the Philadelphia Meeting, leading to the Hicksite schism, in 1827–28, and the formation of a separate Quaker group. There were other divisions too, including the one between the Quaker traditionalists in the Philadelphia Meeting and the Evangelical Quakers, which was driven by tensions over evangelical practices such as revivalism.

Besides the traditional Christian spiritualism of the Quakers, there was a strong surge of popular interest in spiritual and psychic phenomena during the 1840s. Since the earliest colonial times in North America, there had been, on the popular level, deep and abiding interest in folk magic, spiritualism, the occult, and paranormal occurrences—an interest that ran parallel to, and sometimes within, forms of Christianity. Many of these themes surged in popularity in 1848 through widely disseminated and sensationalized reports of the psychic abilities of two teenage girls, Katie and Margaret Fox of Hydesville, New York, who, it was claimed, could contact the spirits of the dead. This renewed interest in such things become a major religious movement in the middle of the nineteenth century.

Renewed Immigration and Immigrant Christianity

When large-scale immigration from Europe resumed in the 1830s and 1840s, new immigrants had to adjust to the religious and societal world that had been developing in America—and this was especially true for immigrants who were coming from outside the Anglo-American sphere. While there were

English-speaking immigrants from Britain during this time, a growing number of the immigrants were Irish and German Roman Catholics and German and Scandinavian Protestants. These immigrants had to adjust not only to pluralism and voluntary church structures—given that their prior experience was largely of monolithic religious cultures and with European state churches—but also to the dominant evangelical Protestantism. The new immigrants, mainly Lutherans and Roman Catholics, also had to negotiate with versions of their traditions that were already established, having been founded during the colonial period.

The colonial Roman Catholic Church was constituted mainly by English settlers in and around Maryland, and their numbers were reinforced by French refugees fleeing the chaos of the French Revolution. Though the bulk of American Protestants were openly hostile to Roman Catholics, and there were a number of tensions and incidents between the two groups, American Roman Catholics were protected by their constitutional right of freedom of religious expression, which they came to appreciate. The Roman Catholics began founding their own educational institutions, staffed mainly by religious orders from Europe, including the Jesuits, and organized new missionary dioceses on the American frontier. Because of the generally Protestant (and anti–Roman Catholic) nature of American public schools, many Roman Catholic parishes organized separate parochial schools to educate their own children.

The territorial expansion of the United States and renewed immigration greatly increased the ethnic diversity within American Catholicism and the numbers of American Roman Catholics. The American purchase of the Louisiana Territory in 1803 had added the French Roman Catholic settlers in southern Louisiana to their ranks, and the annexation of Texas and the territories gained from Mexico (New Mexico to California) in 1848 added large numbers of Spanish-speaking Latin Americans. At that time, the bishops and other leaders of the American Catholic Church were of English and French backgrounds, and they soon came into religious and social conflict with the Hispanic Roman Catholics who were now a part of their church but whose religiosity was markedly different from their own.

The new wave of immigration added to these internal ethnic tensions with the arrival of large numbers of Irish and German Roman Catholics. With the immigration of Germans came the need to develop separate German-language parishes and educational institutions. German and Irish immigrants both came in such numbers that they overwhelmed the earlier Roman Catholic leaders, with whom the new immigrants soon contended for leadership and authority. Because of the structural umbrella of Roman Catholicism, these ethnic tensions and divisions resulted in several separate ethnic "spheres" within the American Roman Catholic Church as a whole.

Immigration also brought larger numbers of German and Scandinavian Lutherans to the United States, resulting in similar types of religious, linguistic, and social tensions between the descendants of the colonial Lutherans and the new immigrants. But without a common, overarching structure, these differences quickly led to the establishment of separate Lutheran denominations. The older, colonial Lutherans had already transitioned to using English in their congregations and had also adopted many of the structural and even theological elements of the evangelical Protestant consensus from their neighbors, including mission societies, Sunday schools, and even elements of revivalism. These English-speaking Lutherans spread into the American midwestern frontier, forming new regional synods. In 1820, under the leadership of Simon S. Schmucker, a number of these regional groups formed a national organization, the General Synod, to coordinate activities among themselves and to be a national presence. But not all Lutheran groups joined this new organization.

There was an inevitable reaction against this new "American" Lutheranism from other Lutherans who wished to retain a traditional, and more strictly confessional, Lutheran theology and practice. Led by clerical members of the Henkel family from southwestern Virginia, more traditional Lutherans formed their own separate synods in competition with already existing Lutheran groups. This dynamic intensified with the arrival of new Lutheran immigrants from Europe and the need for new ethnic and linguistic Lutheran congregations and church structures. One especially strict confessional group that began arriving in Missouri in 1839 were religious refugees from the Saxony region of Germany, who left that area because of religious changes forced by the Prussian government. This group, along with other conservative Lutheran immigrants, formed the German Evangelical Lutheran Synod of Missouri, Ohio, and Other States in 1847 (shortened to the Lutheran Church–Missouri Synod in 1947), to resist the influence of evangelical Protestantism. They were the largest Lutheran denomination formed by the new immigrants, most of whom continued to worship and teach in their first languages. Most of these Lutherans settled in the rural areas of the American Midwest and Upper Midwest, and several states in these regions have been influenced by a large Lutheran presence.

African American Christianity and the Movement for the Abolition of Slavery

In an era of rapid growth for American Christianity, perhaps the most striking gains were among African Americans, both enslaved and free. Many African

Americans became Christians in the Great Awakenings and the camp meetings and revivals of the early nineteenth century, and increasingly they organized their own congregations and distinctive forms of Christianity. These African American Christians came to embody the essence of the evangelical Protestant consensus (and they still do, to a large extent), although they were widely considered outsiders because of their race. Methodist and Baptist preachers, some of them African American, spread the gospel in its revivalistic form, and many African Americans became Christians. But this was not simply an automatic adoption of White Christianity; instead, it involved the conscious adoption and adaptation of Christianity to meet the distinct needs of African Americans, often with some elements of religious customs and practices of older forms of African religion and culture.

The separate institutional forms of African American Christianity were most evident in urban areas of the North, where free African Americans organized their own congregations. These congregations were mainly Methodist and Baptist, but there were also Presbyterian, Episcopalian, and even Lutheran congregations established before the Civil War. There was also the formation of separate denominations, including the African Methodist Episcopal Church (1816) and the African Methodist Episcopal Zion Church (1821), and informal groups of congregations in other traditions. Not all of these congregations were in the North. The First African American congregation in Charleston, South Carolina, claimed 2,400 members by 1830, probably a mix of free and enslaved persons. There were at least five different African American Episcopal parishes established during this time.

However, most African Americans worshiped in segregated sections of White congregations or in informal gatherings around the farms and plantations where they were enslaved. Estimates are that perhaps 20 percent of all Methodists in 1820 were African Americans, and the percentage among the Baptists was probably even larger. Scholars have referred to the informal network of African American Christian communities, especially those unauthorized ones in the South, as an "invisible institution" of licensed and unlicensed preachers and religious revivalists. White citizens tried to maintain control over the religious lives of enslaved African Americans out of fear that the preaching of the Christian gospel would lead the latter to "unfortunate" conclusions. Slave owners frequently had pastors preach on texts from the New Testament that urged obedience, such as Ephesians 6:5 ("Slaves, obey your earthly masters with fear and trembling, . . . as you obey Christ"). But African Americans were too sophisticated to fall for such prooftexting. As one scholar has put it, "Slaves embraced evangelical Christianity as an affirmation of hope and self-respect, of moral order and justice in circumstances where these were scarce and precious."[6] If Christianity were only an alien religiosity to African Americans, it would hardly have made such headway into the community.

White Americans often preached a message of servitude to African Americans; in response, African American Christians quickly developed a rich, distinctive tradition of hymns and stories that expressed what Christianity meant to them, focusing on themes of hope, freedom, and God's justice for all. Especially important to this community were the Old Testament stories of God's liberation of the Israelites and their escape from enslavement to the "promised land." These forms of Christianity drew from the exhortations and revival worship of the camp meeting tradition, combining them with singing, dancing, and shouting.

African American Christian leaders sought to do what they could to assist their communities, both free and enslaved. Although free African Americans were clear of the bondage in which many others were held, they often faced crushing poverty and brutal discrimination. And African American congregations (then as now) served as important sources of mutual aid and encouragement. Some African Americans went to Africa as Christian missionaries, especially to Liberia and Sierra Leone. One of these was Lott Carey (1780–1828), who bought himself and his family out of slavery, became a physician and Baptist preacher, and in 1821 was sent to Liberia by the newly organized Richmond African Baptist Missionary Society. Others took a more active political role in the United States. Organized in 1830, the National Negro Convention Movement (also called the Colored Conventions Movement) was the first African American political group, whose first leader was AME bishop Richard Allen. This group gathered regularly in convention prior to the Civil War to counter discrimination and work for the abolition of slavery. Sojourner Truth (born Isabella Baumfree, ca. 1797–1883), free from her Dutch owner in New York, became an itinerant preacher and lecturer spreading Christianity and abolitionism across the North. Harriet Tubman (born Araminta Ross, 1822–1913), a devout Methodist, escaped a brutal master in Maryland and risked her life numerous times to bring others out of slavery in the South. The activism that was so much a part of the evangelical Protestant consensus was central to the African American religious experience.

Slavery had been a part of American history ever since the first enslaved persons landed in Jamestown in 1619 and had been present in every colony at one time or another. Around the time of the American Revolution there had been some American leaders who suggested that the practice should be abolished or

6. Daniel Walker Howe, *What Hath God Wrought: The Transformation of America, 1815–1848* (New York: Oxford University Press, 2007), 184.

phased out, and certain religious figures, such as the Quaker John Woolman and some early Methodists, spoke forcefully for its abolition. In 1787, English politician William Wilberforce, an Anglican evangelical, began a twenty-year battle to finally end the British transatlantic slave trade. His crusade was supported by some American evangelicals, but steps toward abolition in America petered out in the early nineteenth century. A common proposal at this time was to solve the problem by "colonization," or returning the African Americans to Africa (no one asked them if they wanted to go back!), and the American Colonization Society was formed in 1817. Another proposed solution was the gradual abolition of slavery over time, along with compensation for the slave owners.

While slavery was gradually eliminated in the northern states for a variety of reasons, both pragmatic and principled, slavery actually grew more important in the southern states. The key reason was cotton. The looms of the industrial revolution had an insatiable appetite for cotton, which was needed to turn out

Jarena Lee, African American Methodist Woman Preacher

I now began to think seriously of breaking up housekeeping, and forsaking all to preach the everlasting Gospel. I felt a strong desire to return to the place of my nativity, at Cape May, after an absence of about fourteen years. . . . When within ten miles of that place, I appointed an evening meeting. There were a goodly number came out to hear. The Lord was pleased to give me light and liberty among the people. After meeting, there came an elderly lady to me and said, she believed the Lord had sent me among them: she then appointed me another meeting there two weeks from that night. . . . At the first meeting which I held at my uncle's house, there was, with others who had come from curiosity to hear the woman preacher, an old man, who was a Deist, and who said he did not believe the coloured people had any souls—he was sure they had none. . . . He now came into the house, and in the most friendly manner shook hands with me, saying, he hoped God had spared him to some good purpose. This man was a great slave holder, and had been very cruel. . . . From this time it was said of him that he became greatly altered in his ways for the better.

Ten years from that time, in the neighborhood of Cape May, I held a prayer meeting in a school house. . . . After service, there came a white lady, of great distinction, a member of the Methodist Society, and told me that at the same school house ten years before, under my preaching the Lord first awakened her. She rejoiced much to see me, and invited me home with her, where I staid till the next day.

Jarena Lee, *Religious Experience and Journal of Mrs. Jarena Lee, Giving an Account of her Call to Preach the Gospel* (Philadelphia: 1849), 18–20.

massive amounts of cheap cloth. Enslaved persons were used to grow and pick the cotton, and new technologies, such as the cotton gin, further increased the demand for enslaved persons. Southerners wanted more land for cotton, leading to the annexation of Texas and the Mexican-American War. The debate over slavery, increasingly along regional lines, consumed national politics and many other aspects of national discourse. The Missouri Compromise of 1820, balancing the admission of new states between slave and free territories, saved the union for a time, but the question continued to fester.

6.4. Frederick Douglass.

Beginning around 1830, there were new and more radical calls for the immediate abolition of slavery and the emancipation of enslaved persons. One such call was issued in Boston in 1829 by African American David Walker (1796–1830). Walker's book, entitled *An Appeal to the Coloured Citizens of the World*, called for the immediate abolition of slavery and for African Americans to fight for their freedom. This was a radical move for the time and raised renewed fears in the South of slave rebellions and violence. There were hundreds of such uprisings before the Civil War, including the 1822 revolt led by Denmark Vesey in Charleston and the 1831 rebellion led by Nat Turner, who had been strongly influenced by biblical apocalypticism, in Virginia.

Others pushed for political and social changes they hoped would lead to immediate abolition. In 1831, William Lloyd Garrison started the abolitionist newspaper *The Liberator*, which became an important literary vehicle for the movement. In 1833, Garrison and others founded the American Anti-Slavery Society to further the cause of immediate abolition, which increasingly overtook the earlier calls for colonization and gradual emancipation. Frederick Douglass (1818–95), who was himself African American, was another prominent voice through his lectures and his 1845 autobiography. Southern Quaker sisters Sarah Grimké (1792–1873) and Angelina Grimké Weld (1805–79) were early southern abolitionists who were forced to move north because of their views. Angelina's husband, Theodore Dwight Weld (1803–95), was a strong leader in the movement, lecturing for the cause across the North. The radical calls from these three for immediate abolition greatly raised tensions over slavery in the United States, which elicited a growing divide over the issue and an increasingly strong proslavery reaction. Presbyterian pastor Elijah Lovejoy (1802–37) established an abolitionist newspaper in southern Illinois, only to become a martyr for the abolition cause when he was killed by a proslavery mob in 1837.

The cause of immediate abolition was embraced by only a fraction of the people in the North and virtually no one in the South (at least, virtually no one publicly supported it). Northern churches tended to be cautious about the subject, worrying that too strong of a stance on the issue would divide them from their colleagues in the South. But abolitionists pushed the Northern denominations to adopt the cause, leading to divisions within the Methodist General Conference in 1844 and the formation of a separate denomination called the Methodist Episcopal Church, South. Similar issues among the Baptists led to the formation of the Southern Baptist Convention in 1845. On the other side, impatience with the cautious stance of the northern denominations caused some Methodist, Baptist, Presbyterian, Lutheran, and Quaker advocates of abolition to break away and form their own religious groups.

Almost all Americans agreed on the important authority of the Bible, but they waged an increasingly divisive struggle over what exactly the Bible had to say about slavery and how the Bible did (or did not) apply to the contemporary situation. Southern attitudes hardened in defense of slavery after 1830 in response to immediate abolitionism, and southern Christians wrote books and tracts arguing that both the Old and New Testaments knew about and accepted the institution of slavery and even urged slaves to remain loyal to their masters. Some southern apologists even suggested that slavery was good for enslaved persons, as it allowed them to become Christians (something not likely in Africa). Northern abolitionists countered with publications arguing that the Bible opposed slavery and that the type of slavery seen in the nineteenth-century United States was fundamentally different from the slavery of biblical times. An important work in this vein was Theodore Dwight Weld's *The Bible against Slavery* (1837), which was widely disseminated. Abolitionist authors also issued graphic literary portrayals of the harshness and brutality of slavery itself.

Questions of slavery and its possible abolition consumed all areas of national life during this period and greatly affected the Christian churches. Many of them tried to avoid the issue or develop moderating positions, but increasingly they were pulled by more radical forces on either extreme. Traditionally, American Christians had held that religion and political action were to be kept separate, but the logic of activism and the millennial expectations propelled some of them into increased political action. However, the American political system of the time was stacked in favor of the South, and a series of southern presidents did nothing about slavery, favoring the status quo. Frustration with this situation eventually pushed some abolitionists into direct action, by defying the laws of the nation, laws that they considered immoral, unjust, and against the will of God as they understood it. It was a time and an issue where a moderate position was increasingly difficult to maintain.

───────────────────────── BIBLIOGRAPHY ─────────────────────────

Cross, Whitney R. *The Burned-Over District: The Social and Intellectual History of Enthusiastic Religion in Western New York, 1800–1850.* Ithaca, NY: Cornell University Press, 1950.

Hatch, Nathan O. *The Democratization of American Christianity.* New Haven: Yale University Press, 1989.

Howe, Daniel Walker. *What Hath God Wrought: The Transformation of America, 1815–1848.* New York: Oxford University Press, 2007.

Hutchison, William R. *The Transcendentalist Ministers: Church Reform in the New England Renaissance.* New Haven: Yale University Press, 1959.

Irons, Charles F. *The Origins of Proslavery Christianity: White and Black Evangelicals in Colonial and Antebellum Virginia.* Chapel Hill: University of North Carolina Press, 2008.

Newman, Richard S. *Freedom's Prophet: Bishop Richard Allen, the AME Church, and the Black Founding Fathers.* New York: New York University Press, 2008.

Noll, Mark A. *America's God: From Jonathan Edwards to Abraham Lincoln.* New York: Oxford University Press, 2002.

Numbers, Ronald L., and Jonathan M. Butler, eds. *The Disappointed: Millerism and Millenarianism in the Nineteenth Century.* Bloomington: Indiana University Press, 1987.

Raboteau, Albert J. *Slave Religion: The "Invisible Institution" in the Antebellum South.* New York: Oxford University Press, 1978.

Smith, Timothy L. *Revivalism and Social Reform in Mid-19th-Century America.* Nashville: Abingdon, 1957.

7

Slavery, War, and Immigration, 1850–80

THE YEARS SURROUNDING the American Civil War (1861–65) were pivotal to the history of the United States, and the country's modern foundations were forged out of the terrible agony of that bitter conflict. In 1850, the country was essentially a confederation of agrarian states that were being torn apart over slavery. The Civil War not only settled the question of slavery once and for all; it also permanently welded the union together (by force), and by 1880 the country was moving toward its future as an urbanized, industrial nation.

Despite the carnage of the Civil War, the population of the United States grew from twenty-three million inhabitants in 1850 to fifty million by 1880. This population growth was augmented by increasing numbers of immigrants. During the 1850s, 2.8 million people immigrated to the United States, then 2.3 million more came in the 1860s, and then another 2.8 million in the 1870s. Most of these immigrants came from Europe, although Asian immigration to the West Coast was also beginning during this period. Most of the new immigrants were seeking farmland in the Midwest and Great Plains, but as the best land was soon gone, immigrants began to swell the nation's burgeoning cities. In 1850, only about 15 percent of Americans lived in urban areas, but by 1880 that number had doubled to almost 30 percent. There were regional variations: by 1880, the Northeast was 50 percent urbanized, but the South was only 12 percent urbanized. Older cities like New York, Boston, and Philadelphia grew much larger than they had been, but midwestern cities like Chicago, Detroit, St. Louis, and Cleveland expanded even more dramatically. During and after the Civil War, these cities led the country's increasing growth of factories, as the United States became a major world industrial power.

The Civil War was a costly, four-year struggle over the fate of the American union. Citing their fears of "Northern aggression" and the possible restrictions on or elimination of slavery, eleven Southern states seceded from the union in 1861 to form the Confederate States of America. The Union government and the Northern states sought to prohibit this secession by the use of military force, which the Confederacy resisted. Fought mainly on Southern territory, the war was a brutal affair in which the industrial and demographic power of the North eventually overwhelmed the South, but not before hundreds of thousands of lives were lost on both sides. Though hostilities ended in 1865 and the Southern states were eventually brought back into the union, the South, as a region, continued for many decades to be its own sectional world within the larger United States. Slavery was ended, but African Americans faced bitter discrimination and an uncertain future in both the South and the North.

The westward expansion of the country continued into the Midwest, Great Plains, and West Coast. Added to the thirty states already established in 1850 were eight more during this period: California (1850), Minnesota (1858), Oregon (1859), Kansas (1861), West Virginia (1863), Nevada (1864), Nebraska (1867), and Colorado (1876). Additional territory was added by the Gadsden Purchase from Mexico, in 1854, and the purchase of Alaska from Russia, in 1867. The previously established line of the frontier pushed farther west with the agricultural settlement of the Great Plains (North Dakota to western Texas), and the Pacific Coast states were joined to the rest of the country through the completion of the transcontinental railroad, in 1869, and the establishment of an east-west telegraph link. However, this post–Civil War expansion did cause renewed conflict between White settlers and Native Americans. Despite occasional Native victories—such as the Battle of the Little Bighorn, in 1876—military battles between American forces and Native nations resulted in the increasing loss of Native territory and in Native peoples being confined to reservations. This was a period of great defeat and mistreatment of the Native Americans.

Religious Developments during the 1850s

One early aspect of the growing immigration to the United States was the arrival of Irish Roman Catholics. Leaving Ireland because of poverty, famine, and mistreatment by British landowners, approximately 2.5 million Irish came to America between 1840 and 1880, with almost 900,000 arriving during the 1850s alone. Though the Irish were generally farmers in Ireland, as economic refugees they rarely had the financial resources to farm once they immigrated. Rather, they generally settled in the urban areas of the North and Midwest and became laborers and industrial workers, often at the bottom of the employment spectrum. Their arrival in such great numbers before the Civil War occasioned much civil and religious turbulence, caused mainly by the fact that they were overwhelmingly Roman Catholic. Besides being Protestants, most Americans during the early nineteenth century were distinctly anti–Roman Catholic, a long heritage that stretched back to the sixteenth century in England. Besides this fierce historical Protestant-Roman Catholic antagonism (held on both sides), American Protestants viewed European Roman Catholic leaders, including the pope, as antidemocratic, which at this point in time they generally were. So many Roman Catholics arriving in such a short period raised fears in American Protestants that their country was being overrun. Discrimination and violence against Irish immigrants were common, and there was even a short-lived nativist, anti–Roman Catholic political group, the Know-Nothing Party.

The arrival of so many Irish Roman Catholics also caused turbulence within the small American Roman Catholic Church, which was overwhelmed by their numbers. It set up a situation within American Roman Catholicism where a large number of recent ethnic immigrants vied with older, more established groups for power and control, a situation that would be repeated multiple times in the future. As the Irish organized their own parishes, schools, and religious orders in the United States, they gained a power base from which they would eventually come to control many of the institutions of power in the church.

Another controversial religious group, this one homegrown, was the Church of Jesus Christ of Latter-day Saints, commonly known as the Mormons. An outgrowth of the religious revivals and enthusiasms of the early nineteenth century, this group was organized in 1830 by religious seeker Joseph Smith (1805–44). Smith said he had a religious vision that led him to another book of revelation from God, the *Book of Mormon*, which told of a visit of Jesus Christ to the "lost" Hebrew tribes in North America. Based on Protestantism but going theologically far beyond it, Smith's followers attempted several communal settlements in Ohio and Missouri before settling their community in Nauvoo, Illinois, in 1839. Their settlement in frontier Illinois caused a great deal of resentment from their neighbors, who worried about the growing power of the group. This new religious group was a distinct version of American Protestant Restorationism, but, rather than restoring the New Testament church, the Mormons sought to restore the Old Testament patriarchy, including its organizations and temple rituals. Especially controversial was the gradual introduction of a prophetic revelation by Smith that Mormon men could take multiple wives in what he called "celestial marriage," a practice that continued until publicly ended in 1890.

Joseph Smith was murdered by an angry mob of local "gentiles" (non-Mormons) in 1844, and control over the group passed to his lieutenant Brigham Young. Fearing more violence, the Mormons left Nauvoo in 1847 and made the dramatic and difficult trek overland to the Great Salt Lake basin in Utah, where they created their own self-contained world. Their initial claim of an independent "State of Deseret," encompassing much of the Intermountain West, was dashed by the transfer of this territory from Mexico to the United States in 1848. The Mormons established their particular culture in Utah and

Mrs. Fox's Account of Spiritual Rapping

On Friday night we concluded to go to bed early, and not let it disturb us; it came, we thought we would not mind it, but try and get a good night's rest. My husband was here on all these occasions, heard the noise and helped search. It was very early when we went to bed on this night; hardly dark. We went to bed so early, because we had been broken so much of our rest that I was almost sick.

My husband had not gone to bed when we first heard the noise on this evening. I had just laid down. It commenced as usual. I knew it from all other noises we had ever heard in the house. The girls, who slept in the other bed in the room, heard the noise, and tried to make a similar noise by snapping their fingers. The youngest girl is about 12 years old; she is the one who made her hand go. As fast as she made the noise with her hands or fingers, the sound was followed up in the room. It did not sound any different at that time, only it made the same number of noises that the girl did. When she stopped, the sound itself stopped for a short while.

The other girl, who is in her 15th year, then spoke in sport and said, "Now do this just as I do. Count one, two, three, four," &c., striking one hand in the other at the same time. The blows which she made were repeated before. It appeared to answer her by repeating every blow that she made. . . .

I then asked if it was a human being that was making the noise? and if it was, to manifest it by the same noise. There was no noise. I then asked if it was a spirit? and if it was, to manifest it by two sounds. I heard two sounds as soon as the words were spoken. . . .

I am not a believer in haunted houses or supernatural appearances. I am very sorry that there has been so much excitement about it. It has been a great deal of trouble to us.

A Report of the Mysterious Noises Heard in the House of Mr. John D. Fox (Rochester, NY: E. E. Lewis, 1848), 6–8.

other parts of the region, aided by how remote they were from the rest of the United States. A much smaller group of Mormons, the Reorganized Church of Jesus Christ of Latter Day Saints, broke from Young and remained in Missouri and the Midwest.

Another popular religious movement during the 1850s was spiritualism, or the belief that persons then living could contact and converse with the spirits of the dead, who had transcended this visible world for a realm beyond the living. Not a religion per se, and very resistant to organizational or doctrinal forms, spiritualism was a rather loosely connected mixture of beliefs and practices that could be taken on their own or blended with more conventional religious systems. Beginning with the celebrated example of the Fox sisters in 1848, spiritualism became a very popular movement during the 1850s, even among conventional Christians. Central to spiritualism was the belief that specially attuned persons, called mediums, could serve as conduits between the living and the departed by means of séances and other spiritual practices. Mediums practiced all over the country, and spiritualist magazines, such as the *Spiritual Telegraph* and *The Banner of Light*, spread the news. Editor Horace Greeley of the *New York Tribune* was a great advocate of spiritualism, and showman P. T. Barnum took the Fox sisters on display around the country. Spiritualism was celebrated by many famous Americans, including many women, who found these beliefs and practices congenial. Spiritualism was revived during and after the Civil War, as grieving families sought contact with their dead loved ones, and although it has flourished and waned since then, these beliefs and practices have remained a constant part of American religious culture.

Abolition and the Churches

The political and religious battles over slavery and its abolition intensified during the 1850s. Another grand political solution was attempted through the Compromise of 1850, which brought California into the Union as a free state but allowed the inhabitants of the New Mexico and Utah territories to decide on the issue of slavery for themselves at the time of their statehood. Another part of this attempted solution was the Fugitive Slave Act of 1850, which compelled state officials (especially in the North) to assist federal marshals in recapturing those enslaved persons who had run for freedom. Opposed by hardliners on both sides of the issue, these actions probably delayed the Civil War by a decade, but they also further inflamed tensions. Incensed by the Fugitive Slave Act, many in the North refused to comply with it. Southerners saw this noncompliance as further proof of Northern aggression. The Supreme

Court, dominated by Southerners, issued a famous ruling against the freedom of an enslaved man, Dred Scott, in 1857, which further widened the gap. These federal decisions led some Northern abolitionists into active resistance to those laws they believed ran counter to the will of God.

7.1. Harriet Beecher Stowe.

The Fugitive Slave Act of 1850 also led to the writing of a famous and widely influential novel, *Uncle Tom's Cabin*, in 1852. The writer of this novel, Harriet Beecher Stowe (1811–96), was a staunch abolitionist and a member of the Beecher family, a leading religious family in the North. As the daughter, sister, and wife of prominent Congregational pastors and teachers, she famously claimed about the book that "God wrote it." This book, which graphically portrays the evils of slavery, became a religious classic, giving theological reasons to oppose slavery. In its first year, it sold over three hundred thousand copies, despite being widely banned in the South. It was probably the greatest vehicle for the popularization of the abolitionist movement. When Abraham Lincoln met Stowe during the Civil War, he supposedly said she was "the little woman who wrote the book that made this great war!"[1]

Northern religious resistance to slavery took on an increasingly activist tone during the 1850s. In addition to resisting via noncompliance with and active defiance of the Fugitive Slave Act of 1850, some religious individuals engaged in efforts to assist enslaved persons in reaching freedom in Canada through the famous "Underground Railroad." This was a network of individuals and groups that assisted African Americans who had escaped slavery by providing transportation and safe houses along the routes north. Religious individuals— and even some congregations—sheltered fugitives in direct violation of federal law, justifying their actions with the claim that God's laws superseded the laws of the nation (when the latter were unjust).

Federal law, stemming from the Missouri Compromise of 1820, forbade the extension of slavery into the western territories north of the southern border

---

1. Cindy Weinstein, ed., *The Cambridge Companion to Harriet Beecher Stowe* (New York: Cambridge University Press, 2004), 1.

of Missouri. But Southerners, eager for new states in the West to allow slavery, sought to overturn this ban, arguing that the inhabitants of each new state should decide the issue for themselves (popular sovereignty). When Kansas and Nebraska were organized as territories in 1854, the Missouri Compromise was repealed, touching off a violent conflict in Kansas between supporters and opponents of slavery. There was a rush into Kansas of outsiders who sought to steer the territory in one direction or the other; at one point there were two rival territorial legislatures with two rival constitutions, one slave and one free. Armed bands attacked and murdered the supporters of rival positions, such that the territory came to be known as "Bleeding Kansas." Religious individuals in the North and South rushed assistance to their respective sides; Henry Ward Beecher (1813–87), the brother of Harriet Beecher Stowe, preached for funds to buy rifles for the Free-Staters (those who wanted Kansas to be a state free of slavery), and the legend is that rifles shipped to them were packed in crates labeled "Beecher's Bibles."

The divide over slavery took on increasing religious fervency on both sides. One militant leader on the anti-slavery side was John Brown (1800–59), a Northern businessman who aided the abolitionist cause and the Underground Railroad. He left his business to take up arms in Kansas in 1855, participating in the open warfare (and massacres) in that territory. Brown became increasingly militant and displayed a religiously millenarian position, seeing himself as the "agent of God" to punish the South and the slave owners. In 1859, Brown organized an armed raid on the federal armory in Harper's Ferry, Virginia, intending to seize weapons and organize an armed uprising of enslaved persons in the area against the slave owners. The raid was foiled, and Brown arrested. Southerners rejoiced when Brown was executed, but many in the North considered him a religious martyr for the cause. At the start of the Civil War, Union troops marched into battle singing the popular hymn "John Brown's Body."

The growing animosity between North and South took on definite religious overtones, each party sure that God was on their side. The religious intensity of the Northern abolitionist attacks on slavery occasioned an equally intense and religious response from the supporters of slavery in the South. Since, at the time, the Bible was a ubiquitous authority, both sides attempted to enlist it for their own cause. It must be said, however, that even though Northern abolitionists supported the end of slavery (with a few exceptions), they generally did not believe in anything close to what many today would call racial equality. In fact, some advocates of the abolition of slavery could be rather racist themselves and were against slavery primarily because they believed the practice was injurious to the nation.

The Civil War and Christianity

National politics during the 1850s was fixated on slavery and the sectional conflicts. A new party, the Republicans, brought together a disparate coalition of former Whigs and Free-Soilers (advocates of the containment of slavery), and, although their presidential candidate in 1856 did not win, they were a rising force in American politics. The Democrats were fatefully divided before the 1860 election and ended up with two presidential candidates, while the Republicans nominated a relatively unknown Illinois lawyer, Abraham Lincoln (1809–65). Since Democratic votes were split, Lincoln won a convincing victory, despite carrying none of the Southern states. The election of Lincoln was the last straw for many Southerners, and, beginning with South Carolina, eleven Southern states seceded from the union to form the Confederate States of America in 1861. When Lincoln called up federal troops to quell the secession, the Confederacy called for troops to defend itself, and the American Civil War began on April 12, 1861.

The political division of the country also meant a similar religious division. The issue of slavery had already divided the Methodists and the Baptists into Northern and Southern groups during the 1840s, and the Presbyterians were the only other group to divide before the Civil War (in 1857). But sectional tensions were strong in other denominations, and with the formation of the Confederacy in 1861, separate Episcopal, Roman Catholic, and Lutheran churches were organized in the South. Some denominations—such as the Congregationalists, Quakers, and Unitarians—did not face division because they had very few (if any) congregations in the South. The situation was more complicated for Christian denominations in the border states (Missouri, Kentucky, and Tennessee), where the sectional divisions were less clearly delineated. Groups like the Lutheran Church–Missouri Synod attempted to take a mediating position, and the Christian Church (Disciples of Christ) was the sole major denomination to avoid division.

The onset of the war was met with great religious zeal on both sides. Very few anticipated that it would be as long and bloody as it was. Preachers on both sides delivered impassioned sermons urging listeners to give their all for the war effort and declaring that God was on their side and that their cause was God's cause. The war occasioned intense religious activity and revivals, especially among the troops as the war dragged on. Though there were no formal means for recognizing and regulating them, thousands of Christian pastors (regularly called and self-appointed) traveled with the troops, an estimated twenty-three hundred of them with the Union armies and eight hundred among the Confederate forces. Wartime religious revivals in the military camps were intense, and it has been estimated that close to two hundred thousand Union soldiers and one hundred thousand Confederate soldiers were converted, perhaps close to 10 percent of the combined forces. Sometimes religious figures joined the army directly, such as Episcopal bishop of Louisiana Leonidas Polk (1806–64) and Southern Presbyterian layman Thomas "Stonewall" Jackson (1824–63), as well as others on the Union side.

Chaplains did much more than preach revivals. They aided the soldiers with daily needs, handed out supplies, and tended the wounded and dying. Organized religious benevolent groups—such as the United States Commission, the Sanitary Commission, and the American Tract Society—also ministered to the spiritual and physical needs of the Union soldiers. Similarly, the Union's Freedmen's Bureau aided those African Americans freed from slavery in territories taken from the Confederacy. Among Confederates, religious benevolent activities were also common, though less organized; because the war was fought largely on Southern territory, these needs were addressed on an ad hoc basis by local religious groups. Thousands of Christians—in both North and South—volunteered to serve the soldiers of their respective armies.

Given the religious fervor of the times, it is not surprising that the war itself took on millennial overtones. At least initially in the North, the war was generally less about the abolition of slavery and more about the maintenance of the American union of states. This union took on quasi-religious and millennial overtones; God had brought a new Israel into existence in North America, and the continuation of that union, whole and undivided, was God's work. As the popular wartime hymn composed by Julia Ward Howe (1819–1910), the "Battle Hymn of the Republic" stated,

> Mine eyes have seen the glory of the coming of the Lord:
> He is trampling out the vintage where the grapes of wrath are stored;
> He hath loosed the fateful lightning of His terrible swift sword:
> His truth is marching on.

The Union armies were God's millennial force. Later in the hymn, the soldiers were urged,

> As he [Christ] died to make men holy, let us die to make men free.[2]

It is not too much to say that before the Civil War America was a coalition of states, and that the Civil War made it a country (the Union) with an

---

2. Julia Ward Howe, "The Battle Hymn of the Republic," *Atlantic Monthly* 9, no. 52 (February, 1862), 10, https://www.theatlantic.com/past/docs/issues/1862feb/batthym.htm.

almost religious sense of itself—for good or for ill. This civil religion (religion of the country) bound people together and gave them a sense of the rightness of their cause.

Likewise, many in the Confederacy saw their nation and their cause in religious terms and held that they were defending their society from the godless forces of Northern aggression. They believed the South, as a region, was particularly blessed because of its faithfulness to God. Because the war was fought mainly in Southern territory, the Confederate soldiers were defending the sacred soil of the South. Even though the odds were against them, this fight was held to be a noble and religious duty. Despite the outcome, the conflict forged a new Southern identity that continued after the war.

Abraham Lincoln, "Second Inaugural Address," 1865

Neither party expected for the war the magnitude or the duration which it has already attained. Neither anticipated that the cause of the conflict might cease with, or even before, the conflict itself should cease. Each looked for an easier triumph, and a result less fundamental and astounding. Both read the same Bible, and pray to the same God; and each invokes his aid against the other. It may seem strange that any men should dare to ask a just God's assistance in wringing their bread from the sweat of other men's faces; but let us judge not, that we be not judged. The prayers of both could not be answered—that of neither has been answered fully.

The Almighty has his own purposes. "Woe unto the world because of offenses! For it must needs be that offenses come; but woe to that man by whom the offense cometh." If we shall suppose that American slavery is one of those offenses which, in the providence of God, must needs come, but which, having continued through his appointed time, he now wills to remove, and that he gives to both North and South this terrible war, as the woe due to those by whom the offense came, shall we discern therein any departure from those divine attributes which the believers in a living God always ascribe to him? Fondly do we hope—fervently do we pray—that this mighty scourge of war may speedily pass away. Yet, if God wills that it continue until all the wealth piled by the bondman's two hundred and fifty years of unrequited toil shall be sunk, and until every drop of blood drawn with the lash shall be paid by another drawn with the sword, as was said three thousand years ago, so still it must be said, "The judgments of the Lord are true and righteous altogether."

With malice toward none; with charity for all; with firmness in the right, as God gives us to see the right, let us strive on to finish the work we are in.

Abraham Lincoln, "Second Inaugural Address, March 4, 1865," in *Abraham Lincoln: Speeches and Writings, 1859–1865* (New York: Library of America, 1989), 686–87.

One of the most intriguing religious figures of the Civil War was the Union president, Abraham Lincoln. Despite not being formally religious or even a church member—though he attended church regularly while in Washington, DC—he was perhaps one of the most fascinating theologians in American history. He was raised among Christians on the Indiana frontier, but it is not clear what his personal religious convictions were. Regardless, it is obvious that he knew much of the Bible by heart and that he saw much of the world through the lens of the biblical narrative. Many of Lincoln's writings and speeches are filled with biblical references and demonstrate a basic worldview primarily shaped by the Bible. This is most apparent in his second inaugural address (1865), in which he wrote of the war's combatants, "Both read the same Bible, and pray to the same God; and each invokes his aid against the other. It may seem strange that any men should dare to ask a just God's assistance in wringing their bread from the sweat of other men's faces; but let us judge not, that we be not judged. The prayers of both could not be answered—that of neither has been answered fully. The Almighty has his own purposes." When asked once if God was on the side of the Union, Lincoln replied that rather he hoped the Union was on the side of God.

Such nuance is not only refreshing but also more true to the biblical God than the certitude of so many others that God was definitively on their side. When Lincoln was assassinated on April 14, 1865—which also happened to be Good Friday—he instantly became a messianic Christ-figure in the eyes of many Northerners, God's martyr for the Union cause, literally for the cause of God. One wonders what Lincoln himself would have thought of that.

Reconstruction

The end of the Civil War in 1865 occasioned a furious debate in the North about the reunification of the country and about how the South should be treated. Hardliners in the North urged that the South be treated harshly and that Southern states should only be readmitted to the union after a lengthy period of reconstruction. Lincoln's successor, Andrew Johnson, was from a border state and willing to go light on the South, including allowing their racial subjection of the newly freed African Americans. But radical Republicans in Congress overrode Johnson's policies and passed the Fourteenth (1868) and Fifteenth (1870) Amendments to the Constitution, granting citizenship and rights to African Americans. Federal troops were stationed in the South to oversee this reconstruction, and the Southern states had to conform their constitutions to the national one. Some African Americans were even elected to state legislatures and to Congress during this period. Reconstruction lasted until the tumultuous election of 1876, which was thrown to Congress to decide. A corrupt bargain was struck whereby the Republican candidate could win in return for a pledge to withdraw federal troops from the South. This meant the end of Reconstruction and the beginning of a very dark period for African Americans in the South.

Some Christian denominations that were divided by the war were reunited almost immediately after, including the Episcopalians and the Roman Catholics. For others, it was a longer road. The Lutherans were reunited in 1917, the Methodists in 1939, and the Presbyterians not until 1983. The Baptists of the North and South have not yet reunited, and the Southern Baptist Convention remains the single largest Protestant group in the United States.

One important part of the Reconstruction effort was the work of the Freedmen's Bureau, a federal office under the War Department that was charged with caring for the newly freed African Americans in the South. Under the leadership of General Oliver Otis Howard (1830–1909), sometimes known as the "Christian General" for his fervent piety, the bureau recruited hundreds of local agents (often Northern abolitionists) to provide for the needs and rights of formerly enslaved persons. Despite opposition from President Johnson and local White Southerners, the Freedmen's Bureau worked with benevolent groups in the North to establish three thousand schools for African Americans in the South and to serve the needs of four million newly freed women and men. More controversially, the bureau also often worked to ensure the political rights of African Americans, which resulted, for a brief time, in a thriving Republican Party in the South among this group. This organization was scaled back by Congress after 1869 and ceased operations in 1872.

Other Northern religious and benevolent groups also worked among Southern African Americans after the war, attempting to support the work of the Freedmen's Bureau and other federal efforts. But these Northerners were despised by White Southerners as "carpetbaggers" and agitators, and with the end of Reconstruction many such Northerners were chased out of the South. Strangely, after the war the attention of many Northern abolitionists turned away from African Americans in the South and toward many other social crusades, such as temperance and women's rights. It was as if they considered the legal abolition of slavery to be enough, without considering the needs of the people they had fought so strongly to free.

The defeat of the South in 1865 and their forced reintegration into the union was a bitter blow for Southerners, who had been as convinced of the holiness of their cause as the Northerners had been of theirs. Some questioned whether God had abandoned his people in the Confederacy.

7.2. Reconstruction Voting in the South.

Increasingly, however, many Southerners threw off the effects of the defeat to reaffirm that although they had been militarily conquered by the North, their religious and social causes had not been overcome and in fact were as valid as they had ever been. The military might of the North was likened to the armies of the Assyrians in the Old Testaments: ungodly people who had been used by God to "chastise" the South (the new Israel), but that did not mean that they had been abandoned—they remained the chosen people of God. The society of the South before the war was remembered in a romantic haze as almost Edenic, and Southerners were still convinced that their cause was just. This ideology, often referred to as the "Religion of the Lost Cause," remained an integral part of White Southern culture. Looking at the postwar developments in the North with disdain as an abandonment of both Christianity and civilization, White Southerners retained a deep confidence in their own Christian virtues. While the Civil War became a memory in the North fairly quickly, it became a central part of Southern identity for generations to come. Confederate soldiers and generals were immortalized in bronze and in annual observances as a part of the Southern, regional version of civil religion.

After the war, many White Americans in the South effectively re-enslaved African Americans through economic subjection, legal and social harassment, and violence. After the end of Reconstruction and the withdrawal of federal troops from the South, White Southerners harshly repressed African Americans, and White Northerners did nothing to stop them. Groups based on a perversion of Christianity, such as the Ku Klux Klan, terrorized African Americans into submission. It is important to note that the Klan was also found in Northern areas, and African Americans suffered similar discrimination in the North.

African American Churches

African Americans took advantage of their newfound freedom in many ways, but especially through the formation of their own independent Christian congregations and denominations. Prior to the Civil War, a sizable percentage of the churchgoers in the White-led denominations in the South were African Americans, although they were often relegated to separate sections within the local congregations. After the war there was a definitive split within Southern Christianity as African Americans left or were pushed out (both happened) of White-led churches, and so Christian congregations in the South became highly racially separate. Since segregation was fast becoming the norm in the South, many Whites extended this idea to the churches. But many African Americans left White churches of their own accord, as they longed to escape to independent congregations of their own. It is important to recall that some 90 percent of all African Americans before the First World War lived in the South, and the vast majority of them lived in rural areas.

The strongest African American denominations were those formed in the North prior to the Civil War, especially the African Methodist Episcopal (AME) Church and the AME Zion Church. These denominations started almost immediately at the end of the war to expand into the South, as typified by AME bishop Daniel Payne's triumphant return to Charleston, South Carolina, in 1865. In the city he had fled thirty years previously, Payne sought to organize AME congregations among the African American residents of the area. But the efforts of the Northern-based AME and AME Zion denominations were resisted by some local African Americans who sought to establish their own Methodist organizations. In 1870, a group of African Americans from within the Methodist Episcopal Church, South, withdrew from this denomination to form their own: the Colored Methodist Episcopal (CME) Church (later renamed the Christian Methodist Episcopal Church). The competition between the CME and the AME and AME Zion denominations was intense and, at times, hostile. AME leaders derided the CME as "sellouts" and as the "Rebel Church" or the "Democratic Church." CME leaders resented the AME Church as "carpetbaggers" and "sheep-stealers." Because of the centralized nature of Methodist church organization, this conflict was pronounced. But even with all this, the three groups could (and did) cooperate at times, especially concerning the sponsorship of African American missionaries to Africa later on.

Probably two-thirds of all African Americans after the Civil War were Baptists, but since the Baptists were much less denominationally structured than the Methodists, they were much slower to form regional and national associations. Many of the local African American Baptist congregations organized after the war were created from the informal and independent congregations that already existed. Although an early state association of African American Baptists was formed in North Carolina in 1866, other regional associations were slow to form, and the National Baptist Convention was not established until 1895. Baptists in America have been divided into dozens of different traditional families, and such splintering happened among the African American Baptists as well. A group of African Americans left the Primitive Baptists in 1866 to form their own Colored Primitive Baptist organization, just one of many such splits.

The Baptists were not the only denomination to divide along racial lines. Similar divisions also occurred in other denominations: Presbyterian (e.g., the Colored Cumberland Presbyterian Church, 1874), Episcopal, Lutheran (e.g., the Alpha Synod of the Evangelical Lutheran Church of Freedmen in America, 1889), and even Roman Catholic (in such locations as Louisiana and Maryland). It is difficult to determine the size of these associations, which were outside the organized Methodist groups. By 1880, the AME comprised 400,000 members, the AME Zion 250,000 members, and the CME 120,000 members. Extrapolating from the fact that African American Methodists have historically represented approximately 25 percent of the total religious population, it seems reasonable to estimate that at the time there may have been up to three million African Americans in these independent denominational families.

These congregations and denominations were the central core of the African American community—not only religiously but also socially and, later, politically—as they were some of the few independent organizations allowed to African Americans, especially after Reconstruction and during the brutal repressions of segregation and the "Jim Crow" era. African American preachers and ministers were the de facto leaders of their communities, guiding them through very difficult periods. Some later African American writers have derided these preachers for a perceived lack of resistance to White suppression, even to the point of suggesting that they preached an "otherworldly" gospel of "pie-in-the-sky-when-you-die." But to be fair to these African American pastors, they had a very challenging task in a remarkably hostile time, and the larger society allowed them very little power.

One important aspect of African American Christianity after the Civil War was the formation of schools and educational institutions for their communities. Since public education for African Americans was either totally lacking or wholly inadequate, especially in the South, African American denominations made a priority of forming their own schools and colleges. As early as 1856, the AME formed Wilberforce College (now Wilberforce University) in Ohio, and after the war dozens more African American schools followed. They were aided in this by the American Missionary Association, a Northern abolitionist organization (mainly Congregationalist) formed in 1846. One of the few abolitionist groups active in the South after the war, this association worked with African American leaders to form twenty schools before 1870, including what are now Fisk University, Howard University, and Hampton University.

Postwar Immigration and Religion

Immigration to the United States resumed strongly after the Civil War and accelerated until the First World War (1914–18). Most of these new immigrants were non-English-speakers from Continental Europe: first Protestants, and then an increasing number of Roman Catholics and Jews. As good and available farmland was increasingly settled, later immigrants crowded into the rapidly growing cities or into mining and manufacturing areas. Religion was an important element of immigrant societies, as a means of ethnic and language maintenance if nothing else, but immigrant religion was very complicated. It is sometimes imagined that immigrants headed to the nearest ethnic congregation right after getting off the boat. But this is a myth. Immigrants enjoyed the religious freedom and pluralism of America and exercised their ability to choose different religious options, or often no religion at all. Immigrant pastors and priests had to work extremely hard just to gather in even a fraction of "their" people, who were scattered around the country. Only between 10 and 30 percent of Scandinavian immigrants, for example, joined one of the ethnically based Scandinavian American denominations, and these percentages are on par with those of other groups as well. Often having had little or no religious choices in their home country, immigrants sought to control their own religious destinies in the New World.

One major beneficiary of this wave of immigrants was the Roman Catholic Church, which grew to 3.5 million members by 1880. Immigration from

Library of Congress / Wikimedia Commons

7.3. Immigrants at Ellis Island.

Ireland tailed off after the war, but immigration from Germany, Austria, Italy, and Poland accelerated, leading to an even greater ethnic diversity of Roman Catholics in America. These immigrants formed a complex of ethnic parishes and schools, served by immigrant priests and religious orders of women and men. Since many leaders were members of religious orders, they were often not under the direct control of the local Roman Catholic bishops, which caused complications. While by 1880 there were six thousand Roman Catholic priests in the United States, there were twenty-two thousand women religious (nuns). Additionally, ethnic rivalry was a constant factor in church politics. Irish Americans, having arrived early and in large numbers, were quick to take control of the American Roman Catholic hierarchy, just as they did in urban politics in many cities.

The popes and bishops of the European Roman Catholic hierarchy were dubious of so many of their people going to the United States, which they considered an "ungodly" and Protestant place. Roman Catholic leaders in America were somewhat less concerned but fought hard to see that their people remained good and obedient members of the Church. One huge worry was the generally Protestant nature of public schools, which led to a strong push for every parish to have its own parochial school. American Roman Catholics also began an impressive network of higher schools and colleges, which eventually numbered in the hundreds.

American Roman Catholics also had to deal with persistent anti-Catholicism from Protestant Americans. Roman Catholic aversion to public education, their use of ethnic languages, and their loyalty to the papacy suggested to their Protestant opponents that while immigrant Catholics were in America, they were not becoming Americans. This suspicion was increased by the very conservative (even reactionary) opposition to democracy by European Roman Catholic leaders—especially the popes. The First Vatican Council, in 1870, pronounced as dogma the doctrinal infallibility of the pope, confirming the suspicions of many Protestants. But most American Roman Catholics strongly averred that they could, in fact, be good Roman Catholics and good American citizens simultaneously, despite the skepticism of European Roman Catholic leaders and American anti-Catholics.

Archbishop John Hughes on the Need of Parochial Education, 1840

Besides the introduction of the Holy Scriptures without note or comment, with the prevailing theory that from these even children are to get their notions of religion, contrary to our principles, there were in the class-books of those schools false (as we believe) historical statements respecting the men and things of past times, calculated to fill the minds of our children with errors of fact, and at the same time to excite in them prejudice against the religion of their parents and guardians. These passages were not considered as sectarian, inasmuch as they had been selected as mere reading lessons, and were not in favor of any particular sect, but merely against the Catholics. We feel it is unjust that such passages should be taught at all in schools, to the support of which we are contributors as well as others. . . .

If the public schools could have been constituted on a principle which would have secured a perfect NEUTRALITY of influence on the subject of religion, then we should have no reason to complain. But this has not been done, and we respectfully submit that it is impossible. The cold indifference with which it is required that all religion shall be treated in those schools—the Scriptures without note or comment—the selection of passages, as reading lessons, from Protestants and prejudiced authors, on points in which our creed is supposed to be involved—the comments of the teacher, of which the commissioners cannot be cognizant—the school libraries, stuffed with sectarian works against us—form against our religion a combination of influences prejudicial to our religion, and to whose action it would be criminal in us to expose our children at such an age.

John R. C. Hassard, *Life of the Most Reverend John Hughes* (New York: D. Appleton & Co., 1866), 230–32.

Lutherans were another major group of immigrants in this period. Immigrant Lutherans had the advantage of being Protestants (of a sort) and the disadvantage of using non-English languages. While the longer-settled eastern Lutherans had already adopted English, these new immigrants insisted on using the languages of their European homelands. Though many American Protestants saw these Lutherans as "good" immigrants and promising candidates for assimilation into their own "English" churches, the language barrier and the fact that so many settled in rural ethnic enclaves in the Upper Midwest largely prevented such assimilation.

Internal theological and ethnic tensions were rife within American Lutheranism, and without the overall umbrella of the European state churches, these new Lutherans soon broke up into separate regional and national synods. Between these groups and those stemming from the division of previously established American Lutherans over theological issues and the Civil War, there were soon at least twenty major Lutheran groups and many other smaller ones. One major cluster of tensions involved the renewal and awakening movements in nineteenth-century European Lutheranism, which dominated within the immigrant Lutheran churches in North America. These pietist Lutherans consciously decided that they would not replicate the European state churches; rather, they would build a new form of Lutheranism within the American context. But they did not adopt American models uncritically. The nature and degree of these adoptions became a major sticking point within American Lutheranism, and questions of how far to adhere to the sixteenth-century Lutheran confessional writings became and remained a point of major internal controversy.

Although the Lutherans, in total, were not as numerous as the Roman Catholics, they did parallel them in a number of different ways. For one, as Roman Catholics came to dominate many of the eastern cities, Lutherans came to dominate many rural areas of the Midwest and Upper Midwest. They also established a network of Lutheran schools and colleges, as well as an impressive array of hospitals and social service agencies.

The experiences of the later Calvinist or Reformed Protestant immigrants to the United States were similar to those of the Lutheran immigrants. By the middle of the nineteenth century, the colonial branches of the Reformed tradition (Dutch and German) had switched to the use of English and moved closer to their American Calvinist cousins. The newer Reformed immigrants from Germany and Holland came in the middle of the nineteenth century and formed their own ethnic congregations, mainly in the Midwest. The later German Reformed congregations formed the German Evangelical Synod of North America in 1840, which maintained the German language tradition until the early twentieth century. Midcentury Dutch immigrants likewise formed ethnic congregations, some of which eventually joined the Reformed Church in America. But other Dutch immigrant congregations, led by pastors who had dissented from the Reformed state church in Holland, gathered in Michigan in 1857 to form the Christian Reformed Church. This group was marked by a more conservative and confessionally strict form of Dutch Calvinism and maintained its distance from the Reformed Church in America.

Orthodox Christianity, the dominant form of Christianity in eastern Europe, Russia, and the Middle East, was also established in America by the nineteenth-century immigration of peoples from these regions (although Orthodox immigrants would later come in greater numbers). Like the Roman Catholics, the Orthodox are led by ruling bishops, but unlike the Roman Catholics, the Orthodox have no central leader (like the pope), so the early Orthodox churches in America were divided by ethnicity and relations to their homeland churches and leaders. The earliest Orthodox churches in the United States were Russian, and a Russian Orthodox diocese was transferred from Alaska to San Francisco in 1872. Though this church sought to gather in other Orthodox parishes, ethnic and theological differences meant the eventual proliferation of Orthodox church bodies. Some Orthodox groups transferred themselves under papal control but maintained their own languages and theological and ecclesiastical customs; these groups were then referred to as Uniates or Greek Catholics.

Religion in the West

The push to expand White settlement into the western half of the country, stalled out by the Civil War, strongly resumed after 1865 as new immigrants and those seeking economic advancement poured into these areas. The Homestead Act of 1862 granted millions of acres of land to farmers and ranchers willing to settle on them. The line of settlement expanded into the Great Plains region (the Dakotas, Nebraska, and Kansas) until, by the 1880s, most of the good land was taken. Areas of the Pacific coast (especially Northern California and Oregon) drew more Americans, and the Mormons built their proposed "State of Deseret" in the Intermountain Region around the Great Salt Lake. The completion of the transcontinental railroad in 1869, along with other subsequent rail lines, increased these movements, and telegraph lines were strung across the West. Discoveries of gold, silver, and other important minerals created a number of western "rushes" and boom towns, and forestry and fishing were also important economic engines.

The initial White settlements in the West were often haphazard and filled with transient populations, predominantly men. Religious organizations were gradually developed along eastern patterns by farmers and ranchers on the Great Plains, but religious institutions remained scarce west of this region. Traveling home missionaries often covered vast amounts of territory to meet with scattered groups of believers. The Presbyterian pastor Sheldon Jackson (1834–1909) organized dozens of congregations from Denver to Seattle and then, in 1877, pushed up into Alaska. Roman Catholic priest Pierre-Jean de Smet (1801–73) was an early presence throughout the Dakotas and Montana and set up missions for the Native American populations there. Numerous other Protestant and Roman Catholic home missionaries traveled the region and founded congregations, although shifting populations and lack of resources meant that many of these did not survive. One important marker of success and permanence in these settlements was the eventual presence of women, who were often vital to the continuation of organized religious life on the frontier.

But religious life continued to be weak in the West, and there was no single religious pattern there; specific groups might, at most, be regionally important. The Roman Catholic Church predominated across the Southwest and Southern California, where eastern bishops like Jean Baptiste Lamy (1814–80) reorganized the predominantly Hispanic parishes. The Mormons dominated in the Utah region, though Protestant pastors attempted to establish a presence there. On the West Coast there was the establishment of eastern-style Protestant congregations, especially in the San Francisco-Sacramento region of California and the Willamette Valley of Oregon, but these congregations remained a religious option, rather than dominating the area. And Asian immigrants to the West Coast brought their own religious traditions and institutions. The result was a checkerboard of religious life, with numerous religious options. The options grew only slowly, and in many places organized religious life remained weak. This religious pattern continued to define the region, parts of which are among the least "churched" areas of the country even today.

The late nineteenth-century expansion of White settlement into the West was a complete disaster for the Native Americans in the region. Faced with this threat, many tribes attempted to defend their traditional territories and ways of life by resistance and force, bringing them into armed conflict with federal troops. Although Native American resistance was effective at times, eventually they were militarily defeated and confined to reservations around the West. As a part of this reservation system, the federal government pledged to support the tribes economically and to protect them, but these pledges and peace treaties were often broken or unfulfilled. Native communities were decimated by war, violence, alcohol, disease, and exploitation, destroying many lives and wreaking havoc on their cultures and religious lives.

Christian missionaries sought to assist the Native Americans, but their efforts were often episodic at best, and many of their efforts did more harm than good. The general conception at the time among Whites was that Native Americans needed to be incorporated into the economic, social, and religious patterns of the dominant White communities in the United States or they would not survive. Given the understandable Native resistance to this, officials and missionaries often felt they had to destroy Native cultures and ways of life, especially through education of younger generations, in order to bringing Native Americans into the dominant culture. President Ulysses S. Grant (1822–85) instituted his Peace Policy toward the Native Americans in 1869. This policy granted access to religious organizations (mostly Northern Protestants) who would contract with the federal government to manage up to seventy Native reservations in the West. Religious workers built mission schools and distributed federal aid, and some Native Americans did convert to Christianity. Others resisted, maintaining their traditional religious practices or developing their own creative combinations of Christianity and Native religions.

Change and Diversity within Protestantism

The period after the Civil War saw a continuation of the growth of White Protestantism, even as increasing theological diversity threatened to divide the old, prewar evangelical consensus, especially in the North and Midwest. There was a definite liberalizing trend within the more established Protestant denominations that set in motion a counterreaction among conservatives within these groups, who were dismayed by what they saw as a loss of their original integrity and positions. This was especially true among the Northern Methodists and Baptists, which had grown so quickly, and true to a lesser extent in other denominations.

The old Protestant consensus had been formed on a conversionistic evangelicalism, with revivalism and Arminianism providing its theological base. Such an emphasis on conversion suggested that people in their "natural," preconversion state were lost souls and discernable sinners. Conversion meant a near instantaneous transformation, and those converted often dramatically recounted the darkness of their preconversion lives, in stark contrast with their blessed lives after being awakened. But given the general optimism of the age, even in the church there were some who questioned or downplayed the whole element of dramatic, life-changing conversions and the dismal theology of human beings in their "natural" state. Along the lines of Horace Bushnell's *Christian Nurture*, liberalizers within these Protestant churches envisioned the human person as essentially good and the moral life as a gradual journey toward improvement.

Unlike the Unitarians, most of these liberals did not discard traditional Christian orthodoxy wholesale, but they did begin to downplay a number of doctrines, including the atonement, original sin, and predestination. For them, Christian improvement was tied to moral improvement, following the teachings and example of Jesus, and downplaying those "older" parts of the Bible and Christian faith that seemed increasingly irrelevant.

The most visible transformation, and the greatest internal tensions, can be seen among the Methodists, especially outside the South. It is sometimes difficult to remember how strange and countercultural the early Methodists seemed to the other Christian groups around them. Initially, Methodism was often seen as a dangerous and bizarre sect, which respectable people would not join. But because of their vigor and their message, they became a huge success, growing from nothing to become the largest Protestant group in America by 1850. But success often has within it the seeds of its own decline; not that the Methodists declined, but their dramatic early growth leveled off, and they were eventually surpassed by both the Roman Catholics and the Baptists.

As the Methodists succeeded, they took on all the elements of middle-class Protestant respectability. Traveling circuit riders and homegrown amateur preachers gave way to a regularized and educated clergy. Strict personal holiness standards were increasingly relaxed, and members were allowed personal behaviors that would have been unthinkable in previous generations. The rough-and-tumble revivals of the camp meetings faded, and the camps themselves were gradually transformed into middle-class summer resorts, complete with edifying lectures. Social distinctions crept in, as with the practice of "pew rents," whereby wealthier Methodists paid for prestigious and prominent seats in the church sanctuary, while poorer Methodists were shunted to the back and sides. Humble Methodist chapels gave way to large and impressive brick and stone church buildings, with large pipe organs, rivaling even the buildings of the Episcopalians. Methodists built an impressive system of colleges and seminaries and firmly increased the educational standards for their pastors. And church power was increasingly centralized, especially in the hands of the Methodist bishops. Causation is difficult to prove, and it cannot be said that these factors account completely for the stall in Methodist growth, but that stall went hand-in-hand with the shift of Methodism from countercultural radical movement to respectable middle-class establishment.

Traditional and conservative Methodists decried what they saw as the loss of the original vision and vigor of the early movement. The venerable Methodist circuit rider Peter Cartwright (1785–1872) wrote an autobiographical book in 1856 that lambasted his Methodist colleagues for these changes, and his example was followed by a number of others. In the 1850s, a Methodist pastor and leader in upstate New York, Benjamin Roberts (1823–93), began attacking the leaders of what he called the "New School" of Methodism and eventually was deemed so disruptive that he and some of his followers were expelled from the church. This group eventually formed the Free Methodist Church in 1860. The Wesleyan Methodist Church, which had separated from the northern Methodists in 1843 over the issue of abolitionism, after the Civil War also became a vehicle for those disaffected from the Methodist Episcopal Church. These dissenting groups remained small but represented the concerns of others within the larger Methodist denomination.

One of the traditional distinctives of the Methodist movement—going back to John Wesley himself—was a stress on personal holiness. While holding to the Protestant understanding that one is justified (made right with God) through faith alone, the Methodists also believed that, through the creative work of the Holy Spirit, one could grow in holiness, even to entire sanctification. Many Methodist dissidents seized on this theme as the key teaching they wished to reinvigorate and restore. One of the first major leaders in this "Holiness" movement was the evangelist Phoebe Palmer (1807–74), who urged traditional Wesleyan themes through her popular evangelistic preaching and writings, especially her book *The Way of Holiness*. Concentrating on the traditional practices of revivalism and the camp meetings, others formed the National Camp Meeting Association for the Promotion of Holiness in 1867, with a network of camps and speakers dedicated to such themes. During this time, these dissenters mostly remained as a movement within the larger Methodist Church, but many later would heed the call to "come out" and form separate Holiness and Wesleyan groups. In the wider religious culture, these themes of holiness and personal transformation in Christ were spread through wildly popular gospel hymns. Fanny Crosby (1820–1915) was the leader of this, but she was joined by many others.

Part of the Holiness movement was a renewed emphasis on the personal appropriation of God's Holy Spirit in the life of the believer and the benefits this relationship accrued. One significant publication on this theme came in 1870: *The Baptism of the Holy Spirit*, by Asa Mahan (1799–1889). Mahan was president of Oberlin College until he was forced out; then he became a leader in the Wesleyan Methodist Church. Another important book on the topic was written by Boston Baptist minister Adoniram Judson Gordon (1836–95), whose works explored the "fruits of the Holy Spirit" in the believer, especially faith healing and prophecy. Holiness and these gifts of the Holy Spirit became an

Phoebe Palmer on the Need for Holiness

She [an unnamed sister in the faith] now saw that holiness, instead of being an attainment beyond her reach, was a state of grace in which every one of the Lord's redeemed ones should live—that the service was indeed a "reasonable service," inasmuch as the command, "Be ye holy," is founded upon the absolute right which God, as our Creator, Preserver, and Redeemer, has upon the entire service of his creatures.

Instead of perceiving anything meritorious in what she had been enabled, through grace, to do, i.e., in laying all upon the altar; she saw that she had but rendered back to God that which was already his own.

She looked upon family, influence, earthly possessions, &c., and chidingly, in view of former misappropriation, said to her heart, "What hast thou, that thou hast not received? And if received, why didst thou glory in them as of thine own begetting?" And though with Abraham in the sacrifice of his beloved Isaac, she was called seemingly to sacrifice that of all earthly objects surpassingly dear, yet so truly did she now see that the "Giver of every good gift" but rightfully required his own in his own time, that she could only say, "The Lord gave, and the Lord hath taken away, blessed be the name of the Lord."

And Oh, what cause for deep and perpetual abasement before God did she now perceive, in that she had so long kept back part of that price which, by the requirement of that blessed word, she now so clearly discerned infinite love had demanded; and when the inquiries were presented, "Is God unreasonable in his requirements? Hath he given the command, 'Be ye holy,' and not given the ability with the command, for the performance of it?" Her inmost soul, penetrated, with a sense of past unfaithfulness, acknowledged not only the reasonableness of the command, but also the unreasonableness of not having lived in obedience to such a plain Scriptural requirement.

Mrs. P. Palmer, *The Way of Holiness, with Notes by the Way* (New York: G. Lane and C. B. Tippett, 1845), 33–35.

increasingly common motif. Popular events—such as the annual Keswick Convention in England (beginning in 1875) and the American Bible and Prophecy Conference (in New York in 1878)—furthered these themes.

These conservatives also differed from the mainstream of American Protestants in their increasing embrace of premillennialism—the idea that the world would end in trauma, along the lines of the biblical book of Revelation. Although the Millerite movement disintegrated after the Great Disappointment of 1844, scattered groups continued these themes, which grew in popularity. Ellen G. White (1827–1915) was influenced by the Millerite revivals and founded the Seventh-day Adventist movement in 1860, which embraced a form of premillennialism. Out of a similar trajectory, Charles Taze Russell

(1852–1916) gathered a Bible study movement that eventually became the Jehovah's Witnesses. British preacher John Nelson Darby (1800–1882) embraced premillennialism and popularized it in the United States through seven very popular preaching tours between 1859 and 1874. Darby's teachings were the core of the Niagara Bible Conference, which took place annually from 1875 to 1897. As the nineteenth century moved toward its end, the premillennialist worldview became increasingly common and important among conservative White Protestants in America, eventually dividing them from the mainstream Protestant denominations.

Women and American Christianity

Throughout the history of Christianity in America, women have constituted the majority of church members. And in some times and places, they have outnumbered men by up to two-to-one. Without the presence of women in frontier congregations, such organizations would have hardly been possible. As should be abundantly clear from the narrative so far, the formal leadership of American Christianity continued to be male. But American Christianity depended on women. Although true equality was still a long way off, by the middle of the nineteenth century there were some cracks in the male domination of Christian leadership, and women were organizing in powerful ways to support religious causes important to them.

Some of the most important changes affecting women in Christianity were social and demographic, as the changing nature of American society created new opportunities for them. The shifting nature of the workforce and family meant that women's roles changed. Male workers now increasingly went out from the home to separate workplaces (such as offices, factories, or stores), and the home became a female-dominated realm. Labor-saving devices and greater economic security meant that women now had the time and resources for outside activities in the church and community. Women had a distinct social and religious sphere of their own, and they were increasingly exercising control within it.

Some women sought or took leadership roles for themselves within American Christianity. While women's leadership was not unknown among groups like the Quakers and Unitarians, mainstream Protestants lagged behind in this area. The first woman to become a regularly ordained Protestant pastor was Antoinette Brown (1825–1921), an 1846 graduate of Oberlin College who was ordained by a Congregational church in New York in 1853. She remained a parish pastor for only a few years, but this was an event rather far ahead of its time. Other women were leaders in more commonly accepted ways; they were recognized as evangelists or itinerant preachers, proclaiming the gospel but not having permanent, direct power over a mixed congregation. African American preacher Jarena Lee (1783–ca. 1850) was licensed by the African Methodist Episcopal Church in 1819, and other Methodist women increasingly gained similar power. Women such as Phoebe Palmer (Holiness movement) and Ellen G. White (Seventh-day Adventists) were also active in national leadership outside the mainstream Protestant denominations.

Christian denominations allowed for organized groups of women who were "set aside" for religious service, including the powerful Roman Catholic women's religious orders (including orders for African American women) and the deaconess movement among American Protestants, especially the Methodists, Lutherans, and Episcopalians. In these orders women carried out religious and social services, especially in education and health care, on their own terms. At a time when the social "safety net" was thin at best, these women provided crucial services for church and society. Groups of immigrant women, both Roman Catholic and Protestant, were vital to the establishment of their religious traditions in the United States.

An initial area where women gained power and a voice was in the movement for the abolition of slavery. Women like the Grimké sisters, Harriet Beecher Stowe, Sojourner Truth, and Harriet Tubman were important and nationally recognized figures in this movement. After the Civil War, many of these same women turned their attention to gaining voting rights for women in the suffrage movement. Having gained the right of African American men to vote, now they wanted the same rights for themselves. And these rights were not only sought in the political realm; increasingly, women pushed for a voting role in congregations and denominations, although these were slow in coming. Other women gained a powerful voice through the postwar temperance movement. Frances Willard (1838–98), who was refused ordination in the Methodist Church, turned her considerable talents to the cause of temperance. Out of a series of local temperance crusades in Ohio and New York, the national Woman's Christian Temperance Union was formed in 1874 and became a national force after Willard assumed its presidency in 1879.

Women also formed local and national groups to support domestic and foreign missions. Women were especially important in the missions of evangelism, education, and health care; being sent into traditional cultures, these women missionaries could enter homes and work with women and children where male missionaries could not. In 1873, Presbyterian sisters Sue McBeth (1830–93) and Kate McBeth (1833–1915) began a long-running mission among the Nez Percé tribe in Idaho, and Southern Baptist Charlotte "Lottie" Moon

7.4. Temperance Prayer Meeting in a Saloon.

(1840–1912) commenced mission work in China that same year. The ecumenical Women's Union Missionary Society was formed in New York City in 1861, and by 1865 they had sent ten women missionaries to work in Asia. Other denominational women's missionary societies were founded among Northern and Southern Protestants in the 1860s and 1870s, until almost every Christian group in America had some sort of similar organization.

The successes of these women's mission and reform groups were made possible by local and regional women's groups, which funneled contributions to the national level. Women's societies in the local congregation could be an important (if not crucial) part of its work; indeed, besides sending funds off for missions, the local women raised funds for the operation and ministry of the congregation itself. Often these women's groups had a budget equal to or larger than the congregation or denomination. Wise male pastors knew that the support, or nonsupport, of their ministry by the women's groups could make or break their efforts. In hindsight, perhaps these groups now seem old-fashioned, or like half measures, but in them local women learned and practiced skills in organization, leadership, and fundraising, lessons on which later generations of religious women would build. They also took ownership of their own ministries, including those beyond their congregations. Through their efforts, they educated themselves in their faith and in cultures around the world.

———————— BIBLIOGRAPHY ————————

Braude, Ann. *Radical Spirits: Spiritualism and Women's Rights in Nineteenth-Century America*. Boston: Beacon, 1989.

Goen, C. C. *Broken Churches, Broken Nation: Denominational Schisms and the Coming of the Civil War*. Macon, GA: Mercer University Press, 1985.

Heyrman, Christine Leigh. *Southern Cross: The Beginnings of the Bible Belt*. Chapel Hill: University of North Carolina Press, 1998.

Holifield, E. Brooks. *Theology in America: Christian Thought from the Age of the Puritans to the Civil War*. New Haven: Yale University Press, 2003.

Hutchison, William R. *Errand to the World: American Protestant Thought and Foreign Missions*. Chicago: University of Chicago Press, 1987.

Kerr, K. Austin. *Organized for Prohibition: A New History of the Anti-Saloon League*. New Haven: Yale University Press, 1985.

Rable, George C. *God's Almost Chosen Peoples: A Religious History of the American Civil War*. Chapel Hill: University of North Carolina Press, 2010.

Raser, Harold E. *Phoebe Palmer, Her Life and Thought*. Lewiston, NY: Edwin Mellen, 1987.

Stout, Harry S. *Upon the Altar of the Nation: A Moral History of the Civil War*. New York: Viking, 2006.

Walker, Clarence E. *A Rock in a Weary Land: The African Methodist Episcopal Church during the Civil War and Reconstruction*. Baton Rouge: Louisiana State University Press, 1982.

8

Mass Immigration, New Ideas, and
Tensions over Modernity, 1880–1914

As THE NINETEENTH CENTURY DREW TO A CLOSE, the United
States continued the process of dramatic growth and development that had been
evident since its independence from Great Britain. This period saw the addition
of the last western territories as states, with statehood for North and South
Dakota, Montana, and Washington in 1889; for Wyoming and Idaho in 1890;
for Utah in 1896; for Oklahoma in 1907; and for Arizona and New Mexico in
1912. As of the 1890 census, the frontier was declared "closed," meaning that
population densities had risen to "settled" status throughout the country. The
population of the country doubled over thirty-five years, growing from fifty
million in 1880 to ninety-nine million in 1914.

A substantial portion of this growth was due to immigration, through which
at least fourteen million new persons arrived in the country during this period. The rate of immigration did not peak until the first two decades of the
twentieth century, with an average of one million immigrants arriving each
year in the United States from 1907 to 1914. The percentage of "foreign-born"
Americans in the country rose to 14 percent by the early twentieth century,
raising concerns among many "native-born" citizens. It was not just the percentages that raised concerns, but the fact that many of the newer immigrants
were Roman Catholics and Jews from southern and eastern Europe, or, on
the West Coast, Chinese and Japanese. In 1882 further Chinese immigration

was formally excluded, and in 1892 the facility at Ellis Island in New York was opened—not to welcome immigrants, but to screen out those immigrants who were "undesirable."

The growth in population fueled the continuing trend toward the urbanization and industrialization of the country. Recent immigrants and those relocating from rural areas swelled the cities of the East and Midwest, and nationally the percentage of Americans living in cities grew from 28 percent in 1880 to 46 percent in 1910; in the East it reached 71 percent by 1910. An abundance of natural resources and a growing workforce pushed the continued industrialization of the country, which had become a leading world industrial power by 1914. In 1910, though the number of Americans engaged in agriculture remained steady at about ten million, the number of those engaged in industry and commerce grew to twenty-five million. The trend toward industrialization and urbanization was also propelled by a wave of new inventions and technology, many developed by Americans, including the telephone, movies, recorded music, automobiles, airplanes, and many others. Growing electrical and telephone networks supported much of this growth. Improvements in medicine and sanitation led to longer life expectancies, and the prevalence of diseases such as typhus, cholera, and yellow fever was greatly reduced.

Toward the end of the nineteenth century, the United States expanded its global reach, especially in the Western Hemisphere and Pacific Ocean. The territory of Hawaii was annexed in 1898, and in that same year the United States went to war with Spain over its remaining territories in the Caribbean and the Pacific. With an American victory, Puerto Rico and Guam were annexed as territories and Cuba and the Philippines came under American protection. The United States gained control of the Panama Canal Zone in 1904 and, in a feat of engineering prowess, completed the canal there by 1914. While not formally annexing other territories in Latin America, the United States actively intervened in the internal affairs of many of these countries, sometimes militarily, to preserve or expand American interests. By the beginnings of the First World War, the United States had become a leading world power, though it did not always see itself as such.

The religious composition of the United States was greatly increased and diversified by the new immigration, as well as by new religious options developed within the country. The rate of religious adherence in the country grew from 35 percent in 1870 to 51 percent by 1906. The largest growth came from the immigration of millions of Roman Catholics from southern and eastern Europe; by 1900 there were fourteen million Roman Catholics in the country, making this denomination the largest single religious organization in the United States. But the Protestants also saw substantial growth, and as a whole they still outnumbered the Roman Catholics. At the beginning of the twentieth century, the Baptists led the way in Protestant growth. There were still more Methodists than Baptists at that point, but the Methodist share of religious membership had peaked in 1850, and by the 1920s the Baptists had surpassed the Methodists to become the largest Protestant family in the country. Immigration also fueled the growth of the Lutherans, who become the third-largest Protestant family by 1900, surpassing the Presbyterians, Congregationalists, and Episcopalians.[1]

Protestantism and Urban America

The growth of the American cities during the late nineteenth century created new challenges and opportunities for American Protestantism. While new immigrants added to the population of these cities, the bulk of their growth came from rural and small-town Protestants moving into urban areas. Although it is often assumed that urbanization and secularization went hand in hand and that these burgeoning American cities were largely irreligious places, the reality was that the percentage of people who were church members in these new cities was higher than it was in rural areas. In the 1906 religious census, the American government calculated the rate of religious adherence in the principal urban areas at 56 percent, higher than the 51 percent calculated for the nation as a whole.[2]

The growth of cities necessitated new ways of organizing and spreading religious life. Many new congregations were formed in the growing outer areas of the cities, either as church plants or as "daughter" congregations formed by inner-city congregations, many of whose members were already moving out to the new suburbs. But the influx of young rural Protestants into the cities demanded novel ways of reaching them and bringing them into Protestant congregations. The older revivalism, tailored to small towns and rural areas, had to be adjusted for urban areas. The pioneer in this was Dwight L. Moody (1837–99), a young man from Massachusetts who had moved to Chicago and become the premier urban revivalist. After a surprisingly successful two-year revival in England (1873–75), Moody and his song leader, Ira Sankey (1840–1908), returned to North America where they led hugely successful urban revivals in major cities over the next several decades. Moody's revivals were held in major

---

1. Edwin Scott Gaustad, *Historical Atlas of Religion in America*. rev. ed. (New York: Harper and Row, 1976), 11; and Roger Finke and Rodney Stark, *The Churching of America, 1776–2005: Winners and Losers in Our Religious Economy* (New Brunswick, NJ: Rutgers University Press, 2005), 23, 157.

2. Finke and Stark, *Churching of America*, 202.

8.1. Dwight L. Moody Preaching.

amphitheaters over a series of weeks, drawing in tens of thousands of hearers
every night. Blanketing the local media and featuring the memorable gospel
tunes of Sankey and others, Moody enlisted the aid of local Protestant preachers and rewarded them by referring new converts to their congregations. Just
as Finney before him had adapted revivalism to small-town America, Moody
brought it into the cities. Moody inspired a legion of other revivalists who
followed his example, especially the flamboyant and impassioned ex–base-
ball player William Ashley "Billy" Sunday (1862–1935), who was the leading
American revivalist after Moody's retirement.

   As many of the rural and small-town Protestants moving into the cities were
young, unmarried men and women, Protestant leaders worried about them
succumbing to all the activities that their traditional morality abhorred. Thus,
they sought to create Protestant institutions in the cities that would foster Protestant religiosity and morality. In this, the most important institution was the
Young Men's Christian Association (YMCA). Originally founded in London

in 1844, the first North American YMCA was established in Boston in 1851 and was soon followed by hundreds of local chapters in cities and on college campuses around the country. While the YMCA was a nondenominational movement, it was very much in the evangelical Protestant tradition and was a place where young men could find Christian companionship, Bible studies, recreation, and safe lodgings—in short, community and purpose in large and often unfamiliar cities. The YMCA also trained its members in personal evangelism and benevolent activities: reaching out to members of the military, the urban poor, and others; organizing Bible studies and Sunday schools; and performing social service outreach. The Young Women's Christian Association (YWCA)—a similar, yet separate, organization—was established in 1866. The YWCA and other similar groups were especially important for providing safe housing to young, single Christian women in the cities at a time when it was considered morally suspect for young women to live on their own. Branches of the YMCA and YWCA essentially functioned as islands of small-town Protestantism within the often-dangerous and suspect world of nineteenth-century urban America.

And the world of these new cities *was* often dangerous and harsh, without the protections and social services that are now in place. Poor people and recent immigrants crowded into the older areas of the cities, were housed in tenement houses and fetid slums, and eked out a precarious existence from dangerous jobs in industrial plants. Benevolent organizations had long dedicated themselves to work among the urban poor, but the scale of these needs ballooned with the growth of the cities. New organizations began work in the cities, especially the Salvation Army, which had been founded in England in 1865 and established in North America in 1880. Though organized as an "army," the Salvation Army was in fact an evangelical Protestant church (in the Wesleyan-Holiness tradition) dedicated to social service and evangelism among the poor. Branches of the Salvation Army were organized around the United States, including foreign-language branches dedicated to working among new immigrants. The Salvation Army was particularly successful in working with the urban poor, providing meals, housing, and relief along with religious outreach. Toward the end of the century, Jane Addams (1860–1935) established another Protestant outreach to the same populations, the settlement house movement. Addams founded Hull House in Chicago in 1889 to provide education and support for the poor and immigrants, and there were over 350 such houses across urban America by 1910.

Urban Roman Catholic parishes and religious orders also provided major support for new urban immigrants, who increasingly were coming from Roman Catholic areas of Europe. But many of these new immigrants were only nominally Roman Catholic and were often deeply anticlerical (estranged from the leadership of the church). The harsh working conditions and very poor housing in the cities led to the rise of the labor union movement and socialist groups. The leaders of these groups were also often estranged from organized religion, believing that the traditional churches supported the capital industrialists and not the rights of the working poor. In many places, labor unions and socialist clubs became a substitute for religious organizations. Christian groups worried deeply about the alienation of the poor from religion, and at least some of the motivation for their evangelistic and social service outreach was to combat unions and socialism. Truth be told, some of the Protestant outreach was also motivated by anti-Catholicism and a desire to make immigrants into "acceptable" Protestants.

One element of the Protestant solution to urban ills was the growing effort to end the sale and use of alcoholic beverages, and eventually alcohol's complete prohibition. This social crusade was generally supported across the Protestant spectrum, and even by a few of the Roman Catholic bishops in America. The use of alcohol, especially by the urban poor, was certainly a major contributor to the social ills of late nineteenth-century America, and the liquor industry was a powerful political force. Organizations like the Woman's Christian Temperance Union were ranged against this, and a new and powerful organization, the Anti-Saloon League, was founded in 1893. Under the leadership of Wayne Wheeler (1869–1927), the Anti-Saloon League combined religious fervor and political organizing to push prohibition on a state and national level; it was often referred to as "the Church in action against the Saloon." Although a national Prohibition Party ran presidential candidates starting in 1872, this group did not have a major impact.

Liberal Protestantism

From the beginnings of the nineteenth century, with the formation of the Unitarians, and later with the mediating theology of Horace Bushnell, many of the main Protestant denominations moved in an increasingly liberal direction, especially the Congregationalists, Presbyterians, and, most importantly, many of the Methodists (especially in the North). Most of these liberal Protestants did not go as far as the Unitarians, with their denial of the Trinity and doubts about the divinity of Christ. Rather, these groups tended toward a moderate liberalism that retained many of the trappings of classic Christianity but that reinterpreted some traditional teachings and downplayed others. Following German theologians such as Friedrich Schleiermacher and Adolf von Harnack, these liberals saw Protestant Christianity as true not absolutely but relatively—that is, as true in the sense of being closer to a faithful understanding of God than any other religious option. To them, many of the traditional Christian doctrines represented prior steps along the way to the enlightened present, and the older doctrinal formulations were no longer binding on Christians of their day. These liberal theologians wished to maintain the essential "core" of Christian teachings but to discard the older formulations that they now considered obsolete. Many of them believed that the original religious message of Jesus had been obscured by Paul and later Christian writers, who had developed a Christian theological structure in combination with Greek philosophy.

An important question for these liberals was how to understand the nature and person of Jesus Christ. For them, Christ was the figure most closely attuned to the divine character and teachings of God. They did not necessarily reject

Charles M. Sheldon, "What Would Jesus Do?"

"What I am going to propose now is something which ought not to appear unusual or at all impossible of execution. Yet I am aware that it will be so regarded by a large number, perhaps, of the members of this church. But in order that we may have a thorough understanding of what we are considering, I will put my proposition very plainly, perhaps bluntly. I want volunteers from the First Church who will pledge themselves, earnestly and honestly for an entire year, not to do anything without first asking the question, 'What would Jesus do?' And after asking that question, each one will follow Jesus as exactly as he knows how, no matter what the result may be. I will of course include myself in this company of volunteers, and shall take for granted that my church here will not be surprised at my future conduct, as based upon this standard of action, and will not oppose whatever is done if they think Christ would do it. Have I made my meaning clear? At the close of the service I want all those members who are willing to join such a company to remain and we will talk over the details of the plan. Our motto will be, 'What would Jesus do?' Our aim will be to act just as He would if He was in our places, regardless of immediate results. In other words, we propose to follow Jesus' steps as closely and as literally as we believe He taught His disciples to do. . . ."

Henry Maxwell paused again and looked out over his people. It is not easy to describe the sensation that such a simple proposition apparently made. Men glanced at one another in astonishment. It was not like Henry Maxwell to define Christian discipleship in this way. There was evident confusion of thought over his proposition. It was understood well enough, but there was, apparently, a great difference of opinion as to the application of Jesus' teaching and example.

Charles M. Sheldon, *In His Steps: "What Would Jesus Do?"* (Chicago: Advance, 1898), 20–21.

the divinity of Christ, but they reinterpreted Christological and soteriological doctrines to suit a liberal understanding of him. This line of thought was embodied in an extremely popular religious novel, *In His Steps*, by Congregational pastor Charles Sheldon (1857–1946). Sheldon imagined a local pastor challenging his congregation to consider the moral and social problems of the day and asking them to consider the question "What would Jesus do?" (the source of this popular phrase). The obvious goal was for contemporary Christians to work out their faith in action to right the ills of society, as Jesus would do if he were there among them. Christ as a moral example and guide was the core of this religious vision.

According to Sheldon and others, however, in order to address the social problems of the time, Christians needed to transcend traditional approaches, which depended on religious conversion and individual moral reform. Guided by the emerging discipline of sociology, these reformers pursued a "social gospel" that sought broad reform of societal structures. In liberal Christianity, this became an important movement, known as the Social Gospel movement. Washington Gladden (1836–1918), an influential pastor from Columbus, Ohio, wrote some thirty-eight books urging this approach. But it was pastor and theologian Walter Rauschenbusch (1861–1918), of Rochester Theological Seminary in New York, who wrote the seminal works for the movement, including *Christianity and the Social Crisis* (1907). Rauschenbusch served as a pastor for eleven years in the slums of New York and later studied in Germany, where he was influenced by the writings of the liberal German theologian Albrecht Ritschl. Beyond the Social Gospel movement, there were several small groups that advocated for Christian Socialism, but this movement was unable to flourish in the United States.

Traditionally, formal higher education in the United States had been dominated by Protestant Christianity. The typical educational institution was a small undergraduate institution, with a curriculum based on the liberal arts and classics and headed by a Protestant clergyman. The student experience was strongly influenced by a moral education along Christian lines. Moral discipline was enforced, with the college acting as a student's parent (*in loco parentis*); this was true of both public and private institutions. After the Civil War, the nature of American higher education changed, and along with these older institutions came the development of new graduate research institutions based on the "scientific" model of German universities. These newer programs, such as Johns Hopkins University (founded in 1876), began to consciously distance themselves from the traditions of Christianity in favor of a more secular and scientific approach. Typical of this new trend was the founding president of Cornell University (founded in 1865), Andrew Dickson White (1832–1918), who expressed his views in his influential book *A History of the Warfare of Science with Theology in Christendom* (1896). To White and others, science was the future for humanity, a future that had only been hampered by dogmatic theology.

New studies in Europe and America treated Christianity and the Bible "scientifically" and asked critical questions of both. Scientific theories—such as Darwin's ideas about the evolution of the species—were increasingly explored, although Darwinian evolution was only slowly adopted. In the German universities some scholars began to ask hard questions about the Bible and its history, applying a new method of study called higher biblical criticism, which sought to apply to the Bible the same rigorous critical analysis that would be applied to any ancient human text. Some more daring biblical scholars in America began to apply this new method to their own academic studies. Charles Augustus Briggs (1841–1913), a Presbyterian who taught at Union Theological Seminary in New York, created an uproar in 1891 with his address "The Authority of the Holy Scripture," in which he challenged the traditional understandings of biblical authority. Briggs was tried and expelled by his Presbyterian denomination, which led to Union cutting its ties with that denomination. These developments were then echoed in other places, as American Protestants wrestled with the new scholarship and its implications for their teachings and religiosity.

It was in the major Protestant divinity schools that many of these new ideas took root, especially Union Theological Seminary (New York) and the new University of Chicago Divinity School, founded in 1892. At Union, Briggs and Arthur Cushman McGiffert (1861–1933) were the leading exponents of the new liberal approach to Christianity. But this new approach was especially strong at Chicago, where such scholars as Shailer Mathews (1863–1941) and Shirley Jackson Case (1872–1947) pushed the limits of the new liberal approach, a movement often referred to as the Chicago school of theology. This movement was based on the historical-critical method, the emerging discipline of sociology, and the philosophical systems of William James and John Dewey.

Conservative Protestantism

As religious and secular liberalism took root in the mainline Protestant denominations and new American universities, traditionalists and conservatives pushed back against the changes, which led to tensions and conflicts. Older and more moderate elements within the conservative wings of the established denominations attempted to thwart the growth of liberalism directly. Dwight Moody and frequent presidential candidate William Jennings Bryan (1860–1925) were such conservative leaders. At the same time, newer conservative forces—such as the Holiness, Pentecostal, and fundamentalist movements—sought new paths and institutions outside of establishment Protestantism. Though the liberal-conservative tensions stressed American Protestantism, the final rupture would not occur until after World War I (1914–18).

Traditional conservatives formulated theological rebuttals to secular modernism and the accommodations to it by liberal Protestantism. One center of this restatement of traditional Christian theology was Princeton Theological Seminary. There, theologians Archibald A. Hodge (1823–86) and Benjamin B. Warfield (1851–1921) offered a spirited defense of traditional Christian theology and developed new defenses of the authority of the Bible, formulating its authority around the concepts of biblical inerrancy and divine inspiration. A Princeton New Testament scholar, J. Gresham Machen (1881–1937), then sharpened these concepts and led an attack on liberal theology and higher biblical criticism. Many who followed them remained, for the time being, within the traditional mainline Protestant denominations.

But, increasingly, for others the time was at hand for them to part ways with these denominations. The first major exodus from the Methodist denominations was of those who believed that liberalism and moral laxity had fatally infected these groups. While there had certainly been previous defections from Methodism in the mid-nineteenth century, including the Holiness movement and the traditional camp-meeting organizations, Holiness defections from Methodism intensified toward the beginning of the twentieth century, with the founding of dozens of independent Holiness denominations and associations between 1880 and 1910. One major group, the Church of God (Anderson, Indiana), was founded in 1881 by Daniel Sidney Warner (1842–95) and became a leading Holiness denomination. Another group that eventually became influential was the Church of the Nazarene, founded in 1895 by Phineas F. Bresee (1838–1915), which went through multiple iterations before reaching its final form. The Salvation Army was another Wesleyan defection, as were a significant number of African American Holiness groups formed during this period.

As important as the Holiness movement was, it was eclipsed in the early twentieth century by the new Pentecostal movement, and a significant number of Holiness leaders and groups eventually became Pentecostal. Many elements came together to form Pentecostalism at the beginnings of the twentieth century, including American revivalism, the Holiness movement, fundamentalist and dispensationalist theology, and the Keswick "higher life" tradition. In addition to the traditional conversion experience and baptism, Pentecostalism also urged a second baptism, a baptism of the Holy Spirit, and the indwelling of the

Spirit in the life of the believer. The baptism of the Spirit, the biblical "latter rain," was manifested in the believer in several spiritual signs, such as speaking in tongues, faith healing, prophecy, and power for spiritual warfare (including driving out demonic spirits by way of exorcism). Pentecostal worship was often very free, depending on the presence of the Holy Spirit to lead the congregation. Pentecostal groups were congregational in structure, and there were hundreds of different denominations and associations across the spectrum, including groups that were predominantly White, African American, or Hispanic.

Pentecostalism has several suggested origins, including revivals preached by Charles Fox Parham (1873–1929) in Topeka, Kansas, in 1901, and other manifestations of the Holy Spirit, especially in the southern half of the United States, around that time. But the origins of Pentecostalism have generally been traced to revivals held at a church on Azusa Street in Los Angeles, California, starting in 1906. The itinerant African American preacher William J. Seymour (1870–1922) launched an interracial revival in a rundown building at 312 Azusa Street, which eventually drew large crowds and national attention. The emotionalism of the revivals and the emphasis on the gifts of the Spirit, especially speaking in tongues, occasioned both great interest and great scorn. Both because of their "overly enthusiastic" worship and because they were often poor and working class, these early Pentecostals were viewed as embarrassing and dismissible by the elites of the secular press and the more conventional denominations, who referred to the Pentecostals as "holy rollers." But the revival continued, and it sparked an outpouring of similar Pentecostal revivals around the United States, and later the world.

8.2. Azuza Street Mission, Los Angeles.

Early Pentecostals were often not too concerned with permanent religious structures, seeing this outpouring of the Holy Spirit as a sign of the imminent end of the world. But fairly quickly they formed Pentecostal congregations, associations, and denominations, of which there were three main wings. First, out of the Wesleyan-Holiness wing of the movement came groups like the Church of God in Christ, which was composed mainly of African Americans, and the Church of God (Cleveland, Tennessee), which was predominantly White. Some of these groups had been founded prior to 1900 and later became Pentecostal. The second wing of Pentecostalism came out of the Reformed-Baptist tradition. The largest group in this wing, which also became the largest Pentecostal denomination in the United States, was the Assemblies of God—founded in Hot Springs, Arkansas, in 1914. The third Pentecostal wing was made up of the "Oneness" Pentecostals, whose adherents baptized in the name of Jesus only. Though the Azusa Street revival was interracial and prominently featured women's leadership, as these Pentecostal groups were organized, they were often formed along racial lines, and women's leadership was gradually curtailed.

All these conservative groups had a common goal: the defense of traditional Christian doctrines from liberal and secular critics. As early as 1878, a fourteen-point statement of faith that included the inerrancy of the Bible was adopted at a meeting of the Niagara Bible Conference. Conservative theologians, such as those at Princeton, wrote scholarly defenses not only of the inerrancy of scripture but also of the virgin birth of Christ, his miracles, atoning death, bodily resurrection, and second return at the end of the world. From 1910 to 1915, conservatives contributed theological articles on such topics to a series of twelve booklets that were called *The Fundamentals: A Testimony to the Truth*. Financed by wealthy Christian businessmen, these booklets were printed in large numbers and sent to Protestant pastors around the country as a defense of traditional Christian theology.

One new element of this conservative Protestantism was the rising influence of premillennial and dispensationalist eschatology, arguing for a rather pessimistic view of the world and of a climactic, final battle between the forces of evil in the world and God's heavenly armies, along the lines of what is described in the biblical book of Revelation. Rejecting the optimistic belief in the gradual improvement of the world ahead of Christ's second coming, this view saw the world as slipping into chaos and held that each Christian was to save as many individual people as possible. Larger social reforms were viewed as a waste of time because the world was to end imminently. This eschatology, urged by John Nelson Darby, was popularized by Cyrus Ingerson "C. I." Scofield (1843–1921) in an immensely influential work, the Scofield Reference

Bible (1909), in which this theology was written into the interpretive notes accompanying the biblical text.

As Christian colleges and seminaries were increasingly influenced by liberalism, conservatives also formed their own educational institutions, especially Bible schools and missionary training institutes. Hundreds of these independent schools, most notably Moody Bible Institute in Chicago (1886), were formed to defend traditional Christian doctrines and to educate conservative Christian pastors and teachers. This was just another sign of the gradual splintering of American Protestantism that became permanent in the early twentieth century.

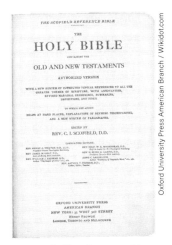

8.3. Scofield Reference Bible

Mind, Health, and Alternate Religions

Americans have always been seekers and explorers when it comes to religion, and each generation seems to have its own preferred brands of religious expression. After the horrors of the Civil War, there was a renewed interest in alternative religions, including willingness to explore religious traditions outside of Christianity, such as spiritualism, the religions of health or the mind, and exported and westernized versions of Eastern religions. All these religious options were increasingly explored by some middle-class White Americans.

Alternative ideas concerning healing and health were increasingly popular toward the end of the nineteenth century, as the regular diets of most Americans were appalling, and the standards of medicine and of medical practitioners were generally low. A number of persons and groups encouraged various schemes for alternative diets and health foods. Some of these—like new breakfast cereals, graham crackers, and peanut butter—were relatively benign and became a part of the standard American diet, while others were more outlandish and even dangerous. Alternative medical practices were also advanced, with the same ratio of common sense and dangerous quackery. The Seventh-day Adventists became prominent advocates of alternative diets and medicines, and they established sanitariums, hospitals, and schools of alternative medicine in locations around the country. Theologically, they were otherwise unremarkable: conservative and premillennial Protestants with roots in the Millerite movement of the 1840s.

Other alternative groups pushed beyond standard Protestant Christianity, especially toward metaphysical religious traditions of healing and the conquest of diseases through the control of the mind. Christian Science gained prominence as a metaphysical religion that sought relief from suffering and illness through mind control. The creator of Christian Science, Mary Baker Eddy (1821–1910), had long suffered illness and pain until she was healed by a religious healer in 1866. Trying to understand this, she searched the Christian scriptures and found what she believed to be coded messages having to do with mind control and metaphysical healing. She published these findings in a book entitled *Science and Health* (1875; in

8.4. Mary Baker Eddy.

1883, it became *Science and Health with Key to the Scriptures*). Christian Science societies, with metaphysical healing practitioners, were established around the country. This movement was centered on the Mother Church, the First Church of Christ, Scientist, which was founded in Boston in 1892, and on a robust publishing ministry. There were fifty-five thousand members of the movement by 1906, which reached a peak in the early twentieth century, and declined from there. Another, more conventionally Protestant, version of metaphysical religion was the Unity School of Christianity, founded in Kansas City, Missouri, in 1889, by Myrtle Fillmore (1845–1931) and her husband, Charles Fillmore (1854–1948). These various alternative religions became very popular on the West Coast, and their membership was predominantly female.

Other religious options abounded. Spiritualism, which had flourished for a time before the Civil War, regained its popularity after the war. Some varieties of spiritualism combined this way of thinking with religious impulses from Asian religions. Helena Petrovna Blavatsky (1831–91) and her partner, Henry Steel Olcott (1832–1907), started the modern movement of Theosophy in 1875 by blending spiritualism with Buddhism, enlivened by Blavatsky's theatrical skills. A Hindu teacher, Swami Vivekananda (1863–1902), brought a metaphysical form of Hinduism to middle-class America through the Vedanta Society. And a universalistic and messianic form of Persian Islam, Bahá'í, was introduced to America in 1894. Much interest in these and other groups was occasioned by the World's Parliament of Religions at the world's fair in Chicago in 1893.

Roman Catholic and Other Christian Immigrants

The shifting patterns of immigration toward the end of the nineteenth century brought millions more Roman Catholics to the United States, including some three million Italians and two million Poles. Though some of these immigrants naturally sought the religious and social comfort of Roman Catholic parishes, many others, especially the Italians, were nominally religious and often disaffected from the church. Roman Catholic leaders had to work hard to form and staff ethnic parishes for these new immigrants, and to gather the immigrants in. But they were successful in this and built a remarkable network of parishes, schools, religious orders, and social service agencies. They also established numerous religious societies and fraternal organizations for laypeople. By 1906, there were sixteen million Roman Catholics in the United States, making up 32 percent of all religious adherents in the country.

Though these adherents were all under the control of a single Roman Catholic hierarchy, beneath this the church was often divided along ethnic lines, with separate parishes and religious orders for various immigrant groups and languages. The dioceses and national church structures were generally in the hands of Irish and German bishops, who clashed at times with the newer immigrants, many of whom had distinctive religious customs foreign to the bishops. Disputes over power and control were common, and one dissident group of Polish Americans, under the leadership of Franciszek Hodur (1866–1953), broke away and in 1897 formed the Polish National Catholic Church, independent of the papacy.

There were also tensions and disputes between American Roman Catholic leaders and the church hierarchy in Rome. Several American bishops who attended the First Vatican Council (1869–70) in Rome were uncomfortable with the declaration of papal infallibility, which came out of that meeting, though they went along with the decision. Nineteenth-century popes took decidedly conservative positions, especially regarding the political and social changes sweeping through Europe, and they tended to view such developments in the United States with alarm. These popes thought that Roman Catholics in America were in grave danger from democracy, from the lack of state support of religion, and from the country's Protestant culture.

American Roman Catholic leaders were divided as to how far they and their members could accommodate themselves to the culture and institutions of America. There was a strong push for separate Roman Catholic parochial education, both on religious and ethnic grounds, the public schools being (rightly) considered "too Protestant." Many Catholic educational institutions were established, the most prominent being the Catholic University of America, in Washington, DC, which was formed in 1887. Some conservative bishops, including Michael Corrigan (1839–1902) of New York, urged a substantial degree of separateness. But other bishops, such as John Ireland (1838–1918) of St. Paul, Minnesota, and John Keane (1839–1918) of Richmond, Virginia, urged a wider degree of Roman Catholic accommodation and participation in American public life, insisting that one could be a good Roman Catholic and a good American citizen at the same time. Bishop Ireland promoted the

Papal Encyclical on "Americanism," 1899

The underlying principle of these new opinions is that, in order to more easily attract those who differ from her, the Church should shape her teachings more in accord with the spirit of the age and relax some of her ancient severity and make some concessions to new opinions. Many think that these concessions should be made not only in regard to ways of living, but even in regard to doctrines which belong to the deposit of the faith. They contend that it would be opportune, in order to gain those who differ from us, to omit certain points of her teaching which are of lesser importance, and to tone down the meaning which the Church has always attached to them. . . .

We, indeed, have no thought of rejecting everything that modern industry and study has produced; so far from it that we welcome to the patrimony of truth and to an ever-widening scope of public well-being whatsoever helps toward the progress of learning and virtue. Yet all this, to be of any solid benefit, nay, to have a real existence and growth, can only be on the condition of recognizing the wisdom and authority of the Church. . . .

From the foregoing it is manifest, beloved son, that we are not able to give approval to those views which, in their collective sense, are called by some "Americanism." But if by this name are to be understood certain endowments of mind which belong to the American people, just as other characteristics belong to various other nations, and if, moreover, by it is designated your political condition and the laws and customs by which you are governed, there is no reason to take exception to the name. But if this is to be so understood that the doctrines which have been adverted to above are not only indicated, but exalted, there can be no manner of doubt that our venerable brethren, the bishops of America, would be the first to repudiate and condemn it.

Pope Leo XIII, "Testem Benevolentiae Nostrae: Concerning New Opinions, Virtue, Nature and Grace, With Regard to Americanism" (1899), *Papal Encyclicals Online*, https://www.papalencyclicals.net/leo13/l13teste.htm.

Faribault Plan, in which Roman Catholic children would attend local public schools while also being granted release time for them to receive religious education in the local parishes.

Alarmed by these accommodating trends, the church hierarchy in Rome issued a series of letters and encyclicals warning against them. In 1899, Pope Leo XIII issued an apostolic letter condemning what he called "Americanism" in the church and warning the American bishops against too great an accommodation to structures in the United States. Ireland, Keane, and others demurred, saying that the attitudes the letter had condemned were not, in fact, what they had been advocating. It was up to the leader of American Catholics, Cardinal James Gibbons (1834–1921) of Baltimore, to smooth relations with Rome and to calm tensions at home.

The great increase in immigration of Roman Catholics also alarmed many American Protestants, and the increased immigration restrictions toward the end of the century were specifically aimed at non-Protestant immigrants. Additionally, there was an upswing in Protestant nativism (hostility to outsiders) seen in the rise of anti-immigrant groups. The Ku Klux Klan, which strongly opposed all non-White and non-Protestant immigrants, was revived in both the South and the North. Another nativist group, the American Protective Association, formed in 1887, blamed the social and economic difficulties of the time on the newcomers. This nativist association was generally located in the rural Midwest and had some political success, but it faded after 1898. There were also some anti–Roman Catholic overtones to the Spanish-American War in 1898.

Though German immigration declined after 1880, the immigration of Scandinavians remained strong until the First World War, swelling the number of Lutherans in America, who became the third-largest Protestant family in the country. Lacking a national hierarchy, these Lutherans divided into numerous ethnically and theologically distinct groups, often referred to as synods. Lutherans also debated among themselves about how much they should accommodate to the general American religious culture dominated by evangelical Protestantism. Some conservatives established separate parochial schools, but most Lutherans did not, sending their children to public schools. Many Americans saw these Lutherans—despite their foreign languages and distinct cultures—as "good" Protestant immigrants and welcomed them. A high point for Lutherans was the celebration, in 1883, of the four-hundredth anniversary of the birth of Martin Luther. Many American religious leaders commented warmly on Luther's legacy and on the presence of Lutherans in the country.

Orthodox Christians from eastern Europe and Russia were also among this wave of immigrants, and they, too, established ethnic parishes and institutions in the United States. The Russian Orthodox were the earliest to organize, and in

1905 moved their diocese to New York City, seeking to provide an institutional home for all Orthodox Christians in the United States. But this did not work, as the Orthodox also divided along ethnic and linguistic lines, buoyed by the stirrings of ethnic nationalism in eastern Europe; many of these groups remained under the leadership of the Orthodox hierarchies in their home countries. The largest group of Orthodox Christians in America were the Greeks, who had established nearly 150 ethnic parishes by 1914, and they resisted the control of the Russian diocese in New York. Though there was growth in the number of Orthodox Christians in America, they still accounted for less than 1 percent of all religious adherents by 1906.

Women and Christianity

As American society developed and changed toward the beginning of the twentieth century, women continued to play a major role in American Christianity. Though there were no dramatic developments in this area during this period, women began to advocate for more formal leadership opportunities in church and society, and many seeds of later changes were sown. Very few American Christian groups of the time allowed women into the ranks of their professional leadership, although some women pushed the boundaries of existing opportunities in areas such as social service, education, and missionary work. In some of the more liberal denominations, women were beginning to be allowed a voice and to vote on congregational and denominational levels, though these developments were slow.

The traditional base for Christian women was still in the mission and social service organizations they themselves had developed. Nearly every congregation and denomination had some form of women's organization, and in many places these groups exercised great power, although mostly indirectly. Women could also provide religious leadership through many ancillary roles: as evangelists, missionaries, social service workers, teachers, deaconesses, and in Roman Catholic religious orders. Some women, dissatisfied with their traditional religious options, found religious meaning and opportunities in the new alternative religious options of the time, such as Adventism, the Holiness movement, Christian Science, the Unity School, and forms of spiritualism. The membership of these groups was predominantly women, and many of their leaders were women.

Women were involved in the new movements to address the myriad social problems of the day. An important voice in the Social Gospel movement was Vida Dutton Scudder (1861–1954), a professor of English at Wellesley College.

She was very active in Christian social action and socialism and was a co-founder of the College Settlements Association. Her wider influence came through her writings, including through the novel *A Listener in Babel* (1903), which was set in an urban slum. From more traditional beginnings, the leader of the Woman's Christian Temperance Union (WCTU), Frances Willard (1839–98) led that organization to expand its single focus on alcohol to include addressing many of the societal ills that beset American women. Jane Addams and hundreds of other Christian women worked in the settlement houses to address the needs of the urban poor. In numbers equal to—or even greater than—their male

Elizabeth Cady Stanton, *The Woman's Bible* (1898)

These familiar texts are quoted by clergymen in their pulpits, by statesmen in the halls of legislation, by lawyers in the courts, and are echoed by the press of all civilized nations, and accepted by woman herself as "The Word of God." So perverted is the religious element in her nature, that with faith and works she is the chief support of the church and clergy; the very powers that make her emancipation impossible. When, in the early part of the Nineteenth Century, women began to protest against their civil and political degradation, they were referred to the Bible for an answer. When they protested against their unequal position in the church, they were referred to the Bible for an answer. . . .

This led to a general and critical study of the Scriptures. Some, having made a fetish of these books and believing them to be the veritable "Word of God," with liberal translations, interpretations, allegories and symbols, glossed over the most objectionable features of the various books and clung to them as divinely inspired. Others . . . came to the conclusion that all alike emanated from the same source; wholly human in their origin and inspired by the natural love of domination in the historians. . . .

There are some general principles in the holy books of all religions that teach love, charity, liberty, justice and equality for all the human family, there are many grand and beautiful passages, the golden rule has been echoed and re-echoed around the world. There are lofty examples of good and true men and women, all worthy our acceptance and imitation whose lustre cannot be dimmed by the false sentiments and vicious characters bound up in the same volume. The Bible cannot be accepted or rejected as a whole, its teachings are varied and its lessons differ widely from each other. . . . A few of the more democratic denominations accord women some privileges, but invidious discriminations of sex are found in all religious organizations, and the most bitter outspoken enemies of woman are found among clergymen and bishops of the Protestant religion.

Elizabeth Cady Stanton, introduction to *The Woman's Bible*
(New York: European Publishing Company, 1898), 2:8–14.

counterparts, young Christian women responded to the evangelical call of missions to Africa and Asia, and many went abroad as nurses, teachers, evangelists, and as the wives and partners of male missionaries.

A primary focus of many Christian women was the cause of temperance or, increasingly, the call for the legal prohibition of the production and sale of alcohol. Groups like the WCTU and the Anti-Saloon League had thousands of local chapters with a predominantly female membership. These groups developed a strong political power base, which allowed them to campaign successfully for the prohibition of alcohol on the local and state levels in several instances. The movement for women's rights—most notably suffrage (the right to vote)—was also on the minds of many women, although there were varying degrees of support for such causes. The temperance movement itself eventually prompted some women to support the suffrage movement, as it was believed that obtaining voting rights for women would strengthen the political "muscle" for the temperance cause.

However, relations between the women's rights movement and traditional Christians were often strained. Many male religious leaders, grounded in traditional gender roles, resisted suffrage and the expansion of women's rights. Often their resistance was grounded in a certain reading of the Bible, especially passages that expressed male domination over women. Meeting this attitude, beginning in 1895 suffrage leader Elizabeth Cady Stanton (1815–1902) and others published *The Woman's Bible*, a commentary on portions of the Bible that hoped to "correct" interpretations that subjugated women. Though the publication was an instant bestseller, it was also rather controversial, and some suffrage groups disavowed it.

African Americans and Native Americans

This period was a bleak one for African Americans, and even worse for Native Americans. The end of Reconstruction in 1877 and the withdrawal of federal troops from the South allowed these states to swiftly reverse African American civil rights and impose harsh restrictions, including segregation of the races. Supreme Court decisions in 1883 and 1896 further eroded the gains in civil liberties that had come briefly to African Americans after the Civil War, and African Americans were subjugated economically and subjected to terror campaigns, which included lynching. For Native Americans, this was a tragic period, when their final attempts at military resistance were crushed and they were involuntarily confined to bleak reservations. Their cultures and ways of life were destroyed in the name of integrating them into the modern world, and they suffered from government mistreatment and neglect.

For many African Americans, religion was one of the few areas of independence and self-expression left to them, and religious institutions became a central focus of their communal life. African American pastors were often leaders in their communities and attempted to help their communities deal with poverty, repression, and violence. Different leaders attempted different strategies to deal with these traumas, either working as well as they could within the present realities or resisting the present realities and seeking to become as independent of the larger culture as possible. Two major figures of this time represent these two different paths. Booker T. Washington (1856–1915) was an African American educator and leader who, in 1881, formed the Tuskegee Normal School for Colored Teachers (now Tuskegee University) in Alabama. He urged his community to embrace education, self-discipline, and moral improvement and to work as much as possible within the current system. AME bishop Henry McNeal Turner (1834–1915), on the other hand, was outspoken in opposition to repression and violence and supported African American independence. He made four trips to Africa during the 1890s, supported the Back-to-Africa movement, and famously declared in 1898 that "God is a Negro" to shock the religious consciences of Americans. From different positions, both men attempted to ameliorate the dire situation of their community.

The growth of African American religious organizations continued. African Americans were more likely than the general population to be church members, and, by 1906, this community constituted 11 percent of all religious adherents in the United States. The African American Methodist denominations were already formed by this time, and though the Baptist congregations were more numerous, they were also slower to form national associations. A milestone was the formation of the National Baptist Convention in 1895, but this denomination was split into two groups in 1915. There was also the organization of numerous African American Holiness and Pentecostal denominations toward the end of this period. The largest of these was the Church of God in Christ, but there were dozens of other smaller groups, which often shifted and re-formed, alternating between Holiness and Pentecostal identities. As an alternative, there were the African American Roman Catholic parishes and religious orders, and many other independent congregations across the religious spectrum. Many of these denominations, especially the Methodists and Baptists, also organized significant mission activity to Africa.

After the Civil War, the vast majority of African Americans (some 90 percent) lived in the southern states, but the harsh conditions there led some to consider other options. In the first decades of the twentieth century, there were the beginnings of what would come to be called the Great Migration—African Americans moving from the South to the cities of the East and Midwest. Conditions and job opportunities were somewhat better there than in the South, and African Americans established their own religious congregations in these new homes. Although urged by Turner and others, the Back-to-Africa option was not very popular, and those who did return to Africa often found very difficult conditions there.

For Native Americans, this period was a total disaster. After 1880 there were pockets of Native American military resistance, but these were systematically

A Native American, Firsthand Account of the Massacre at Wounded Knee, 1890

The following morning the soldiers began blowing their bugles and began to stand around us in ranks, but I thought nothing of it, as it was their natural custom to do so. And then we [the men] were told to come out and sit down at a place near the door of Big Foot's tent, which we did. Then a lot of soldiers got in between us and our camp, separating us from the women and children.

An officer then told us he wanted our guns, and as soon as we gave them up, he would give us provisions, and we could go on our way. We, the older men, consented willingly and began giving them up; we had all given them up, as I thought, when I saw an Indian with a gun under his blanket, and the soldiers saw it at the same time, and they took it away from him. They [the soldiers] commenced searching the Indians at the same time.

Meanwhile, the medicine man was going through the incantations of the Ghost Dance, stopped and began speaking to the younger Indians, but I paid no attention to what he said, as I had not the least fear of any trouble; so I pulled my blanket over my head and did not see anything until I heard much talking and loud voices. I uncovered my head, and I saw everyone had arisen on his feet, and I heard a shot coming from where the young Indians stood. Shortly after that I was shot down, and I laid there as I fell.

The firing was so fast and the dust and smoke so thick, I did not see much more of the fight until it was over. . . . I raised my head and saw a man standing among the dead, and I asked him if he was the man they called Fox, and he said he was, and I said, "Will you come to me?" And he came to my side. I then asked him who was that man lying there half burned, and he said, "I understand it is the medicine man." . . . I then said to Fox, "He has caused the death of all our people."

Quoted in Robert Bateman, "Firsthand Accounts from Wounded Knee Tell a Chaotic Tale of Fear, Terror—and Indiscriminate Gunfire," Historynet, November 5, 2018, https://www.historynet.com/wounded-knee-what-really-happened/.

crushed by federal troops (including several African American cavalry regi-
ments, the so-called buffalo soldiers). These efforts included forcing the last
resisters onto reservations and massacres, such as the one at Wounded Knee,
South Dakota, in 1890. In Native American communities, religion and culture
are integrated and constitute a single way of life. To try to pacify the Native
Americans, and to begin to integrate them into the larger American culture and
economic world, federal officials sought to destroy traditional Native American
cultures and ways of life. On many reservations, White religious workers and
missionaries opened schools and mission agencies to work among the Native
populations and, despite their often-good intentions, were complicit in this
destruction of Native cultures in the name of Christianizing and "civilizing"
Native peoples.

Traditional Native American religion was often suppressed or outlawed,
and in many places was forced underground. Some Native peoples converted
to forms of Christianity but continued to practice traditional religions as well.
Christian influences also infiltrated Native religious practices. Christian messianism and apocalypticism were an important element in the Ghost Dance
movement envisioned by a Paiute shaman, Wovoka (ca. 1856–1932). This movement swept through reservations in the 1880s and 1890s, but it also led to the
massacre at Wounded Knee. Starting in the 1870s, the religious use of peyote
(a hallucinogen) came into use among southwestern and Plains tribes, forming
the core of a pan-tribal religious movement that became known as the Native
American Church. This religious path, sometimes referred to as the Peyote Way,
combined traditional Native religiosity with Christian themes, especially sacra-
mentalism. The early leaders in this movement included a Caddo shaman, John
Wilson (ca. 1845–1901), and a Comanche chief, Quanah Parker (ca. 1845–1911).

Christian Mission Activity

The American Christian enthusiasm for missions continued to expand after
the Civil War, and increasingly this interest turned toward mission work in
foreign countries. Hundreds of new denominational and independent mission
boards were formed, and these organizations sent thousands of (mostly young)
American Christians overseas to proclaim the gospel, first in Asia and Africa,
then also in Latin America. Almost every Christian congregation had a local
branch of a missionary society, and many Americans brought the spirit of missions into their homes by subscribing to one or more of the hundreds of available
missionary publications. Junior mission societies were developed for children,
student mission societies recruited and supported volunteer missionaries, and

women supported other women in their mission work. Though it was not an intended effect of this movement, missionary publications and furloughed mission personnel widened the worldviews of countless American Christians by drawing their attention to world peoples and cultures.

Much of this mission work, especially its geographic expansion, was made easier or even possible through the expansion of Western colonial influence in Asia and Africa toward the end of the nineteenth century. Expanded transportation and communication made the movement of missionaries much easier, and advances in medicine and sanitation allowed them to work in areas hitherto impossible. In the 1884–85 Berlin West Africa Conference, the Western European powers brought almost all of Africa under European control, and much of Asia was either colonized or subjected to Western domination. The relation between Western colonialism and Christian missions during this time is complex. Western missions were certainly aided by colonialism, and sometimes the missionaries themselves were complicit with it. On the other hand, some missionaries rejected colonial protection and special privileges, and some acted in defense of Native peoples against colonial abuses. Besides the gospel message, Western missions often brought education and health care to Indigenous peoples, raised up local religious leaders, and sparked an incredible expansion of Christianity in the Global South by the end of the twentieth century.

Earlier Protestant mission boards continued their work and were joined by hundreds of new mission organizations, together sending thousands of Americans into mission fields. In 1900, Americans made up some 27 percent of Protestant missionaries overseas. At that time, there were approximately forty-five hundred American Protestant missionaries, and 60 percent of them were women, either single or the wives of male missionaries. One of the first major waves of new missionaries arose from the activities leading to the formation of the Student Volunteer Movement for Foreign Missions, formally organized in 1886, which attracted sixteen hundred young men and five hundred young women to pledge to go overseas in mission work. The motto of this organization was audacious: "The Evangelization of the World in This Generation." The primary leader of this movement, YMCA Secretary John R. Mott (1865–1955), became a leading figure in Protestant missions.

Missionaries were still recruited and supported by the mainline Protestant missionary boards, but increasingly new groups and models emerged, many based on the example of Hudson Taylor's China Inland Mission. These new missionaries pledged to develop their own funding and to work in interior regions of Asia and Africa, beyond direct colonial support. Conservative Protestants began to organize and support these independent mission societies because of their distrust of mainline denominational mission boards, which they feared had been "infected" with liberalism and modernism. New Holiness and Pentecostal denominations also developed their own mission work in Latin America by the 1910s. African American Methodists and Baptists began their own mission work in western and southern Africa by the 1880s, especially in Liberia, Sierra Leone, and South Africa. More than one hundred African American missionaries were also employed by mainline Protestant mission boards, although these missionaries sometimes suffered from discrimination and restrictions by colonial officials. And, despite the daunting challenges facing this period's new immigrant groups (both Protestant and Roman Catholic) in establishing themselves in the United States, even these groups and their young people caught the "missions bug" and developed their own mission activities, either independently or in conjunction with established mission societies in their home countries. In 1911, the Roman Catholic Maryknoll order established the American Foreign Missionary Society, which worked mainly in Asia. Lutheran denominations formed their own mission societies and sent missionaries to China, India, Liberia, Madagascar, and South Africa.

The expansion of Christian missionary activity was also boosted by the American territorial gains from the Spanish-American War, of 1898, and by the dramatic expansion of American interests in Latin America after that time. Traditionally, Protestant missionaries had avoided mission work in Latin America—not because they had scruples about "stealing sheep" from the Roman Catholics (they hardly considered Roman Catholics to be real Christians), but because many of these countries had severe restrictions on Protestant activities. But with greater American influence in the region, especially in the Caribbean and Central America, Protestant missionaries began to work there and to attract local converts to extend the reach of these Protestant missions. There was a strong belief in the superiority of Anglo-Saxon Protestant Christianity, as typified in *Our Country* (1885), the influential book by Josiah Strong (1847–1916). Many supposed that it was the duty of these Christians to convert and civilize the other parts of the world, bringing civil liberty and pure, spiritual Christianity.

Growth of Protestant Ecumenism

Ecumenism is the idea that—despite their differences in theology, polity, and worship—Christian groups and families ought to come together with as much unity as possible and cooperate while facing the common challenges and opportunities they encounter. With religious diversity among American

Christians increasing, ecumenism came to be seen more and more as a necessity. Although, as has been seen, there was a great degree of consensus among American Protestants during the first several decades of the nineteenth century, denominational and theological differences increased through the century, especially the growing tensions between liberal mainline Protestants and conservative evangelicals, and little commonality existed between Protestants and Roman Catholics.

What ecumenical relations there were during the nineteenth century were generally accomplished by nondenominational groups working together for common purposes, such as winning converts, distributing Bibles, social reform, abolition, and temperance. Some American Protestant leaders participated in the formation of the Evangelical Alliance in 1846, but the American branch of this ecumenical group was not formed until 1867. An international General Conference of this alliance was held in 1873 in New York, and national meetings of the group were held between 1877 and 1893, but after that this movement declined. There were a number of pan-Protestant groups that met regularly, including the Student Volunteer Movement for Foreign Missions, the YMCA and YWCA, and the Young People's Society of Christian Endeavor.

One large impetus for ecumenical cooperation was the widely perceived need for the coordination of mission activities, especially in foreign missions. After its founding in 1886, the Student Volunteer Movement for Foreign Missions began in 1891 to hold large meetings (Quadrennials) every four years. In 1900, an Ecumenical Missions Conference was held in New York City, followed in 1910 by a much larger World Missionary Conference held in Edinburgh, Scotland, in which over a thousand delegates, mainly from Anglo-American mission societies, participated. This meeting was a high point for the Western mission movement and produced volumes of information regarding and analysis of missionary efforts and challenges. It also led to the formation of a permanent organization, the International Missionary Council, and eventually to most other Western ecumenical organizations in the twentieth century.

In America, mainline Protestants sought greater ecumenical cooperation. After an initial meeting in 1905, the Federal Council of Churches of Christ in America (FCC) was formed in 1908 by thirty-three denominations that represented eighteen million American Christians. The constituent groups were mainly the northern mainline Protestant denominations, most African American denominations, and a number of Eastern Orthodox groups; Roman Catholics, most evangelical Protestants, and most immigrant denominations did not participate. The FCC was formed on a rather vague doctrinal basis, declaring "the essential oneness of the Christian Churches in America in Jesus Christ as their Lord and Savior."[3] Initially, social concerns were a major impetus for the establishment of the FCC, and so the council formed the Commission on Church and Social Service. In 1908 the FCC issued a policy document, "The Social Creed of the Churches," which urged progressive and liberal positions on social issues and labor relations and advocated for a minimum wage, pensions, limited workweeks, and other regulations on business and industry. The FCC was effectively the religious wing of the American progressive movement.

Though the FCC was only an advisory organization to its member denominations and comprised only a fraction of American Christians, it represented some of the most powerful and socially prominent groups. The FCC had an oversized agenda and an overinflated view of itself, claiming to speak for American Christianity as a whole and to set its agenda. It believed that there were too many "redundancies" because of competition among various denominations, and it urged the consolidation of efforts though interdenominational organizations, with the FCC at the head, of course. One gets a strong feeling from the activities and positions of the council that they sought to control American Christianity and to freeze out those they did not agree with, especially the conservative evangelical and Pentecostal denominations.

America as a Colonial Power and the Lead-Up to the First World War

As the United States expanded westward across North America to the Pacific Ocean, a number of American leaders imagined a further expansion of the country into the Pacific and southward into Latin America. Southern politicians had cast a covetous eye on Mexico, Central America, and the Caribbean as possible new territories for slavery, and later business interests had sought commercial control over the same areas. Having bought Alaska from Russia and annexed Hawaii, the United States also sought further bases in Asia. The defeat of the Spanish in 1898 brought Puerto Rico and Guam under permanent American control, and Cuba and the Philippines came under American protection and influence. The United States also limited the activities of European powers in the Western Hemisphere, emphasizing that this was its region of control and intervening regularly in the affairs of other countries in the Americas to maintain its control.

3. "Preamble to the Constitution, Federal Council of Churches" (1908), in Elias B. Sanford, *Origin and History of the Federal Council of the Churches of Christ in America* (Hartford, CT: S. S. Scranton, 1916), 464.

With its defeat of Spain, the United States became recognized as a significant military power, and American diplomats were active in defending American interests. During 1899 and 1900, Secretary of State John Hay pushed the European powers to maintain an "Open Door" policy on China, allowing for equal access to the country for trade purposes and fending off European attempts to dismember China between them. President Theodore Roosevelt was active internationally, helping to negotiate an end to the Russo-Japanese War in 1905 and sending a naval fleet around the world to demonstrate American military strength. But American expansion also brought about troubling moral issues, as in the case of the American suppression of a guerrilla uprising in the Philippines between 1899 and 1902, when reports of military atrocities led to criticism and congressional hearings.

There had been a long tradition of peace movements in the United States, many based in religion, from the founding of the American Peace Society in 1828. There were also historically pacifist churches, including the Quaker, Mennonite, Amish, and Brethren churches. The traumas of the Civil War lent further impetus to these movements, and a number of American religious and reform leaders, including Frances Willard of the WCTU, attended an international peace conference in Paris in 1889. The Spanish-American War was unpopular in certain circles, leading to the formation of the Anti-Imperialist League in 1899, whose participants included William Jennings Bryan, William James, Jane Addams, and Andrew Carnegie. Carnegie was a leader in the international peace movement, establishing the Carnegie Endowment for International Peace in 1910 and the Church Peace Union—an interfaith coalition of Protestants, Roman Catholics, and Jews—in 1914.

Pacifism and the peace movement were, however, not widely popular among American Christians, although many did share a common commitment to efforts to derail the outbreak of war and to develop mechanisms for the resolution of conflicts. But it was very clear in the opening years of the twentieth century that, despite efforts to the contrary, the European powers were hurtling toward war, although few conceived of just how terrible that war would actually be. Most American Christians were not pacifists, but quite a few of them were isolationists who felt strongly that the United States should not be entangled in the war between the European powers. The wars that the United States fought in the nineteenth century were one-on-one conflicts within the perceived American sphere of influence and were thus not considered "foreign entanglements," something most Americans sought to avoid.

The Religious Situation on the Eve of the First World War

American Christian denominations traditionally avoided taking overt and direct political stances, a practice that paired naturally with the free exercise and establishment clauses of the First Amendment to the Constitution. But churches frequently took positions on moral issues that had political implications, so the division between church and state was, in reality, less definite than it might seem. The first major issue to test the traditional separation of church and state was that of the abolition of slavery. Decisions made by the Supreme Court and Congress around abolition infuriated activists and made them consider whether direct political involvement might be necessary. Toward the end of the nineteenth century, other issues—including Prohibition, women's rights, reforms of industrial and commercial operations, and American expansionism—also caused religious advocates to consider political intervention.

The Social Gospel movement, as seen in the FCC's Social Creed, seems to have been an additional step in this direction, and the more conservative opponents of the FCC charged that the council had, in fact, stepped away from the core of Christianity and that its message was much more social and political than it was gospel. At the beginning of the twentieth century, such divisions were hardening and presaged battles yet to come. American Christianity was continuing to grow and becoming ever more diverse in its organizational and theological forms. But this growth and diversification increasingly raised the question of whether American Christian groups could work together. There were common purposes that brought many of them together, to be sure, but they had trouble articulating a common theological position that most or all could share.

─────────────── BIBLIOGRAPHY ───────────────

Curtis, Heather D. *Faith in the Great Physician: Suffering and Divine Healing in American Culture, 1860–1900*. Baltimore: Johns Hopkins University Press, 2007.

Hutchison, William R. *The Modernist Impulse in American Protestantism*. Cambridge, MA: Harvard University Press, 1976.

Kuklick, Bruce. *Churchmen and Philosophers: From Jonathan Edwards to John Dewey*. New Haven: Yale University Press, 1985.

Marsden, George M. *Fundamentalism and American Culture*. 2nd ed. New York: Oxford University Press, 2006.

Marty, Martin E. *Modern American Religion*. Vol. 1, *The Irony of It All, 1893–1919*. Chicago: University of Chicago Press, 1986.

Robert, Dana L. *American Women in Mission: A Social History of Their Thought and Practice*. Macon, GA: Mercer University Press, 1997.

Sandeen, Ernest R. *The Roots of Fundamentalism: British and American Millenarianism, 1800–1930*. Rev. ed. Grand Rapids: Baker, 1978.

Szasz, Ferenc Morton. *The Protestant Clergy in the Great Plains and Mountain West, 1865–1915*. Albuquerque: University of New Mexico Press, 1988.

Wacker, Grant. *Heaven Below: Early Pentecostals and American Culture*. Cambridge, MA: Harvard University Press, 2001.

Warren, Louis S. *God's Red Son: The Ghost Dance Religion and the Making of Modern America*. New York: Basic Books, 2017.

9

War, Prohibition, and the Great Depression, 1914–41

BY 1914, WHEN WORLD WAR I broke out in Europe, the United States had become a world power, although its inhabitants did not always recognize it as such. America was a leader in terms of industrial output and economic power, but despite its victory in the Spanish-American War in 1898, it had not sought appreciable territory in the great European race to grab colonies in Africa and Asia. The United States had grown its navy considerably, but its other military forces were very modest compared to those of the European powers. America considered the Western Hemisphere its zone of influence, and it intervened in this region economically and sometimes militarily, but it did not develop many traditional colonies. Territorially, the United States had reached its full extent, and with the admission of Arizona and New Mexico as states in 1912, the lower forty-eight states were complete. The only territories added after this were minor: the US Virgin Islands were purchased from Denmark in 1917, and groupings of Pacific islands were added after World War II.

The national trends of urbanization and industrialization continued. The population of the United States grew from 99 million in 1914 to 133 million in 1941, and the percentage of citizens living in urban areas went from 51 percent in 1920 to 56 percent by 1940. The rapid pace of European immigration to the United States came to an abrupt halt in 1914 with the beginning of the war in Europe, and did not recover due to strict limits imposed in the

1920s and because of the Great Depression in the 1930s. A significant internal migration was that of African Americans from the rural South to the cities of the Northeast and Midwest; 1.6 million African Americans made this Great Migration between 1916 and 1940, drawn by industrial jobs and slightly better living conditions.

Although World War I began in Europe in 1914, America resisted joining this war until April 1917, after attacks on Atlantic shipping caused significant American deaths. Initially, the country was woefully unprepared for war, but eventually American military forces were sent to Europe, and by 1918 they had tipped the balance of power, which led to the defeat of Germany and Austria-Hungary. This period saw important political developments, including amendments to the Constitution allowing for a national income tax (Sixteenth), popular election of senators (Seventeenth), the prohibition of alcoholic beverages (Eighteenth), and the right of women to vote (Nineteenth). Progressive activism and laws led to better working conditions, the rights of labor unions, antitrust actions, and many important financial and consumer regulations.

American technological and industrial innovation continued its rapid expansion, with new and greatly expanded access for ordinary citizens to electricity, automobiles, and many other new consumer goods. Advances in wealth, improved access to food and health care, and innovations in medicine meant that the average American life span rose from fifty-four years in 1915 to sixty-two years in 1940, despite the great influenza pandemic of 1918 and 1919. Americans embraced a new era of mass communications during this time, with the widespread adoption of movies and radio broadcasting, which also led to increasing social changes in the 1920s.

After World War I, the nation longed for "normalcy" and an isolationist withdrawal from the world, including the rejection of membership in the new League of Nations. Very tight immigration restrictions in the 1920s cut the flow of new arrivals to a trickle. Fear of communism and socialism, along with a general fear of "undesirable outsiders," added to this withdrawal from the wider world, and isolationism and pacifism once again became popular. A laissez-faire attitude toward government and the economy was commonplace, although the enforcement of Prohibition regulations tended to divide the "wets" from the "drys."

The popular national mood of complacency throughout the 1920s ended abruptly with the great stock market crash in October 1929. There had already been a long-running agricultural depression through the 1920s, but the dramatic economic crash of 1929 spread the depression throughout the rest of the economy. Depressions were a regular feature of American economic life, but this one, the *Great* Depression, was different, both in its length and in its depth. Traditional means of addressing the hardships of depression—local efforts and private charities—were overwhelmed by the sheer magnitude of the event; at its lowest point, nearly 25 percent of American households were without employment income. Franklin Delano Roosevelt was elected president in 1932 and implemented a series of national measures—called the New Deal—to address the crisis; these measures gave hope, but the country did not fully recover economically until World War II.

The Great Depression was a worldwide event, and it increased social and military unrest around the world, which led to the rise of Adolf Hitler in Germany, mass starvation and deportations in Russia, and new militarist leaders in Japan and Italy. Military conflicts and other hostilities increased during the 1930s, including the Spanish Civil War in 1936, the Japanese invasion of China in 1937, and the 1938 German annexation of Austria and the Sudetenland (previously a German-majority region of Czechoslovakia). World War II formally began in 1939 with the German invasion of Poland, and Germany conquered much of western Europe in 1940. The British held out, but they were severely tested by German bombing campaigns in 1940 and 1941. Still, the isolationist mood in the United States was not overcome until the Japanese surprise attack on the American military base at Pearl Harbor, Hawaii, on December 7, 1941, after which America formally entered the war.

World War I

Despite the growing tensions within American Christianity and newer, secular challenges to religion in general, the period before World War I saw perhaps the peak of Christian influence on American public life. Mainline Protestant groups, especially, controlled many aspects of society and politics, while the growing presence of American Roman Catholicism dominated in important areas, most notably the major cities. A kind of popular melding of religious and political visions of the country had been on display in the Spanish-American War in 1898. This kind of melding, called public religion or civil religion, assumed that the goals of Christianity and the goal of the United States were practically the same. Further, building on traditional Christian postmillennialism, the goal of the country was seen as bringing its model of religion and democracy to the world. America was considered the best example of Christian civilization the world had ever seen, a beacon to everyone else. Two influential Democratic politicians of the time, William Jennings Bryan (1860–1925) and Woodrow Wilson (1856–1924), typified this vision of the country. Both were traditional Presbyterians who had had conversion experiences and who believed that the United States had something akin to a messianic position in the world.

Political and military tensions had been simmering in Europe for at least a decade before 1914, and a spark in an obscure corner of the Balkans was all it took to bring the continent to all-out war. After an initial German thrust into France, the conflict stalemated in trench warfare, a new form of industrial warfare in which hundreds of thousands of soldiers were slaughtered with little movement of the lines. Americans watched in horror and vowed that their country would never be drawn into such a senseless European conflict. The dominant mood of the country was isolationist, and Wilson himself campaigned for reelection to the presidency in 1916 with the boastful slogan, "He kept us out of the War." Pacifist groups, like the Church Peace Union, formed by Andrew Carnegie in 1914, were very popular. Even though America envisioned itself as savior to the world, most Americans would not support sending their sons to fight in a futile European war.

Nevertheless, America was slowly drawn into World War I. News reports and other media emphasized German atrocities committed against civilian populations in the battle zone, especially in neutral Belgium, and the "Hun" became a figure of terror. German submarines sank many ships in the Atlantic Ocean, including ones with Americans onboard. Finally, in April 1917 America entered the war on the side of the United Kingdom and France, which were both desperate for military assistance. Though the United States Navy had been built up over the previous decades, the American army was small and ill-supplied. The country prepared itself for war: a civilian draft was instituted, and new military training facilities were built around the country.

Previous positions notwithstanding, American Christians jumped eagerly into the national war effort, and church leaders urged support for the war. Almost every group dedicated itself to the war effort, except the historically pacifist churches (such as the Quakers and the Mennonites) and a few others, such as the Jehovah's Witnesses. The initial practical need was to bring Christian ministry to the troops by means of military chaplains and other Christian workers. National Christian groups—including the Federal Council of Churches (FCC), the YMCA, the YWCA, and the American Bible Society—developed systematic outreach programs. And denominational families came up with their own programs. The home-front activities that supported the war effort (such as rationing and fundraising) were strongly urged from many pulpits.

However, the rush to support the war and demonize the enemy led to a number of unfortunate developments. Since Germany was the primary enemy, German Americans were immediately suspected of disloyalty; and a similar suspicion was extended to other foreigners as well, an instance of the general xenophobia that has arisen periodically in America. Immigration had peaked shortly before 1914, and by that year up to 13 percent of Americans were first- or second-generation immigrants, a historic high. Speaking a language other than English was suddenly seen as a sign of potential disloyalty. Many of the immigrant religious groups primarily used their native languages in their congregations, schools, and other institutions, so those ministries were targeted. Laws were passed in several states to prohibit the use of languages other than English in education and even in public gatherings or during worship, though these laws were eventually ruled to be unconstitutional. "Foreigners" were investigated for possible disloyalty, and some were sent to internment camps. There were even scattered instances of mob violence.

Immigrant religious groups rushed to demonstrate their support for the war effort, and in many cases became hyperpatriotic. American Lutherans had hoped to mount major celebrations in 1917 of the four-hundredth anniversary of the Protestant Reformation, but, given the Reformation's German roots, they wisely turned their attention to supporting the war effort instead. Wartime xenophobia accelerated the transition in many immigrant denominations from speaking native languages to primarily using English, but these changes took into the 1920s and 1930s to complete. Roman Catholics and Lutherans quickly developed efforts in military chaplaincy, which after the war were turned into continuing organizations, the National Catholic Welfare Council and the National Lutheran Council, respectively.

With the latter stages of the war came another deadly event, the great influenza pandemic of 1918 and 1919, which killed 50 million people worldwide, 650,000 of whom were in the United States. Influenza (commonly known at the time as grippe or catarrh) was nothing new to the world, but it was generally not counted among the most dangerous diseases. This new viral strain, however, was different because of its speed of dissemination and lethality. The influenza was first seen among the military before it appeared among the general population, and the widespread movement of troops around the globe spread it quickly. Another distinctive element of this influenza was that it was particularly deadly among young adults, aged eighteen to forty, prime military ages. Doctors could do little but let the disease run its course, and those worst affected died quickly. The only effective responses were public health strategies, including quarantine and shutting down public gatherings. During the fall of 1918, when the pandemic was at its worst, churches and schools were shuttered, and religious leaders risked their lives to attend to the sick and dying.

American Christian missionary efforts in Africa and Asia also expanded during the war. European mission agencies and churches had been the primary leaders in these efforts, but their leadership faltered because of the war. German colonies were taken over by the British and the French, and German missionaries were interned. Many European missions could not get their personnel to the mission fields or did not have the funds to support them. American mission agencies stepped up to fill the gaps for these "orphaned missions" and began taking a leading role, a trend that continued after the war.

Religious and Social Developments after World War I

Two amendments to the US Constitution were passed and took effect immediately after the war: the Eighteenth, prohibiting the manufacturing and sale of alcoholic beverages (Prohibition), and the Nineteenth, granting women the right to vote (suffrage). Prohibition had deep religious roots and was supported across denominational lines, and though women's suffrage had fewer overt religious ties, this amendment and the spirit behind it would eventually have profound effects on American Christianity in the twentieth century.

The movement for Prohibition was perhaps one of the last great social and religious crusades of the nineteenth century, and one with broad Protestant support. Even as deep fissures were opening between conservative and liberal Protestants, each side had its own religious reasons for supporting Prohibition. Eventually, organizations like the Anti-Saloon League and the Woman's Christian Temperance Union were able to gain enough political leverage on the national level, and the Eighteenth Amendment was passed by enough states to come into effect in 1920. Not all religious groups supported it, however. Most Roman Catholics and many of their leaders opposed the measure, as did a few Protestant groups, such as the Lutheran Church–Missouri Synod.

The amendment granting women the right to vote was passed around the same time, and women were able to vote in the 1920 national election. There was no explicit religious tie to this amendment, although some religious leaders supported it because they felt that women might be more willing to vote for Prohibition candidates. But the recognition that women had the right to make their voices heard in political elections eventually had a huge impact on the shape of American Christianity. Most Protestant denominations and congregations were organized along the lines of a representational democracy, and power within them was based on voting. Even before the Nineteenth Amendment there had been some movement to grant women the vote in congregational and denominational elections, although this was generally limited. But now, with women receiving the vote in political elections, there was a slow but discernable movement to grant them the vote in religious elections as well. Women even began to argue for the right to hold offices in congregations and to become

9.1. Anti-Saloon League March.

delegates to regional and national assemblies, although progress here was even slower.

This increasing push for women's rights in religious organizations was countered by other movements looking to curtail women's power in other ways. Such movements especially targeted the financial and religious power of separate women's religious organizations, such as mission societies and boards. Christian women had been successful in organizing themselves during the nineteenth century, and in many congregations and denominations the organizations they developed wielded significant power—especially financial power. Women had always been the majority in American religion, and their growing influence worried many male leaders. In 1911, a broad coalition of Protestant church leaders formed the Men and Religion Forward Movement. The explicit goal of this movement was to evangelize boys and men, but its implicit goal was to make religion more "manly" and to counter the power of women. After World War I, in the name of "greater efficiencies" there was a general push to merge women's mission boards into their denominational counterparts; unspoken in this initiative was the desire to bring these groups under male control. However, these merger efforts succeeded only occasionally, since women generally resisted them.

Although Americans quickly came together to support the war effort and national unity was preached from many Christian pulpits, there were underlying social and religious tensions, both long-standing and new, that erupted after the end of the war. With many of these tensions, a primary concern of the Protestant majority was that their power and control over national life were being eroded by other religious or nonreligious groups. The chaos around the world after World War I added to these anxieties.

The Russian Revolution in 1917, which brought the communists to power, created great anxieties in the United States, as well as fears of political and social radicalism. There had long been socialist, communist, and even anarchist groups in the United States, sometimes related to the labor union movement, but they had gained little political power. Nevertheless, the fear of radical groups blossomed into the Red Scare of 1917 to 1920, when the federal government moved to curtail their power and even deport some of their leaders. Despite the efforts of some, American Christianity had not had a good relationship with the labor movement, and the communists and some of the socialists had rejected organized religion altogether; for some, the labor unions were their "church." That many union members and leaders were of immigrant and Roman Catholic backgrounds increased the tensions. American Roman Catholics made some attempt to influence the labor movement, most notably through the Knights of Labor, but this organization was viewed with suspicion by some in the church hierarchy.

The Ku Klux Klan, which first emerged after the Civil War, was revived in 1915 and grew rapidly into the 1920s. It targeted African Americans as well as immigrants, Roman Catholics, Jews, socialists, communists, and others. The Klan had widespread support around the country, not just in the South, and claimed over 4 million members at its peak, although the organization fell apart almost as rapidly as it had grown, its membership plummeting in the 1930s. It claimed to be based on Protestant and Christian principles, though many American Christian leaders disavowed it.

Anti-Semitism was another common element of the postwar period. The later stages of the great nineteenth-century immigration included large numbers of Jews from eastern Europe and Russia, many of whom were escaping religious persecution. The arrival of so many Jews not only unnerved Christians but also threatened to overwhelm the already acculturated Reform Jews. A number of the leaders of the labor union movement and the radical political groups were Jewish in background, though many were nonpracticing Jews—which added to anti-Semitic Americans' distrust of the labor movements and the left-wing political groups. But modern anti-Semitism is generally based on specious racial categories rather than religious ones. The Red Scare included denunciations of supposed international Jewish conspiracies to take over the world, circulated by some prominent Americans, including Henry Ford.

Nativist suspicions also applied to recent immigrants, especially Roman Catholics and other non-Protestants. Coming out of the sixteenth-century English Reformation, American Protestantism had a long-running strain of anti-Catholicism, and the rapid growth of American Roman Catholicism into the early twentieth century stoked such attitudes. With Roman Catholic leaders preoccupied with the basic need of gathering in and organizing the masses of immigrants, American Catholicism's leaders and organizations (e.g., the Knights of Columbus) sought to counter these nativist attitudes by emphasizing the "Americanness" of resident Roman Catholics. Though Roman Catholics often dominated political power in the large cities, their national presence lagged. When Al Smith ran as the first Roman Catholic candidate for president in 1928, he faced a nativist backlash and lost decisively.

These fears and anxieties led to drastic restrictions on immigration during the 1920s. There had already been restrictions on immigration from Asia and the screening for "undesirable" immigrants at Ellis Island during the late nineteenth century, and, in 1924, Congress passed the Johnson-Reed Act (also known as the Immigration Act of 1924), which completely shut down immigration from Asia and subjected European immigration to stringent quotas that virtually eliminated immigration from southern and eastern Europe. As a result, the number of new immigrants to the United States plunged.

The Growth and Organization of American Christianity

The nineteenth century saw a dramatic growth of organized religion, and, contrary to the perception of many, this growth continued well into the twentieth century. In 1906, 51 percent of the American population belonged to a religious organization, and by 1926 this number had risen to 56 percent. Since the turn of the century, the Roman Catholics had been the largest single religious group, although the Protestants as a whole were still substantially larger. By 1926, the fast-growing Baptists had overtaken the Methodists as the largest grouping of Protestants, a position they still maintain. The Methodists slipped into second place, followed by the Lutherans, the Presbyterians, and the Christian Church (Disciples of Christ). Across this multiplicity of denominations, there was an increasing push to merge many of them together.

One of the major ecumenical efforts after World War I was the Interchurch World Movement (IWM). This effort was instituted in December 1918 by 135 representatives of church and mission organizations, principally from White, mainline Protestantism. Funded initially by a grant from oil magnate and devout Baptist layman John D. Rockefeller (1839–1937), this movement was an ambitious ecumenical attempt to survey and respond to the needs of the world. It was dedicated to the traditional goal of the evangelization of the world, but also to a scientific and sociological approach to the issues of church and world. The staff of the IWM developed ambitious plans and suggested courses of action. They advocated for the consolidation of small rural congregations, strategies to meet the religious challenges of churches in urban areas, and other initiatives. To support these efforts, as well as to bring relief to the churches of Europe and to expand foreign missions, the leaders of the IWM set an extremely ambitious fundraising goal of $400 million. But despite well-crafted advertising campaigns, this effort was a complete failure. The IWM did not even raise enough funds to cover its administrative costs, so it collapsed in 1920. Parallel fundraising efforts within the various denominations did somewhat better, raising about $200 million between them. But denominational loyalty usually trumped a single ecumenical vision, even for the mainline Protestants.

As America and American Christianity grew, there was a perceived need for better and larger organizations. The model for all of this was American business, especially the developing American corporations and conglomerates. Efficiency and scale were the watchwords of the day, and it was believed that the larger and more unified an organization was, the better it could meet its responsibilities. Of course, consolidated corporations led the way in this, but the same mantra was applied to government, education, social service organizations, and, of course, religion. The FCC, the IWM, and the various programs for church mergers all followed this model.

As they grew larger, many denominations adopted a centralized business model for their own organizations. Most American Protestant denominations had not traditionally had much in the way of permanent staffing beyond their elected leaders. They conducted their main business at annual meetings, and continuing work was carried out by committees of pastors and laypeople. There were usually no permanent church headquarters. But by the 1920s or so, many denominations, mission boards, and ecumenical agencies had grown large enough to require permanent administrative staff, and they formed church headquarters largely based on business models. In effect, the leaders in these new denominational structures functioned as chief executive officers (CEOs), and the pastors took on the role of a sales force. In this way, the centralization of power and efforts in these church headquarters moved away from the older organizational models.

But American Christianity drew more than an organizational model from early twentieth-century business practices; it also adopted a new way of presenting its message. The example of the Interchurch World Movement shows directly how the commercial language of the time pervaded its essential approach.

Bruce Barton, *The Man Nobody Knows* (1925)

The kindly lady . . . would have been terribly shocked if she had known what was going on inside the little boy's mind.

"You must love Jesus," she said every Sunday, "and God." . . .

Jesus was the "lamb of God." The little boy did not know what that meant, but it sounded like Mary's little lamb. Something for girls—sissified. . . .

Years went by and the boy grew up and became a business man.

He began to wonder about Jesus.

The more sermons the man heard and the more books he read the more mystified he became. One day he decided to wipe his mind clean of books and sermons. He said, "I will read what the men who knew Jesus personally said about him. I will read about him as though he were a new historical character, about whom I had never heard anything at all."

The man was amazed. A physical weakling! Where did they get that idea? Jesus pushed a plane and swung an adze; he was a successful carpenter. He slept outdoors and spent his days walking around his favorite lake. His muscles were so strong that when he drove the money-changers out, nobody dared to oppose him! . . .

A failure! He picked up twelve men from the bottom ranks of business and forged them into an organization that conquered the world.

When the man had finished his reading he exclaimed, "This is a man nobody knows." "Someday," said he, "someone will write a book about Jesus. Every business man will read it and send it to his partners and his salesmen. For it will tell the story of the founder of modern business."

So the man waited for someone to write the book, but no one did. Instead, more books were published about the "lamb of God" who was weak and unhappy and glad to die. The man became impatient. One day he said, "I believe I will try to write that book, myself."

And he did.

Bruce Barton, introduction to *The Man Nobody Knows* (Indianapolis: Bobbs-Merrill, 1925).

The work of the church was to be subjected to "scientific" study to make sure that it was as efficient as possible. Publicity for the IWM campaign suggested that Christianity was the "biggest business of the biggest man [i.e., Christ] in the world." It said that Christ "was always about His Father's business" and that he "needs big men for big business."[1] A very successful biography of Christ, titled *The Man Nobody Knows* (1925), was written by Congregational

1. "Bulletin from the Interchurch World Movement," April 1920, quoted in Eldon G. Ernest, *Moment of Truth for Protestant America: Interchurch Campaigns Following World War One* (Missoula, MT: Scholar's Press, 1974), 89.

layman and advertising executive Bruce Barton (1886–1967). Barton felt that other treatments of the life of Christ were hopelessly old-fashioned and liable to alienate modern audiences. Barton pictured Christ as the greatest business organizer the world had ever seen, one who took a ragtag bunch of losers (the disciples) and turned them into the greatest sales force the world had ever seen. Barton's subsequent books on the Bible and the apostle Paul were developed along similar lines. Calvin Coolidge, the American president during this time, famously declared in 1925 that "the chief business of the American people is business." Apparently, some religious leaders agreed with this sentiment.

Popular religious messaging of the time sometimes followed the sentiment put forward by Barton and others. One of the most famous preachers of the age was Norman Vincent Peale (1898–1993), who in 1932 became the pastor at the prestigious Marble Collegiate Church in New York City. Though his most influential book, *The Power of Positive Thinking*, did not appear until 1952, he published a string of books in a similar vein during the 1930s. Peale's message was a combination of popular therapeutic psychology and religious prescriptions drawn from the Bible. He argued that aligning one's life with the purposes of God's world would bring personal happiness, physical health, and even financial success, something that has been dubbed by critics as the health and wealth gospel, or the prosperity gospel. Peale was by no means the only proponent of this mode of religious thinking during this period. Russell H. Conwell (1843–1925), pastor at the Baptist Temple in Philadelphia and founder of Conwell School of Theology (a predecessor of today's Gordon-Conwell Theological Seminary), was a famous religious lecturer best known for his sermonic lecture titled "Acres of Diamonds," which he delivered over six thousand times, reaching hundreds of thousands of listeners. In this lecture, he asserted that there were "acres of diamonds" in one's own backyard, there for the taking, and that it was the possibility and the duty of every Christian to become rich in order to be able to serve the cause of Christ. Like Peale (and Andrew Carnegie), Conwell intimated broadly that there were connections between personal advancement and success and Christian piety and devotion.

Theological Disputes and Developments

Within American Protestantism, the tensions between liberals (modernists) and conservatives (fundamentalists) had been growing for decades before World War I, but overt disputes were limited during the war. After the war, however, these tensions broke out into open disputes, mainly in certain northern denominations, especially the Northern Presbyterians, Northern

Baptists, and the Christian Church (Disciples of Christ). Other denominations either had fewer conservatives (Congregationalists and Episcopalians) or fewer liberals (Southern Baptists and Lutherans). It must be said that most pastors and church members in all these denominations were probably neither decidedly modernist nor decidedly fundamentalist, and the disputes within the denominations were generally settled by how the largest group of centrists happened to lean.

The basic theological elements of fundamentalism had been set down in a series of booklets issued between 1910 and 1915 called *The Fundamentals*, which were eventually distilled into five nonnegotiable points. The most important of these points was the inerrancy of the Bible. By this was meant that the Bible did not, and could not, contain any errors, whether doctrinal or otherwise. The events described in the Bible—including God's creation of the world in six days and Jesus's miracles—all had to be literally true. It was thought that even a single error was enough to call the authority of the whole Bible into question. However, liberals were embracing modern theories about geology and evolution and admitting that many parts of the Bible were not literally true—that they were, rather, prescientific myths. This conflict went to the core of Protestant Christianity because Protestantism was built on the sole authority of the Bible. An explosion was brewing over these differences.

Fundamentalism as a movement began after World War I, characterized by an aggressive defense of the authority of the Bible and an unwillingness to join or cooperate with anyone who did not share the fundamentalist commitment to biblical inerrancy. In 1919, William Bell Riley, Reuben Torey, and others founded the World's Christian Fundamentals Association in Philadelphia, which became the leading fundamentalist organization. Besides disseminating their theological views, one main purpose of the organization was to support state-level laws prohibiting the teaching of evolution in public schools. Such laws were passed in several states, including Tennessee, which led to a major controversy in 1925: the so-called Scopes Monkey Trial.

John Scopes was a science teacher in Dayton, Tennessee, and in 1925 he was charged with teaching evolution in school. His trial mushroomed into a national media spectacle, covered extensively in the press and broadcast live on the radio. The prosecution was led by none other than William Jennings Bryan, and the defense was led by famed trial lawyer Clarence Darrow (1857–1938). The trial ended up being less about Scopes, who admitted that he had taught evolution and paid a fine, than it was a national referendum on biblical inerrancy and science. In the court of national public opinion, Darrow and the press, especially the journalist H. L. Mencken (1880–1956), subjected Bryan—and by extension the biblical inerrantists—to scorn and ridicule and won decisively.

9.2. Clarence Darrow and William Jennings Bryan, Scopes Trial, 1925.

Biblical literalists and fundamentalists were portrayed as uneducated, backwoods southern people who were simply not all that bright.

This was an unfortunate caricature, because many fundamentalists were none of these things, and there were numerous people outside of fundamentalism who held to similar positions on the authority of the Bible. One leading figure defending the literal authority of the Bible was Princeton Theological Seminary professor J. Gresham Machen (1881–1937). His book *Christianity and Liberalism* (1923) offered a spirited defense of traditional views of the Bible and Christian doctrines and charged that while modernist Christianity was certainly modern, it was in fact not Christian at all. In 1929, when Princeton Seminary was reorganized to allow more diverse theological positions, Machen and a core of conservative professors left Princeton to form Westminster Theological Seminary in Philadelphia.

The other main action in what became known as the fundamentalist-modernist controversy was a series of intradenominational battles during the 1920s over control of denominational and mission boards, mainly within the Northern Presbyterians and Northern Baptists. In 1922, well-known pastor Harry Emerson Fosdick (1878–1969) sparked an offensive against

Harry Emerson Fosdick, "Shall the Fundamentalists Win?" (1922)

These two groups exist in the Christian churches and the question raised by the Fundamentalists is—Shall one of them drive the other out? Will that get us anywhere? Multitudes of young men and women at this season of the year are graduating from our schools of learning, thousands of them Christians who may make us older ones ashamed by the sincerity of their devotion to God's will on earth. They are not thinking in ancient terms that leave ideas of progress out. They cannot think in those terms. There could be no greater tragedy than that the Fundamentalists should shut the door of the Christian fellowship against such.

I do not believe for one moment that the Fundamentalists are going to succeed. Nobody's intolerance can contribute anything to the solution of the situation which we have described. If, then, the Fundamentalists have no solution of the problem, where may we expect to find it?

Nevertheless, it is true that just now the Fundamentalists are giving us one of the worst exhibitions of bitter intolerance that the churches of this country have ever seen. . . . Opinions may be mistaken; love never is.

As I plead thus for an intellectually hospitable, tolerant, liberty-loving church, I am, of course, thinking primarily about this new generation. We have boys and girls growing up in our homes and schools, and because we love them we may well wonder about the church which will be waiting to receive them. Now, the worst kind of church that can possibly be offered to the allegiance of the new generation is an intolerant church.

Harry Emerson Fosdick, "Shall the Fundamentalists Win?," *Christian Century*, June 8, 1922, 713–17.

fundamentalism with a ringing sermon, "Shall the Fundamentalists Win?," which achieved national dissemination. In these fights over denominational control, the fundamentalists indeed did not win, not so much because the modernists were more powerful, but because the centrist elements within the denominations refused to side with the fundamentalists. Unwilling to remain within these mainline denominations, many fundamentalists left them to form new ones, including Machen's Orthodox Presbyterian Church. Fundamentalists went on to form their own Christian subculture in America, with its own networks of educational institutions, mission boards, and publishing houses. Not all conservatives who left were classic fundamentalists, however. Many shared fundamentalism's theology and opposition to modernism but not its militant tactics. They increasingly came to prefer the label *evangelicals* (rather than *fundamentalists*), and they probably constituted the majority of conservative Protestants. American Protestantism was thus split into two camps: the old "mainline" Protestants, still culturally strong, and the newer evangelical groups, who offered a different Protestant vision. As mainline Protestants began pulling away from traditional models of evangelism, especially on the overseas mission fields, conservatives founded their own independent mission boards and agencies dedicated to traditional "soul-winning" approaches.

It should be noted that the Protestant modernists were not a large group. They were mainly found among the faculty of the leading mainline Protestant seminaries and divinity schools. Liberal Protestants (such as Fosdick) made up a larger group; while somewhat sympathetic to the modernists, they were definitely reacting against the conservatives. Their theological positions were a continuation of nineteenth-century liberalism: a generally optimistic, postmillennial Protestantism focusing on Jesus as the moral and religious guide and on the "core" doctrines of the faith, but open to modern developments, such as the "higher" criticism of the Bible. They had moved away from the conversionist narrative of revivalism and saw the Christian life as a continuous upward movement toward greater faith, principally through education and moral training.

But the tragic events of World War I—especially the mass slaughter on the Western Front—caused many in Europe and North America to question this classic liberal narrative, both within Christianity and in the wider culture. The spectacle of the leading, most "modern," Western democracies sacrificing an entire generation of their young men in such a useless war caused many to rethink their positions. The fact that many liberal Christians had so strongly supported their governments' war efforts was also troubling. Karl Barth (1886–1968), a Swiss Reformed pastor and theologian, came to reject the Christian liberalism of his theological teachers and, in his influential commentary *The Epistle to the Romans* (1919, 1922), called the optimistic, progressive schema of liberal Protestantism into question. Barth called for a serious and renewed theological encounter with the Bible and with classic, premodern Protestant orthodox theology. While his commentary and subsequent books were slow to be translated into English, his attack on Protestant liberalism radiated outward and inspired a new generation of Protestant theologians.

American modernist theologians typically rejected Barth and his "theology of crisis." But many others took notice, including American theologians (and brothers) H. Richard Niebuhr (1894–1962) and Reinhold Niebuhr (1892–1971), who eventually took prestigious theological positions at Yale and at Union Theological Seminary (New York), respectively. In numerous theological works from the 1920s onward, the Niebuhrs attacked the optimistic Christian theology of the liberals without retreating into fundamentalism. They charged that the liberal theology of their age was a pale and lifeless religion, virtually indistinguishable from the Western societies in which it was lodged and unable to critique them. In his influential book *Moral Man and Immoral Society* (1932), Reinhold Niebuhr criticized the optimistic theological anthropology of the liberals and called for a serious reappropriation of the Christian doctrines of sin and evil. And H. Richard Niebuhr, in his 1938 book *The Kingdom of God in America*, argued strongly against the prevalent assumption that the kingdom of God could be equated with the nature and purposes of American civilization. Their approach to Christian theology and ethics—which some have called neoorthodoxy—represented a break both with fundamentalists and with liberals; it attracted other theologians and pastors and became a leading form of Protestant theology in America through the middle of the twentieth century.

H. Richard Niebuhr's Criticism of Liberal American Protestantism (1937)

It is evident that the kingdom of Christ into which the revivalists bade men press in dependence on God's grace was not identified with the visible church. It was more than ever the invisible church. . . .

With the cessation of the movement and the turn toward institutionalism the aggressive societies became denominations. . . . [A denomination] may be defined as a missionary order which has turned to the defensive and lost its consciousness of the invisible catholic church. These orders now confused themselves with their cause and began to promote themselves, identifying the kingdom of Christ with the doctrines and practices prevalent in the group. . . .

The old idea of American Christians as a chosen people who had been called to a special task was turned into the notion of a chosen nation specially favored. . . . Thus institutionalism and imperialism, ecclesiastical and political, go hand in hand. . . .

Christ the redeemer became Jesus the teacher or spiritual genius in whom the religious capacities of mankind were fully developed. . . .

A God without wrath brought men without sin into a kingdom without judgment through the ministrations of Christ without a cross. . . .

At the very time when the paralysis of institutionalization seemed most evident in the Christian movement in America signs were not lacking of a new spirit stirring . . . [that] manifested increasing interest in the great doctrines and traditions of the Christian past, as though they were aware that power had been lost because the heritage had been forgotten, or that there was no way toward the coming kingdom save the way taken by a sovereign God through the reign of Jesus Christ.

H. Richard Niebuhr, *The Kingdom of God in America* (New York: Harper, 1937), 104, 177, 179, 192–93, and 198.

During the 1920s and 1930s, American Roman Catholics were continuing their struggle over their adaptation to American culture and religiosity. The virtual end to immigration from Europe at the beginning of World War I meant that the dramatic growth of Roman Catholicism slowed, but in 1926 Roman Catholics still represented 37 percent of all religious adherents and 20 percent of the total population. With the end of immigration, the transition to the use of English and acculturation into American society more broadly intensified, pushed by widespread xenophobia and anti-Catholicism. Although "Americanism" as an ideal had been rejected by the Vatican in 1899, American Roman Catholics continued to face the question of how they fit in with a national culture that was still mainly Protestant. Like many other non-Protestant immigrants, they sought to fully embrace and maintain their religious traditions while also fully embracing their American nationality. But it was a struggle.

Theologically, Roman Catholics were still constrained by a church hierarchy that was strongly traditional and conservative. Yet there were signs within the tradition of new growth and vitality, especially a new theological tradition coming from Catholic Europe: neo-Thomism, a re-appreciation of the core theology of Thomas Aquinas. This new movement, particularly influential in Roman Catholic higher education after the war, somewhat paralleled Protestant neoorthodoxy in its strategy by going back to a core orthodox theologian. From this base, it sought to creatively engage with modern culture without being swallowed up by it.

Changes in American Culture during the 1920s

After the energy and push for national unity during World War I, the postwar period seemed restless, diffused, and contentious. Though the servicemen coming home from the war longed for things to return to normal, as did practically everyone else, the world had changed, and there was little agreement about what "normal" actually meant. The frantic pace of industrial and agricultural production during the war led to an inevitable slump afterward, and jobs were not so easy to get. The agricultural depression after the war lingered on through the 1920s, affecting rural Americans and accelerating the ongoing flow of people into urban areas. Labor unions had been growing since the late nineteenth century, often by means of strikes, but now employers were pushing back by curbing wages and trying to break the power of the unions. There were several high-profile strikes immediately after the war, many of which were put down with repression and sometimes violence. The rise of communism and the resulting Red Scare created a heated and uncertain environment in the country and added to the general sense of unease.

The implementation of Prohibition in 1920 added to the general discontent. Though many American Protestants were strongly in favor of Prohibition and cheered on its enforcement, there were many others in the country who opposed the new measure. These people enjoyed their beer and wine, and Protestant support for Prohibition led them to resent both the government and those religious groups that so fervently supported the measure. An underground economy developed almost at once, with smugglers and bootleggers providing illegal alcohol to "speakeasies" and other outlets. Organized crime flourished through control of this illicit industry, the growth of which was abetted by ordinary Americans who just wanted a drink. One popular icon of the age was a *flapper* (a 1920s term referring to a young woman who flouted conventional standards of behavior) drinking bathtub gin in an illegal speakeasy while listening to hot jazz.

This is sometimes characterized as an age of unrest, hedonism, and cynicism. As with most characterizations, there is a grain of truth to this. It was an age in which there were ongoing denigrations of and attacks on conventional religiosity in the popular media, some of which received widespread attention. Some of the most popular novels of the day lampooned conventional religion and middle-class, middle-American culture. These included the popular works by Sinclair Lewis (1885–1951): *Main Street* (1920), *Babbit* (1922), and *Arrowsmith* (1925). Lewis's 1927 novel, *Elmer Gantry*, took direct aim at entrepreneurial religion with a searing portrayal of a corrupt preacher. Journalist H. L. Mencken and others savagely satirized conservative Protestantism in the press and openly cheered what they saw as the decline of religion in general. These writers portrayed religious people as backward, uneducated hypocrites whose religiosity was slowly dying because of modernity and education. These attacks were based on a form of secularization theory, which held that modern, progressive people were likely to outgrow their need for religion (something that has rarely been the case in the United States). On top of this was the growth in popularity of therapeutic psychology, especially Freudianism, which saw adult religious belief as a neurosis, or psychological maladjustment. For some, popular psychological therapy and books became a substitute for religion (or, rather, a substitute religion!).

The trend toward urbanization continued, and agricultural employment declined as industrial and commercial employment rose. The movement of people into the cities meant their continued growth, and, as immigrants and African Americans moved into the core urban areas, White middle-class Americans moved out toward new suburban developments. Contrary to secularization theories, organized religion was actually stronger in the cities than in the rural areas. But in the cities, older forms of Protestantism were significantly challenged by aggressive, newer forms of Christianity. Many middle-class Americans were attracted to new forms of religion that often were not conventionally Christian, such as Christian Science and Unity, as well as to non-Christian movements like Bahá'í, Vedanta, and many others. In the cities, people simply had a greater variety of religious choices, and the new groups catered to this reality.

One of the most important elements of the 1920s was the rise of national mass communications, something that had a profound effect on American culture. The spectacular popularity of radio broadcasting and motion pictures (movies) during this period was the beginning of American national popular culture. These new media, and the people who ran and starred in them, became the arbiters of national culture. A radio set became a domestic standard, such that almost every home in the country had one. Americans flocked to the movie theaters, and movies provided a new world for people to emulate, if they could. Radio and motion pictures also promoted other new forms of entertainment and popular culture, including jazz and swing music.

American Christians and their leaders were cautious about, and often even hostile toward, these new media and the popular culture they were creating, especially because of the hedonism and sexual openness that they often glorified. Preachers and priests often railed against the "glorification of immorality" that they saw in movies and heard on the radio. Movies were the biggest target of concern, and the industry reacted cautiously toward these criticisms. A number of states explored implementing restrictions on the content of movies. In 1929, a Roman Catholic priest named Daniel Lord (1888–1955) drafted a potential list of moral regulations for the film industry—standards that, in 1930, were adopted into the regulations of the Motion Picture Production Code by the Motion Picture Producers and Distributors of America (popularly known as the Hays Office; now formally the Motion Picture Association). Concerned about its reputation and its audience's reactions, the industry chose self-censorship instead of having censorship imposed on it. The National Legion of Decency, a Roman Catholic organization formed in 1934, also provided a moral rating system for media for American Catholics.

Radio broadcasting was a different case. Although religious leaders rarely liked what they heard on the radio, they did recognize radio's potential for mass religious communication and evangelism. Early local efforts at religious broadcasting used existing radio stations as well as stations they established, such as the Moody Bible Institute's station, WMBI, in Chicago (which was founded in 1926). But the radio industry was soon consolidated into influential national networks, including the Columbia Broadcasting System (CBS), the National Broadcasting Company (NBC), and the Mutual Broadcasting System. Religious broadcasting on these networks made media stars out of some religious broadcasters, such as the Roman Catholic bishop Fulton Sheen (1895–1979) with *The Catholic Hour* (aired from 1930 to 1950), Lutheran theologian Walter A. Maier (1893–1950) with *The Lutheran Hour* (started in 1930 and still airing), and evangelical pastor Charles Fuller (1887–1968) with the *Old Fashioned Revival Hour* (aired from 1937 to 1968), all of which were extremely popular.

Note the lack of mainline Protestantism here, something that deeply concerned the Federal Council of Churches and its Department of Religious Radio. The FCC worked with a number of networks (but not Mutual) to regulate religious broadcasting by insisting that the networks carry only programming by "responsible" FCC member denominations and that they not sell airtime to any other groups. This was an open attempt to monopolize religious broadcasting and freeze out others, most notably Protestant evangelicals. Evangelicals responded by forming their own radio stations and networks, which became much more popular than the "approved" programming carried by the established networks. Typical was the *Voice of Prophecy*, begun in 1929 by Seventh-day Adventist H. M. S. Richards (1894–1985). Starting with a single station, this program grew into a large national network. The FCC's attempt at monopolization was a complete failure, and evangelicals came to dominate the airwaves.

New Religious Movements and Groups

During the 1920s and 1930s there was solid—and sometimes spectacular—growth of established alternative religious groups, such as Christian Science, Latter-day Saints, Unity, Jehovah's Witnesses, and Theosophy. These years were also a time of religious experimentation and the development of dozens of new, smaller religious groups, often on the fringes of established denominations. Many of the new groups were clustered around a single charismatic leader who often was revered to the point of godhood and maintained tight control over the lives of adherents. The development of these groups excited great concern among both the mainline religions and secular critics, and though many books were written to warn people of the supposed dangers of such groups, these efforts seemed to have little effect in stemming their growth.

The Great Migration of African Americans to the cities in the North and Midwest also saw the development of new religious options within their communities. Although the established African American denominations (Methodists and Baptists) began many new congregations in the cities, hundreds of independent Holiness and Pentecostal congregations were also developed there. These new independent congregations were often started by self-ordained, independent religious entrepreneurs and located in whatever spaces were available, such as storefronts and otherwise unoccupied buildings. Some of these new congregations grew to be well-established institutions within the African American urban communities. As in the rural South, these religious institutions were central to the African American communities, and their pastors were recognized community leaders.

The harshness of segregation and racial discrimination remained, and it continued to fuel a strategic debate within the African American community between those who pushed for greater rights and integration and those who rejected White society and called for African American separateness and self-sufficiency. During this period, the latter position was urged by Marcus Garvey (1887–1940), founder of the Universal Negro Improvement Association (UNIA). Originally from the West Indies, Garvey preached the need for his community to become self-reliant and independent from White society. His religious and business efforts flourished for a while, including a steamship line that acted as a large-scale venture in African American economic self-determination as well as a means for African Americans to emigrate back to Africa. But Garvey's efforts began to collapse in 1922 when the US government indicted him for mail fraud. Religiously, Garvey preached the necessity of African Americans to conceive of God as Black (not White) and that they had to reject the dominant White theologies, which he felt were oppressing them. Some UNIA members formed their own denomination, the African Orthodox Church, which prominently featured images of a Black Christ, Madonna, saints, and angels.

Others who advocated for African American separateness went beyond this to reject Christianity altogether as a White religion. These leaders rejected African American Christianity as a "slave religion" and sought what they felt were more authentically African religious models. During this period, a number of Black Jewish or Hebrew communities flourished, and the Moorish Science Temple of America was founded in 1913 in Newark, New Jersey; it drew on Islam and eventually splintered into several factions. The Nation of Islam grew out of this splintering and was established as an organization in its own right around 1930, in Detroit. None of these groups were traditionally Jewish or Muslim in the typical sense. Instead, they added elements of esoteric religion, Masonry, and new beliefs, such as that God was Black and that White religious leaders had hijacked this original religion.

On the other side were a number of urban African American religious messiahs who preached integration and multicultural congregations. The most

9.3. Father Divine.

famous of these was Father Divine, born George Baker (ca. 1876–1965), a charismatic figure who began to preach in 1915 that God was present in and through his person. Using funding from several wealthy patrons, Father Divine organized interracial communities in and around New York City, with satellite groups elsewhere. These communities developed local efforts to feed the poor and meet their needs, and Father Divine organized his Peace Mission movement to have a larger impact. Another similar figure was Charles Emmanuel Grace (1881–1960), commonly referred to as Sweet Daddy Grace by secular critics and critics from mainline denominations. He began preaching in New York around 1919 and soon developed his own organization, the United House of Prayer for All People, which eventually had about twenty congregations on the East Coast. This movement combined traditional elements of Holiness and Pentecostalism with a focus on Sweet Daddy Grace as a quasi-messianic figure.

Established forms of these new religious movements flourished during the 1920s. In the period between 1916 and 1926, membership in Christian Science rose by 67 percent, in various spiritualist groups by 74 percent, in theosophy by 27 percent, and in Mormonism by 11 percent. Christian Science transcended the death of its founder in 1910 and had 267,000 adherents by 1936. The Unity School also grew, and, in 1927, Charles Fillmore built a large Unity complex near Kansas City, Missouri. Christian Science and Unity both developed extensive centralized publishing and merchandising operations that supported their work, as did many other religious groups of the period.

Several new groups began during this time, including the Jehovah's Witnesses and the International Church of the Foursquare Gospel. The roots and theology of the Jehovah's Witnesses go back to the 1870s, but with the death of leader Charles Taze Russell in 1916, control of the movement fell to Joseph Franklin "Judge" Rutherford (1869–1942), who took the movement from a loose association to a tightly centralized group. This organization, formally named the Jehovah's Witnesses in 1931, developed a massive publishing operation, along with radio broadcasting and other enterprises, all of which were centrally controlled from its headquarters in Brooklyn. Because Jehovah's Witnesses believed that the devil controlled the governments and churches of the world, they refused to cooperate with civil authorities. Their pacifism and noncompliance during World War I brought government investigations and repression, and Jehovah's Witnesses were widely reviled by many in American society.

The International Church of the Foursquare Gospel was a more conventionally Christian denomination, with roots in Holiness and Pentecostalism. The founder of this movement was a flamboyant evangelist, Aimee Semple McPherson (1890–1944), who built her empire from Southern California beginning in 1918. McPherson was a dramatic and effective revival preacher whose work revolved around her five-thousand-seat Angelus Temple in Los Angeles and a radio station, KFSG, which was the core of a national radio broadcasting network. Despite McPherson's involvement in a 1926 scandal—which included reports of kidnapping and fraud—her movement continued to grow, and the denomination was established in 1927.

The growth of such groups and their stances sometimes raised questions about the boundaries of freedom of religion under the First Amendment. During this time, the Jehovah's Witnesses and Christian Science were involved in several important court cases concerning some of their practices, and they pushed the envelope on what was permissible religious expression. They also tested the boundaries of what is considered Christianity. Although Christian Science, Unity, the Latter-day Saints, and the Jehovah's Witnesses all consider their traditions forms of Christianity (often the highest form of Christianity), the rest of the Christian denominations in the United States do not, finding that their theology and practices do not conform with the historical norms of the faith.

American Christianity and the Great Depression

The Great Depression of 1929 to 1941 is so named because of its length, depth, and sheer persistence. Americans were used to economic cycles of boom and bust; these were expected elements of its mostly unregulated capitalistic system. But this depression was different. It actually began after World War I, when overproduction in the farm economy crashed commodity prices and plagued the rural economy through the 1920s. But it was the thinly regulated capital markets that really did the damage, when, in October 1929, a speculative stock-market bubble burst, and a cascade of bank and industrial failures plunged the economy into a deep hole. President Herbert Hoover tried all the traditional remedies, to no avail, and was ousted by Franklin Delano Roosevelt in 1933. In his New Deal programs, Roosevelt instituted wide-ranging reforms of banking and finance and began the Social Security system. His various relief programs brought hope to people, but the economy lagged, and the Depression was ended only by increased defense spending after 1940.

American churches and religious organization had been on the front lines of social relief during previous depressions, but the size and length of this depression quickly overwhelmed their resources. The mainline Protestant churches saw a "religious depression" during the 1930s, where giving plunged and church attendance went down. The financial troubles of the mainline were extended by how expensive their sometimes-monumental church buildings and well-salaried clergy were to maintain. Denominational and congregational programming were cut, and pastors often had their salaries reduced or deferred. The mainline churches prided themselves on being leaders in society, but they were helpless in the face of the depression. The repeal of Prohibition in 1933 was another blow to their prestige.

The trend toward merger and consolidation continued during this period. The largest merger was the reunion of the Northern and Southern Methodists in 1939, reversing the split that had occurred in 1844. Among American Congregationalists, the National Council of the Congregational Churches and the General Convention of the Christian Church merged in 1931 to become the General Council of Congregational Christian Churches. There were other, smaller mergers as well, including that of two German Reformed groups into the Evangelical and Reformed Church in 1934, and three Lutheran synods into the American Lutheran Church in 1930. As is often the case, these mergers also resulted in the break off of disaffected congregations into small splinter groups.

Some conservative Protestant churches actually did much better through the Depression than the mainline churches, at least in terms of membership growth and attendance. From 1926 to 1936, the size of the Assemblies of God tripled to

A Pastor in Distress, to His Superior (1933)

September 11, 1933

The undersigned and his family, is living under very uncomfortable circumstances here at Trade Lake, West Sweden, Wis. And I have decided to write you
for advice. I am not getting my salary, it seems to me as I should get it. My two
congregations are now in arrears on my salary to the amount of $1,315.00, in lieu
of the fact that I have waived a percent of it equal to the percent of reduction
of salaries for the professors at our colleges since 1930.

This year, 1933, I offered to refund 25% of my salary to both of my congregations. Trade Lake refused to accept my offer. They want "35% or more" refunded.
So I decided to rely upon their mercy to me and let them decide to pay me as
salary for 1933 a sum equal to 55% of all the congregational income. So far
they have paid me only $25.00, instead of original $80.00 per month. To me this
kind of treatment of their pastor seems unkind and unchristian for kindness
and loyal service. . . .

I have given my whole life to the Lord's work since I was nineteen years old,
in school and in active pastoral work. During all these years I have not managed
to lay anything to live on and am dependent entirely on my salary, myself, my
wife, and three children in minor ages.

Do you think my people can break the contract of my call, in view of my fair
and reasonable refund of it each year, on account of the depression, without
my own personal concent? And what would you advise me to do about their
getting so very far in arrears on my salary? Could you possibly get me a call to
some other field, so I could move away from here?

Fraternally Yours, E. O. Valborg

E. O. Valborg to G. A. Brandelle, September 11, 1933. G. A. Brandelle Presidential
Papers, Augustana Synod Collection, ELCA Archives, Elk Grove Village, IL.

148,000 members, and the Church of the Nazarene doubled to 135,000 members. It is hard to say whether their premillennial theology and charismatic worship were especially attractive to people during hard times, but these churches
often were financially leaner than mainline churches and therefore better able
to withstand the economic downturn. The new subculture and structures of
these conservative Protestant churches were also emerging during these times,
as were significant attempts at self-definition. There was an increasing divide
between those who wanted to claim the label *fundamentalist* and those who
preferred the term *evangelical*. Overall, there was little theological difference
between the two groups; the main difference was that of strategy and approach
to the outside world. Fundamentalists prided themselves on a militant stance

against the liberal and secular world, while evangelicals (eventually a much larger grouping) were less combative. Led by militant leader Carl McIntire (1906–2002), the fundamentalists formed an umbrella organization in 1941, the American Council of Christian Churches. Evangelicals formed their own organization in 1942, the National Association of Evangelicals. Both of these organizations saw themselves as counterweights to the mainline FCC, as the divisions within American Protestantism continued and were formalized.

Hard times, like the Great Depression, often lead to social unrest and radicalism of various kinds. It is actually rather amazing that the United States did not see more unrest and radicalism during the 1930s than it did. The New Deal, with its "alphabet soup" of relief initiatives (the AAA, WPA, NRA, TVA, etc.), may have kept some of the potential unrest at bay, but it greatly increased government spending, and the specter of socialism cheered some but disturbed others. Mainline Protestants were traditionally Republican, and most of them voted against Roosevelt through the decade. Conservative White Protestants, especially in the South, leaned Democratic and tended to vote for Roosevelt. Roman Catholics were traditionally Democratic. And African Americans, drawn by Roosevelt's policies, deserted the Republican Party in droves.

Radical religious conservative and populist critics of Roosevelt were deeply worried about the threat of socialism, even while some of them pushed populist solutions that mirrored some of his New Deal programs. Frank Buchman (1878–1961) appealed to educated elites through his Moral Re-Armament (MRA) movement, popular on college campuses and among upscale White Americans. But others used mass media to appeal to larger audiences. Fundamentalist pastors Gerald Winrod (1900–1957) and Gerald L. K. Smith (1898–1976) both developed periodicals for wide distribution and sternly warned against the dangers of socialism and communism. Smith was also involved in the Share Our Wealth populist movement started by Huey Long. The most influential of these religious leaders who turned to mass media during this period, interestingly enough, was a Roman Catholic priest from Royal Oak, Michigan: Father Charles Coughlin (1891–1979). Coughlin's radio audience reached forty million listeners at its peak. He was initially sympathetic to Roosevelt and his programs but then quickly became vehemently opposed to them, as well as anti-British and isolationist. Coughlin's Roman Catholic superiors could do little to rein him in. These elements on the right also tended toward anti-Semitism.

On the liberal end of the spectrum, a number of Christian groups supported Roosevelt but felt his programs were not going far enough. They called for a full implementation of socialism in America, including the nationalization of industries, transportation, and banking. Most of these groups emphasized socialism as a platform in opposition to both Marxist communism and fascism, and they were strongly in favor of labor unions, isolationism, and pacifism. Christian Socialists formed the Fellowship of Socialist Christians in 1932 and the United Council for Christian Democracy in 1936. Both organizations called for the full implementation of socialism, and the theologian Reinhold Niebuhr was one of their prominent leaders. Patrician southerner Lucy Randolph Mason (1882–1959) was a prominent leader in the National Religion and Labor Foundation, which advocated for workers' rights, and she also advocated for civil rights for African

9.4. Dorothy Day.

Americans. This movement tended to be most influential among educated elites, but there were no real socialist counterparts to the media presence of Mason, Winrod, and Coughlin.

American Roman Catholics fell along a broad spectrum, including voices on both extremes. There were many on the right who listened to Father Coughlin and other traditional conservatives who worried about socialism and communism. In the Spanish Civil War (1936–39), many American Catholics supported the Nationalist forces of General Francisco Franco over the Republicans. But there were also Roman Catholics on the left, including the Catholic Worker Movement and its periodical, *The Catholic Worker*. This movement, which organized hostels, relief efforts, and intentional communities, was led by Dorothy Day (1897–1980) and Peter Maurin (1877–1949). Day was a socialist who converted to Roman Catholicism in 1927 and oversaw the organizational operation of the group and its activities. More mainstream social efforts were spearheaded by Father John Ryan (1869–1943), the long-time head of the Social Action Department of the National Catholic Welfare Council, the main national organization for American Roman Catholics.

American Christianity and Global Conflicts

During the 1930s, military conflicts raged around the world. Benito Mussolini and his Italian Fascists came to power in 1922 and invaded Ethiopia in 1935.

Japanese militarist leaders invaded Manchuria, China, in 1931 and then began a war with China in 1937. Adolph Hitler came to power in Germany in 1933 and militarily pressed German expansionism. The civil war in Spain was a prelude to further military conflict. But despite their possible sympathies with one side or the other, most Americans were decidedly isolationist, and the pacifist movement was popular. Many pacifist religious groups, especially the Fellowship of Reconciliation (formed in 1915), were developed as a reaction against the trauma of World War I. Many groups on the left were in this same camp, including the Catholic Worker Movement. Father Ryan formed the Catholic Association for International Peace in 1927. Radical groups on the right also pushed isolationism, including several "America First" movements and the fascist group the Silver Legion of America (commonly known as the Silver Shirts), which was organized by William Dudley Pelley (1890–1965). Many newer immigrants, especially Irish-American Roman Catholics, were bitterly opposed to the British Empire and especially to American efforts to support it. Pacifism and isolationism often drew together those who would not agree on much of anything else. Although most American Christians were not radicals, there was broad support among them for nonintervention and isolationism, and popular figures (such as the famed aviator Charles Lindbergh) supported this path. Though World War II began in earnest in 1939 and Roosevelt was personally sympathetic to the British cause, he had to bow to noninterventionist sentiments in his 1940 campaign for president.

Then, on the morning of December 7, 1941, Japanese forces attacked the American naval base at Pearl Harbor, Hawaii, destroying much of the American Pacific naval fleet. The United States was thereby drawn into another world war, despite its inclination to avoid it.

——————————— BIBLIOGRAPHY ———————————

Carpenter, Joel A. *Revive Us Again: The Reawakening of American Fundamentalism*. New York: Oxford University Press, 1997.

DeBerg, Betty A. *Ungodly Women: Gender and the First Wave of American Fundamentalism*. Minneapolis: Fortress, 1990.

Dorrien, Gary. *Soul in Society: The Making and Renewal of Social Christianity*. Minneapolis: Fortress, 1995.

Gleason, Philip. *Keeping the Faith: American Catholicism, Past and Present*. Notre Dame, IN: University of Notre Dame Press, 1987.

Hutchison, William R., ed. *Between the Times: The Travail of the Protestant Establishment in America, 1900–1960*. New York: Cambridge University Press, 1989.

Marty, Martin E. *Modern American Religion*. Vol 2, *The Noise of Conflict, 1919–1941*. Chicago: University of Chicago Press, 1991.

Miller, William D. *A Harsh and Dreadful Love: Dorothy Day and the Catholic Worker Movement*. 2nd ed. Milwaukee: Marquette University Press, 2005.

Ribuffo, Leo P. *The Old Christian Right: The Protestant Far Right from the Great Depression to the Cold War*. Philadelphia: Temple University Press, 1983.

Roof, Wade Clark, and William McKinney. *American Mainline Religion: Its Changing Shape and Future*. New Brunswick, NJ: Rutgers University Press, 1987.

Sernett, Milton C. *Bound for the Promised Land: African American Religion and the Great Migration*. Durham, NC: Duke University Press, 1997.

10

The Growth of American Christianity in War and Peace, 1941–65

THE QUARTER CENTURY BETWEEN the beginning of American involvement in World War II and the middle of the 1960s was a time of unparalleled growth, not only for the country as a whole but also for American Christianity. The United States population grew from 132 million people in 1940 to 194 million in 1965, propelled by a demographic surge that came to be known as the baby boom. From 1946 to 1964, over 76 million babies were born. At the height of the baby boom, there was a new baby born in the United States every seven seconds. After the economic decline of the Great Depression, the American economy started a steady rise during the war years, and this expansion continued through the postwar years. Buoyed by both economic and demographic expansion, religious life in the United States reached historic heights by 1965. In 1940, about half of all Americans claimed a specific religious adherence or membership; but by 1965, this rate had risen to two-thirds of all Americans.

Coming out of the ravages of the Great Depression, the United States was once again thrust into a major world war with the Japanese surprise attack at Pearl Harbor on December 7, 1941. The country rapidly sprang into action to prepare for war; nevertheless, the first year of American involvement was very difficult. Gradually, however, the United States brought its full economic and military power to bear against Japan, Italy, and Germany, and by 1945 the United States and its allies had crushed these opponents and brought the war to an end. The United States emerged from the war as a world superpower only to then enter a prolonged "Cold War" between the capitalist countries of the West and the communist countries of Eastern Europe and Asia, including its former allies the Soviet Union and China. This conflict, beginning in 1947, lasted for much of the rest of the century.

After the end of World War II, most Americans yearned for a return to "normal." The Americans who had fought in and won the war, known as the "Greatest Generation," sought to finally build their lives, lives that had been put on hold through the Great Depression and the war. With the postwar economy expanding at an average of 3.5 percent a year, Americans were able to purchase consumer goods and housing like never before. The burgeoning suburbs around major cities grew at breakneck speed, and the center of American population spread south and southwest into the Sun Belt. General prosperity and wage growth were such that, by the middle of the 1950s, some 60 percent of Americans were considered middle-class. Ownership of automobiles, homes, and major appliances shot up, as these items were now within most Americans' budgets. Fueled by postwar prosperity and the financial support of the G.I. Bill (formally, the Servicemen's Readjustment Act), the number of Americans with college degrees increased from 4.6 percent in 1940 to 9.4 percent in 1965. This economically prosperous postwar America came to be labeled the "Affluent Society." The baby boom and suburban expansion brought about a parallel boom in the building of schools, colleges, and religious congregations.

Though it was a time of general prosperity, it was not a comfortable time. The end of World War II ushered in the Cold War and the specter of annihilation through atomic weapons. The Cold War flared hot during the Korean War (1950–1953) and through other conflicts, such as the Cuban Missile Crisis of 1962. Fears of communist infiltration of the United States led to a new Red Scare and to political and social unrest. With the "space race" between the Soviet Union and the United States came the development of nuclear missiles and satellites, and, by 1962, the human exploration of outer space. But there were other traumas. A polio outbreak (especially among children) caused a great deal of fear for Americans, until the development of effective vaccines by Jonas Salk and Albert Sabin.

Despite the generation's general prosperity, social conservatism, and compliance, some mocked the dominant corporate culture and suburban life as hollow. Cultural critics disparaged the period as vacuous, and restless youth, such as the "beatniks," pushed back against cultural norms. By the end of the period, a new youth culture was emerging, fueled by the raw musical power of rock and roll.

African Americans sought their own slice of the American "pie," pushing for integration into American public life and for the civil rights that were enshrined in the Constitution but had yet to be extended to them. The struggle for civil rights was conflicted and sometimes violent. With the integrations of the US military in 1948 and public schools in 1954 and the protests and demonstrations of the 1950s and 1960s, however, the dream of integration slowly (and often painfully) began to be realized. Civil rights leaders, such as Dr. Martin Luther King Jr., leveraged social and political pressure, including with large-scale events such as the March on Washington for Jobs and Freedom in 1963.

After the administration of Democrat Harry Truman, the nation was led through the 1950s by moderate Republican Dwight D. Eisenhower. But the election of the young Democratic president John F. Kennedy in 1960 promised to deliver something of a social revolution. Kennedy and his wife Jackie brought a new and youthful style to the nation's capital, but his presidency was cut short in 1963 when he was assassinated in Dallas, Texas. His successor, Lyndon B. Johnson, delivered socially progressive legislation with his Great Society programs of the early 1960s, the Civil Rights Act of 1964, and the Voting Rights Act of 1965. It was a time of great expansion of governmental social programs and institutions.

American Christianity and World War II

The nation had turned inward after World War I, displaying a decidedly isolationist posture. Dismayed at the carnage of that war and regretful for their support of it, many religious leaders embraced pacifism. American isolationism and pacifism were largely swept away after Pearl Harbor, however, when an attack on American armed forces shook the nation into action. Support by religious leaders for American involvement in World War II was strong, although it generally lacked the excessive rhetoric that was all too frequent during the previous war. In part, this may have been due to the influence of Protestant neoorthodox theology and the Roman Catholic just war doctrine, both of which claimed a "realistic" view of human nature and society and allowed for the reasonable use of force to counter evil and aggression. Xenophobia flared up during the Second World War, most notably with the shameful detention of Japanese Americans in internment camps in the West. Leading up to the war, there were still a number of religious figures on the right who opposed the war, including the Roman Catholic radio personality Father Charles Coughlin; these figures were quickly silenced, however—Coughlin, by his religious superiors in 1942.

Other religious groups opposed the war, and military service in general. They included the Quakers and other historically pacifist churches (such as the Mennonites and the Church of the Brethren). The Catholic Worker Movement also opposed the war and military service, as did the Jehovah's Witnesses. Since the latter did not claim a religious exemption (because they would not cooperate with a government they considered evil), about five thousand Witnesses were imprisoned during the war for refusing to enter the armed forces. Although the Selective Training and Service Act of 1940 allowed for religious exemptions to armed service, a large majority of draft-eligible young men from the peace churches still enlisted in the military.

Christian denominations in the United States quickly contributed religious leaders to serve as official chaplains in the military, who were commissioned as officers in the armed forces. From fewer than two hundred before the war, the number of these chaplains climbed to over eleven thousand by the end of the war. About 70 percent were Protestant, and about 30 percent were Roman Catholic. Major ecumenical organizations, such as the Federal Council of Churches (FCC) and the National Association of Evangelicals, coordinated much of this work. As in previous wars, other religious organizations—the YMCA, YWCA, American Bible Society, and many others—developed civilian ministries to military installations, especially in the United States, as did many congregations located near these bases. Of course, the movement of so many clergy into the armed forces created large problems for Christian denominations and their congregations. To make things work, older pastors continued to serve congregations for the duration of the war, though they might have retired sooner under normal circumstances, and seminaries accelerated their programs of study to help get new religious leaders trained and serving in congregations (or the military) as quickly as possible.

The religious rhetoric surrounding this war was different from that which surrounded previous American wars. It mirrored changes that had taken place in American society during the interwar period. There had been a slow but growing acceptance of the reality of religious pluralism and an increasing integration of Roman Catholics and Jews into the mainstream of American society. The nation had by no means overcome anti-Catholicism and anti-Semitism, but the sheer size of American Roman Catholicism and the social and intellectual contributions of American Jews were hard to dismiss. One major incident during the war came to symbolize this new acceptance. In 1943, when the SS *Dorchester* was torpedoed, four chaplains (two Protestant, one Roman Catholic, and one

10.1. Four Chaplains from the SS *Dorchester*.

Jewish), handed their life jackets to other soldiers, giving their lives to save others. This episode received widespread acclaim and symbolized the growing acceptance of the "three faiths." In his wartime speeches, President Roosevelt rallied the nation to support the "Four Freedoms," one of which was the freedom of Religion. Roosevelt sometimes cast the war as a struggle against the enemies of religion, accusing Nazi Germany and imperial Japan of irreligiosity and religious repression.

The entire nation was mobilized to support the war effort, especially to produce the materials needed to fight. On the home front, this mobilization occasioned huge social disruptions, as a significant number of women went to work in war industries. Some Americans migrated to the South and Southwest to work in defense industries, where extreme housing limitations meant that families often had to live in trailers or other makeshift housing. Religious groups tried to deal with these social disruptions within their congregations, and some denominations provided outreach ministries to defense-industry workers and their families. Tight restrictions on printing, travel, and building materials constrained new and existing ministries for the duration of the war, although religious leaders began to plan for postwar expansion.

Although the war was generally supported by religious leaders, the events of the war itself raised difficult social and theological issues. The growing awareness of the Holocaust in Europe was deeply disturbing to many religious leaders, including Christians, for whom it gradually forced an uncomfortable reappraisal of the ways that Christians and Christian teaching had, for centuries, supported anti-Semitism. And the internment of Japanese Americans and the continuing segregation of African Americans, even in the military, seemed to belie the rationale for the war that the United States was a beacon of righteousness and freedom. Other religious leaders were concerned about some of the technologies and strategies of modern warfare that were being employed, including massive aerial bombing campaigns that devastated Germany and Japan. The development of American atomic weapons was shrouded in deep secrecy, but when they were used on Japanese cities, that terrifying new capacity for violence on a previously unimagined scale then had to be reckoned with as well.

Religion and the Postwar Era

During World War II, American religious leaders were already planning for the postwar future and were optimistic that it would be bright. Religious growth in the United States had stalled, or even declined somewhat, from the 1920s onward. During the Great Depression, both religious attendance and financial giving declined, and congregations and religious institutions struggled to survive (some did not). The sudden advent of World War II meant a huge jump in Americans' finances, but the war effort siphoned off much of their time and disrupted their lives. Thus, after two decades of restraint, the hope was that things would return to "normal" and American religious organizations and congregations could again experience the kind of growth they had enjoyed during the nineteenth century.

But religious groups and their leaders faced huge postwar challenges as well. Many parts of Europe and Asia were devastated by the war, and their churches had suffered badly. Newer mission churches in Africa and Asia had been cut off from Western funding and faced immense challenges. The churches of the United States were relatively unscathed and faced pressure to assist in the rest of the world. Many American religious groups, both Roman Catholic and Protestant, initiated major fund drives among their members for postwar relief, and they raised millions of dollars (although, per capita, American Jews raised far more than American Christians). Religious organizations worked with displaced persons in Europe who were fleeing war and communism and sought to resettle them in western Europe and the United States. The postwar resumption of missionary activity in Asia and Africa was greatly complicated by the collapse of European colonialism and the push toward national independence for former European colonies. As these countries became independent, their churches also pushed for autonomy from Western mission organizations.

Much hope was invested in the United Nations, after it was founded in 1945, but these hopes were dimmed by the expansion of communism into eastern Europe and Asia—especially China, which became communist in 1949. Since communism was officially atheistic and antagonistic toward religion, churches in these areas suffered doubly: first from the war, then from communism. China had been a major focus of mission activity, but Western missionaries were expelled after 1949. Pyongyang, the capital of North Korea, was once home to so many Korean Christians that it was known as the "Jerusalem of the East." But Western missionaries had been expelled from the countries in this region in the lead-up to and early years of the war, so new mission fields had to be developed in Asia, especially in places like Taiwan, Hong Kong, Malaysia, and South Korea. By the end of World War II, the United States was the leading supplier of Christian missionaries to the rest of the world.

In the United States, the war had caused huge social disruptions, and the postwar period saw even more. The generation of young women and men who had grown up during the Depression and then mobilized to fight the war had known only times of disruption and hardship. Many had put their lives on hold for the duration of the war, and with the coming of peace, these Americans hoped that they would finally be able to get on with their lives, that things would finally return to "normal." For many of these young adults, "normal" meant getting an education, finding a job, getting married, having kids, and buying a house. There was an incredible pent-up demand for all these things, especially having children, lots of children. The seventy-six million children born between 1946 and 1964, a time known as the baby boom, was a massive demographic bubble that would come to define much of American life for the rest of the century and beyond.

In terms of American church attendance, there has been a historical pattern of church adherence and attendance being tied to the human life cycle. The very young and the very old have been the most likely to attend church, with the 18-to-25-year-old category having the lowest percentage of attendance. Adherence and attendance have typically risen among young adults when they marry and especially when they have children. The baby boom was a time when lots of young Americans were settling down and having children, so it also occasioned a surge in religiosity, and religious organizations were stretched to their limits to accommodate it.

The postwar boom seriously stretched the available housing stock, leading to an explosion of home building in the suburban areas surrounding American cities. The long-standing trend of Americans moving to urban areas continued, but city dwellers themselves were attracted to these new suburbs by the promise of affordable home ownership. Modestly priced suburban homes were made even more affordable through the assistance of government housing programs run by the Federal Housing Administration and the US Department of Veterans Affairs. The demographic shift of Americans to the South and Southwest that had begun during the war also continued. A number of those who had gone to work in defense industries in those regions decided to stay there, in the warm weather and with the affordable housing prices.

These trends had huge impacts on American religious groups, which struggled to organize and supply enough congregations in the areas with rapidly expanding local populations. Older churches sought to expand their facilities to accommodate these needs, and many congregations added new educational wings to their buildings to meet the demand for children's religious education. Denominations traditionally based in the North, especially mainline Protestant denominations, struggled to open new congregations in states like Florida, Texas, Arizona, and California, where many young Americans were putting down roots. These new congregations were often initially outposts of Northern religious culture in the South.

Religious education was also affected by these trends. Roman Catholics and others who promoted parochial primary education scrambled to open new schools in the suburbs. Religious higher education was also stressed by the sudden demand, but many institutions became eligible to receive partial government funding for dormitories and classroom buildings, which fueled their expansion. Returning servicemen and servicewomen were eligible for education assistance through the G.I. Bill, which also benefited these schools. Even seminaries saw a large upturn in enrollment and tried to move seminarians through their programs as quickly as possible to help meet the demand for new pastors and priests.

Religion and the Postwar Society

The end of World War II resulted in a global rearrangement of power and, unfortunately, the beginnings of new geopolitical tensions. The alliance of the United States, the United Kingdom, the Soviet Union, and China that had defeated Germany and Japan fractured over postwar disputes, especially over the clashes between the communist powers and the Western democracies. The Soviet Union's domination of the eastern European countries and its establishment of communist regimes in them led to the development of the North Atlantic Treaty Organization (NATO) by the Western powers (including West Germany) with the goal of resisting communist advances. In 1949 the communists took control in China, fracturing China's relationship with the United States and motivating a renewed alliance between the United States and Japan. These new tensions, dubbed the Cold War, resulted in a prolonged low-grade conflict that flared up at times, such as in the Korean War. The development of atomic weapons in Russia and China, along with missiles to carry them, made the stakes of this new conflict extraordinarily high.

In the United States, the Cold War led to renewed anti-communist activities within the government and society. Just as after World War I, there was a new Red Scare in the late 1940s and early 1950s. Despite the genocides under Stalin in the Soviet Union during the 1930s, socialist (and even communist) groups had become established in the United States, and the Soviet Union was America's wartime ally. But the postwar anti-communist wave cast grave suspicions on these domestic groups, and many people (some guilty and others innocent) were caught up in the investigations. Postwar trials for treason and espionage, especially those of Alger Hiss in 1950 and Julius and Ethel Rosenberg in 1951, inflamed the situation, which climaxed with anti-communist congressional

Billy Graham on the Communist Threat

Ladies and gentlemen, for some time I have been stating to this radio audience that communism is far more than just an economic and philosophical interpretation of life. Communism is a fanatical religion that has declared war upon the Christian God. To a striking degree this atheistic philosophy is paralleling and counterfeiting Christianity. . . . At this moment it appears that communism has all the earmarks of this great anti-Christian movement. Communism could be only a shadow of a greater movement that is yet to come. However, it carries with it all the indications of anti-Christ. Almost all ministers of the gospel and students of the Bible agree that it is master-minded by Satan himself who is counterfeiting Christianity.

Christianity has a Bible; so does communism in the manifests. Christianity demands repentance from sin; communism demands a confession on the part of new converts concerning their past activities, errors and failures. Christianity demands the acceptance of certain cardinal doctrines as prerequisites for entrance into the Kingdom of God; so does communism. Christianity demands the complete surrender of body, soul, and will to Christ; so does communism demand complete surrender to the philosophy of communism. Christianity demands absolute loyalty; Jesus Christ said, "If a man is to follow me, he must take up his cross and deny himself daily." So does communism demand absolute loyalty to its leadership. Christianity demands the winning of new converts; the Christian is to ever be witnessing for his Lord. So does communism demand that every communist try to win others to the communistic way of life. . . .

Humanly speaking, faith can be overcome only by faith, courage by courage, loyalty by loyalty, devotion by devotion. The communist stands as a challenge to the Christian to bring to their leader a greater fight, a greater loyalty, a greater devotion, a greater discipline, a more glorious self-denial than anything that communism can show.

Billy Graham, *Christianity vs. Communism* (Minneapolis: Billy Graham Evangelistic Association, 1951), 3–4.

hearings led by Senator Joseph McCarthy (1908–57). The Korean War also contributed to the tensions, as did the specter of atomic warfare.

The religious dimension of anti-communism was very important, as this conflict was perceived as more than political—it was viewed as a grand struggle between two mutually incompatible worldviews. Communism was officially atheistic, and communist countries often persecuted religious believers or put harsh restrictions on them. Thus, any conflict between communist countries and Western powers was inevitably seen as an existential struggle between religion and atheism. In the United States it was extremely common to see the term *godless* affixed before the term *communism*, and it was not a far leap to infer that if an American was an atheist or an unbeliever, they could be suspected of not being in full support in the struggle against communism. For many in the United States, being religious was held as almost a patriotic duty, and rates of religiosity climbed steadily during the 1950s. In 1952, President Dwight D. Eisenhower (1890–1969) famously declared that religion was a good thing, and everyone should have one, but that he did not care which one it was. During this time, the motto "In God We Trust" was added to American currency, and the phrase "under God" was added to the Pledge of Allegiance.

Even though Protestants were still in the majority in 1950s America, Roman Catholics had become a leading religious group, and Judaism had become an important national presence. This situation of religious pluralism meant that it was no longer realistic to claim that the United States was solely a Protestant—or even a Christian—nation. Many relied on the American Enlightenment tradition that saw religion as inculcating a common ethical morality, and thus religiosity was a public benefit to the country.

The civil religion (religion of the nation) needed some sort of center to it, something to bind the country together religiously despite its growing religious

Dwight D. Eisenhower on Religion in America

Speaking of his conversation with Soviet General Zhukov.
I must say that in just a matter of immediate dialectic contest, let's say, I didn't know exactly what to say to him, because my only definition was what I believed to be the basic one, the basic reason for its existence. I know it would do no good to appeal to him with it, because it is founded in religion. And since at the age of 14 he had been taken over by the Bolshevik religion and had believed in it since that time, I was quite certain it was hopeless on my part to talk to him about the fact that our form of government is founded in religion.

Our ancestors who formed this Government said in order to explain it, you remember, that a decent respect for the opinion of mankind impels them to declare the reasons which led to the separation between the American colonies and Britain. And this is how they explained those: "we hold that all men are endowed by their Creator . . ." not by the accident of birth, not by the color of their skins or by anything else, but "all men are endowed by their Creator." In other words, our form of Government has no sense unless it is founded in a deeply felt religious faith, and I don't care what it is. With us of course it is the Judeo-Christian concept but it must be a religion that all men are created equal. So what was the use of me talking to Zhukov about that? Religion, he had been taught, was the opiate of the people.

"Text of Eisenhower Speech," *New York Times*, December 23, 1952, p. 16, cols. 3–6.

pluralism. Starting in the 1930s, some had begun to describe the United States as a "Judeo-Christian" nation, pulling together the three major religious groups in a common religiosity growing out of the Hebrew Bible. Jewish author Will Herberg (1901–77), a former Marxist turned religious conservative, wrote his influential book *Protestant, Catholic, Jew* in 1955. In it, he delineated the common religious root of America and reinforced the idea that there was an essential religious center to the nation. Catholic intellectual John Courtney Murray (1904–67) also supported American religious pluralism and identity, even when conservative forces in the Roman Catholic hierarchy objected.

Still, despite this line of thought, traditional religious tensions remained. Protestants worried about the growing strength and influence of Roman Catholicism and strongly objected to attempts made by the government to establish diplomatic relations with the Vatican. Anti-Catholicism was widespread in certain corners of American Protestantism, and more conservative elements within Roman Catholicism maintained a deep suspicion of what they saw as an essentially Protestant nation. These Catholics did not consider religious freedom and pluralism and the separation of church and state laudable values. The Holocaust and the formation of the State of Israel in 1948 created some sympathy for Judaism in America after World War II, but much anti-Semitism remained entrenched in American culture. It was one thing to discuss a common religious culture and the Judeo-Christian tradition (whatever that meant), but the day-to-day living out of American religious pluralism was as difficult as it had ever been.

American Christianity in the 1950s

This period was a flush time for America in general, and particularly for American Christianity. All the postwar elements—including the demographic expansion, the desire for a return to normal, the baby boom, and the anti-communist crusade—pushed Americans into churches by the millions. In the period between 1945 and 1965, Christianity in America grew to numerical levels that it had never seen before, and that it has not seen since. There was talk of a postwar revival in religion, and the revival was real, although critics (then and since) questioned just how deep the religiosity went.

Although such data do have their faults and limitations, survey and numerical data are essential for getting a reasonably accurate sense of the vast and complex developments of American Christianity by the middle of the twentieth century. By any measure, the growth was impressive. By the mid-1950s, when asked whether they had attended religious services in the past week, 49

Will Herberg on Religion in 1950s America

This is at least part of the picture presented by religion in contemporary America: Christians flocking to church, yet forgetting all about Christ when it comes to naming the most significant events in history; men and women valuing the Bible as revelation, purchasing and distributing it by the millions, yet apparently seldom reading it themselves. Every aspect of contemporary religious life reflects this paradox—pervasive secularism amid mounting religiosity, "the strengthening of the religious structure in spite of increasing secularization." The influx of members into the churches and the increased readiness of Americans to identify themselves in religious terms certainly appear to stand in contrast to the way Americans seem to think and feel about matters central to the faiths they profess.

The paradox is there, and it would be misleading to try to get rid of it by suppressing one or the other side of the apparent contradiction. It will not do to brush aside the evidences of religious revival by writing off the new religiousness as little more than shallow emotionalism, "escapism," or mere pretense. The people who join the churches, take part in church activities, send their children to church schools, and gladly identify themselves in religious terms are not fools or hypocrites. They are honest, intelligent people who take their religion quite seriously. Of that there cannot be much doubt.

Nor, on the other hand, can there be much doubt that, by and large, the religion which actually prevails among Americans today has lost much of its authentic Christian (or Jewish) content. Even when they are thinking, feeling or acting religiously, their thinking, feeling, and acting do not bear an unequivocal relation to the faiths they profess. . . .

It is the thesis of the present work that both the religiousness and the secularism of the American people derive from very much the same sources, and that both become more intelligible when seen against the background of certain deep-going sociological processes that have transformed the face of the American people in the course of the past generation.

Will Herberg, *Protestant, Catholic, Jew: An Essay in American Religious Sociology* (New York: Doubleday, 1955), chap. 1.

percent of all Americans—nearly half the population—said yes. Forty-five percent of Protestants answered yes to this question, as did 75 percent of Roman Catholics, making Catholics the group with the highest percentage of weekly service attenders.[1]

Asking about belief in God was another way of gauging the religiosity of the overall population. In 1947, some 94 percent of Americans said they believed in

1. Jackson W. Carroll, Douglas W. Johnson, and Martin E. Marty, *Religion in America: 1950 to the Present* (San Francisco: Harper & Row, 1979), 10–22.

God, while by 1953 this number had grown to 98 percent, and when pushed to give a more precise definition, over 90 percent of Americans claimed to believe in God as a personal being.[2] In 1957, when asked, 69 percent of Americans said that the influence of religion in American life was increasing.[3]

Rates of membership and other affiliation with religious groups were clearly on the rise. Membership went up from 49 percent in 1940 to 69 percent in 1965. When asked a more general question—whether they had a religious "preference"—over 90 percent of Americans in this period answered yes.[4] This rise in religious affiliation and membership was seen across the religious spectrum: from Roman Catholics to mainline Protestants to evangelical Protestants. The postwar wave of religiosity was a rising tide that lifted all boats. See the following figures of denominational membership growth between 1955 and 1965:

Assemblies of God: up 43 percent

Episcopal Church: up 20 percent

Lutheran Church in America: up 22 percent

Lutheran Church—Missouri Synod: up 34 percent

Presbyterian churches: up 17 percent

Roman Catholic Church: up 38 percent

Seventh-day Adventists: up 31 percent

Southern Baptist Convention: up 27 percent

Methodist churches: up 10 percent

There were only a few major denominations that did not enjoy much growth during this period, including the American Baptist Convention (up 2 percent) and the United Church of Christ (down 2 percent).[5] With all the new families and young children, many churches had to construct new buildings and expand existing ones. In 1945, when wartime restrictions were still in effect, only $26 million was spent on church construction. By contrast, in 1950, $409 million was spent on church construction. And slightly over $1 billion was spent on it in 1960.[6] By any indication, participation in religious life in the United States was rising dramatically.

2. Carroll, Johnson, and Marty, *Religion in America*, 29.

3. Carroll, Johnson, and Marty, *Religion in America*, 33.

4. Sydney E. Ahlstrom, *A Religious History of the American People* (New Haven: Yale University Press, 1972), 952; and Carroll, Johnson, and Marty, *Religion in America*, 9.

5. Carroll, Johnson, and Marty, *Religion in America*, 15.

6. Ahlstrom, *Religious History of the American People*, 953.

Even as religious pluralism was expanding and new denominations were being formed, mainline Protestants continued their push for denominational consolidation and merger. Although the large-scale merger of Methodist denominations envisioned in the 1930s did not come about, the Southern and Northern Methodists did join to form the Methodist Church in 1939. More denominations consolidated in the following decades: the Church of the United Brethren in Christ merged with the Evangelical Church to form the Evangelical United Brethren Church (1946); two northern Presbyterian denominations combined to form the United Presbyterian Church (U.S.A.) (1958); and the Congregational Christian Churches combined with the Evangelical and Reformed Church to form the United Church of Christ (1957). But not all merger attempts were successful. During the 1950s, ambitious plans to merge two-thirds of American Lutherans derailed, resulting in two new denominations: the American Lutheran Church (1960) and the Lutheran Church in America (1962).

The impetus for these mainline Protestant mergers (and those yet to come) came from the corporate and institutional culture of conglomeration, as seen in American businesses and governments. This was an age of consolidation, from school districts to corporations. For many religious groups seeking to maintain their privileged positions of societal leadership, it seemed that having fewer—but larger—denominations would give Christians more power to influence American society. But these consolidations were often also driven by a desire to make sure the "right" and "proper" religious voices (that is, theirs) would be heard. From the 1940s on, mainline Protestant leaders, through the FCC, sought to restrict religious broadcasting to their own members. As we have seen, evangelical Protestants and others soon found ways around these restrictions. And, ironically, the result was an American media landscape in which the mainline Protestant presence was relatively small.

The postwar religious revival in the United States was personified by a single person: William Franklin "Billy" Graham (1918–2018). Billy Graham became perhaps the best-known religious figure in the country during the second half of the twentieth century. Graham was an unlikely candidate for this position. He was a born-again Protestant evangelical from rural North Carolina, and an evangelist in the style of Dwight Moody and Billy Sunday. After graduating from Wheaton College, in Illinois, Graham began his career as an evangelist in Los Angeles with the evangelical organization Youth for Christ. With a dynamic preaching style and rugged good looks, Graham soon became nationally known for his 1949 revivals in Los Angeles and was featured in the national media (with a push from powerful publisher William Randolph Hearst Sr.). Graham founded the Billy Graham Evangelistic Association in

10.2a and b. Billy Graham Crusade.

1950 and quickly published several best-selling books and started airing a television show, *The Hour of Decision*.

Graham's public "crusades" in the United States and around the world were meticulously planned well in advance to achieve maximum publicity. His 1957 New York Crusade at Yankee Stadium was planned three years in advance. Graham's willingness to work with Protestant leaders across the spectrum brought criticism from fundamentalist leaders, and his long association as an adviser to American presidents sometimes caused controversy. But he remained widely popular and influential even into the early twenty-first century.

Though he may have been the most well-known, Graham was not the only religious media star of the 1950s. Catholic bishop Fulton Sheen (1895–1979) was a religious writer popular with many across the religious spectrum, and he achieved great influence through his television show, *Life Is Worth Living* (1951–57), which had an estimated audience of thirty million viewers. Mainline Protestant preacher Norman Vincent Peale (1898–1993) was a prolific media star and author: his 1952 book *The Power of Positive Thinking* spent three years at the top of the New York Times bestseller list. The 1950s was a decade of religious media stars.

Cooperation, Mergers, and Ecumenism

The postwar period was an exciting time for those who had dreamed of closer relations between the various Christian denominations in the United States. Many considered it a scandal that American Christians were so fragmented, and they thought that Christians would have more influence in society if they were more united. At the very least, it was thought, the separate Christian groups should work together in cooperative ecumenical arrangements. But the ideal was that the overall number of distinct Christian groups would be reduced through mergers and other consolidations, especially among the Protestants.

One of the most important ecumenical developments of the period was the formation of the National Council of the Churches of Christ in the USA (NCC; also known as the National Council of Churches) in 1950. Rooted in older organizations such as the Evangelical Alliance (established in 1846) and the Federal Council of Churches (established in 1908), at its inception, the NCC brought together twelve different interdenominational agencies—including organizations focused on missions, education, and communications—along with twenty-five Protestant denominations and four Orthodox Christian groups. The NCC thus represented thirty-three million American Christians. Like the FCC, the NCC predominantly comprised the old mainline Protestant groups (Methodist, Northern Baptist, Episcopal, Presbyterian, and Congregational), although there were also newer additions. Because the Roman Catholic Church and almost all conservative Protestant churches would not join, however, the NCC has never represented the majority of American Christians, although it has presumed to speak for them.

Conservatives were wary of the NCC for many reasons, including what they saw as the influence of liberal Christianity in the organization. By design, the NCC's foundational theological documents were rather vague, especially about traditional doctrines that conservatives held dear. Conservatives also resented the presumption of the new organization to speak for all American Christians. The organizing convention of the NCC was held in a large hall under a banner proclaiming "One Nation Under God." Some conservative critics in the early 1950s charged that the NCC was a communist/socialist front, an accusation based on the fact that some NCC leaders had been active in Christian Socialist groups in the 1930s. In 1952, when the NCC introduced a new translation of the Bible (the Revised Standard Version), conservative critics charged that its translations of certain passages undercut the virgin birth and divinity of Christ. The NCC's support for the Civil Rights Movement in the 1950s was also controversial with many conservatives.

On the world scene, the ecumenical gatherings from the early twentieth century, such as the international conferences on Faith and Order and Life and Work, resulted in the formation of the World Council of Churches (WCC) in Amsterdam in 1948. A number of American Christian denominations, mainly those in the NCC, participated in the founding of the WCC. Various Protestant "families" began to develop their own world organizations, such as the Lutheran World Federation and the World Alliance of Reformed Churches.

Further consolidation and cooperation were signaled in 1958 with the construction of a nineteen-story office building in Manhattan, across from the prestigious mainline Protestant Riverside Church. This office building, called the Interchurch Center, was built in cooperation with John D. Rockefeller and was intended to provide offices for the NCC and its various agencies along with national headquarters for many of the mainline Protestant denominations and their affiliated agencies. The fact that President Eisenhower and Secretary of State John Foster Dulles were present for the laying of its cornerstone testifies to the importance of this building, sometimes referred to by nicknames like the "God Box" and the "American Vatican." The symbolism was clear: this building was intended be the nerve center of American Christianity, unity symbolized in stone.

Despite the acceleration of mergers and consolidations among American Protestants after World War II and the formation of cooperative bodies like the NCC and WCC, some still fretted that there were too many Protestant denominations. The leading proponent of further consolidation was Eugene Carson Blake (1906–85), Presbyterian leader and president of the NCC. In a 1960 sermon in San Francisco, California, "A Proposal Towards the Reunion of Christ's Church," Blake put forth an expansive vision of a united American Protestantism, a vision that was then taken up in 1962 by the formation of the Consultation on Church Union (COCU). The COCU developed commissions to organize future gatherings and to explore theological and organizational factors relevant to denominational consolidation. There were important examples of church consolidations from around the world that the commissions could learn from, including the newly formed Church of South India and the "uniting" churches in Canada and Australia, all of which brought together disparate Protestant churches.

In these merger and consolidation efforts, which mainly involved mainline Protestants, there was an undercurrent of concern—sometimes openly expressed—that the mainline was losing its control of American religion and society. Roman Catholics and conservative Protestants were gaining power and status, as evidenced by the popularity of Billy Graham and Bishop Fulton Sheen. Catholics and conservative Protestants had long outnumbered mainline Protestants, and they were now challenging mainline power. Efforts at mainline-Protestant unity were partly motivated by the conviction that mainline Protestants had to join together to counteract this challenge to their power and prestige.

Postwar American Roman Catholicism

Boosted by immigration and demographic growth, by the beginning of the twentieth century Roman Catholicism had become the single largest organizationally unified religious body in the United States. For much of the twentieth century, Roman Catholics represented around 20 percent of the total American population, although Protestants were still more numerous when considered in the aggregate. Roman Catholic growth and traditional Protestant anti-Catholicism led to conflicts and resentments. Many Roman Catholic leaders, especially European officials in the state churches and the Vatican, were still extremely wary of the religious freedom and pluralism in the United States, which they believed to be based on Protestantism. These leaders thought American democracy was incompatible with the establishment and flourishing of Roman Catholicism in the country, and some had actively tried to discourage Catholics from immigrating to the United States. While some Roman Catholic leaders in America pushed for greater integration of their flock into American society, conservative elements in the Vatican soon quashed this movement.

Despite these worries, Roman Catholicism was established and flourished in the United States, forming a huge network of parishes, religious orders, educational institutions, and social service agencies. Up through the middle of the twentieth century, this network formed a distinctive religious subculture in the United States separate from the main public institutions of the country—a Catholic America. Though Roman Catholicism was institutionally organized from the top, this subculture was divided by ethnicity and languages further down, resulting in separate linguistic parishes and institutions in many areas. Even with their eventual transition to the use of English, many of these ethnic divisions remained strong. Irish Americans dominated the religious hierarchy, but other groups pushed back.

This American Roman Catholic subculture and the religious institutions that supported it were largely built through the financial sacrifices of its laypeople and by the work of Catholic priests, nuns, and monks who were organized in large numbers of religious orders. Many Roman Catholic families of the time had large numbers of children, and devout parents frequently intended one or two of them for the priesthood or the religious life. These religious taught in the parochial schools, staffed the hospitals and social service agencies, and served the immigrant populations.

For lay Roman Catholics, the subculture of Catholic America was built on large numbers of voluntary religious groups: devotional groups such as sodalities and rosary societies, fraternal organizations such as the Knights of Columbus, immigrant aid and burial societies, and social groups. Many were organized along ethnic and linguistic lines, often replicating Catholic institutions from immigrants' former home countries. American Roman Catholics were intentionally separated from the rest of Christian America by these groups and by prohibitions from the religious hierarchy limiting exposure to certain movies, books, publications, and other media. Their observance of religious festivals, days of fasting, and many other daily religious habits also separated American Roman Catholics from their neighbors and defined their subculture.

Through the twentieth century, Roman Catholics were gaining power in the United States, mainly in the urban areas of the Northeast and Midwest, where their power as a voting bloc elected local mayors and city council and congressional members. Though this power was significant, Catholics still lacked political influence on the national level and faced discrimination and limitations in several ways. Popular anti-Catholicism was widespread and limiting, as Al Smith learned in his 1928 presidential run. In 1939, President Roosevelt encountered a storm of criticism when he appointed an ambassador to the Vatican. Some Americans charged that the appointment was a violation of the separation of church and state. When President Truman tried to appoint a successor for that ambassador in 1951, the storm of criticism was such that he abandoned the appointment, which then stayed empty for the next twenty years. And when John F. Kennedy ran for president in 1959, he had to assure wary Protestant voters that he would not be swayed or influenced by pressure from Roman Catholic officials.

After World War II and the social and demographic changes of the 1950s, the walls of Catholic subculture began to erode, as immigrants were increasingly acculturated and assimilated. The war had brought together people from many

10.3. Second Vatican Council Session.

different religious backgrounds. Many Roman Catholics moved out to the new suburban developments and into mixed neighborhoods with Protestants, Jews, and others. Huge new parishes were built in the suburbs that blurred the old ethnic lines. Some Roman Catholic intellectuals chafed at the strict restrictions on what they could read and what they could publish. In the 1950s there was a sense among American Roman Catholics of a looming change, though many were cautious about naming it.

Change came in a very unexpected way. In 1958, the elderly cardinal of Venice, Angelo Giuseppe Roncalli (1881–1963), was elected pope as John XXIII. Many observers expected him to do little, to act as a caretaker until the election of another pope. But he surprised everyone by calling for a general council of church leaders and by charging this council, the Second Vatican Council (1962–65), to consider wide-ranging and even fundamental changes in the Roman Catholic Church. With the 1960 election of John F Kennedy as the first Roman Catholic president of the United States and the dramatic changes in global Roman Catholicism that would unfold over the next decades due to Vatican II, American Roman Catholicism came of age.

African American Christianity and the Civil Rights Movement

Christian congregations continued to play a central role in the African American community during the twentieth century. The congregations of the African American denominations—Baptist, Methodist, Holiness, and Pentecostal—had traditionally served as the social cores of their communities, and their pastors were important local leaders. A national coordinating organization, the Fraternal Council of Negro Churches, was formed in 1934. After World War II, the traditional roles of Black churches and church leaders were augmented by new initiatives as some became influential in the struggle for civil rights. This new movement created some tensions within the African American churches, many of which were traditionally conservative and wary of the new activism. But the post-1945 push for an end to discrimination and segregation was something that most African Americans supported.

The African American community and its churches were hit hard by the economic ravages of the Great Depression, and they usually had fewer resources in place to sustain them than their White counterparts did. The situation during World War II was an improvement, as many jobs in the defense industries were made available to African Americans, and millions of African Americans served in the US military. Yet even as African Americans served their country in these ways, segregation and discrimination continued. African Americans were shunted into separate military units. The rising expectations for prosperity and a comfortable home life that many Americans had after the war were shared by many African Americans, but change was hard won and slow.

The first major legal action against segregation came in 1948 when President Truman signed an executive order to integrate the armed forces of the United States, though this integration was only slowly achieved. Then in 1954, the United States Supreme Court ruled against school segregation in the case of *Brown v. the Board of Education*, overturning a previous ruling from 1896 (*Plessy v. Ferguson*). Though the ruling was narrowly focused, it signaled that the court rejected legal segregation and discrimination on the basis of the Fourteenth Amendment to the Constitution, leading to a flood of other, similar litigation. But it took more than legal rulings to overcome segregation. Direct protests and actions were necessary, including the Montgomery, Alabama, bus boycott, in 1955–56, and the use of federal troops to force the integration of schools in Little Rock, Arkansas, in 1957.

The rising activism of young African American ministers was an important part of the Civil Rights Movement. During and after World War II, Baptist pastors Adam Clayton Powell Sr. (1865–1953) and his son Adam Clayton Powell Jr. (1908–72) pushed for civil rights from their positions as the pastors of the Abyssinian Baptist Church in Harlem. In 1945, Powell Jr. was elected to the House of Representatives, where he served for decades. Other African American pastors joined the Civil Rights Movement as well, and the Baptist pastor from Atlanta, Georgia, Martin Luther King Jr. (1929–68) would become the most prominent. From his position at the Ebenezer Baptist Church in Atlanta, King became the leading national voice in the Civil Rights Movement of the 1950s and 1960s, spearheading efforts around the country to push for integration and expanded rights for African Americans. In 1957, King, Baptist pastor Ralph David Abernathy (1926–90), and others formed the Southern Christian Leadership Conference (SCLC) to coordinate civil rights efforts. King himself became nationally known for his leadership of protests, boycotts, and marches, including efforts in Birmingham and Selma, Alabama. His "I Have a Dream" speech, from the 1963 March on Washington for Jobs and Freedom, and his "Letter from a Birmingham Jail," of the same year, became famous and influential. King was awarded the Nobel Peace Prize in 1964.

Not everyone in the African American community agreed with King, however, and his nonviolent—but disruptive—tactics. Many traditional African American pastors were very cautious about advocating for social changes so directly and were worried about the tactics of King and the SCLC. In 1963, some African American church leaders formed the National Negro Evangelical Association (now the National Black Evangelical Association) to focus efforts

Martin Luther King Jr.'s "I Have a Dream" Speech (1963)

I have a dream that my four little children will one day live in a nation where they will not be judged by the color of their skin but by the content of their character. . . .

That one day . . . little Black boys and Black girls will be able to join hands with little white boys and white girls as sisters and brothers. . . .

That one day every valley shall be exalted, and every hill and mountain shall be made low, . . . and the glory of the Lord shall be revealed. . . .

With this faith we will be able to work together, to pray together, . . . to stand up for freedom together, knowing that we will be free one day. . . .

Let freedom ring.

When we let it ring . . . , we will be able to speed up that day when all of God's children . . . will be able to join hands and sing in the words of the old Negro spiritual: Free at last. Free at last. Thank God Almighty, we are free at last.

Martin Luther King Jr., "I Have a Dream" speech, August 28, 1963, Lincoln Memorial, Washington, DC, https://www.npr.org/2010/01/18/122701268/i-have-a-dream-speech-in-its-entirety.

on more traditional soul-winning efforts. On the other side of the spectrum, some civil rights proponents thought King and his allies were not confrontational enough and pushed for more direct action. Radicals such as Malcolm X (1925–65) dismissed King's vision of integration and called, rather, for Black separatism, the building up of Black institutions, and direct responses against racial violence.

Some White church leaders gave their support and encouragement to the Civil Rights Movement, although it must be said that there were many others who either opposed the movement or watched from the sidelines. The National Council of Churches (NCC), which included some of the African American denominations, was an early supporter of the Civil Rights Movement and made this cause an important part of their activities in the 1950s and 1960s. Young people joined the Freedom Rides into the South beginning in 1961, and some White pastors and seminarians joined the protests or traveled south as observers. Most of them faced hostility, arrest, and violence alongside African Americans, and several of them, including pastors James Reeb and Bruce Klunder, were killed.

The Civil Rights Movement won important political support during the administration of President Lyndon Johnson, who engineered major accomplishments in civil rights legislation over determined opposition. The passage of the Civil Rights Act in 1964 and the Voting Rights Act in 1965 signaled a major change in federal policies on civil rights and integration, though the

10.4. Representatives of the National Council of the Churches of Christ in the USA at the 1963 March on Washington for Jobs and Freedom.

implementation of these policies, especially on the local level, came only slowly and painfully. The integration of Christian churches, which were voluntary organizations, came much slower. In 1963, King observed that "11:00 am on Sunday morning" was the most segregated hour of the week[7]—a challenge to predominantly White denominations. But some African American church leaders defended the necessity of their own distinct denominations and congregations as being central to the health and identity of the African American community.

Christian Theology after the War

In the early twentieth century, American Protestantism was divided between the dominant liberal theology of the mainline denominations and the conservative and fundamentalist theologies that opposed them. The former sought to embrace the challenge of modernity and change with it, while the latter rejected any element of modernity that conflicted with what they took to be traditional

7. Interview with Martin Luther King Jr., "Meet the Press," NBC, April 17, 1960, https://www.youtube.com/watch?v=1q881g1L_d8.

Christian theological understandings. But the events of World War II and after suggested that neither of these two approaches was altogether viable. The modern world brought great advances, certainly, but also war on an unimaginable scale, the Holocaust, and the specter of nuclear annihilation. Liberalism seemed incapable of critiquing modernity, and fundamentalism seemed equally incapable of engaging it. American Christians wrestled with new approaches that attempted to do better.

Many of the new theological possibilities originated from European Christian theologians, especially those associated with the movement known as neoorthodoxy. Beginning with the work of Swiss theologian Karl Barth (1886–1968), this rather broad family of theological approaches attempted to reclaim the central theological insights of the sixteenth-century Protestant Reformers and to restate them to meet the modern situation. Working out his disillusionment with classic liberal theology after World War I, Barth rooted his theology in the primacy of the revelation of the Word of God, rather than beginning with the human experience of the world. As an alternative to liberalism, his theology started with Jesus as the world-determining revelation of God and the Bible as the divinely given witness to that revelation, and it centered on the classic categories of human sinfulness and divine redemption. Barth became popular in the United States in the 1950s as his massive, multivolume *Church Dogmatics* began appearing in English translation. Barth was especially popular among American Presbyterians, with Princeton Theological Seminary in New Jersey serving as the center of American Barthianism. Barth's Swiss colleague Emil Brunner (1889–1966) was also influential.

As we've seen, in America neoorthodoxy had as its main proponents two brothers: H. Richard Niebuhr (1894–1962) and Reinhold Niebuhr (1892–1971). Their version of neoorthodoxy, sometimes called Christian Realism, used traditional Christian themes and categories while also attempting (contrary to fundamentalism) to engage the world as modernity had revealed it to be with a frank understanding of the possibilities and limits for human life considering the theological, moral, and political factors at play.

The Niebuhr brothers issued a steady stream of influential theological works during and after World War II. Reinhold Niebuhr, who taught at Union Theological Seminary in New York, published his major, two-volume work, *The Nature and Destiny of Man* (1943), as a rebuke to both liberalism and fundamentalism. H. Richard Niebuhr, who taught up the road at Yale, wrote important works on the nature of modern society and on Christian ethics. In his 1960 book, *Radical Monotheism and Western Culture*, H. Richard restated the neoorthodox theme of the centrality and "otherness" of God and God's revelation as over and against human and cultural constructions. In his *The*

Responsible Self (1963), he attempted to outline a Christian ethical stance that could engage with the world's problems without becoming defined by the world.

The Niebuhr brothers were influential in American Protestantism during the 1950s and even had some influence on American Cold War policy. Reinhold Niebuhr was active in the Christian-socialist movement but was realistic about what engagement with the world was all about, understanding the paradoxes of life and how engagement sometimes meant choosing the lesser of two evils. John Foster Dulles (1888–1959), secretary of state during the Eisenhower administration (and an active lay Presbyterian), was one of a number of political leaders influenced by the Niebuhrs. But few embraced the Niebuhrs' version of neoorthodox theology. Critics on the left faulted it as not liberal enough, and critics on the right rejected it as simply rehashed liberalism.

Other theologians sought to deal with the traumas and realities of the postwar situation by reimagining the human condition and its relation to the divine. Building on the work of nineteenth-century Danish theologian Søren Kierkegaard, a generation of philosophers and theologians sought to focus on the human experience of encountering God and truth, not as an *intellectual* choice but as a *personal* commitment and choice (as Kierkegaard put it, a "leap of faith"). This movement came to be known as Christian existentialism, after the philosophy of postwar intellectuals such as Martin Heidegger and Jean-Paul Sartre. In America, the leading Christian existentialist was a German exile, Paul Tillich (1886–1965), who taught at Union Theological Seminary and Harvard before ending up at the University of Chicago. In a number of books, such as *The Courage to Be* (1952) and his three-volume *Systematic Theology* (1951–63), Tillich sought to redefine Christian theology in existentialist terms. The revelation of God was the answer to human questions, but it was appropriated by humans searching for meaning and truth in the modern world.

There were other noteworthy theological influences in this era. The writings of German theologian and anti-Nazi martyr Dietrich Bonhoeffer (1906–45) were gradually translated into English after the war and were especially important in the areas of ethics and social engagement. More radical was the new biblical hermeneutic of German scholar Rudolf Bultmann (1884–1976), who held that people no longer lived in the "mythic" world of the Bible and that it was time to "demythologize" the biblical text for the modern world. Even more radical yet, some liberals—including the French Protestant theologian Gabriel Vahanian (1927–2012), who taught at Syracuse for twenty-six years—felt that even traditional theism was no longer of use to modern humans. This was the beginning of what would eventually be called death-of-God theology.

Among Protestant conservatives, a group known as the Neo-Evangelicals tried to restate traditional Protestant theology. This group wished to retain traditional theology, more or less as fundamentalists understood it, while also engaging the world in a more direct and constructive way through their faith. The leading theologian of this group was Carl F. H. Henry (1913–2003), whose book *The Uneasy Conscience of Modern Fundamentalism* (1947) sought to establish a new engagement with the modern world. When Billy Graham and L. Nelson Bell (1894–1973) started a new periodical in 1956, *Christianity Today*, as a counterpoint to the mainline's *Christian Century*, they chose Henry as their editor. Neo-Evangelical institutions, such as Wheaton College (Wheaton, Illinois) and Fuller Theological Seminary (Pasadena, California), rose to prominence among these conservative American Protestants.

The English literary scholar, lay theologian, and Christian apologist Clive Staples "C. S." Lewis (1898–1963) was also very popular with these new evangelicals. In more than three dozen popular and influential books, with tens of millions of copies in print, Lewis sought both to defend traditional Christian theology and to make it accessible and relevant to persons in the modern world. Some Christians declared that Lewis's books had brought them to the Christian faith or had saved that faith for them. While Lewis was very popular among American evangelical Protestants, his influence also extended far beyond those circles.

Contentment and Disaffection in the Postwar Era

The postwar era was dominated by an overwhelming desire of many Americans to resume "normal" lives after the Great Depression and World War II. The urge to find jobs, set up homes and families, and establish careers was pervasive and fueled the postwar expansion of American religion. Yet this period was also filled with unease, with new and lingering fears nagging at the general sense of prosperity. And there were many Americans who could not find the peace and success they sought or who came to reject the general vision of conventional society.

The general prosperity of the postwar period is undeniable. Despite some instability and painful adjustments immediately after the war, the American economy expanded consistently through the 1950s and early 1960s. Jobs were available, and many people were able to afford homes and significant consumer goods for the first time. Expectations were high for continuing prosperity, and many were realizing the "American dream." Conventional religiosity played a large role in these expectations. Many Americans considered their country favored and blessed by God.

The general optimism of the time was also fueled by popular self-help works that were overlaid with a veneer of vague religiosity. Above all, the works of Reformed pastor and author Norman Vincent Peale reached their peak, with books like *A Guide to Confident Living* (1948) and *The Power of Positive Thinking* (1952) becoming perennial bestsellers. Other, similar writers were also read widely, including Emmet Fox (1886–1951) and Glenn Clark (1882–1956), who combined self-help, psychology, and New Thought religiosity in a soothing blend. For some, psychology became a religion unto itself. These works added to a general sense of agency—a sense that a person could achieve their dreams if only they worked hard enough and smart enough. God was blessing them and giving them the tools to succeed.

And yet, there were many reasons to be fearful. The postwar world order was quickly upset by the new, fundamental struggle between the Western democracies and the communist powers, Russia and China. The postwar expansion of communism into Eastern Europe and Southeast Asia was frightening to many, especially when Russia and then China developed nuclear weapons. The continuing Cold War flared hot during the Korean War and in tensions over Cuba in the early 1960s. Fears of communism also flared within the United States, with accusations of communist influence in government and education, and revelations of those who were spying for the communist powers. The specter of possible nuclear war and annihilation added greatly to the fear, as did the polio epidemics of the 1940s and 1950s. It was impossible to completely bar these fears from creeping in through the safe walls of American homes.

This age has often been depicted as one of conformity and allegiance to organizations, including churches. Some critics attacked this culture, finding it shallow and insipid. Critics from within Christian circles often attacked the average American congregation and its worship as being boring and inconsequential, geared more toward pacifying people than toward helping them deal with personal and societal problems. Other critical attacks—including the influential study *The Organization Man* (1956), by William H. Whyte Jr. (1917–1999), and the popular novel *The Man in the Gray Flannel Suit* (1955), by Sloan Wilson (1920–2003)—were aimed at the culture in general.

Some Americans could not or would not take up their expected roles in conventional postwar society. Some suffered the lingering traumas of military service or of disrupted youth during the previous decades. There was a restlessness among some and a desire to "walk on the wild side"—as seen in the postwar motorcycle gangs. An American subculture sprang up that was built on nonconformity, jazz music, and other edgy cultural elements. In 1948, writer Jack Kerouac (1922–69) dubbed this subculture the Beat movement. Another major influence in this movement was the poet Allen Ginsberg (1926–97), who lamented, in his work "Howl": "I saw the best minds of my generation destroyed by madness."[8] Kerouac and Ginsberg's explorations of Asian religions, such as Buddhism and Hinduism, also fueled a new American interest in the Zen school of Buddhism.

Some of those disaffected, especially among the youth, did not quite know how or why they were disaffected—they just knew they were. The lives of these youth were captured in the 1955 film *Rebel Without a Cause*, which depicted their emotional and social estrangement. The film's star, James Dean, became a symbol of such youth, and he achieved cult status after his death in a 1955 auto accident. Many were drawn to the new and powerfully raw music of rock and roll pioneers like Elvis Presley, Roy Orbison, and Little Richard, who became idols for a new generation of youth. Other youth were drawn into the gentler world of folk music—which also had, however, a definite edge of social critique.

The religious world of the United States was expanding, but the old order, dominated by mainline Protestantism, was not. Much of the control that these groups had (or thought they had) came through the enshrinement of a general Protestant religiosity in many institutions of public life, especially the public schools. But the United States Supreme Court increasingly chipped away at this. In several court decisions during the 1940s, the court moved to apply the Free Exercise and Nonestablishment Clauses of the First Amendment to units of state and local government for the first time. In 1943, the court struck down local restrictions on religious activities by outsider groups (Jehovah's Witnesses, in the case in question). But the major rulings came in the early 1960s, when the court struck down compulsory school prayer and other religious devotional practices. This led to a large public outcry claiming that the court was attacking the religious foundations of American society, although, if truth be told, the offending "religious" practices were already so watered down as to be almost meaningless. But symbolism is important, and these rulings were important for just that reason.

Conclusion

By the early 1960s, participation in organized religious life in the United States was at the highest level it had ever reached. Religious leaders and publications were influential, and even the national news magazines regularly commented on religious themes and stories. Consolidations and mergers created new national denominations, and innovative Christian theology was influential in academic

8. Allen Ginsberg, "Howl," Poetry Foundation, https://www.poetryfoundation.org/poems/49303/howl.

and cultural life. American Christianity faced criticism both from within and from out, but there was an expansive and optimistic feeling among many Christian leaders across the spectrum. Little did they know that the coming decades would rock the very foundations of American Christianity and transform it.

──────────── BIBLIOGRAPHY ────────────

Butler, Jon. *God in Gotham: The Miracle of Religion in Modern Manhattan*. Cambridge, MA: Harvard University Press, 2020.

Dorsett, Lyle W. *Serving God and Country: U.S. Military Chaplains in World War II*. New York: Berkeley, 2012.

Ellwood, Robert S. *The Fifties Spiritual Marketplace: American Religion in a Decade of Conflict*. New Brunswick, NJ: Rutgers University Press, 1997.

Finstuen, Andrew S. *Original Sin and Everyday Protestants: The Theology of Reinhold Niebuhr, Billy Graham, and Paul Tillich in an Age of Anxiety*. Chapel Hill: University of North Carolina Press, 2009.

Hudnut-Beumler, James. *Looking for God in the Suburbs: The Religion of the American Dream and Its Critics, 1945–1965*. New Brunswick, NJ: Rutgers University Press, 1994.

Ling, Peter J. *Martin Luther King, Jr.* 2nd ed. London: Routledge, 2015.

Lotz, David W. *Altered Landscapes: Christianity in America, 1935–1985*. Grand Rapids: Eerdmans, 1989.

Marty, Martin E. *Modern American Religion*. Vol. 3, *Under God, Indivisible, 1941–1960*. Chicago: University of Chicago Press, 1996.

Niebuhr, Reinhold. *The Nature and Destiny of Man: A Christian Interpretation*. Louisville: Westminster John Knox, 1996.

Sittser, Gerald L. *A Cautious Patriotism: The American Churches and the Second World War*. Chapel Hill: University of North Carolina Press, 2010.

Thuesen, Peter J. *In Discordance with the Scriptures: American Protestant Battles over Translating the Bible*. New York: Oxford University Press, 1999.

Wacker, Grant. *America's Pastor: Billy Graham and the Shaping of a Nation*. Cambridge, MA: Belknap, 2014.

11

Conflict and Change, 1965–95

THE THIRTY-YEAR PERIOD FROM 1965 TO 1995 was a time of turmoil, change, and growth in American society and around the world, as the post–World War II era fundamentally reshaped life politically, socially, and technologically. As the baby boomer generation came of age, their ideals and aspirations pushed this reshaping and were often in conflict with the expectations of the older generations. With the collapse of European colonialism, newly independent countries in Africa and Asia challenged the Western powers, and the eventual end of communism in Russia and Eastern Europe further reshaped the world order.

In the United States, the optimistic and youthful atmosphere of the early 1960s was sundered by the assassination of President John F. Kennedy on November 22, 1963. Kennedy was succeeded by his vice president, Lyndon B. Johnson, who went on to be elected in his own right in 1964. Though not the cultural icon Kennedy was, Johnson was much more effective in passing sweeping social legislation, including his Great Society programs and civil rights laws. Kennedy had been strongly anti-communist, challenging Russia and Cuba and beginning military involvement in Vietnam. Beginning in 1965, Johnson greatly escalated the war in Vietnam. But the war became increasingly unpopular, and civil rights tensions broke out into race riots in major cities from 1966 to 1969. The year 1968 was the *annus horribilis* (horrible year) and a watershed, as protests became widespread and sometimes radicalized, and the country came close to fracture, especially with the assassinations of Martin Luther King Jr. and Robert F. Kennedy.

Johnson decided not to run for president in 1968, and he was succeeded by Republican Richard M. Nixon, who also won reelection in 1972. Nixon inflamed anti-war tensions by incursions into Cambodia in 1970, but he also began the process of withdrawing troops from Vietnam. In 1971, the conservative Nixon stunned the world by traveling to China and normalizing relations with that country. But Nixon was engulfed by controversy surrounding political scandals in 1973 and 1974, and he eventually resigned as president. Nixon was succeeded by Gerald Ford. Ford ran for president in 1976 but was defeated by Democrat Jimmy Carter. The events of the ten years leading up to the two-hundredth anniversary of American independence in 1976 soured what became a very muted celebration.

The late 1960s began a period of social change in the United States, with many shifts that are still under way almost sixty years later. The push for civil rights brought substantial, yet incomplete, changes for African Americans. The growing concern over environmental pollution, signaled by the establishment of Earth Day in 1970, brought new governmental action and public awareness to the problem. The "sexual revolution" of the 1960s and later brought new personal freedoms but great social turmoil. And the women's rights movement would, in the coming decades, fundamentally transform American life.

The 1970s was a period of general disillusionment and drift. The twin perils of stagnation and serious monetary inflation sapped the American economy, which was also pummeled by oil crises brought on by events in the Middle East in 1973 and 1979. The social changes of the time were highly divisive. The Supreme Court ruled in favor of the right to abortion in 1973. And conservatives blocked a proposed equal rights amendment to the Constitution. South Vietnam fell to the communists in 1975, adding to the general national ennui, and refugees flocked into the United States from Southeast Asia. Resurgent nationalism in the Middle East challenged American policy in the region, especially the Islamic Revolution in Iran in 1979.

In 1980, Republican Ronald Reagan defeated Carter for the presidency, signaling a conservative trend in American politics and social life. Reagan cut taxes, implemented conservative policies, pushed the "War on Drugs," and actively pushed back against communist powers, especially against Russia and Eastern Europe. Though many feared that Reagan's actions against communism were pushing the world to the brink of nuclear war, European communism eventually collapsed with the fall of the Berlin Wall and the reunification of Germany in 1989, the fall of the Soviet Union in 1991, and the resurgence of nationalism in Eastern Europe. These events signaled the end of the Cold War.

The 1980s saw a renewal of the American economy and monetary policies that brought inflation under control. Americans concentrated on "getting ahead" in their jobs and careers. The economy boomed, despite a stock market crash in 1987 and the emergence of China as a new world economic power to challenge the United States. The computer revolution, especially the development of affordable personal computers, transformed business and technology. And the development of the World Wide Web in the 1990s similarly transformed communications and culture.

As communism faded as a key rival, America's attention was drawn to developments in the Middle East. Israel, America's ally, had dramatically defeated its enemies in wars in 1967 and 1973, but this increased regional tensions. Islamic militancy became a major problem, and terrorists struck in the United States in the World Trade Center bombing in 1993 and in airplane hijackings during this period. President George H. W. Bush intervened in the Middle East via the Gulf War in 1991. Domestic radicalism and bombings were also an issue during this time.

Societal Conflicts and American Christianity, 1965–75

Much of the social change and turmoil of this entire period has its roots in events that took place during the ten turbulent years from 1965 to 1975. The openness and general optimism of the first half of the 1960s quickly evaporated, and American society was plunged into chaos and factionalism, the likes of which it had not seen since the Civil War one hundred years earlier. American religious leaders struggled to respond to the fast-changing events, unsure of how to speak to the new realities and provide leadership to their congregations.

The political and social advances in the Civil Rights Movement from 1954 to 1965 were dampened by the strength of the resistance to them and the realization of the difficulty of the tasks ahead. The nonviolent direct action of Martin Luther King Jr. was admired by many, but some in the African American community felt that their actions needed to be stronger and more direct. Radical Black nationalist leaders, such as those in the Black Panther Party, pushed for more rapid and substantial changes. The struggle for integration and civil rights had also moved into the cities of the North, where frustrations led to violence and rioting between 1965 and 1968. In 1968, King was assassinated—a major turning point that rattled the nation and further inflamed racial tensions.

American religious officials attempted to respond to the situation. The leaders of the National Council of Churches (NCC) and many mainline Protestant denominations signaled their support of civil rights, although their own

congregations were often slow to follow. Frustrated by inaction, in 1969 some
African American activists, including James Forman (1928–2005), developed
the Black Manifesto, which called for religious organizations to give $500 mil-
lion in reparations to the African American community. Forman presented his
demands one Sunday at Riverside Church in New York City. These demands
were not met, but many denominations did increase funding for civil rights
and anti-poverty efforts. Radicals also attacked historic Black churches for their
timidity and failure to act. These churches responded by reminding radicals of
the crucial leadership that historic Black churches had long provided within
the community.

Many White Christians were divided by the increasingly strident tone of the
Civil Rights Movement. Some supported the cause but worried about whether
the larger society could handle the pace and scope of change. Some churches
traditionally avoided taking public stances on controversial social and political
issues. And some congregations were opposed to the Civil Rights Movement.
In response to school integration, for example, some White Christian congregations sponsored their own private Christian schools as an alternative to the
public schools.

The escalated US involvement in the war in Vietnam, beginning in 1965,
necessitated a greatly increased military draft. This sparked further social conflict, and an active anti-war effort was organized almost immediately, mainly by
youth and college students. Protests and violence quickly broke out on college
campuses, and marches and demonstrations were common, as was resistance
to the draft. The furor over the Vietnam War reached a peak in the summer of
1968 with massive demonstrations in Chicago—at the site of the Democratic
Party convention—and again across the country in 1970 after the killing of
four anti-war protesters at Kent State University in Ohio.

Christian denominations in America were deeply divided over the Vietnam
War. Except for the historic peace churches, these denominations had mainly
supported previous American wars within certain limits. Traditional just war
theory imagined wars fought only in certain extreme situations and only as
constrained by rules of war. But modern warfare was often difficult to fit into
such limits, and many questioned whether any war could be justified. Increasingly, some American Christian leaders, such as Protestant pastor and activist
William Sloane Coffin Jr. (1924–2006) and Roman Catholic brothers Philip
Berrigan (1923–2002) and Daniel Berrigan (1921–2016), rejected any support
for the war and instead worked actively against it.

Leading the way in the anti-war activities was a countercultural movement
of young people who came to be known as "hippies." An outgrowth of beat-
nik culture, the hippies were a movement of young people who dismissed the

traditional social order and its mores and envisioned a radically new world of love and peace. Though this movement was not necessarily religious in orientation, it did employ Hindu and Buddhist thought patterns, especially the idea of visualization; for example, the hippies believed that the peaceful new world order they sought would become a reality if enough people visualized it. Their use of psychedelic drugs and jettisoning of traditional sexual mores were, in part, means of freeing their minds from the "bad vibes" of traditional society. In 1967 the hippies proclaimed the "Summer of Love," a "be-in" in San Francisco that was to begin this new reality, but this event soon collapsed into chaos, as did many hippie communes that were established at this time.

Most American youth were not full-fledged hippies, but many were deeply questioning their parents' world and the society their parents' generation had created after World War II. Youthful rebellion was manifested in anti-war and countercultural attitudes, all backed up with a soundtrack of the rock music that many of their parents detested. The high point of this culture was a multiday rock-music festival in Woodstock, New York, in the summer of 1969, which drew tens of thousands of young Americans. Later that year, another such event, this one at the Altamont Speedway in California, collapsed into drugs and violence. The anti-war movement also splintered, and a small fraction of it devolved into bombings and terrorism.

The element of the new youth culture that probably disturbed the older generations the most was the sexual revolution of the 1960s, which was a direct challenge to traditional religious teachings about sexuality. Innovations, such as "the pill" (oral contraceptives) and wider availability of legal abortions, removed some of the perceived dangers of sexual activity. Drawing on the theories of psychologist Sigmund Freud and those of anthropologist Margaret Mead (whose work was eventually debunked), the leaders of this revolution suggested that the root of the world's problems was repressive attitudes toward sex and that "free love" would lead to better and happier relationships, and probably world peace.

Another element of the rebellion against traditional society and its norms was the women's rights movement. Of all the social rebellions of the 1960s, this one was probably the most far-reaching. In the early 1960s, women activists began to question traditional gender roles and attitudes in society and pushed for new freedoms for women. By the late 1960s, this had become known as the women's liberation movement. Many aspects of this, but especially the increasing movement of women into the paid workforce, had immense long-term effects on American Christian denominations and congregations. Traditionally, women's volunteer labor had been essential to the functioning of congregations and religious schools; increasingly, however, congregations and religious schools had to offer women paying, professional jobs if they wanted them to carry out these responsibilities. Working women also had less time to spend taking part in their traditional religious activities and societies. During this time, mainline Protestant denominations began to ordain women as pastors—some Methodists and Presbyterians in the 1950s, some Lutherans in 1970, and Episcopalians in 1976. But conservative Protestants and Roman Catholics, which represented the majority of American Christians, did not follow their lead and still do not formally ordain women as pastors or priests.

New Theological Trends

The 1960s and 1970s saw the development of new theologies that sought to challenge the traditional postwar theological order, and especially the neoorthodoxy of Barth and the Niebuhr brothers that had previously been dominant. These new theologies built on the older American Protestant liberalism of the early twentieth century but often pushed beyond it to openly question many of its fundamental assumptions. These new theologies were activist in nature, applying theological understandings to the transformation of life in this plane of existence; they were about power and organizing people to change this present world.

Drawing from the social trends after World War II, some believed that modern society was becoming dominated by secular (nonreligious) rationalities and that modern persons increasingly no longer believed in a transcendent (otherworldly) being called "God" or in an afterlife, heaven, or eternal reward or punishment. Some of these theorists, pointing to the decline of organized religion in postwar Europe, proclaimed that "God is dead," or that the traditional God of Christianity was obsolete. This direct attack on traditional Christian theism suggested that religion needed to be radically refocused on following the teachings of the human Jesus and his models of love and the ethical life. Theologians Paul van Buren (1924–98), William Hamilton (1924–2012), and, especially, Thomas J. J. Altizer (1927–2018) published provocative books, leading to a cover story in the April 8, 1966, issue of *Time* magazine, which asked, "Is God Dead?" Though this movement was limited to a small circle of academic theologians, this question caused quite a public stir.

Another set of new theologians drew on other ideologies outside Christianity, including Marxism. Traditionally, Marxist ideology was dismissive of the idea of a transcendent God, or really anything beyond this material world. Marxism was militantly atheistic, believing that religion was a drug (an "opiate") fed to the workers by the bosses to keep them from rising up to overthrow capitalism. But some theologians believed it was possible to employ Marxist

Death of God Theology

Radical theology is a contemporary development within Protestantism—with some Jewish, Roman Catholic, and non-religious response and participation already forming—which is carrying the careful openness of older theologies toward atheism a step further. It is, in effect, an attempt to set an atheist point of view within the spectrum of Christian possibilities. While radical theology in this sense has not yet become a self-conscious "movement," it nevertheless has gained the interest and in part the commitment of a large number of Christians in America, particularly from students of all disciplines, and from the younger ranks of teachers and pastors. The aim of the new theology is not simply relevance or contemporaneity for its own sake, but to strive for a whole new way of theological understanding. Thus it is a theological venture in the strict sense, but it is no less a pastoral response to those who have chosen to live as Christian atheists.

The phrase "death of God" has quite properly become a watchword, a stumbling-block, and something of a test in radical theology, which itself is a theological expression of a contemporary Christian affirmation of the death of God. Radical theology thus best interprets itself when it begins to say what it means by that phrase. The tasking of clarifying the possible meanings of the phrase, "death of God," is scarcely begun in the essays of this volume. . . .

Perhaps the category of "event" will prove to be the most useful answer to the recurring question, "Just what does the 'death of God' refer to?" . . . One could list a range of possible meanings of the phrase. . . . It might mean . . . that there once was a God to whom adoration, praise, and trust were appropriate, possible, and even necessary, but now there is no such God. This is the position of the death of God, or radical theology. It is atheism, but with a difference.

J. J. Altizer and William Hamilton, *Radical Theology and the Death of God* (Indianapolis: Bobbs-Merrill, 1966), ix–x.

analysis of social power inequities and its critique of capitalism within a theistic religious framework. This approach, which came to be named liberation theology, was first developed in the early 1960s by young Roman Catholic priests and theologians in Latin America. These religious leaders believed that the role of the church was to be on the side of the poor and oppressed, something that was labeled the "preferential option for the poor." One of the leading proponents of liberation theology was Gustavo Gutiérrez (1928–), whose book *Theology of Liberation* was released in English in 1973. Through Gutiérrez and others, liberation theology became influential, especially among liberal Roman Catholic and Protestant theologians.

Liberation theology was adapted for use beyond its original setting among the rural and urban poor in Latin America, being extended to other communities in need of liberation. Women theologians made use of many of its elements in developing a new feminist theology in the 1970s and 1980s. Prominent theologians such as Rosemary Radford Ruether (1936–2022) and Elisabeth Schüssler Fiorenza (1938–) sought to change traditional Christian theology in light of the new insights of the women's movement of the time. A few, more radical theologians, such as Mary Daly (1928–2010), eventually concluded that Christianity was too patriarchal for redemption and moved in a post-Christian direction. Liberation theology was also an important element in the newly emerging Black theology of the same period, sparked by the book *Black Theology and Black Power* (1969) by James Cone (1938–2018). While many African American Christians remained rather theologically conservative, Cone and others argued for a Black theology of liberation that would empower social changes.

Roman Catholicism after Vatican II

As Roman Catholicism had changed little in the four hundred or so years prior, the wide-ranging changes that came out of the Second Vatican Council (1962–65) were dramatic and, for some, disconcerting. The council was defined by the term *aggiornamento* (update); the goal was a Roman Catholicism for the modern world. The council did not make major doctrinal or structural changes in the church. The reforms were characterized as "pastoral" adaptations of the ways Roman Catholics had long practiced their faith.

American Roman Catholicism had defined a particular subculture in America, with distinctive practices and pieties that had marked Catholics as a separate group within the broader American religious culture. With Vatican II, however, fasting and other devotional practices that had previously been mandatory were made optional, and the piety—especially concerning the veneration of Mary and the saints—was streamlined. Confession was urged, but strictures around it were relaxed. The Latin Mass was eliminated; worship was now to be in the languages of the people, and priests were now to put more emphasis on preaching within the worship services. The Roman Catholic Church also began a series of ecumenical dialogues, marking a new openness in relations with Orthodox, Anglican, Lutheran, and other Protestant churches. These ecumenical dialogues lessened tensions and differences between the groups, but the basic Roman Catholic position that it alone was the one, true, universal church did not change.

For Roman Catholics in religious vocations (priests, nuns, and monks), the changes were very dramatic. Traditionally, their positions within parishes and congregations had been carefully delineated, and their holiness and separation from the world was marked by distinctive dress and other practices. But, in order to play down their separation from the laity, Vatican II swept away many of these distinctions and liberalized others, including making the traditional religious habits (garments) optional. Whether intended or not, these changes also signaled to many a loss of power and prestige for those in religious vocations—they were now more like lay Roman Catholics. The numbers of religious vocations in the American Roman Catholic Church declined dramatically during the 1960s and 1970s. There were ten thousand fewer priests and thirty-five thousand fewer nuns at the end of the 1970s than there were at the beginning of the 1960s. The resulting shortage of priests and nuns was felt strongly in the local parishes and parochial schools, which had to find alternate staffing.

All these changes came about within a broader trend of American Roman Catholics moving more into the mainstream of general American society. White Roman Catholics were moving into the middle class and into the suburbs. And in levels of education and income, they were matching their Protestant neighbors. The patterns of worship and piety that had marked their distinctiveness were relaxed, something that many Roman Catholics welcomed. Traditionally, they had attended weekly worship at much higher levels than Protestants, but by the 1970s Roman Catholic attendance at worship had declined to levels that matched those of Protestants. Rates of participation in the Sacrament of Confession also declined dramatically.

Roman Catholicism was—to a great extent—built on obedience, tradition, and continuity, which made change very difficult to manage. Reform on this scale raised fundamental questions about the whole system: traditionalists decried the changes as going much too far, while liberals felt the changes did not go nearly far enough. This created tensions within the church. With the post–Vatican II changes and tensions occurring at the same time as the larger cultural revolutions of the 1960s and 1970s, many American Catholics were asking new and pressing questions. Pope Paul VI (r. 1963–78) attempted to steer a moderate course through this period, but in 1968 he reaffirmed traditional Roman Catholic social teachings against contraception. The church also maintained its opposition to abortion, even as abortion was legalized in the United States. And, despite the women's revolution, the church continued to maintain a male and celibate priesthood, although some new roles in the church for women were opened. Pope Paul VI also attempted to rein in more liberal elements of the American Roman Catholic Church, including activist priests such as the Berrigan brothers.

Perhaps encouraged by the new openness, many Roman Catholic laypeople began to move away from total obedience to church leaders and positions, choosing a more selective approach instead. They increasingly chose those elements of the faith that they agreed with and ignored those elements with which they disagreed. It was becoming common for American Catholics to express disagreement with the pope on particular points even while they held him up appreciatively as a spiritual leader. Perhaps Catholics, living in a country where religious life had been deeply formed by Protestantism, were picking up some "Protestant" religious attitudes. In a religious organization that traditionally emphasized hierarchy and absolute obedience, these shifts in Catholic posture led to conflict.

In 1978, a Polish cardinal became Pope John Paul II (r. 1978–2005) and continued the trend of moderation and reining in liberalizing elements in the church. Pope John Paul II was very popular in America and visited the United States in 1979 and 1987, but he used those trips to criticize the trends toward selectivity, reminding Roman Catholics that the church expected obedience to church teachings and doctrines. Despite their positive feelings for the new pope, American Catholics continued to exercise individual judgment and selectivity.

As White ethnic Roman Catholics moved into the religious and cultural mainstream of the United States, there was a growing trend of them leaving the church altogether due to such factors as mixed marriages, divorce, and disagreements with church officials and church teachings. The percentages of White Roman Catholics declined, though overall membership levels remained steady because of the influx of Roman Catholic immigrants.

Immigration and the American Churches

Throughout its history, the United States has had complicated stances toward new immigrants. Immigration was largely unregulated until the end of the nineteenth century, when restrictions were tightened in response to increasingly large numbers of non-Protestant newcomers. After World War I, Congress drastically restricted new immigration, allowing only limited numbers of displaced persons and refugees into the country. But a few decades later, in 1965, Congress passed legislation allowing for a significant easing of immigration restrictions. However, the ease of restrictions did not mean that immigration went back to its pre–World War I state. While most immigrants to the United States before World War I had been from Europe, the majority of post-1965 immigrants hailed from Latin America, lesser numbers from Asia, and a small (but growing) number from Africa. Two-thirds of all these new immigrants were Christians, and only about 15 percent were Muslims, Hindus, or Buddhists. The post-1965 immigration reforms thus helped keep the United States a majority Christian nation by bringing in Christians from other parts of the world.

The majority of Hispanic immigrants were from Mexico (60 percent), and many also came from the Caribbean and Central America—all overwhelmingly Roman Catholic areas. The religious backgrounds of Asian Americans were much more varied; Muslim, Hindu, Buddhist, and Christian immigrants, as well as a significant number of nonreligious persons, were included in this group. The growing numbers of African immigrants were mostly Christian, but there were also significant numbers of African Muslims, especially refugees from East Africa. Large numbers of refugees emigrated from Southeast Asia (Vietnam, Cambodia, and Laos) in the 1970s, and during the 1980s there were new immigrants from Cuba and Haiti.

Historically, religious organizations have played a crucial role in aiding the settlement and acculturation of new immigrants. Religious ties bound together new ethnic communities, and those communities helped newcomers settle and find work. Immigrant congregations played a key role in maintaining the languages and social customs of immigrants' former home countries, all the while gradually introducing their community members to American social, cultural, and religious norms. Immigrant religious congregations were the largest ethnic organizations in their respective communities.

The vast majority of Hispanic immigrants arrived in the United States as Roman Catholics but often practiced varieties of Roman Catholicism that were significantly distinctive from, and often at odds with, the existing American Roman Catholic hierarchy. Large numbers of Hispanic Roman Catholics were incorporated into the United States through the annexation of Texas, California, and the Southwest, and later Puerto Rico and the Philippines. These Hispanic Roman Catholics were deeply devoted to the popular religious piety and customs of their home countries, but they were also strongly anticlerical, deeply suspicious of and resistant to the clerical leadership of their local Roman Catholic churches. These tensions led to a serious lack of Spanish-speaking priests, especially from among the broader levels of society. And Hispanic Roman Catholicism in the Americas has been characterized by rich and complicated blends of European Catholic customs and other religious traditions and practices—some indigenous, others brought from afar. Catholic spirituality in Mexico has often included strong devotion to the rituals of the Day of the Dead (*Día de los Muertos*) and the veneration of the Virgin of Guadalupe (*Nuestra Señora de Guadalupe*), but the popular Mexican Revolution (1910–20) stripped the church of much of its power and wealth. Other forms of Hispanic popular religion are fusions, such as Santería, from Cuba, and Voodoo, from Haiti—each of which melds popular local Roman Catholicism with Western African religious traditions that were brought to the Caribbean by enslaved persons.

11.1. A Jesus People Rally and Concert in Toronto, May 1971.

From the late twentieth century to today, there has been a growing number of Hispanic Protestants in the United States, mainly Baptists and Pentecostals. Today, about 25 percent of all American Hispanics are Protestants, and most have converted from Roman Catholicism to Protestantism after immigrating. Entrepreneurial Hispanic Protestant pastors in the United States have worked aggressively to recruit new members into their (usually conservative) congregations. These congregations traditionally have been strongly anti–Roman Catholic, although this sentiment seems to have faded as the American Hispanic community has diversified.

Asia is by far the most religiously diverse continent, and no one religious group constitutes a majority in the region. Some Asian immigrants during this time were Muslim, Hindu, or Buddhist; others (especially from China) were nonreligious; and many were Christian. In the United States, about 60 percent of all Asian Americans are Christians, which is a much larger percentage than in Asia itself. The reasons for this are many. Some Asian immigrants came from countries that were already strongly Christian, such as the Philippines or South Korea. Other Asian Christians were religious minorities in their former home countries and selected the United States as their destination because they viewed it as a Christian nation. Still others were Southeast Asians who converted to Christianity in refugee resettlement camps or Chinese immigrants who converted in the United States after getting connected with Chinese Christian congregations.

The growing number of African immigrants have come mostly from areas of the continent that are Christian. Christianity has been growing in Sub-Saharan Africa since the beginning of the twentieth century, and the region is now home to over four hundred million Christians. African Christians are divided between Protestants, Roman Catholics, and independent African-initiated churches, all of which are found in the African immigrant communities in America.

The Christian communities formed by these various immigrant populations have often been at odds with their more long-established counterparts in the United States. Immigrant congregations are often socially and theologically much more conservative than non-immigrant congregations, which can lead to tensions and spark disputes. American denominations sometimes wish to absorb immigrant congregations (for the sake of their own diversity), but immigrant congregations often have good reasons for wanting to remain independent.

Christianities at the Cultural Margins

Much of the countercultural revolution of the 1960s—the hippies and the youth culture—was not particularly tied to organized religion. Some cultural revolutionaries rejected God and religion altogether. Some, like the hippies, were attracted to forms and thought patterns found in Asian religions such as Hinduism and Buddhism. Others found themselves attracted to organized Asian-inspired religiosity, such as Zen Buddhism and the International Society for Krishna Consciousness (ISKCON, or the Hare Krishna movement). But there were some youths and pastors who worked among the cultural revolutionaries and who employed a countercultural sensibility to develop new forms of Christianity in the United States.

There were a number of young Christian leaders who began outreach ministries among the hippies in California in the mid-1960s. These leaders—including Ted Wise (1936–), Richard L. York (1940–94), and Arthur Blessitt (1940–)—set up coffee houses, street ministries, and other forms of outreach to the transient youth populations in the San Francisco and Southern California regions. Beginning around 1967, the resulting groups became known as the Jesus People (or Jesus Freaks or Hippies for Jesus). They blended countercultural sensibilities with evangelical Protestantism, drawing young people away from drugs and toward Jesus, whom they envisioned as the original hippie. Some

Christian communes and other intentional communities were also formed, though they tended not to last very long.

Some offshoots of these efforts had long-term success. In 1965, Chuck Smith (1927–2013) began an outreach ministry within the youth culture of the beaches and surfers of Southern California, eventually forming a congregation called Calvary Chapel in Costa Mesa, California. To reach these youths, Smith abandoned formal ministerial clothing and traditional Christian worship. His Calvary Chapel was informal and blended folk-rock music with Christian lyrics to develop a new, "contemporary" genre of Christian worship music that would eventually sweep through American Christianity. The success of the Costa Mesa congregation inspired numerous other pastors to form similar congregations around the country. These churches were gathered into the Calvary Chapel Association, which by 2016 claimed over seventeen hundred congregations. Its contemporary Christian music was marketed by Calvary Chapel's subsidiary, Maranatha! Music.

A similar movement in Southern California began in 1974 with the formation by Kenn Gulliksen (1945–) of the first Vineyard Church in West Los Angeles, which grew to eight congregations by 1982. In that year, the Vineyard movement was joined by John Wimber (1934–97) and his Calvary Chapel congregation of Yorba Linda, California, and Gulliksen handed over leadership of the movement to Wimber. This movement, too, went nationwide, and by 2020 the Association of Vineyard Churches claimed twenty-four hundred congregations. The loose structure of the Vineyard movement (like the Calvary Chapel Association) led to problems, especially in disciplining local Vineyard pastors who strayed, either doctrinally or morally. A very successful Pentecostal revival in the 1990s at the Vineyard congregation in Toronto, Ontario, gained international recognition, but controversies that arose during this revival led to the congregation leaving the association.

In the 1970s and 1980s, these two associations and others like them set off a revolution in the way many American Christians worshiped: the beginnings of the contemporary Christian music genre and contemporary worship styles. Taking the folk music of the early 1960s and adding rock music styles and idioms, contemporary worship music introduced a whole new form of Christian worship, with guitars, drums, and synthesizers replacing the traditional organs and pianos. The worship was informal, eschewing the traditional liturgies and clerical robes. Pastors moved out from behind their pulpits and wandered around the worship areas. These worship styles were often effective and popular, especially among younger generations, but they also drew huge pushback from traditionalists and the older generations. This clash of styles was dubbed the "worship wars." Many congregations, if they had the resources, decided to offer different worship services, one traditional and the other contemporary, to cover all the bases.

Many of these movements and their congregations were organized around a single charismatic pastor or leader. While most of them remained within the bounds of Christian orthodoxy, sometimes such charismatic leaders took on messianic personas, either by their own claiming or in the eyes of their followers. In the 1960s and 1970s, several new movements, often derived from Christianity, followed these authoritative leaders far outside Christian bounds.

Among those working with the hippies and the countercultural generation was David "Moses" Berg (1919–94), who dubbed his group the Children of God (now the Family International). This group was initially formed into Christian communes spread across the country, held together with "letters" from Berg, who increasingly claimed messianic status among them. This group has gone through numerous reinventions of itself, buffeted by disputes over doctrine and leadership and, most dramatically, by claims of sexual license and abuse, especially of children. After Berg's death, control of the group passed to his second wife, Karen Zerby (pen name Maria Fontaine).

Another leader who veered into personal messianism was South Korean pastor Sun Myung Moon (1920–2012), who claimed that Christ had chosen him to complete his work by unifying all the world's Christians under his leadership. Those who followed Moon were gathered into the Unification Church (the "Moonies"), which had grown in the United States, especially after Moon moved to America in 1971. The Unification Church strictly controlled the lives of its members, who worked very long hours raising funds for the church. Moon served a sentence for tax fraud in the 1980s, and the remaining group, now greatly reduced, is currently controlled by other Moon family members.

Sometimes these groups ended badly. A pastor from Indianapolis, Jim Jones, began a popular interracial ministry in the 1960s and later moved this ministry to the Bay Area of California, where his outreach to the poor and minorities had success. Though Jones was praised by local politicians and leaders, he began to slip into messianic delusions and paranoia, and he increasingly exercised strict control over his followers' lives. Obsessed by apocalyptic fears, Jones eventually led his group to a new settlement—called Jonestown—in the country of Guyana, in South America. When US officials arrived to investigate claims of abuse, Jones ordered them killed. Then, on November 18, 1978, he ordered his nine hundred followers to consume a beverage laced with cyanide, in a mass suicide.

A similarly tragic ending came to the Branch Davidians in Waco, Texas. This group was a 1930s offshoot of the Seventh-day Adventists, and it was taken over by a charismatic young man, Vernon Howell (1959–1993), who took the name David Koresh. Like Jim Jones, Koresh exercised strict control over

11.2a and b. Jim Jones and the Peoples Temple Tragedy.

the group and insisted on their isolation. When federal officials besieged and eventually raided the Branch Davidian compound in 1993 over concerns that the group had been stockpiling illegal weapons, the Davidians died in a fire and a hail of bullets.

The Resurgence of Evangelical Protestantism

As we have seen, the division of American Protestantism in the 1920s, as a result of the fundamentalist-modernist controversy, resulted in a sizeable number of conservative evangelicals and fundamentalists leaving mainline Protestant denominations. They formed new congregations, denominations, and educational institutions, constituting a new conservative-evangelical subculture, one that was marked by a distinct withdrawal from American public life. Shorn of these dissidents, mainline Protestantism attempted to secure its control over religious life in the United States, especially through ecumenical organizations like the NCC. Some scholars at the time believed that such "backward" conservative Protestantism would wither away, with remaining pockets in the rural south eventually dying out from the effects of modernity. Except for evangelist Billy Graham and his widespread fame during the 1950s and 1960s, there were few evangelicals of the period on the national scene.

But the scholars were wrong, and conservative Protestantism grew apace with the rest of American Christianity in the boom years between 1945 and 1965. Then, after the high point of the middle 1960s, mainline Protestant denominations began a precipitous decline from numerical and public prominence. But conservative Protestant denominations continued to grow. The Pentecostal Assemblies of God grew 43 percent between 1955 and 1965, and 37 percent between 1965 and 1975, making it (by far) the fastest growing American denomination of the time. Similar growth was seen in other conservative Protestant denominations, such as the Church of the Nazarene, the Seventh-day Adventists, and the huge Southern Baptist Convention. The substantial growth of megachurches that were founded during this period—Willow Creek, Calvary Chapel, and Vineyard, along with many other such churches—added substantially to evangelical numbers. African American Protestantism—which shared many conservative theological positions (but not political or social ones) with these largely White denominations—retained its prominence. And entrepreneurial Hispanic evangelical pastors formed substantial Baptist and Pentecostal congregations during this time, pulling members from among Roman Catholic parishes and from the religiously unaffiliated. By the 1990s, almost one-quarter of all Hispanics in America identified themselves as Protestant. It was during this period that evangelicals claimed the label "Christian" for the institutions of their subculture: Christian books, Christian music, Christian schools, and so forth.

Of all this evangelical growth, the most surprising was the resurgence of Pentecostalism. Long derided as "primitives" and "holy rollers," many observers thought that the core practices of Pentecostalism—such as speaking in tongues, faith healing, prophecy, and exorcism—were utterly incompatible with the religious sensibilities of "modern" Americans. They were wrong. The steady growth of Pentecostalism continued, and even accelerated, into the 1970s, matching a similar surge of Pentecostalism around the world, especially in the Global South. The growing prominence of Pentecostalism in the United States was also seen in the rise of major Pentecostal media personalities who came to dominate religious broadcasting. First and foremost was Oral Roberts (1918–2009), who forged a national religious broadcasting empire beginning in the 1960s and formed an eponymous university in Tulsa, Oklahoma, in 1965. But there were many other such evangelists. Jimmy Swaggart (1935–) established a similar ministry based in Baton Rouge, Louisiana, preaching upbeat musicality in the same vein as his cousin, rocker Jerry Lee Lewis. Two similar evangelists of the "Word of Faith" movement founded congregations and evangelistic ministries in the Southwest: Kenneth Hagin (1917–2003) in Tulsa, Oklahoma, and Kenneth Copeland (1936–) in Fort Worth, Texas. Millions of viewers tuned into their television programming and saw speaking in tongues, healings, exorcisms, and other spiritual practices.

Even more interesting was the growth of Pentecostal practices among some in mainline Protestant and Roman Catholic congregations. Preferring the term *charismatic* to the term *Pentecostal*, some began an exploration of these spiritual practices in their congregations, beginning in 1959 with an Episcopal rector in California. By the early 1960s, there was a growing charismatic movement

Oral Roberts on the Pentecostal Revival

The Holy Spirit in the now is beginning a new march across the earth. Millions are being touched by His magnificent power. People are feeling a touch of the Spirit. It's crossing all denominational lines, all social barriers, all levels of education. It's great and I'm thrilled about it.

There is no doubt in my mind that the Holy Spirit has something unusual for YOU. . . . You are going to feel something from God. I cannot tell you exactly what it will be, but the Spirit himself will make it known in your inner being in a way so real that you cannot doubt it. . . .

I'm very interested in your understanding the teachings of the Holy Spirit throughout the Bible until the baptism in the Holy Spirit explodes in your being. I want you not only to have the experience of the baptism in the Holy Spirit in your life but also to have an understanding of it—to have a workable knowledge of it. I want you to know better how to apply the power of the Holy Spirit to practical problems that you face in your daily existence.

It seems everyone is paying a lot of attention today to the word charismatic or charisma. But when we use the word charisma we do not use it in the same way that the secular world does. . . .

The word charisma as used in reference to the Holy Spirit is simply GOD LOVING A HUMAN BEING. It is God believing in that human being and imparting to him a gift of the Holy Spirit a gift which he has not earned, . . . a gift which he cannot buy, . . . a gift which is not given because of his individual merit. It is a gift given by the grace of God—unmerited favor. GOD HAS SMILED UPON THAT INDIVIDUAL SO THAT HE, IN TURN, CAN SMILE UPON THE WORLD. The gift works through him but he can never take personal credit for it.

Oral Roberts, *The Holy Spirit in the Now* (Tulsa: Oral Roberts University, 1974), 1:9.

among the mainline Methodists, Lutherans, Presbyterians, and American Baptists, as well as in some Roman Catholic parishes. This movement peaked in the 1970s, and these charismatics formed distinctive groups within their respective denominations. Denominational leaders were not sure what to make of this unexpected development, but they were, in the main, cautiously accepting of these charismatic Christians in their midst.

In the 1960s and 1970s, more evangelicals gained a national following via religious television programming. The mainline Protestant attempts at freezing evangelical television programs off the major networks failed, as evangelical media stars developed their own networks and programming distribution venues. Changes in Federal Communications Commission rules meant that, by 1980, most religious programming on television was by evangelical Protestants. The leader in this was a fundamentalist preacher from Lynchburg, Virginia,

Jerry Falwell Sr. (1933–2007), who began broadcasting his services in the 1960s as the *Old-Time Gospel Hour*. Falwell became a leading figure in American evangelicalism and formed Lynchburg Baptist College (now Liberty University) in 1971 and the political arm of evangelicalism, the Moral Majority political organization, in 1979. Another major media figure was Pat Robertson (1930–2023), who began his show, *The 700 Club*, in 1963. Robertson also started his own Christian network to carry it, the Christian Broadcasting Network. *The 700 Club* was like a talk news show, with Robertson giving his conservative religious perspectives on the events of the day. Robertson's standing was such that he even launched a bid for election as president in 1988. A more notorious figure was Jim Bakker

11.3. Jerry Falwell Sr.

(1940–), who developed a major media empire with his then wife, Tammy Faye Bakker (1942–2007), around their popular show *The PTL Club*, founded in 1974, and Trinity Broadcast Network. The Bakker empire, which included a theme park, collapsed in the 1980s under the weight of Jimmy's sexual and financial indiscretions, and Jimmy was imprisoned for five years. The prominence of evangelists was a mixed blessing, especially in light of their frequent personal failings and incessant fundraising to keep their multimillion-dollar empires afloat.

Conservative American Protestantism was also marked at this time by the growing embrace of premillennial dispensationalism—a distinctive theological vision of the end of the world (the *eschaton*) that anticipates that Christ will return, suddenly and unmistakably, to judge the world and establish a thousand-year reign, and that this will be preceded by wars, natural disasters, and various kinds of corruption, all signs of the impending cataclysm. Many evangelicals of the 1960s and 1970s interpreted events of the time as such signs. Although details varied within this line of thought, it was widely concluded and proclaimed that Christians were then living in the final days of the end of the world and that Satan (or the power of evil) had taken control of many of the world's institutions.

This premillennial dispensational theology, which had been around since the late nineteenth century, achieved new life in 1967 with the release of a new, revised version of the Scofield Reference Bible, which was infused with it. As they observed the nuclear standoffs and fears of the Cold War, the Arab-Israeli conflicts of the Six-Day War (1967) and the Yom Kippur War (1973), and dramatic social changes, many became convinced that the end of the world was indeed near. The first major statement of this perspective was a wildly popular book by Hal Lindsey (1929–), *The Late Great Planet Earth*, first published in 1970. This book, which the *New York Times* declared the best-selling nonfiction book of the 1970s, sold millions of copies and brought premillennial thinking into the popular imagination. In a similar way, an evangelical movie, *A Thief in the Night*, released in 1972, portrayed the end of the world in a fictionalized form and had millions of viewers. A later version of premillennial dispensationalism was the basis of the Left Behind series of novels by Tim LaHaye (1926–2016) and Jerry B. Jenkins (1949–), a series of twelve novels and many other spin-offs. A conservative estimate is that there were at least thirty major predictions of the end of the world between 1967 and 1995, many by leading evangelical figures.

The Rise of the Christian Right in American Politics

As we have seen, in the late nineteenth century, conservative American evangelicals were active in politics, especially in the temperance movement. Evangelical William Jennings Bryan was a leading presidential candidate during this period. But after 1920, stung by defeat in battles with the modernists, evangelicals largely withdrew from participation in public life. Premillennialism imagined an increasingly evil world, in which governments were corrupted by the devil, and many evangelicals concluded that the best thing for them to do was to focus on soul winning and remaining untainted by the world. Though Billy Graham was a national figure and a confidant of several American presidents, he remained determinedly out of political life.

Beginning in the 1970s, however, American evangelicals suddenly returned to active participation in political life. Because evangelical leaders could mobilize millions of evangelical voters to support specific issues and candidates, they became a formidable power in American politics. Contemporary observers anguished aloud about the outsized impact of these new evangelical voters and political organizations. In truth, however, these voters were not new. They had simply ended their self-imposed exile from public life and were participating once again in ways commensurate with their numbers.

Formerly, evangelicals had been split between the two major political parties, with northern evangelicals supporting the Republicans and southern

Francis A. Schaeffer, "A Christian Manifesto" (1982)

I think the Church has failed to meet its obligation in these last 40 years for two specific reasons. The first is this false, truncated view of spirituality that doesn't see true spirituality touching all of life. The other thing is that too many Christians, whether they are doctors, lawyers, pastors, evangelists—whatever they are—too many of them are afraid to really speak out because they did not want to rock the boat for their own project. . . .

We must absolutely set out to smash the lie of the new and novel concept of the separation of religion from the state which most people now hold. . . .

Now we have turned it over and we have put it on its head and what we must do is absolutely insist that we return to what the First Amendment meant in the first place—not that religion can't have an influence into society and into the state—not that. But we must insist that there's a freedom that the First Amendment really gave. Now with this we must emphasize, and I said it, but let me say it again, we do not want a theocracy! . . . But that's a very different thing while saying clearly we are not in favor of a theocracy in name or in fact, from where we are now, where all religious influence is shut out of the processes of the state and the public schools. . . .

Now, I come toward the close, and that is that we must recognize something from the Scriptures. . . . When the government negates the law of God, it abrogates its authority. God has given certain offices to restrain chaos in this fallen world, but it does not mean that these offices are autonomous, and when a government commands that which is contrary to the Law of God, it abrogates its authority. . . .

Christ must be the final Lord and not society and not Caesar.

Francis A. Schaeffer, "A Christian Manifesto," an address delivered in 1982 at the Coral Ridge
Presbyterian Church, Fort Lauderdale, Florida. https://peopleforlife.org/francis.html.

evangelicals supporting the Democrats. But, beginning in the 1960s, with Democratic support for civil rights and other social causes, southern evangelicals began to desert the Democratic Party in droves. The rapid social changes of the decade—along with Supreme Court rulings on prayer in schools and other issues—raised grave concerns among evangelicals about the moral direction of the United States. Evangelical theologian Francis Schaeffer (1912–1984) authored an influential call to arms, *How Should We Then Live?* (1976), and urged American evangelicals to enter the political arena to fight for their ideals and causes.

A series of hot-button social issues caught evangelicals' attention. In 1972, Congress passed the proposed Equal Rights Amendment to the Constitution and sent it to the states for ratification. Fearing the erosion of traditional understandings of gender relations, conservatives successfully defeated the ratification efforts under the leadership of Phyllis Schlafly (1924–2016) and her organization STOP ERA (Stop Taking Our Privileges-ERA). In 1973, the Supreme Court legalized abortion on the national level with the decision in *Roe v. Wade*, which further alarmed and mobilized religious conservatives. In 1977, singer Anita Bryant (1940–) led a successful opposition to a proposed Dade County, Florida, gay-rights ordinance. Many of these single-issue social groups included conservatives across the religious spectrum (Schlafly herself was a Roman Catholic), but evangelicals had an important role in these movements.

The election of Democrat and active Southern Baptist layman Jimmy Carter (1924–) as president in 1976 was a disappointment to many evangelicals, mainly because of the socially liberal positions of many in his administration. Increasingly, evangelicals turned to the Republican Party, and, in 1978, they became a force in the congressional elections. This marked the birth of what came to be known as the New Christian Right. In 1979, several evangelicals organized well-funded, single-interest groups to become active in politics: Beverly LaHaye (1929–2024) founded the Concerned Women for America, Jerry Falwell Sr. established the Moral Majority, and Randall Terry (1959–) began his pro-life (anti-abortion) activities that culminated in the organization Operation Rescue in 1987.

But the strength of the New Christian Right was seen dramatically in 1980 when they helped Republican candidate Ronald Reagan (1911–2004) defeat Carter for the presidency. Reagan was an unlikely candidate for evangelical affections—he was a divorced Hollywood actor and a mainline Protestant. But Reagan was a staunch conservative and supported the social and political causes dear to evangelicals, who voted for him in droves, well above the national average. Falwell, Robertson, and others became influential in American political life. Thus began the evangelical migration to the Republican Party and their influence within it, which has only grown stronger over the ensuing fifty years. In 1988, evangelical leader Pat Robertson himself campaigned for the Republican nomination for president but lost. Many evangelicals concluded that although they could help elect a president, they probably could not elect an evangelical to the presidency. Many evangelicals were elected to Congress, but even there they could not dominate.

The late 1980s saw a change in strategy by American evangelical leaders. Falwell disbanded the Moral Majority in 1989, claiming the organization of millions of people had fulfilled its purposes. Rather, evangelical political leaders focused their attention on grassroots efforts and state and local politics, where they came to be dominant in many areas. Robertson formed the Christian Coalition in 1989, with Ralph Reed (1961–) as executive director, to focus more tightly on evangelical voters and their issues. The personal and financial failings of a number of televangelists (Bakker, Swaggart, and others) hurt the national image of evangelicals, but their media and political organizations remained formidable political and social forces, especially within the Republican Party.

Cultural Changes in American Congregations

The social and cultural upheavals of the 1960s and 1970s had serious effects on American Christian congregations as they moved into the 1980s and 1990s. Sociologists charted changing patterns of community, belief, and denominational affiliation that placed these congregational changes within the context of larger societal changes affecting many other institutional groups and organizations. These societal changes affected how Americans related to their organizations and to one another.

Probably the most far-ranging changes involved the women's rights movement and the role of women in the United States. Certainly, there were activists in the 1960s who led the way in advocating for increased rights and opportunities for women, and some of these activists took rather extreme positions. There certainly was not a uniformity of agreement among American women over the nature and extent of the desired changes, and there were religious women who led the way in opposition to the Equal Rights Amendment, abortion, and other such causes. But there was an increasingly widespread acceptance of women seeking paid employment outside the home and of the basic rights of women to equal compensation and opportunities, an acceptance that transcended religious lines.

Millions of women, especially younger women, sought employment and careers—not as a substitute for marriage and family life, but in addition to it. This had a major effect on American religious organizations. Traditionally, the majority of congregation members were women, and many of them had volunteered significant amounts of time to keep their congregations operating. With increasing numbers of women seeking paid employment, congregations lost the volunteer labor that was vital to their operation. Increasingly, congregations had to pay women for work done in congregational and religious settings and accord these women professional status. In the Roman Catholic Church, the number of women in religious orders (nuns) dropped dramatically after 1965, with many nuns leaving that life and drastically reduced numbers of young women entering it. This meant that Roman Catholic educational and social organizations, which had traditionally relied on the low-cost labor of nuns, were forced to replace them with better-paid lay women workers. Traditional

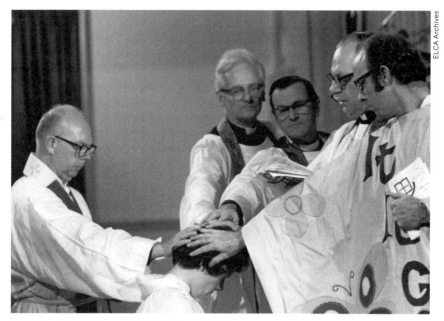

11.4. The Ordination of Elizabeth Platz, 1970.

religious groups for missions and parish life, ubiquitous in earlier generations, also markedly declined, creating further stresses on the lives and finances of American congregations.

Lutherans began ordaining women as pastors in 1970, and Episcopalians began ordaining them as priests in 1976, thereby joining other mainline Protestant denominations that had already made this change. Conservative Protestants did not follow suit, but even among their ranks there were some new opportunities for female leadership. The Roman Catholic Church reaffirmed in the 1970s that the priesthood was only for men, but it did begin to allow for some expanded women's roles, especially as the number of priests declined appreciably.

These changes were part of large societal patterns in which Americans were changing the ways they affiliated with, and remained loyal to, social and religious institutions. Sociologist Robert D. Putnam (1941–) chronicled the loss of social and religious capital that occurred with this shift in his book *Bowling Alone: The Collapse and Revival of American Community* (2000). Traditionally, many Americans were known by the social and religious organizations in which they participated, but these affiliations—whether religious or societal— declined beginning in the 1960s due to disinterest and the increased pace of life. Christian congregations suffered, along with many other organizations, as a part of these trends.

There were important changes in the ties that bound Americans to their religious organizations. Historically, religious groups had counted on the loyalty and denominational affiliations of their members. Methodists had a distinctive identity as Methodists, and when they moved to a new town, they would seek membership in a local Methodist congregation. And the same went for members of other denominations. But postwar Americans were very mobile, and they switched congregations and denominations far more frequently. There was a marked decline in denominational loyalty as Americans "shopped" for new congregations, valuing particular preachers or congregational offerings (such as youth programs) above denominational labels. While this kind of searching for religious identities and congregational homes had always been a part of American religious life (Americans have always been religious "seekers"), this trait has greatly expanded since the 1960s. This religious individualism was observed in 1985 by sociologist Robert N. Bellah (1927–2013) in his book *Habits of the Heart: Individualism and Commitment in American Life*. This book explored how many Americans were coming to develop their own religious (and social) identities by pulling together their own combinations of disparate religious beliefs and practices. Polling data demonstrated that many Americans had rather eclectic sets of religious beliefs, sets that often conflicted with the traditional beliefs of the congregations and denominations to which they belonged.

Increasingly, Christian congregations sought to do whatever they could to attract religiously restless Americans, such as eliminating denominational labels and offering services in a variety of worship styles. Megachurches, including Willow Creek in suburban Chicago, led the way in systematically reevaluating practices to make sure that religious seekers would be comfortable and engaged. Some congregations eliminated the word *church* from their titles, preferring to refer to themselves with generic terms such as *Christian Life Center*. The emphasis was on religious experience, rather than doctrinal or denomination particularity.

Changes in American Denominations, 1965–95

Overall, the percentage of Americans who were members of a Christian denomination grew steadily (if unspectacularly) through the twentieth century, from about 50 percent in 1900 to almost 70 percent in the 1990s. But this overall figure does not show the constantly shifting patterns of Americans' denominational affiliations. As some religious groups grew numerically, others stagnated, and still others declined. After World War II, there was a general rise in membership across the board, which peaked around 1965. However, membership in the old mainline Protestant denominations declined, in some cases dramatically, from 1965 to 1995, while conservative and evangelical churches continued to gain members. Roman Catholic numbers remained generally steady, with losses among White Roman Catholics being matched by a rise in immigrant Catholics from Latin America and Asia.

The postwar pattern of mergers and consolidations among mainline Protestant denominations continued through this period. In 1968, the Methodist Church and the Evangelical United Brethren Church merged to form the United Methodist Church. That same year, two other denominations in this tradition joined to form the Wesleyan Church. In 1983, northern and southern Presbyterians—the United Presbyterian Church in the U.S.A. and the Presbyterian Church in the U.S., respectively—merged to form the Presbyterian Church (U.S.A.), and, in 1988, three Lutheran denominations formed the Evangelical Lutheran Church in America. This last merger generally signaled the end of the period of mainline Protestant mergers, as most of these traditions had already consolidated.

Though this consolidation was externally impressive, these mergers brought with them new problems. Denominational mergers are difficult to achieve, and there are often many within the new denominations who feel that they have lost something. Mergers disrupt old patterns of loyalty and cohesiveness and pull together often disparate groups; old fights between denominational traditions are often thus internalized within the new denominations. Mergers also often result in the formation of small breakaway denominations, usually more conservative than the uniting churches. Additionally, new moderate and conservative movements are sometimes formed within the resulting denominations, seeking to correct what they see as liberal "drift." In the second half of the twentieth century, all these factors were at play in the mainline denominational mergers, combining to create serious internal conflicts at a time when the new denominations were trying to come together.

There were several examples of denominational splintering and schism during this period. Small groups of traditionalist Roman Catholics, upset by the changes of Vatican II, formed their own communities, sometimes on the fringes of the Roman Catholic Church, and sometimes outside of it. Two Protestant schisms occurred because moderates within denominations resisted the majorities' increasingly conservative trajectories: within the Lutheran Church–Missouri Synod, in 1976, and within the Southern Baptist Convention, in 1991.

But most mainline Protestant denominations—along with the Roman Catholic Church, in a sense—were trending in theologically and socially liberal directions. Following the social movements of the 1960s and 1970s, liberal mainline Protestant leaders continued to embrace new causes, including civil rights and women's rights, the new ecology movement, the campaign against nuclear and conventional armaments, and opposition to the conservative policies of Ronald Reagan in the 1980s. There was a growing divide within mainline Protestantism between the clergy, who embraced these liberal causes, and the laity, who tended to be much more conservative. This added to the already-existing tensions within these denominations.

After mainline Protestant membership peaked in 1965, there came a steady, and sometimes dramatic, decline. The losses from 1965 to 1995 were as follows:

American Baptists: down 3 percent

Christian Church (Disciples of Christ): down 51 percent

Episcopal Church: down 27 percent

Evangelical Lutheran Church in America: down 9 percent

Presbyterian churches: down 13 percent

Reformed churches: down 20 percent

United Church of Christ: down 28 percent

United Methodist Church: down 22 percent

When seen in the context of the population growth of the United States during this thirty-year period (1965–95)—when the population increased by 32 percent, from 200 million to 265 million—these losses in the share of the religious "market" for mainline Protestants were dramatic. These denominations historically claimed to represent the core of American Christianity, but now they represented an increasingly small minority of the American population.

The conservative and evangelical ranks continued to grow after 1965, in their traditional denominations as well as in the newer "non-denominational" and megachurch congregations. The gains from 1965 to 1995 were as follows:

Assemblies of God: up 306 percent

Church of God (Cleveland, TN): up 252 percent

Church of the Nazarene: up 74 percent

Southern Baptist Convention: up 45 percent

By 1995, almost 40 percent of Americans claimed they were "born again," a key concept within evangelicalism (although many of these did not share other evangelical positions).

This startling reversal brought great consternation among many in the mainline Protestant community. Some mainline leaders ignored these numbers,
dismissed them, or tried to explain them away as temporary aberrations. But
other observers took the trends seriously. In 1972, Dean M. Kelley (1926–97),
a Methodist executive in the NCC, wrote a groundbreaking study titled
Why Conservative Churches Are Growing, which caused great controversy but

Dean M. Kelley on the Growth of Conservative Churches (1972)

The mainline churches are weakening while the rapidly growing [conservative]
churches are becoming stronger.

These groups not only give evidence that religion is not obsolete and churches
not defunct, but they contradict the contemporary notion of an acceptable religion. They are not "reasonable," they are not "tolerant," they are not ecumenical,
they are not "relevant." Quite the contrary!

They often refuse to recognize the validity of other churches' teachings,
ordinations, sacraments....

The liberal branches seem more attuned to the social and demographic
trends of the modern population. They are more urbanized and cosmopolitan.
They enjoy greater affluence and mobility. Their members have more education
on the average than do those of the conservative branches. One would expect
them, therefore, to appeal more successfully to an increasingly urban, affluent,
educated, and mobile population than could the conservative branches, and
thus to attract more members and grow more rapidly.

But in every case... the conservative branches are increasing proportionately
more rapidly than the liberal!...

Some would say that they are all declining because they have not modernized
rapidly enough; others consider it a regrettable but temporary trauma accompanying rapid change, which will subside when things settle down.

Is it possible that it is neither, but instead a direct *consequence* of modernization? Churches that have not tried to adjust to the times—to ingratiate
themselves with the world—in many cases are not declining. In them we see
no indication that religion is obsolete, churches outdated, or modernization
helpful. They cause us to suspect that the declining churches are not victims of
changing times but of internal failure—the inability to provide a needed product
or service. They have not adequately understood or performed their essential
business: the dispensing of religion. What is this business, and why does it
matter whether it is performed?...

By this important index of spiritual vitality, the mainline churches are weakening while the rapidly growing churches are becoming stronger.

Dean M. Kelley, *Why Conservative Churches are Growing: A Study in
Sociology of Religion* (New York: Harper & Row, 1972), 25–27, 35.

eventually proved to be prophetic. Kelley suggested that with their embrace of liberal social causes and religious pluralism and their distancing themselves from traditional theological doctrines, mainline denominations were left with nothing particularly interesting to offer. Conservative churches were growing, on the other hand, because they offered people theological positions and religious assurances that were distinctive and that the general society did not already have.

This period also saw a dramatic expansion of ecumenical efforts, although evangelical Protestants were not involved in most of these conversations. Inter-Protestant ecumenical efforts continued, mainly among the denominations in the NCC. The most ambitious of these conversations, the Consultation on Church Union (COCU), was between six mainline Protestant denominations and three African American Methodist denominations. The COCU began in 1962, and the dream expressed in its documents from 1966 to 1970 was of an organic merger of these groups. But this vision ran into organizational and ideological difficulties. In 1988, the COCU scaled back its vision to focus on a new concept of "covenanting" toward cooperation and interconnected ministries among its member denominations, but even this was difficult to achieve.

On the international scale, in 1982 the World Council of Churches launched an attempt at closer unity at a conference in Lima, Peru. At this conference, the WCC member churches formally adopted an ecumenical document titled "Baptism, Eucharist and Ministry" (BEM), which expressed common ground between the member churches on these three sacraments and envisioned unity around their shared understanding and practice. Like the COCU's efforts, however, this effort by the WCC gained little traction.

After Vatican II, the 1960s and 1970s saw a large number of bilateral and multilateral ecumenical dialogues, the purpose of which was to work toward greater theological and ecclesiastical understanding between various denominations. Roman Catholic theologians established dialogues with the Orthodox churches, the Anglicans, the Lutherans, and others. There were also discussions between various Protestant groups, both within the United States and internationally. The progress achieved by these discussions varied, but there were no dramatic breakthroughs. Some Protestant denominations established new procedures for the interchangeability of pastors and communications between them, but progress even in these areas was slow. The ecumenical excitement of the 1960s seems to dwindle toward the end of the twentieth century.

The twentieth century also saw a dramatic shift of Christianity toward the rapidly growing churches of Latin America, Africa, and Asia (known collectively as the Global South). These churches, often more traditional and theologically conservative than their counterparts in the Global North, began to influence global denominational families and ecumenical discussions. Their influence on the Roman Catholic Church and the Lutheran, Anglican, Methodist, and Reformed communions has been substantial. And most of the growth of Christianity in the Global South, as in the United States, has been among evangelical and Pentecostal Christians, who were too busy making disciples to have taken much interest in ecumenical discussions.

BIBLIOGRAPHY

Allitt, Patrick. *Religion in America Since 1945: A History.* New York: Columbia University Press, 2003.

Eskridge, Larry. *God's Forever Family: The Jesus People Movement in America.* New York: Oxford University Press, 2013.

Hoge, Dean R., Benton Johnson, and Donald A. Luidens. *Vanishing Boundaries: The Religion of Mainline Protestant Baby Boomers.* Louisville: Westminster John Knox, 1994.

Noll, Mark A. *The Scandal of the Evangelical Mind.* Grand Rapids: Eerdmans, 1994.

Sarna, Jonathan D., ed. *Minority Faiths and the American Protestant Mainstream.* Urbana: University of Illinois Press, 1998.

Stein, Stephen J., ed. *The Cambridge History of Religions in America.* Vol. 3, *1945 to the Present.* New York: Cambridge University Press, 2012.

Steinfels, Peter. *A People Adrift: The Crisis of the Roman Catholic Church in America.* New York: Simon & Schuster, 2003.

Sutton, Matthew Avery. *American Apocalypse: A History of Modern Evangelicalism.* Cambridge, MA: Belknap, 2014.

Williams, Daniel K. *God's Own Party: The Making of the Christian Right.* New York: Oxford University Press, 2012.

Wind, James P., and James W. Lewis, eds. *American Congregations.* Vol. 2, *New Perspectives in the Study of Congregations.* Chicago: University of Chicago Press, 1994.

12

Growing Pluralism and Shifts in American Christianity, 1995–2022

As THE UNITED STATES MOVED into a new millennium, the twenty-first century, the country grew increasingly socially and politically diverse, which led at times to polarization and conflict. Geopolitically, the United States remained the dominant world power, but it faced new challenges from China and a regionally resurgent Russia, as well as the threat of terrorism and asymmetrical attacks in the Middle East. The United States intervened several times in conflicts in the Middle East, mostly notably in Afghanistan and Iraq, but it struggled to define clear goals in these regional conflicts. Other regions—such as the Balkan countries, Somalia, and Iran—also drew American military attention. The lines of conflict in these areas were often unclear, leading to debates at home about the wisdom of intervention in these and other international conflicts.

American politics grew ever more divided and fractious, with control of Congress and the presidency shifting between the Republican and Democratic parties. The election of Republican George W. Bush to the presidency in 2000 was extremely narrow and caused much political turmoil. Bush served until 2008, when he was succeeded by Barack Obama, a Democrat and the first African American president. In 2016, Republican Donald Trump won the presidency, but he was defeated by Democrat Joe Biden in 2020. Control of Congress shifted back and forth, and often the opposing party wrested back control during midterm elections, frustrating the legislative plans of the current president. The two political parties grew further apart. Republicans impeached President Bill Clinton in 1998, and Democrats impeached President Donald Trump twice (once in 2019 and then again in 2021), though neither president was convicted and removed from office. Republican presidents appointed several new Supreme Court justices, and the balance of the court swung in a more conservative direction.

The growing threat of Islamic radicalism became a major issue through the 1990s and came home to the United States with the events of September 11, 2001 (9/11), when four hijacked planes were flown into American targets, including the World Trade Center towers in New York and the Pentagon near Washington, DC, causing great destruction and the loss of thousands of lives. In response, the United States, as a part of the Global War on Terrorism, invaded Afghanistan in 2001 and Iraq in 2003, seeking to destroy the bases of terrorism. After initial successes, these missions got bogged down in protracted conflicts. The mastermind of the 9/11 attacks, Osama bin Laden, was hunted down and killed in 2011, but threats of terrorism continued. Domestic extremists also continued to be a problem, as illustrated by the deadly bombing at the Boston Marathon in 2013.

The American economy grew through the 1990s, fueled by the rise of new tech companies, many of which crashed dramatically in 2000, throwing the American economy into recession. A number of prominent companies had to declare bankruptcy. The American economy recovered from this crash only to be similarly dashed by a crash in housing prices in 2008, in which millions of Americans lost substantial investments in their homes. The American economy recovered, and the stock market grew substantially during the 2010s.

The United States continued to grow more ethnically diverse during this period, as millions of immigrants from Latin America, Asia, and (increasingly) Africa arrived in the United States—some by legal means, others by illegal means. Those arriving by illegal means became the focus of much political and social debate, dividing the two political parties and the American public. Conflicts around the world caused millions of refugees to flee their countries and added pressure on immigration. At home, racial tensions flared in the United States, especially with the high-profile deaths of several African Americans at the hands of police during the 2010s, leading to widespread protests and rioting in some American cities. Issues of racial justice continued to roil the country, as activists pushed for sweeping social and economic reforms.

Much of the growth of the American economy revolved around an explosion of new technologies. By this time, computers had become standard in many businesses and homes, but the real innovation was linking them together with the internet, which revolutionized the ways Americans shopped, communicated, and consumed entertainment. The miniaturization of technology furthered this revolution with the introduction of "smart" cell phones, literally handheld computers that could go everywhere. These technological revolutions had social and economic impacts that have just begun to be realized. Because of them, future generations of Americans will live lives quite different from those of their parents. There were also continuing concerns about changes in the physical environment caused by human activity, and the phrase "climate change" became ubiquitous as the nation struggled to decide what to do about such challenges.

The social changes in American life paralleled in rapidity the technological ones. The proliferation of information and entertainment on cable and the internet led the society to become both more diverse and more fractured. More information did not always mean better information. As Americans of different ethnic and racial backgrounds married and had children, there was a rise in individuals who identified as "multiracial" or "other," instead of one of the traditional survey categories. A growing acceptance of homosexuality was recognized in 2015 by a Supreme Court decision recognizing the legality of same-sex marriage. And some Americans pushed beyond traditional gender identities and monogamous relationships. Society was further stressed by a viral pandemic that spread the disease known as COVID-19 all across the globe. The COVID-19 pandemic drove many Americans—along with others the world over—into involuntary isolation. The long-term effects of this pandemic on American society as a whole, and on American Christianity specifically, have yet to be fully determined.

Changes in American Christianity, 1995–2020

Trends for American Christian denominations have continued in the same general directions since the 1965 peak in membership. Mainline Protestant denominations have continued to decline since 1965, with many of these seven denominations reporting dramatic membership losses. The major increase of American evangelical membership continued into the early twenty-first century, although during the 2010s this growth slowed or stagnated. American Roman Catholic membership declined somewhat, although Catholic numbers have been bolstered by waves of new immigrants. New immigrant Protestantism grew as recent arrivals from Latin America, Asia, and Africa formed their own ethnic-specific congregations, usually along evangelical or Pentecostal lines. African American denominations maintained their prominent

place within their community, while Orthodox immigrants from eastern
Europe and the Middle East increased the American Orthodox total. While
the percentage of Americans claiming some sort of religious membership
remained steady through the first decade of the twenty-first century, a significant drop in membership occurred during the 2010s, especially among
younger Americans, who were more likely to report no religious adherence
(the "Nones"). The rates of attendance at religious services also trended down-
ward during this time.

The situation among the mainline Protestant denominations became particularly dire during this period. In fifty years (from 1965 to 2015), these seven
major denominations went from representing 30 percent of the American population to representing only 10 percent. During the 2010s, these denominations
continued to bleed members:

American Baptists: down 4 percent
Christian Church (Disciples of Christ): down 40 percent
Episcopal Church: down 29 percent
Evangelical Lutheran Church in America: down 22 percent
Presbyterian Church (U.S.A.): down 40 percent
United Church of Christ: down 26 percent
United Methodist Church: down 15 percent

These declines were on top of already major declines in previous decades. Some
of these losses can be attributed to congregants and congregations leaving these
denominations for other groups, often because of the theological and social
liberalism of the mainline denominations. Other losses are from those who
were only loosely religiously affiliated in the first place moving into the "None"
category.

The situation among American Roman Catholics was more complex. The
percentage of Americans who were Roman Catholic declined from 25 percent
in 1965 to around 20 percent in 2015. But this overall statistic masked a significant loss of White American Roman Catholics, a loss that happened to be
compensated for by an increase of non-White, immigrant Roman Catholics.
By 2020, the percentage of Roman Catholics who were White was declining,
especially among younger generations. The younger Roman Catholics were increasingly non-White immigrants: Hispanics, Asians, and Africans. Immigration helped maintain Roman Catholic numbers, although a growing percentage
of Hispanics were (or became) Protestant. This represented a significant loss
for Roman Catholic numbers in America.

The tremendous growth of American evangelicalism since 1965 slowed and even perhaps stagnated in the twenty-first century, but between 20 and 30 percent of Americans are still considered evangelicals. These estimates vary depending on how exactly one defines what an evangelical is and on how one accounts for the independent evangelical congregations (those that are not a part of any denomination or association). A significant portion of the evangelical wing of American Protestantism is African American, and growing numbers are Hispanic and Asian. There are also some conservative congregations within mainline Protestantism that might be considered evangelical in a broader sense. Sometimes, to get an accurate picture of evangelicals in America, it is necessary to examine attitudes and beliefs rather than institutions. For example, in recent surveys, up to one-third of all Americans claim to be "born again" (a marker of evangelicalism), although this may be a rather loose way of measuring.

American evangelicalism also grew more diverse in expression over this period. The classic evangelical denominations remained strong and powerful, such as the Southern Baptist Convention (at sixteen million, the largest Protestant denomination in the US) and the Assemblies of God, along with the large African American denominations (Baptist and Methodist). Yet there were hundreds of smaller groups and thousands of independent evangelical congregations that often claimed to be nondenominational (but in fact were generally Baptist or Pentecostal in character). Newer nondenominational congregations often eschewed denominational labels and even sometimes the word *church* when referring to themselves; they preferred nondescript titles like *Christian Family Center*, thinking that the word *church* was off-putting to many Americans. A new development recently is that many of the larger of these congregations have developed satellite campuses around their base congregations in order to extend their reach.

The growth of evangelicalism has also come through a new generation of celebrity preachers, based in large local megachurches, who have developed multimedia empires on television and cable, via the internet, and through popular publishing enterprises. Perhaps the best known are Joel Osteen (1963–) and his Lakewood Church, in Texas, and Rick Warren (1954–) and his Saddleback Church, in California. Both are nationally known through their media empires, as are two African American preachers, T. D. Jakes (1957–), of The Potter's House in Texas (and elsewhere), and Creflo Dollar (1962—), with his World Changers Church International, in Georgia (and elsewhere), and Creflo Dollar Ministries. There are dozens of other regional examples of megachurches, often in the South and Southwest.

Osteen and Warren typify a new, softer evangelicalism that seeks to avoid controversy by use of positive religious messaging that blends evangelical

New-Style Congregations for a New Millennium

In the typical new paradigm church, most members are relatively young. The church meets in a building that has no stained glass, steeple or pews. In fact, most of these worship spaces are either converted warehouses, theaters or rented school auditoriums. People (including the pastors) come dressed as if on their way to a picnic. The music is what one might hear on a pop radio station, except the lyrics are Christian. The sermon is informal and focused on exposition of a passage of scripture. The pastors are not required to have a seminary education. Typically they are individuals whose lives have been radically transformed by God and who wish to share the good news of their Christian convictions. They view God as capable of supernatural intervention in our lives; hence, they have no difficulty affirming the miracles described in the Bible and they hold to a fairly literal view of scripture.

But the worship environment is not legalistic or rigid. Sunday morning is a time of celebration. The focus is not on theological doctrines but on finding analogues in one's life to the biblical narratives. During the week, members meet in small groups where they worship, study the Bible and care for each other. For many, this small group is the extended family that they never had. These churches also offer a myriad of programs that deal with everything from divorce recovery to child rearing, money management, social outreach ministries to prisoners and unwed mothers, and food distribution. Far from being fundamentalistic, new paradigm churches tend to be tolerant of different personal styles, even while members hold to rather strict moral standards for themselves.

This type of church is culturally hip. Lay members are given tremendous freedom to develop programs. The pastor is a teacher, visionary and trainer, but the people do the basic work of ministry. Many of these churches are independent, and if they do have a denominational affiliation they are part of a movement, not of a church.

Donald E. Miller, "The Reinvented Church: Styles and Strategies; New Paradigms and Renewed Churches," *Christian Century*, December 22, 1999, https://www.christiancentury.org/article/2011-07/reinvented-church.

spirituality with popular self-help themes—think, perhaps, of a combination of Billy Graham and Norman Vincent Peale. Their media preaching tends to be casual and down-to-earth, almost more like a religious lecture than a traditional worship service. Jakes and Dollar may be considered more traditionally evangelical in style, but their message carries beyond their traditional African American base.

Eastern Orthodox Christians in America number about two to three million members, often divided along ethnic and theological lines carried from eastern Europe and the Middle East. Some of these Orthodox denominations are independent (*autocephalous*, meaning "self-headed"), while others are under the ultimate direction of church leaders from their home countries. Recent migration from eastern Europe and religious refugees fleeing from conflicts and terrorism in the Middle East have bolstered Orthodox numbers, but the fall of communism has also led to intense evangelical proselytism in Orthodox countries and the rise of eastern European Protestant churches, especially Baptist churches. There has, however, been a counterflow of some young American evangelicals—often students—into Eastern Orthodox churches, drawn by their liturgical and theological ethos. This has not been a large movement, but it is one that bends traditional theological and ecclesiastical lines in new and interesting ways.

Religion, Nationalism, and Violence

There were a number of high-profile cases of government action against suspected extremist groups during the early 1990s, and some of these groups had religious themes or overtones. Government officials had been on the watch for extremist threats and fringe religious groups since the Jonestown mass murder-suicide in 1978, but it was very difficult for them to tell in advance whether a group would turn violent. Federal officials were involved in a siege of a residence in Ruby Ridge, Idaho, in 1992, in which several people were killed. The next year, 1993, there was an even more high-profile siege of the Branch Davidian compound in Waco, Texas, where eighty members of the group and four federal agents were killed by gunfire or in the accidental burning of the compound. There were worries about a religious compound in Montana, the Church Universal and Triumphant, led by Elizabeth Clare Prophet (1939–2009), where members stockpiled weapons and built fallout shelters, but no conflict happened in this case. As a reaction to these incidents, in 1995 anti-government extremists Timothy McVeigh (1968–2001) and Terry Nichols (1955–) set off a bomb that destroyed the Alfred P. Murrah Federal Building in Oklahoma City, Oklahoma, and killed 168 people. Not all these incidents had religious overtones, but some of them raised questions about religious freedom and American society.

Homegrown religious extremism was a threat, although it was not always clear which groups just spouted hateful rhetoric and which ones were willing to act on their hatred. During the 1960s, the radicalism was on the far-left fringe of American society, but, since the 1990s, more of the radicalism has come from far-right groups (these two different radicalisms share some interesting similarities). The religious element of this far-right radicalism was divided between Christian and non-Christian groups. The non-Christian groups, such as the Aryan Nations and neo-Nazi factions, saw Christianity as a "slave religion"

12.1. Branch Davidian Compound, Waco, Texas.

foisted on Anglo-Saxon White people and rejected Christianity in favor of pre-Christian Germanic religions. But others, especially those in the Christian Identity movement, saw Christianity as the "White man's religion" through an idea called British Israelism, which held that the Anglo-Saxon tribes of northern Europe were actually descended from the Ten Lost Tribes of Israel and thus were the true Hebrews. This belief spawned the Christian Identity movement's racism and anti-Semitism, which relegated non-Whites to an inferior position in the world. In the minds of this movement's adherents, the true White Christians had lost control of their homeland (the United States) to Jews and other interlopers. They sought to rebuild a homeland for true White Christians in the United States, sometimes envisioned to be in the Pacific Northwest region. These Christian Identity groups were found in loose local organizations, tied together through underground publications and websites.

A similar series of terroristic attacks in the name of religion, in this case Islam, also intensified during the 1990s. The military intervention of the United States in conflicts in the Middle East and the Balkans—along with continuing American support for the state of Israel—inflamed tensions within Muslim extremist groups in the Middle East, especially the group called al-Qaeda. Though many Muslims rejected these forms of violence, there were attacks on American interests by radicals in the name of Islam, including the bombing of the World Trade Center in 1993, the bombing of American embassies in Africa in 1997, and an attack on the USS *Cole* in 2000. There was always the temptation to frame these attacks in terms of a continuing struggle between a Christian America and the Islamic world, especially in the context of the ongoing struggles between these two religious groups in parts of Africa and Asia.

Some in Europe and America saw this struggle in terms of an international struggle between two major world cultures: the Christian West (Europe and North America) and the emerging Islamic world in Asia and Africa. With the collapse of the Soviet Union in the early 1990s, the focus of many shifted to challenges from the Islamic world. These perceived threats to Christian America were often joined with perceived internal threats to Christian America from liberals and secularists, who advocated a nonreligious, pluralistic nation. A new movement, Christian nationalism, arose to defend the vision of America as a Christian nation and to maintain it as such from all enemies, foreign and domestic. This ideology believed that America was founded as a nation on Christian principles, and that it was their duty to restore and defend these principles. Supporters believed that, in the United States, it was right and proper for the nation to support and give precedence to Christianity in the public sphere. It is important to delineate this movement from that of Christian Identity. Christian nationalism was not necessarily racially based, and it accepted religious pluralism (to a degree) and supported the constitutional freedoms of religion (also to a degree). But adherents believed that Christianity was slowly being driven out of American life and society, something they vowed to resist.

Much of this struggle involved Christian symbols in American public life—including the display of the Christian cross, the Ten Commandments, and the Lord's Prayer in public settings—and Christian symbolism surrounding Christmas and Easter. Secular groups pushed to eliminate any such displays on public property and public life, and some Christian groups pushed to retain them. The American courts struggled to determine the proper balance between the Free Exercise and Establishment Clauses of the First Amendment to the Constitution, sometimes handing down decisions that pleased neither side.

Millennialism and the Year 2000

In its simplest sense, a millennium is simply a span of one thousand years. The mere turning of the calendar from the final year of the twentieth century to the first year of the twenty-first had no particular importance in and of itself. But given the Christian symbolism of the change of the millennium, this event was seen by some as an auspicious—even potentially cataclysmic—occurrence. A traditional (prescientific) reckoning of the age of the earth was that it began around 4000 BC, making the end of the twentieth century the end of the sixth millennium. Given the biblical symbolism of the number seven, some Christians concluded that the seventh millennium would usher in the foretold thousand-year reign of Christ on earth. Some Christians who held to a premillennial theology believed that the year 2000 might witness the terrible events predicted in the biblical book of Revelation—namely, the great apocalyptic battle between the forces of good and evil and the return of Christ.

Apocalypticism and the Rapture: The Left Behind Novels

If only Irene hadn't gone off on this new kick.

Would it fade, her preoccupation with the end of the world, with the love of Jesus, with the salvation of souls? Lately she had been reading everything she could get her hands on about the Rapture of the church, "Can you imagine, Rafe," She exulted, "Jesus coming back to get us before we die?"

"Yeah, boy," he said, peering over the top of his newspaper, "that would kill me."

She was not amused. "If I didn't know what would happen to me," she said, "I wouldn't be glib about it."

"I *do* know what would happen to me," he insisted. "I'd be dead, gone, *finis*. But you, of course, would fly right up to heaven."

He hadn't meant to offend her. He was just having fun. When she turned away he rose and pursued her. He spun her around and tried to kiss her, but she was cold. . . .

He returned to his chair and his paper. "If it makes you feel any better, I'm happy for you that you can be so cocksure."

"I only believe what the Bible says," Irene said. . . .

He believed in rules, systems, laws, patterns, things you could see and feel and hear and touch.

If God was part of all that, OK. A higher power, a loving being, a force behind the laws of nature, fine. Let's sing about it, pray about it, feel good about our ability to be kind to others, and go about our business. Rayford's greatest fear was that this religious fixation would not fade like Irene's Amway days, her Tupperware phase, and her aerobics spell. He could just see her ringing doorbells and asking if she could read people a verse or two. Surely she knew better than to dream of his tagging along.

Irene had become a full-ledged religious fanatic.

Tim LaHaye and Jerry B. Jenkins, *Left Behind: A Novel of the Earth's Last Days* (Wheaton: Tyndale, 1995), 3–5.

Although there was widespread fascination about what might happen with the commencement of the new millennium, there were only a few scattered Christian leaders who openly predicted that the world would end in 2000. Small groups of believers gathered around such predictions and readied themselves for the events of the Apocalypse, but, like many others before them, they were disappointed when the end of the world did not to arrive that year. However, these premillennial expectations were great fodder for those Christian leaders, TV evangelists, and other preachers who linked the developments they decried in the contemporary world, which they saw as increasingly wicked and godless, with the events described in the apocalyptic biblical writings.

The late twentieth century also witnessed the rise of secular forms of premillennial apocalypticism, shorn of its religious content. Beginning in the 1960s, some authors and commentators predicted the terrible consequences of human activity on the planet, consequences that would lead to a grim dystopian future for humanity. This human activity was variously predicted to lead to vast ecological devastation, crippling human overpopulation and starvation, and nuclear winter and destruction. Ironically, one early form of climate change predictions suggested that human activity was leading the world into a new ice age. Popular books and media amplified these fears in fictionalized accounts of life under such harsh conditions. While the effects of human activity on the planet certainly have led to serious consequences that need to be addressed, it is interesting how some leaders have seized on the language of religious apocalypticism to frame the environmental and climate catastrophe they foresee.

Around the year 2000, one form of secular apocalypticism involved something as arcane as computer coding and design, suggesting that the way computers were developed early on would not allow their internal calendars to cope with the change from the year 1999 to the year 2000; this was dubbed the Y2K bug. Given the dramatically increasing reliance of the global economy on computers, some forecast the traumatic events of a world in which all the computers suddenly failed, wiping out immense amounts of data and pushing human civilization to the brink of collapse. Much like their religious counterparts, some secular apocalypticists went into a survivalist panic and stockpiled basic resources to meet the expected imminent disaster that never arrived.

When disaster did arrive, however, it came in 2001 in a series of terrorist attacks in the American Northeast. Under the orders of radical Islamicist Osama bin Laden, al-Qaeda operatives hijacked four American airliners on September 11, intending to crash them into significant targets. Two airplanes struck the World Trade Center towers in New York City and destroyed them, while a third airplane crashed into the Pentagon, causing damage and loss of life there. A fourth plane, intended for the White House, was diverted by the heroic efforts of passengers and crashed in a field in Pennsylvania. Thousands of people died in these attacks, mainly in New York City, and the country (and the world) were stunned by these traumatic events.

The response of the United States in 2001 was to strike at al-Qaeda bases in the Middle East, especially in the country of Afghanistan, which the American military invaded in 2001 to carry out this mission. In 2003, American and allied leaders determined that Iraq, under the leadership of Saddam Hussein, posed a similar danger, and coalition forces invaded that country too. Although these invasions were initially successful, American and coalition forces were eventually bogged down by attacks from insurgents and asymmetric warfare.

The religious repercussions of the 9/11 terrorist attacks (as they came to be known) were felt mainly by Muslim Americans and in Christian-Muslim relations. Since the al-Qaeda terrorists were radicals on the fringes of the Islamic community, American Muslims and their Christian supporters attempted to make the argument that these terrorists did not represent the vast majority of Muslims around the world. Some asserted that militants were not truly Muslims at all. They stressed that true Islam was, instead, a religion of peace. But others pointed to the wider context of Islamic radicalism in the Middle East, Africa, and Asia, where local Christians were coming under constant attacks and persecution, to argue against this claim.

There was a notable upturn in anti-Muslim attitudes and activities after 9/11, even though many Christian leaders urged restraint and forbearance. These tensions came amid the post-1965 wave of immigration, when increasing numbers of Muslim immigrants and refugees started settling in the United States and building their own mosques. These Muslims were a small fraction of the immigrants of this period, but they tended to be more noteworthy to the American public imagination than the majority of new arrivals, who were Christians. There were some attacks on Muslims in America and on their places of worship.

Some conservative Christian commentators did not focus primarily on the Muslim aspect of 9/11, instead suggesting that these terrorist attacks were God's way of punishing the United States for a host of liberal social and religious developments they decried. In their minds, God was using these terrorists as a punishment for America's drift away from God, much like God used the "pagan" Babylonians in the Old Testament to punish the wayward Israelites.

Part of the context of all this was a distinct trend of growing support among American evangelical Protestants for the state of Israel. The establishment of Israel in 1948 was seen by some as one of the signs of the end times portrayed in the Bible, and, for these (and other) reasons, evangelicals became some of the strongest American supporters of Israel outside the American Jewish community. Support for Israel had been waning among mainline Protestants, some of whom had become more supportive of the rights of Palestinians in the Holy Land. In the intricate politics of the Middle East, the one constant was strong American support for Israel, and American evangelical politicians and leaders were at the forefront of this.

Religion and Public Life

Beginning in the 1960s, there had been increasing polarization about the place of religion (predominantly Christianity) in American public life. Advocates for the strict separation of church and state (both secular and religious) continued to challenge in court anything that looked like state establishment or support of religion, and a series of Supreme Court decisions largely went in favor of these advocates. Prayers of any kind in public schools and displays of religious symbols or texts on public property were eliminated, and, in many other cases, anything religious was banned from the public square. Public schools were especially targets of this litigation, and references to religion in them were increasingly curtailed. But, beginning with the rise of the Christian Right in the 1980s, advocates for traditional religiosity began to win a series of court battles that revolved not around the Establishment Clause of the First Amendment but around the Free Exercise Clause. They claimed that restrictions on religion in the public square violated their constitutional rights to practice their religion freely. As the Supreme Court trended in a more conservative direction during the 1990s and beyond, the court loosened certain restrictions. Religious schools could receive public funding for things such as student transportation and special education, and certain states allowed parents to spend educational tuition vouchers on whatever schools they wished, including religious schools. But no matter what the courts decided, it seemed, there were always new rounds of litigation, from advocates on both sides.

Within various religious groups, there was also a growing polarization between some clergy and their congregations over social and political issues. Whereas in evangelical congregations ministers and laypeople generally shared similar views, among the mainline Protestants clergy adopted ever more liberal social and political positions, resulting in a gap on these issues that increasingly divided them from their congregants. As an example, in the presidential election of 2016, over 80 percent of the mainline clergy voted for the Democratic candidate, while their laypeople were divided between the two candidates fifty-fifty. This gap was seen on hot-button social issues as well.

There was also a growing gap between the two major political parties, Democrat and Republican, over their supporters' attitudes toward religion. After the rise of the Christian Right in the 1980s, the evangelical vote swung gradually but relentlessly toward the Republican Party, a process that was virtually complete by the 2000 election. On the other hand, the Democratic Party swung inexorably toward nonreligious voters, who became an important part of their base (with the exception of African American religious voters, who remained firmly in the Democratic camp). By the presidential elections of the 2010s, the

The "God Gap"

The best predictor of vote choice, according to work by political scientists Robert Putnam of Harvard and David Campbell of Notre Dame, is religiosity, *not* religious affiliation; Putnam and Campbell call it the "God gap."

Religiosity, as the two describe it, includes the three B's: belonging, behaving and believing. The stronger a person's sense of belonging, the more frequent her church attendance and prayer, and the stronger her belief, the greater her religiosity is. . . .

This "God gap" is relatively new. As the scholars observe, "American history teaches us that religion is neither exclusively left nor right, progressive nor conservative." Religion was invoked on both sides of the slavery debate in the 19th century, and it was a vital piece of both Prohibition and the progressive movement. . . .

Pew Research Center has found the same thing, showing that during the 2014 midterm elections, frequency of religious service attendance was an increasingly good predictor of casting a Republican vote. . . .

There have been some changes in patterns of religious identification and religious service attendance over the past 30 years. In the 1970s and '80s, fewer people identified themselves as mainline Protestant, while an increasing number identified as evangelical. However, by the 1990s, this denominational shift was over. What continued to change was the frequency of attendance at religious service. As Putnam and Campbell write, "what the evangelical churches have lost in adherents over the last two decades has mostly been made up for by the evangelicals' zeal."

At the same time that religious Americans became more religious, younger Americans increasingly identified as nonreligious. As Pew found, this growing group of "nones"—those who claim no religious affiliation—are largely part of the millennial generation and, most importantly in terms of the political landscape, are the single largest group in the survey to identify as Democrats. . . . And "evangelicals" are the largest group to identify as Republicans. . . .

Religion itself, and not denomination, has become one of the central dividing lines in American politics.

Anne Pluta, "The Rise of the 'God Gap,'" FiveThirtyEight, January 31, 2016, https://fivethirtyeight.com/features/the-rise-of-the-god-gap/.

most reliable marker of how a person would vote was their self-reported pattern of church attendance. Two-thirds of those who claimed to attend religious services weekly or more voted Republican, while two-thirds of those who said they never or very seldom attended voted Democratic. This remarkable political divergence was labeled by political scientists the "God gap," although it is not agreed whether this benefits one political party or the other. But it did mean that the two political parties came to have very different views on religion and its expressions in public life.

A number of the elements of the sexual revolution of the 1960s had become engrained in American public life by this period, although there were countervailing trends. But though supporters of rights for gay and lesbian people began their push for acceptance in the early 1970s, their positions were slow to gain public acceptance. The AIDS epidemic of the 1980s and beyond, seen initially in gay men, may have contributed to this, although it may also have elicited some sympathy. Public attitudes had shifted some by the 2000s, and advocates for gay rights pushed for same-sex marriages, something that the Supreme Court enabled in a 2015 decision (*Obergefell v. Hodges*). Through the 2010s there were also movements to recognize the rights of transgender individuals, but this, too, has been slow to gain acceptance.

The issue of homosexuality in Christian churches became a very divisive series of battles, mainly within the mainline Protestant denominations. Although some of them had quietly ordained gay and lesbian pastors, the public debate was intensified in 2003 when an openly gay man, Gene Robinson, was elected as the Episcopal bishop of New Hampshire. The question of the ordination of non-celibate gay and lesbian clergy rocked and divided a number of denominations. While the Evangelical Lutheran Church in America (ELCA) voted in 2009 to allow for such ordinations, as a denomination it took no official position on the subject, accepting that there was within the ELCA a difference of opinion on the matter. Led by conservatives from the United States and the Global South, the United Methodist Church voted down the ordination of gay and lesbian pastors several times, but advocates for such action pushed for a controlled separation of the denomination, which led to the formation of two separate ("disunited"?) Methodist denominations. But since most evangelical denominations and the Roman Catholic Church do not ordain non-celibate gay and lesbian individuals, a large majority of American Christians still belong to churches that do not recognize or ordain gay and lesbian clergy.

A major public issue for American Christianity since the 1990s has been high-profile cases of sexual abuse of congregants by clergy. Unfortunately, this is nothing particularly new in American religion. There were several prominent, public cases related to sexual abuse by ministers in the nineteenth century, so it is hard to know whether such activity has increased over time. What is clear is that public attitudes toward sexual abuse by clergy have hardened, and these cases are now being dealt with in a much more open fashion. In the past, these types of charges were often dismissed or hushed up by denominational officials who pressured victims into silence. Since the 1990s, however, sexual abuse cases in general have been increasingly brought out into the open, and victims have been encouraged to report experiences of sexual abuse, in some cases even decades after the fact. These cases have increasingly ended up in court, with the filing of criminal charges or civil lawsuits.

Cases of clergy sexual abuse have occurred across the spectrum of American Christian denominations, and no denomination has been exempt from them. But, since the 1990s, there have been multiple high-profile cases that have especially rocked the Roman Catholic Church, and, in some cases, successful group litigation has led to multimillion-dollar settlements. Some Roman Catholic dioceses around the country were required to sell assets to cover such settlements, and a number of them were forced into bankruptcy. A single predatory priest could have an untold number of victims. In addition to the trauma and suffering of the victims and the financial toll on denominations, this issue has led to a painful erosion of public trust and confidence in religious leaders in general and negatively affected congregants' relationships with their faith traditions.

There has also been an interesting shift in the public faces and voices of religion in America. Through much of the twentieth century, the public influencers of American religion were the leading figures and theologians of mainline American Protestantism and the National Council of Churches. When the media wanted comments from religious leaders, they turned to such individuals. But, beginning in the 1960s, this had begun to change, and the shift accelerated with the dramatic numerical decline of the mainline. By the 1990s, if the media wanted the opinions of American religious leaders, they would almost certainly feature a Roman Catholic bishop, an African American religious leader, or some major evangelical figure (likely a televangelist or megachurch pastor). Mainline Protestant leaders struggled in vain to make their views on issues widely heard in the public square.

Roman Catholics and evangelicals were more prominent in public perhaps because of their media savvy and existing media platforms, but also because they could be counted on to offer a dissenting voice to elements of American social change (the media liking to dig up conflict by focusing on dissenting voices). Religious conservatives pushed back against liberal-leaning social changes, including on issues like abortion, gender roles, and sexuality. These conflicts have come to be called the "culture wars."

12.2a and b. Promise Keepers Rally.

One major element in these culture wars was a conservative group for men known as Promise Keepers, which came to national prominence during the 1990s. This group was the idea of a prominent college football coach, Bill McCartney (1940–), who founded the organization to encourage American Christian men to live up to their responsibilities to their wives, families, and communities. Though the organization worked hard to keep their message positive, uplifting, and nonpolitical, some critics felt that the group was reinforcing traditional gender roles and attitudes. The organization held sold-out rallies in football stadiums across the country, and in 1997 it held a massive rally on the National Mall in Washington, DC. But the rapid institutional growth of this organization could not be sustained, and it entered the twenty-first century as a much smaller, yet still viable, organization.

The continuing growth of separate Christian organizations, especially Christian schools, was also an important factor in the culture wars. Roman Catholic parochial schools had long been an option for those who were worried about the social and political attitudes in American public schools. But there was also a steady proliferation of private religious schools established by evangelical Christian congregations, some of which were organized as public charter schools in states where this was allowed. Other disaffected Christians chose to educate their children at home, a part of the burgeoning homeschool movement.

American Christianity and Post-1965 Immigration

Understanding the past half century or so of American history would be impossible without taking account of the wave of immigrants that came into the United States after the immigration reforms of 1965. Millions of new immigrants from Latin America, Asia, and Africa formed their own ethnic institutions, especially religious organizations. Most came from Latin America, a significant number from Asia, and a smaller (yet growing) number from Africa.

These immigrants contributed to the growing ethnic diversity of the United States, and they had a significant impact on the shape of American Christianity.

These immigrants brought their own religious traditions to America and counted among their numbers are Muslims, Buddhists, Hindus, and others. Yet the number of non-Christian immigrants is small compared to the total number of immigrants: as of 2012, only about 25 percent of new immigrants practice one of these traditional world religions, while another 14 percent claim no religion whatsoever. A solid majority of these new immigrants, approximately 61 percent, are Christians. And this is just counting legal immigrants—the percentage of undocumented immigrants who are Christian is estimated to be 83 percent. Given the slow decline of long-term Americans who are Christians, these new immigrant Christians are helping to prop up the total membership of Christians in the United States and—despite popular attitudes toward the new immigrants (which usually vastly overestimate the percentages of non-Christians)—helping to keep America a majority Christian nation.

Given that the largest number of new immigrants come from the countries of Latin America, this should not be surprising. These countries tend to be overwhelmingly Christian, primarily Roman Catholic. But the surprise came with immigrants from other continents. In Asia, Christians represent only about 8 percent of the total population of the continent, yet around 60 percent of Asian Americans are Christian. And although most Arabs in the world are Muslims, over 60 percent of Arab Americans are Christian. A number of different factors help explain this. First, there seems to be a definite self-selection by Asian Christians to come to what they perceive as a Christian America. Whereas only 30 percent of South Koreans are Christian, over 70 percent of Korean Americans are Christian. Second, some minority Christian groups in Asia, especially in the Middle East, were granted special refugee and immigration status, allowing them easier entry into the United States. And certain majority Christian nations in Asia, notably the Philippines, also have special access to settlement in the United States.

Yet even this is not the full story, because Christian immigrant congregations formed in the United States are generally the largest and most active organizations in their respective ethnic communities, religious or otherwise. Chinese Christian congregations are a good example of this. Immigrants from China are the second-largest segment of the new immigration (after those from Mexico), but a vast majority of these new Chinese immigrants have no religious affiliation (as a result of fifty years of Chinese communist atheism). Yet nearly one-third of all Chinese Americans are Christian, probably because of the extensive Chinese American Christian outreach to their fellow immigrants,

Rev. Thomas Kim / United Methodist News

12.3. A Praise Team from Central Korean United Methodist Church in Dallas, Texas.

most notably on college and university campuses. Similar dynamics can be seen among other immigrant groups.

Ethnically specific Christian congregations are vital to many new immigrants. Sometimes it is not clear whether the ethnicity or the religious identity of these congregations is more important. Ethnic congregations function as the hubs of entire immigrant communities, and they offer familiar language, food, and customs in a new and often strange culture. These congregations function as meeting places and provide networking, advice, and help with governmental and social services. They are important "labs" for learning new organizational and leadership skills that can be carried out into the wider American sphere.

But ethnic congregations can also sometimes be places of conflict, where old norms and practices are challenged by new ideas. In the minds of many immigrants, one of the most important tasks of these congregations is to pass along the language and culture of the ethnic homeland to younger, US-born members of the community. But this is often difficult, as second- and third-generation members are torn between the ethnic community and the wider American world. The maintenance of immigrant languages and customs is often very difficult for younger generations, which can lead to conflict with older generations.

Many older and more settled American Christian groups have long yearned to gather these Christian immigrants into their congregations and denominations, to increase both their ethnic diversity and their numbers. But this is less important for immigrant Christian communities. They appreciate the financial and organizational assistance, but they are often not interested in giving up their independence by joining established denominations. There is also often a clash of cultures and competing agendas. The new immigrant groups often are socially more conservative than their American counterparts. When mainline Protestants have taken liberal social positions, they have often alienated their immigrant counterparts in the process.

New immigrant Christianity is also fluid, forming and reforming with regularity. Immigrant communities can be very transitory, with people (and even whole communities) moving geographically to find better jobs or living conditions. An ethnic congregation can sometimes lose most of its members in a short period of time. Switching denominational identities is also common. Just because an immigrant came into the United States with a particular Christian identity does not mean that they will keep it. Though most Latin American immigrants come into the United States as Roman Catholics, they do not always remain in that tradition. Among Hispanic Americans, almost one-quarter of them have become Protestants, drawn by aggressive evangelization from Spanish-speaking Baptist and Pentecostal congregations led by entrepreneurial pastors.

Christian churches and groups from the Global South are also finding a foothold in the United States, mostly among their immigrant counterparts, but also among settled American populations. Some of the most active are from Christian Africa: Aladura ("praying people") Christianity, one group of which, the Redeemed Christian Church of God (from Nigeria), is perhaps the most impressive example, claiming over seven hundred local congregations in the United States. While this denomination attracts mainly West African immigrants, they have also drawn in some American adherents from wider ethnic spheres.

The globalization of Christianity has brought with it social and theological conflicts that have affected American Christians. The number of Anglicans in the world is now far greater in Africa and Asia than it is in Europe and North America, which has led to great tensions within that communion, as Anglicans in Africa and Asia tend to be significantly more conservative than those in Europe and North America. When the Evangelical Lutheran Church in America decided in 2009 to ordain gay and lesbian clergy, a very large Lutheran church in Ethiopia broke relations with it. Korean-American Presbyterians have often distanced themselves from other Presbyterians over matters of LGBTQ+

affirmation. And global and immigrant Methodists, along with their conservative counterparts in the longer-settled American population, have caused such turmoil in the United Methodist Church over the ordination of gay and lesbian clergy that this denomination has been forced into a division. The vision of a global and ethnically diverse Christianity is very attractive, but the reality of that diversity has proven much more difficult to manage than many expected.

Growing Divisions within American Christianity

Many of the large mainline denominations as they are known today were formed in a series of mergers that stretched from the late 1950s through the late 1980s: the United Church of Christ (1957), the United Methodist Church (1968), the Presbyterian Church (U.S.A.) (1983), and the Evangelical Lutheran Church in America (1988). The consolidations that brought these denominations into being were generally hailed as triumphs of ecumenism and Christian unity. But the construction of these new organizations out of older, separate groups often meant that internal tensions and difficulties stressed the denominations' development going forward. Also generally identified as mainline denominations are the Reformed Church in America, the Episcopal Church, and the American Baptist Churches USA. In these large denominations with millions of members, there have been continuous conflicts over social and theological issues that mirrored the debates within the larger American society.

In these denominations, the moderate-to-liberal wings have long held the reins, while conservatives have worried about what they see as the erosion of traditional Christian theological positions. Since the 1960s, conservatives have formed internal movements to fight this "liberal drift." Although hot-button social issues have usually been the flash points for conservative-liberal interdenominational conflicts, conservatives have insisted that they are fundamentally motivated by a deep concern to maintain a strong and traditional sense of biblical authority.

Traditionalists did have reason to be concerned, as elements within mainline Protestantism and sections of Roman Catholicism were indeed seeking to understand the nature and authority of the Bible in new ways. The most striking example of this was the Jesus Seminar. This group of academic theologians and biblical scholars, led by Robert Funk (1926–2005), was active between 1985 and 2006 and sought to "scientifically" determine the historical authenticity of the sayings and stories about Jesus Christ in the Gospels. Over one hundred scholars participated, voting with colored marbles to determine the "true" life and teachings of the historical Jesus. This second "quest for the historical Jesus" (the first was around the beginning of the twentieth century) judged most of the miracle stories and transcendent theological claims of the Gospel accounts unhistorical, leaving various pictures of Jesus as a first-century Jewish prophet. Critics charged that the end results simply codified the ideologies of the seminar participants and had very little to do with the historical Jesus. Liberal theological ideas about Christian theology and the Bible were promulgated by such authors as Roman Catholic John Dominic Crossan (1934–); Marcus Borg (1942–2015); and, most provocatively, Episcopal bishop John Shelby Spong (1931–2021). Thinking along the lines of classic Protestant liberalism that stretched back over two hundred years, these authors warned that Christianity had to cast off traditional theologies and modernize, or it would die.

Though the liberal elements within the mainline denominations were generally in control, opposition from conservatives and institutional inertia slowed the rate of liberalizing change, as denominational leaders struggled to hold these organizations together. The ordination of women was generally accepted without too much distress or opposition, although the actual integration of women clergy into the denominations was a much longer struggle. But the ordination of LGBTQ clergy was much more controversial, and winning official acceptance of it was a difficult task. Dismayed by the lack of progress on this issue, a number of activist groups formed within the mainline denominations to push for greater and faster changes. They had to contend with passages in scripture that seemed to oppose homosexual activity, and their cases for LGBTQ acceptance sometimes employed understandings of biblical authority that were unacceptable to conservatives or moderates. For a time, they held "irregular" ordinations and defied denominational authorities to place LGBTQ clergy into congregations. Most of the mainline Protestant denominations eventually did decide to ordain LGBTQ clergy.

At the time of the mergers that formed the mainline Protestant denominations as we now know them, some disaffected conservative congregations decided not to enter the new organizations. And others left shortly thereafter. These defections were not particularly numerous. But subsequent developments encouraged further defections, beginning in the 1980s. In the cases of the United Church of Christ and the American Baptist Churches USA, which have congregational polities, it was relatively easy for individual congregations to leave the denominations. In other mainline denominations, however, the processes for congregations that wanted to leave were much more complicated. In some cases, congregations had to fight for the right to leave. The Episcopal Church, for example, claimed the right to retain the properties of congregations seeking to leave, which resulted in a number of court cases.

From the Episcopal Church, disaffected members and congregations formed several breakaway denominations, some of which sought the episcopal oversight of Anglican churches in the Global South. A number of these denominations came together in 2009 to form the Anglican Church in North America, which claimed some 975 congregations and 125,000 members. In Presbyterian circles, a breakaway group that came to be known as the Presbyterian Church in America left the southern Presbyterian Church in the U.S. in 1973; the Reformed Presbyterian Church, Evangelical Synod, then joined the Presbyterian Church in America in 1982, and the denomination now claims about 394,000 members in 1,600 congregations. From the Evangelical Lutheran Church in America (formed in 1988), dissidents organized two different Lutheran denominations: Lutheran Congregations in Mission for Christ (2001), with 975 congregations and 350,000 members, and the North American Lutheran Church (2010), with 325 congregations and 140,000 members. The division of the United Methodist Church was scheduled to happen after the denomination's General Conference in 2022, guided by a framework for division, the "Protocol for Reconciliation and Grace through Separation." It is unclear what the size of the two new denominations will be, but some indication might come through the fact that conservatives mustered a majority of votes to block LGBTQ ordination.

These new breakaway denominations were much smaller than the denominations they left, but their size belied a deeper problem for mainline Protestantism. The mainline denominations often made it difficult for congregations to leave, forcing disaffected congregations to remain within their ranks. Yet this strategy may have been counterproductive. By keeping angry congregations trapped within their organizations, the denominations created a continual source of trouble. And all these organizational changes do not account for conservative members who simply walked away from mainline congregations. This is an untold number, but all these defections—congregational and individual—certainly contributed to the stunning numerical and financial decline of the mainline denominations since 1965.

Demographic Trends in American Religiosity in the Twenty-First Century

Contrary to conventional wisdom, which tends to think that people were more connected to organized religion in the past than they are now, the broad picture of American Christianity over the past 250 years shows a distinctive and sustained pattern of the growth of organized religion. Formal membership in religious organizations in the colonial period was under 20 percent. By 1900, rates of adherence to organized religion had increased to about half the population, and they further increased to about two-thirds by midcentury, where they leveled off. However, in the 2010s there was a marked decline in religious adherence and a rise of those who say they have no attachment to organized religion (the "Nones"). It is difficult to project trends over a single decade into the future, but there are some troubling signs for Christian groups when looking at this data, especially as distributed over the various generational cohorts.

To understand these trends, it is important to think about the ways that Americans have thought about religion and religious affiliation. Since the early nineteenth century, there have been no political establishments of religion—that is, direct state support and funding for religion. But, interestingly, there has been broad cultural support for religiosity, something that might be described as a "cultural establishment" of religion. A cultural establishment of religion is when it is widely believed that organized religion is an important and positive thing for a healthy society and that every good citizen should have a religious identity. President Dwight D. Eisenhower stated this expectation in 1952, when he remarked that religion was a good thing and everyone should have one. The dog tags issued to American soldiers and sailors traditionally noted religious affiliation; there was no option for "no religion."

The roots of this cultural establishment of religion go back to an implicit bargain made between organized religion and the Enlightenment deists who organized the United States in the late eighteenth century. Coming out of the English Enlightenment tradition, these deists were not anti-religious; they believed in some sort of God and thought that a measure of religious faith was good for society. When they considered organized religion, they felt that its main purpose was to inculcate a common morality—to make people into moral citizens. The various organized Christian groups accepted this bargain: they would teach this morality, and in return, the nation would support them in any number of ways (short of direct government subsidy).

So, it came to be widely held that, to be a good citizen, one needed to be an adherent of some organized religion. This social pressure toward organized religion meant that it became advantageous to join one denomination or another, and particular religious groups gained considerable social prominence. The mainline Protestant groups were the most prominent early on, and Roman Catholicism became so by the mid-twentieth century. There were also regional aspects of this "cultural Christianity," with the Baptists dominating in the southern Bible Belt, the Lutherans in the Upper Midwest, and the Mormons in the Intermountain West. People sometimes joined religious groups for nonreligious reasons: for social or business connections, or to provide moral instruction for their children.

But in the first decades of the twenty-first century, there have been signs that the cultural establishment of religion is weakening. The self-proclaimed "Nones" (those with no particular religious affiliation) and "Dones" (those who have left organized religion) grew from 17 percent of the US population in 2007 to 23 percent of the population in 2020. Even if the terms are new, there have always been sizeable numbers of Americans in these categories. But the most troubling sign for organized religion is when these numbers are broken down by generational cohort. Over 20 percent of those in Generation X (born between 1965 and 1979) identify as Nones, but over 30 percent of millennials (born in the 1980s and 1990s) identify as Nones. Some observers believe this points to a trend of Americans increasingly disaffiliating with organized religion, or never forming such affiliations in the first place, while others suggest that the younger generations are simply settling down, marrying, and having children much later in life than their parents and grandparents did (these life milestones often correlating with a return to organized religion).

Some research on the Dones has shown that they are often former members of mainline Protestant denominations or Roman Catholic parishes. Many were marginal or cultural members of these or other organized religious groups, and the decline of the mainline and of White Roman Catholicism may well be attributed, in part, to their leaving. Similar disaffection has not been noted among evangelical Protestants and non-White Christians, but some expect that it may be around the corner.

Importantly, those who identify as Nones are not necessarily, or even usually, atheists. Polls have suggested that close to 80 percent of Nones believe in some form of God or another, and many consider themselves to be good religious people—just not adherents of a particular organized religion. Some of this may be attributed to a decline in membership in all sorts of organizations—fraternal and social groups, advocacy and political groups, as well as religious denominations. Perhaps, this line of thinking goes, some want to participate in religious organizations on their own terms, but not join them. They might have an eclectic religious identity, drawing from a number of different religious traditions (in a sort of a buffet model).

Some of the Nones surveyed wished to consider themselves "spiritual but not religious." This generally meant that they believed in some form of God, in a kind of religious morality (usually some form of the Golden Rule), prayer and meditation, and forms of religious practice that they find personally fulfilling. The claim is that they do not need to join with others in a formal religious setting to be believers; they can worship God on their own, at home or out in nature. A 2005 study of American youth by Christian Smith and Melinda Lundquist Denton coined the term "Moral Therapeutic Deism" (MTD) for this

Private Modern Religion: "Sheilaism"

We interviewed, in the research for *Habits of the Heart*, one young woman who has named her religion after herself.

> Sheila Larson is a young nurse who has received a good deal of therapy and describes her faith as "Sheilaism." This suggests the logical possibility of more than 235 million American religions, one for each of us. "I believe in God," Sheila says. "I am not a religious fanatic. . . . I can't remember the last time I went to church. My faith has carried me a long way. It's Sheilaism. Just my own little voice." Sheila's faith has some tenets beyond belief in God, though not many. In defining what she calls "my own Sheilaism," she said: "It's just try to love yourself and be gentle with yourself. You know, I guess, take care of each other. I think God would want us to take care of each other." Like many others, Sheila would be willing to endorse few more specific points.

I am glad that Sheila does have at least a second point besides taking care of herself and loving others and I suspect that that is a remnant of something she learned somewhere else earlier on.

But the case of Sheila is not confined to people who haven't been to church in a long time. On the basis of our interviews, and a great deal of other data, I think we can say that many people sitting in the pews of Protestant and even Catholic churches are Sheilaists who feel that religion is essentially a private matter and that there is no particular constraint on them placed by the historic church, or even by the Bible and the tradition. . . . The notion that religious belief ought to be a purely internal thing, and then you go to the church or synagogue of your choice, shows how deeply ingrained a kind of religious privatism is.

Robert N. Bellah, "Habits of the Heart: Implications for Religion" (lecture, St. Mark's Catholic Church, Isla Vista, CA, February 21, 1986), http://www.robertbellah.com/lectures_5.htm.

attitude.[1] MTD was a form of deism that envisioned that God wants people to be good, nice, and fair to one another, as taught in the Bible and by most world religions, and that the central goal of life is to be happy and to feel good about oneself. God is involved directly only when requested, and "good" people go to heaven when they die. This way of thinking also avoids the thorny issues raised by religious pluralism: religiosity or spirituality is merely a matter of personal taste, and no one particular form of religion is any more normative than any other. Although MTD as a category has been articulated only recently, it represents a long-standing approach in American society, especially among those who have not joined or identified with any particular form of organized religion.

1. Christian Smith and Melinda Lundquist Denton, *Soul Searching: The Religious and Spiritual Lives of American Teenagers* (New York: Oxford University Press, 2005).

The trends of the 2010s are too recent to venture any long-term predictions from them—and, indeed, some polling in the 2020s has suggested a moderation or even reversal in some of them. Perhaps many of the Nones were only ever nominally religious in the first place and have now simply dropped the pretense of religiosity altogether. Perhaps religious adherence or membership is no longer a helpful way of measuring the health of American religion, if it ever was. But some of these trends from these recent years have been of great concern to American religious leaders.

American Religion and the COVID-19 Pandemic

Toward the end of the 2010s, a new and aggressive viral disease, now known as COVID-19 (short for coronavirus disease 2019), created a worldwide pandemic that severely disrupted all aspects of life. First seen in China in late 2019, the new virus (SARS-CoV-2) quickly spread around the world, eventually causing millions of deaths. The globalized economy and frequent international travel spread the virus. At first, the main victims were older adults and those with underlying conditions and compromised immune systems. Viral epidemics were nothing new to the modern world: influenza viruses swept through the world annually, and previous new viruses, like the swine flu (H1N1) and SARS had come and gone, but without anywhere near the kind of disruption and loss of life that came with COVID-19. This new disease was different. Its attack on the human respiratory system could be intense. It was highly contagious and, for many, lethal. For most people, a case of COVID-19 was comparable to a bad attack of influenza. But for a significant number of others, the virus caused severe debilitation and even death.

Governments around the world began taking the virus seriously in the spring of 2020, and, short of any effective cure, began instituting public health measures to slow the spread of the virus. The goal was to keep hospitals from being overwhelmed by patients. Many localities instituted partial or total lockdowns—closing schools and nonessential businesses, telling people to stay in their homes, and isolating older adults in their care centers. Travel was curtailed. Employment fell as businesses were closed, and the economic consequences of these lockdowns were severe. The United States government worked with pharmaceutical companies to develop vaccines for the COVID-19 virus. Eventually, vaccines were developed and distributed, but it was well into 2021 before the majority of the population was vaccinated.

COVID-19 hit American Christian congregations very hard, as many churches were completely closed for months at a time. The virus spread quickly

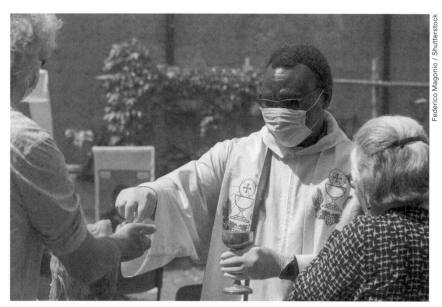

Federico Magonio / Shutterstock

12.4. Receiving Holy Communion during the COVID-19 Pandemic, 2020.

through close gatherings of people (such as at religious services) and especially through aerosol transmission; singing together in a group of people was a major source of infection. Beginning in the spring of 2020, during the Lenten and Easter seasons, many churches canceled all worship services and other activities; many did not open again to in-person worship until 2021. Some congregations held worship services outside, where the risk of transmission was significantly lower, but that was not always possible. Many congregations canceled sacramental services, including baptisms and Holy Communion, and weddings and funerals were postponed.

Congregations tried to compensate. Live or recorded worship services were broadcast online on such platforms as Facebook and YouTube or on congregational websites. Pastoral care was provided (imperfectly) by phone or online video chat. Many congregations and their leaders received a crash course in online church, although many of their initial attempts were quite clumsy. Questions arose, especially over the sacrament of Holy Communion: Could viewers administer the bread and wine to themselves, or should they wait until congregations could reopen in person? Fears of an economic catastrophe for these congregations were real, but many members continued their financial contributions throughout 2020.

Eventually, some congregations and religious leaders pushed back against public health measures. Several Christian entities successfully sued state governments and had lockdown limitations officially lifted. In the spring of 2021, many churches that had sought to abide by public health policy began cautiously to reopen, but there were still sometimes very restrictive limits on the number of congregants allowed to gather in any one building, singing was sometimes still off the table, and facemasks were often required.

The introduction of successful vaccines in 2021 raised other questions: Should vaccine status be required for attendance at worship? What about those who claim to have religious and moral objections to vaccination? A new wave of COVID-19 variants hit the country in 2021, just as churches began to reopen. At the time of this writing, the long-term consequences of the COVID-19 pandemic on American Christianity are unclear. Will COVID-19 have brought permanent changes for American Christians? And if so, will those changes be for good or for ill? Only time will tell.

─────────────── BIBLIOGRAPHY ───────────────

Bowler, Kate. *Blessed: A History of the American Prosperity Gospel*. New York: Oxford University Press, 2013.

Carter, Stephen L. *The Culture of Disbelief: How American Law and Politics Trivialize Religious Devotion*. New York: Basic Books, 1993.

Frykholm, Amy Johnson. *Rapture Culture: "Left Behind" in Evangelical America*. New York: Oxford University Press, 2004.

Fuller, Robert C. *Spiritual, But Not Religious: Understanding Unchurched America*. New York: Oxford University Press, 2001.

Griffith, R. Marie. *Moral Combat: How Sex Divided American Christians and Fractured American Politics*. New York: Basic Books, 2017.

Patel, Eboo. *Sacred Ground: Pluralism, Prejudice, and the Promise of America*. Boston: Beacon. 2012.

Porterfield, Amanda. *The Transformation of American Religion: The Story of a Late Twentieth-Century Awakening*. New York: Oxford University Press, 2001.

Putnam, Robert D., and David E. Campbell. *American Grace: How Religion Divides and Unites Us*. New York: Simon & Schuster, 2010.

Smith, Christian, and Melinda Lundquist Denton. *Soul Searching: The Religious and Spiritual Lives of American Teenagers*. New York: Oxford University Press, 2005.

Warner, R. Stephen, and Judith G. Wittner, eds. *Gatherings in Diaspora: Communities and the New Immigration*. Philadelphia: Temple University Press, 1998.

Epilogue

"So, WHERE ARE WE NOW, and where are we going?" This is the familiar conclusion to many historical narratives. Certainly, history is interesting and enlightening for its own sake, and understanding the past is a joy of its own. Yet many readers—Christian, non-Christian, and secular alike—want history to have meaning, to have lessons that can be taught and learned. Many people understand history to be *teleological*—a word that derives from the Greek word *telos*, or end. This common view of history is that it is moving toward a goal or an end and posits that if the arc of the historical narrative were only to be correctly understood, the trajectory of the past could be projected into the future, illuminating the path forward. Who wouldn't want to have such a crystal ball? There are all sorts of clichés about the understanding of history and the future, most of which contain small grains of truth but are generally simplistic and misleading. But historians make lousy prophets! They like to revel in the complexities and ambiguities of the past but are hesitant to draw larger inferences from their studies. Historians are all too aware, from their studies of the past, how those who try to predict the future are often wrong—sometimes spectacularly wrong. And yet, certainly, better knowledge of the past ought to have implications for the future. Otherwise, the entire enterprise would be nothing more than dabbling in arcane trivialities.

There are two common ways of understanding history, quite often present in American Christianity, that illuminate the misunderstandings of the relation of history to the present and the future. The first, often seen in more conservative circles, is the longing for a past "golden age." This suggests that there is, somewhere in the past, a perfect time, a golden age, when human society flourished and things were great. The time between the golden age and the present is one of distressing regression from that wonderful period. The goal of history, then,

349

is to, as best as possible, use the past to replicate the golden age in the present and future. This can be seen in the strong and enticing movement in American Christianity called Restorationism, or the idea of restoring the ideal church. There are two problems with this. First, those who would restore some sort of golden age cannot agree among themselves what and when that golden age was. Each group has its own idea, but they do not and cannot agree. Second, really understanding the past often makes one very appreciative of the present. If you truly understood what it was like to live in past centuries, would you really want to go back there?

The other common misuse of history, often seen in more liberal circles, is the denigration of the past as having little or no positive use. This viewpoint understands history as a definitive progression from darkness to light, from ignorance to knowledge. The present is a definite upgrade from the past, and inevitably the future will be better than the present. This is seen in American Christianity in postmillennial thought, where, by means of God's agency and human cooperation, the glorious kingdom of God will eventually be established on earth. Onward and upward! So then, why is knowing about the past, the historical record, valuable? All the past can be is a cautionary tale and proof that this progression to a glorious future is assured. However, though things do change—and there are certainly improvements—human beings are essentially the same across history, and technological and social advances are so often corrupted by these essential flaws in human nature. The old saying is often true: "The more things change, the more they remain the same."

Another saying about history is perhaps closer to the truth, although in another way it too can be misleading. This is the saying, attributed to a number of different sources, "Those who cannot remember the past are condemned to repeat it." Historical amnesia is a real problem, and some problems might be avoided if the mistakes of the past were remembered. But again, pesky human nature rudely intrudes. Often, though humans know what may be best for themselves and their societies, in spite of this knowledge and their best intentions, they stubbornly repeat their mistakes and act in ways that are counterproductive. Yet another old adage says it all: "We have met the enemy, and he is us."

All this raises again the question that was posed at the beginning—namely, the question of the reason for all this history. If nothing else, the study of our history should focus on two distinct elements that would seem to be in tension: history should empower us, and history should humble us. These two exist side by side, and like the yin and yang, one exerts a cautionary pull on the other. Certainly there is much good in the past. People have acted in ways that were noble and good, and we ought not lose these inspirations. And yet, there is much to be decried in the past, and we ought not forget this either.

Most of all, this historical record helps us understand that we too are human, with all the limitations that this brings. And when we arrogantly believe that we would have somehow done better, in their world and in their time, than our predecessors did, we are deluding ourselves.

In terms of the history of American Christianity, three points emerge from the narrative given in this book: The first is the overwhelming diversity of American Christianity, elements of which were present from the beginning, though this diversity has mushroomed dramatically since the end of the eighteenth century. The sheer number of different Christian groups in the country is staggering, and this seems to be expanding further. The voluntary system, freedom of religion, and the positive acceptance of religious pluralism has led to this diversity. America is a "religious supermarket," with nearly endless options to choose from. Religious entrepreneurs have taken the opportunities afforded by the religious marketplace to attract members to their religious visions and to create new communities and movements.

The second element is, perhaps paradoxically, the underlying unity and continuity to American Christianity despite the multiplicity of Christian options. The basic forms and structures of Christianity in the United States have not really changed all that much in the last 250 years, despite the many changes in religion and society that have occurred in that time. The basic theological and ecclesiastical elements of American Christianity have certainly morphed into the religious realities we now know in the early twenty-first century, but the American religious "DNA" remains surprisingly consistent. A churchgoer of the early nineteenth century, transported to the present, would still recognize much within today's Christian communities as familiar.

The third element is that the history of Christianity in America often pushes against, and sometimes even contradicts, our assumptions. Most Americans, religious or not, are quite surprised to find out, for example, that organized religion was much weaker in the colonial period than it is today. This fact undoes the narrative of religious decline that is so common in today's accounts. Of course, there could be further fundamental shifts in the future in how Americans relate to their religious institutions. The lesson to learn is that sweeping metanarratives, positive or negative, are often wrong.

For Christians in the United States, their histories are a part of their present and future in important ways, and learning about their history is crucial, if only to understand the ways Americans have been religious and continue to be religious. The story continues, and we try to make sense of it in ways that can strengthen both individual and communal existence. And history is a growth area. There is always more of it being made!

For Further Reading

———————— GENERAL REFERENCE WORKS ————————

Kurian, George Thomas, and Mark A. Lamport, eds. *Encyclopedia of Christianity in the United States*. 5 vols. Lanham, MD: Rowman & Littlefield, 2016.

Melton, J. Gordon. *Melton's Encyclopedia of American Religions*. Edited by James A. Beverley, Constance M. Jones, and Pamela Susan Nadell. 8th ed. Detroit: Gale Cengage Learning, 2009.

Noll, Mark A., Nathan O. Hatch, George M. Marsden, David F. Wells, and John D. Woodbridge, eds. *Eerdmans' Handbook to Christianity in America*. Grand Rapids: Eerdmans, 1983.

Piepkorn, Arthur C. *Profiles in Belief: The Religious Bodies of the United States and Canada*. 3 vols. New York: Harper & Row, 1977.

Queen, Edward L., II., Stephen Prothero, and Gardiner H. Shattuck Jr. *The Encyclopedia of American Religious History*. 2 vols. New York: Facts on File, 1996.

Reid, Daniel G., Robert D. Linder, Bruce L. Shelley, and Harry S. Stout, eds. *Dictionary of Christianity in America*. Downers Grove, IL: InterVarsity Press, 1990.

Stein, Stephen J., ed. *The Cambridge History of Religions in America*. 3 vols. New York: Cambridge University Press, 2012.

———————— SPECIALIZED REFERENCE WORKS ————————

Bender, Harold S., Cornelius Krahn, Cornelius J. Dyck, and Dennis D. Martin, eds. *The Mennonite Encyclopedia*. 5 vols. Hillsboro, KS: Mennonite Brethren; Scottdale, PA: Herald Press, 1955–90.

Bowden, Henry Warner. *Dictionary of American Religious Biography*. Westport, CT: Greenwood Press, 1977.

Burgess, Stanley M., Gary B. McGee, and Patrick H. Alexander, eds. *Dictionary of Pentecostalism and Charismatic Movements*. Grand Rapids: Regency Reference Library, 1988.

Demy, Timothy J., and Paul R. Shockley, eds. *Evangelical America: An Encyclopedia of Contemporary American Religious Culture*. Santa Barbara, CA: ABC-CLIO, 2017.

Foster, Douglas A., Paul M. Blowers, Anthony L. Dunnavant, and D. Newell Williams, eds. *Encyclopedia of the Stone-Campbell Movement*. Grand Rapids: Eerdmans, 2004.

Glazier, Michael, and Thomas J. Shelley, eds. *Encyclopedia of American Catholic History*. Collegeville, MN: Liturgical Press, 1997.

Harmon, Nolan B., Albea Godbold, and Louise L. Queen, eds. *Encyclopedia of World Methodism*. 2 vols. Nashville: United Methodist Publishing House, 1974.

Hart, D. G., and Mark A. Noll, eds. *Dictionary of the Presbyterian and Reformed Tradition in America*. Phillipsburg, NJ: P&R, 2005.

Hill, Samuel S., Charles H. Lippy, and Charles Reagan Nelson, eds. *Encyclopedia of Religion in the South*. 2nd ed. Macon, GA: Mercer University Press, 2005.

Hillerbrand, Hans J., ed. *Encyclopedia of Protestantism*. 4 vols. New York: Routledge, 2004.

Miller, Timothy, ed. *America's Alternative Religions*. Albany: State University of New York Press, 1995.

Murphy, Larry G., J. Gordon Melton, and Gary L. Ward, eds. *Encyclopedia of African American Religions*. New York: Garland, 1993.

New Catholic Encyclopedia. 2nd ed. 15 vols. Detroit: Thompson Gale, 2003.

Wengert, Timothy J., Mark A. Granquist, Mary Jane Haemig, Robert Kolb, Mark C. Mattes, and Jonathan Strom, eds. *Dictionary of Luther and the Lutheran Traditions*. Grand Rapids: Baker Academic, 2017.

ATLASES

Carroll, Bret E. *The Routledge Historical Atlas of Religion in America*. New York: Routledge, 2000.

Carroll, Jackson W., Douglas W. Johnson, and Martin E. Marty. *Religion in America: 1950 to the Present*. San Francisco: Harper & Row, 1979.

Gaustad, Edwin S. *Historical Atlas of Religion in America*. Rev. ed. New York: Harper & Row, 1976.

Gaustad, Edwin S., and Philip L. Barlow. *New Historical Atlas of Religion in America*. Rev. ed. New York: Oxford University Press, 2001.

BIBLIOGRAPHIES AND STATISTICS

Burr, Nelson R. *Religion in American Life*. New York: Appleton-Century-Crofts, 1971.

———. *A Critical Bibliography of Religion in America*. 2 vols. Princeton: Princeton University Press, 1961.

Grammich, Clifford, Kirk Hadaway, Richard Houseal, Dale E. Jones, Alexei Krindatch, Richie Stanley, and Richard H. Taylor, eds. *2010 U.S. Religion Census: Religious Congregations & Membership Study*. Kansas City, MO: Association of Statisticians of American Religious Bodies, 2012.

Lindner, Eileen W., ed. *Yearbook of American and Canadian Churches: Compilation of Statistical Pages, 1916–2000*. New York: National Council of the Churches of Christ in the United States of America, 2001.

Sandeen, Ernest R., and Frederick Hale. *American Religion and Philosophy: A Guide to Information Sources*. Detroit: Gale Research, 1978.

United States Bureau of the Census. *Census of Religious Bodies*. 1890, 1906, 1916, 1926. Washington, DC.

ANTHOLOGIES AND READERS

Butler, Jon, and Harry S. Stout, eds. *Religion in American History: A Reader*. New York: Oxford University Press, 1998.

Gaustad, Edwin S., Mark A. Noll, and Heath W. Carter, eds. *A Documentary History of Religion in America*. 4th ed. Grand Rapids: Eerdmans, 2018.

Hackett, David G., ed. *Religion and American Culture: A Reader*. New York: Routledge, 1995.

Ruether, Rosemary Radford, and Rosemary Skinner Keller, eds. *Women and Religion in America*. 3 vols. San Francisco: Harper & Row, 1981–86.

Smith, H. Shelton, Robert T. Handy, and Lefferts A. Loetscher, eds. *An Historical Interpretation with Representative Documents*. 2 vols. New York: Charles Scribner's Sons, 1960.

STANDARD HISTORIES

Ahlstrom, Sydney E. *A Religious History of the American People*. 2nd ed. New Haven: Yale University Press, 2004.

Albanese, Catherine L. *America: Religions and Religion*. 5th ed. Boston: Wadsworth, 2012.

Byrd, James P., and James Hudnut-Beumler. *The Story of Religion in America: An Introduction*. Louisville: Westminster John Knox, 2021.

Corrigan, John, and Winthrop S. Hudson. *Religion in America*. 9th ed. New York: Routledge, 2018.

Handy, Robert T. *A History of the Churches in the United States and Canada*. New York: Oxford University Press, 1977.

Hannah, John D. *Invitation to Church History: American*. 2 vols. Grand Rapids: Kregel, 2019.

Koester, Nancy. *Introduction to the History of Christianity in the United States*. Rev. ed. Minneapolis: Fortress, 2015.

Marty, Martin E. *Pilgrims in Their Own Land: 500 Years of Religion in America*. Boston: Little, Brown, 1984.

Noll, Mark A. *A History of Christianity in the United States and Canada*. 2nd ed. Grand Rapids: Eerdmans, 2019.

Williams, Peter W. *America's Religions: From Their Origins to the Twenty-first Century*. 4th ed. Urbana: University of Illinois Press, 2015.

INTERPRETATIONS

Clebsch, William A. *From Sacred to Profane America: The Role of Religion in American History*. New York: Harper & Row, 1968.

Finke, Roger, and Rodney Stark. *The Churching of America, 1775–2005: Winners and Losers in Our Religious Economy.* New Brunswick, NJ: Rutgers University Press, 2005.

Gaustad, Edwin Scott. *Dissent in American Religion.* Chicago: University of Chicago Press, 1973.

Handy, Robert T. *A Christian America: Protestant Hopes and Historical Realities.* 2nd ed. New York: Oxford University Press, 1984.

Hatch, Nathan O. *The Democratization of American Christianity.* New Haven: Yale University Press, 1989.

Hughes, Richard T. *Myths America Lives By.* Urbana: University of Illinois Press, 2003.

Marsden, George M. *Religion and American Culture.* New York: Harcourt Brace Jovanovich, 1990.

Marty, Martin E. *A Nation of Behavers.* Chicago: University of Chicago Press, 1976.

———. *Righteous Empire: The Protestant Experience in America.* New York: Dial, 1970.

Mead, Sidney E. *The Nation with the Soul of a Church.* New York: Harper & Row, 1975.

Moore, R. Laurence. *Religious Outsiders and the Making of Americans.* New York: Oxford University Press, 1986.

Sarna, Jonathan D., ed. *Minority Faiths and the American Protestant Mainstream.* Urbana: University of Illinois Press, 1998.

Tweed, Thomas A., ed. *Retelling U.S. Religious History.* Berkeley: University of California Press, 1997.

Williams, Peter W. *Popular Religion in America: Symbolic Change and the Modernization Process in Historical Perspective.* Urbana: University of Illinois Press, 1989.

DENOMINATIONAL HISTORIES

Casey, Michael W., and Douglas A. Foster, eds. *The Stone-Campbell Movement: An International Religious Tradition.* Knoxville: University of Tennessee Press, 2002.

Feldmeth, Nathan P., S. Donald Fortson III, Garth M. Rosell, and Kenneth J. Stewart. *Reformed and Evangelical across Four Centuries: The Presbyterian Story in America.* Grand Rapids: Eerdmans, 2022.

Granquist, Mark. *Lutherans in America: A New History.* Minneapolis: Fortress, 2015.

Hamm, Thomas D. *The Quakers in America.* New York: Columbia University Press, 2003.

Hennesey, James. *American Catholics: A History of the Roman Catholic Community in the United States.* New York: Oxford University Press, 1981.

Hughes, Richard T. *Reviving the Ancient Faith: The Story of Churches of Christ in America.* Grand Rapids: Eerdmans, 1996.

Land, Gary, ed. *Adventism in America: A History.* Grand Rapids: Eerdmans, 1986.

Leonard, Bill J. *Baptist Ways: A History.* Valley Forge, PA: Judson, 2003.

Prichard, Robert W. *A History of the Episcopal Church: Complete through the 78th General Convention.* 3rd ed. New York: Morehouse, 2014.

Richey, Russell E., Kenneth E. Rowe, and Jean Miller Schmidt. *The Methodist Experience in America: A History.* Vol. 1. Nashville: Abingdon, 2010.

Synan, Vinson. *The Holiness-Pentecostal Tradition: Charismatic Movements in the Twentieth Century*. Grand Rapids: Eerdmans, 1997.

Wenger, J. C. *The Mennonite Church in America: Sometimes Called Old Mennonites*. Scottdale, PA: Herald, 1966.

Youngs, J. William T. *The Congregationalists*. New York: Greenwood, 1990.

——————— CHRISTIAN THEOLOGY IN AMERICA ———————

Ahlstrom, Sydney E., ed. *Theology in America: The Major Protestant Voices from Puritanism to Neo-Orthodoxy*. Indianapolis: Bobbs-Merrill, 1967.

Carey, Patrick W., ed. *American Catholic Religious Thought: The Shaping of a Theological and Social Tradition*. New York: Paulist Press, 1987.

Goff, Philip, Arthur E. Farnsley II, and Peter J. Thuesen, eds. *The Bible in American Life*. New York: Oxford University Press, 2017.

Holifield, E. Brooks. *Theology in America: Christian Thought from the Age of the Puritans to the Civil War*. New Haven: Yale University Press, 2003.

Noll, Mark A. *America's God: From Jonathan Edwards to Abraham Lincoln*. New York: Oxford University Press, 2002.

Schell, Hannah, and Daniel Ott. *Christian Thought in America: A Brief History*. Minneapolis: Fortress, 2015.

Thuesen, Peter J. *Predestination: The American Career of a Contentious Doctrine*. New York: Oxford University Press, 2009.

Toulouse, Mark G., and James O. Duke, eds. *Sources of Christian Theology in America*. Nashville: Abingdon, 1999.

Warner, Michael, ed. *American Sermons: The Pilgrims to Martin Luther King Jr*. New York: Library of America, 1999.

——————— CHRISTIANITY AND AMERICAN CULTURE ———————

Bohlman, Philip V., Edith L. Blumhofer, and Maria M. Chow, eds. *Music in American Religious Experience*. New York: Oxford University Press, 2006.

Dean, William. *The Religious Critic in American Culture*. Albany: State University of New York Press, 1994.

Dillenberger, John. *The Visual Arts and Christianity in America: From the Colonial Period to the Present*. Rev. ed. New York: Crossroad, 1989.

Lundin, Roger, ed. *Invisible Conversations: Religion in the Literature of America*. Waco: Baylor University Press, 2009.

Marini, Stephen A. *Sacred Song in America: Religion, Music, and Public Culture*. Urbana: University of Illinois Press, 2003.

McDannell, Colleen. *Material Christianity: Religion and Popular Culture in America*. New Haven: Yale University Press, 1995.

Smidt, Corwin E., Lyman A. Kellstedt, and James L. Guth, eds. *The Oxford Handbook of Religion and American Politics*. New York: Oxford University Press, 2009.

Wilson, John F. *Church and State in American History*. Boston: D. C. Heath, 1965.

Witte, John, Jr., and Joel A. Nichols. *Religion and the American Constitutional Experiment.* 4th ed. New York: Oxford University Press, 2016.

─────── WOMEN IN AMERICAN CHRISTIANITY ───────

Brekus, Catherine A., ed. *The Religious History of American Women: Reimagining the Past.* Chapel Hill: University of North Carolina Press, 2007.

Collier-Thomas, Bettye. *Jesus, Jobs, and Justice: African American Women and Religion.* New York: Knopf, 2010.

Lindley, Susan Hill. *"You Have Stept out of your Place": A History of Women and Religion in America.* Louisville: Westminster John Knox, 1996.

Lindley, Susan Hill, and Eleanor J. Stebner, eds. *The Westminster Handbook to Women in American Religious History.* Louisville: Westminster John Knox, 2008.

─── AFRICAN AMERICANS IN AMERICAN CHRISTIANITY ───

Aaseng, Nathan. *African-American Religious Leaders.* New York: Facts on File, 2003.

Callahan, Allen Dwight. *The Talking Book: African Americans and the Bible.* New Haven: Yale University Press, 2006.

Evans, Curtis J. *The Burden of Black Religion.* New York: Oxford University Press, 2008.

Murphy, Larry G., ed. *Down by the Riverside: Readings in African American Religion.* New York: New York University Press, 2000.

Pinn, Anne H., and Anthony B. Pinn. *Fortress Introduction to Black Church History.* Minneapolis: Fortress, 2001.

Raboteau, Albert J. *Canaan Land: A Religious History of African Americans.* New York: Oxford University Press, 2001.

Sernett, Milton C., ed. *Afro-American Religious History: A Documentary Witness.* Durham, NC: Duke University Press, 1985.

─── LATIN AMERICANS IN AMERICAN CHRISTIANITY ───

Badillo, David A. *Latinos and the New Immigrant Church.* Baltimore: Johns Hopkins University Press, 2006.

Espinosa, Gastón, and Mario T. García. *Mexican American Religions: Spirituality, Activism, and Culture.* Durham, NC: Duke University Press, 2008.

Martínez, Juan Francisco. *Los Protestantes: An Introduction to Latino Protestantism in the United States.* Santa Barbara, CA: Praeger, 2011.

Walsh, Arlene M. Sánchez. *Latino Pentecostal Identity: Evangelical Faith, Self, and Society.* New York: Columbia University Press, 2003.

─── ASIAN AMERICANS IN AMERICAN CHRISTIANITY ───

Alumkal, Antony W. *Asian American Evangelical Churches: Race, Ethnicity, and Assimilation in the Second Generation.* New York: LFB Scholarly, 2003.

Ecklund, Elaine Howard. *Korean American Evangelicals: New Models for Civic Life*. New York: Oxford University Press, 2006.

Phan, Peter C. *Christianity with an Asian Face: Asian American Theology in the Making*. Maryknoll, NY: Orbis Books, 2003.

Williams, Raymond Brady. *Christian Pluralism in the United States: The Indian Immigrant Experience*. New York: Cambridge University Press, 1996.

Yang, Fenggang. *Chinese Christians in America: Conversion, Assimilation, and Adhesive Identities*. University Park: Pennsylvania State University Press, 1999.

─────── IMMIGRANTS IN AMERICAN CHRISTIANITY ───────

Carnes, Tony, and Fenggang Yang, eds. *Asian American Religions*. New York: New York University Press, 2004.

Ebaugh, Helen Rose, and Janet Saltzman Chafetz, eds. *Religion and the New Immigrants: Continuities and Adaptations in Immigrant Congregations*. Walnut Creek, CA: AltaMira, 2000.

Foley, Michael W., and Dean R. Hoge. *Religion and the New Immigrants: How Faith Communities Form Our Newest Citizens*. New York: Oxford University Press, 2007.

Gornik, Mark R. *Word Made Global: Stories of African Christianity in New York City*. Grand Rapids: Eerdmans, 2011.

Leonard, Karen I., Alex Stepick, Manuel A. Vasquez, and Jennifer Holdaway, eds. *Immigrant Faiths: Transforming Religious Life in America*. Lanham, MD: AltaMira Press, 2006.

Ludwig, Frieder, and J. Kwabena Asamoah-Gyadu, eds. *African Christian Presence in the West: New Immigrant Congregations and Transnational Networks in North America and Europe*. Trenton, NJ: Africa World Press, 2011.

Olupona, Jacob K., and Regina Gemignani, eds. *African Immigrant Religions in America*. New York: New York University Press, 2007.

Index

Abernathy, Ralph David, 279. *See also* Civil Rights Movement, the; King, Martin Luther, Jr.

abolitionism, 162–68, 180, 224, 227
  and African American education, 184
  African American leaders of, 164
  and the American Anti-Slavery Society, 166
  and the American Civil War, 177, 180
  and the American Colonization Society, 165
  controversies over, 148, 173–74
  and denominational schisms, 167, 192
  and evangelicals, 165
  and immediatists, 166–67
  Northern support of, 132
  popularization of, 174
  print culture of, 166—67, 174
  and Quakers, 160, 165–66
  Southern responses to, 167, 175–76
  and violence, 175
  women's support of, 195
  See also American Civil War, the; Garrison, William Lloyd; slavery; Truth, Sojourner; Tubman, Harriet; Walker, David; Wilberforce, William

Adams, John, 11, 94, 109, 114, 116. *See also* deism; Enlightenment, the

Addams, Jane, 203, 217, 226

African Methodist Episcopal (AME) Church, 132, 163, 182, 195. *See also* Allen, Richard; Methodism

African Methodist Episcopal Zion Church, 134, 163, 182. *See also* Methodism

Allen, Richard, 132, 164. *See also* African Methodist Episcopal (AME) Church; Methodism

al-Qaeda. *See* Islam

Altizer, Thomas J. J., 294

American Baptist Churches USA. *See* Baptists

American Bible Society, 151, 232, 262

American Board of Commissioners for Foreign Missions (ABCFM), 149–50. *See also* missions

American Civil War, the, 152–53, 158, 166, 190, 291
  and abolition, 195
  and Abraham Lincoln's theology, 179
  and African American Christianity, 163–64, 182–84
  and alternate religions, 211–12
  and American industrialization, 170
  begins, 176
  carnage of, 169
  context of, 169–75, 177
  and denominational schisms, 176, 192
  effects of, 19, 169
  end of, 179
  and higher education, 206
  and immigration, 184, 187–88
  and John Brown, 175
  and Lutheranism, 187
  and migration, 219–20

361

and the American Civil War, 176
and the American Revolution, 108, 136
and Anglicanism, 86, 106–7
Calvinist theology in, 87, 89, 147
church structure of, 73, 87
in colonial America, 7, 71, 85–86, 96,
    106–7, 135, 147
divisions within, 102, 147
and ecumenism, 274
and education, 94
and evangelicalism, 148
and the First Great Awakening, 96, 101,
    123, 147
liberalism in, 204, 241
mergers within, 253, 272
and missions, 149
and Presbyterians, 73, 136
prominence of, 19, 85, 144
and Puritanism, 7, 59, 68, 85, 87, 94
receding of, 136, 144
and religious freedom, 118, 120, 122
and religious rationalism, 138
and the Second Great Awakening, 123, 147
Separatists in, 71, 87, 129, 138
and slavery, 174, 176
women's ordination in, 194
See also First Great Awakening; Puritan-
    ism; United Church of Christ
Constantine, 3
Consultation on Church Union (COCU),
    275, 317
Conwell, Russell H., 240
Coolidge, Calvin, 240
Cooper, James Fenimore, 143
Copeland, Kenneth, 305. See also
    Pentecostalism
Cornwallis, Charles, 113–14. See also
    American Revolution, the
Coronado, Vázquez de, 44
Corrigan, Michael, 214. See also Catholicism
Cortés, Hernán, 36
cotton, 38, 165–66. See also slavery
Cotton, John, 66–67. See also Hutchinson,
    Anne; Puritanism
Coughlin, Charles, 255–56, 261. See also Ca-
    tholicism; New Deal, the
Council of Trent (1545–63), 5, 33. See also
    Catholicism; Protestant Reformation
COVID-19, 321, 345–47

Cranmer, Thomas, 4, 56. See also Calvin,
    John; Church of England; Luther, Mar-
    tin; Protestant Reformation
Cromwell, Oliver, 59. See English Civil War
Cromwell, Thomas, 56
Crosby, Fanny, 192. See also Holiness
    movement
Crossan, John Dominic, 340. See also
    Catholicism
Cutler, Timothy, 86, 106

Daly, Mary, 296
Darby, John Nelson, 194, 210. See also Sco-
    field, Cyrus Ingerson
Darrow, Clarence, 241–42. See also
    fundamentalism
Davenport, James, 100, 102. See also First
    Great Awakening; Whitefield, George
Davenport, John, 67. See also Puritanism
Day, Dorothy, 256. See also Catholicism;
    socialism
Dean, James, 286
deism, 76, 158, 344–45
    and disestablishment, 12, 119–20, 123
    and the Founding Fathers, 11–12, 94,
        109–10, 114
    God's benevolence in, 10
    and Jesus Christ, 137, 156
    moralism of, 109, 137, 342
    and revelation, 10, 109
    and traditional Christianity, 94, 109–10,
        123, 137
    and trinitarianism, 156
    and Unitarianism, 138
    See also Enlightenment, the; religious free-
        dom; Unitarianism
Denton, Melinda Lundquist, 343
Descartes, René, 92. See also Enlightenment,
    the
Dewey, John, 207
Dias, Bartolomeu, 35
Diderot, Denis, 92. See also Enlightenment,
    the
Disciples of Christ. See Christian Church
    (Disciples of Christ); Restorationism
Dollar, Creflo, 323–24
Dominicans, 34, 41. See also Catholicism;
    Franciscans; Jesuits; missions
Dones, 24, 343